걸프 사태

유엔안전보장이사회
동향 3

걸프 사태

유엔안전보장이사회 동향 3

| 머리말

　걸프 전쟁은 미국의 주도하에 34개국 연합군 병력이 수행한 전쟁으로, 1990년 8월 이라크의 쿠웨이트 침공 및 합병에 반대하며 발발했다. 미국은 초기부터 파병 외교에 나섰고, 1990년 9월 서울 등에 고위 관리를 파견하며 한국의 동참을 요청했다. 88올림픽 이후 동구권 국교 수립과 유엔 가입 추진 등 적극적인 외교 활동을 펼치는 당시 한국에 있어 이는 미국과 국제사회의 지지를 얻기 위해서라도 피할 수 없는 일이었다. 결국 정부는 91년 1월부터 약 3개월에 걸쳐 국군의료지원단과 공군수송단을 사우디아라비아 및 아랍 에미리트 연합 등에 파병하였고, 군·민간 의료 활동, 병력 수송 임무를 수행했다. 동시에 당시 걸프 지역 8개국에 살던 5천여 명의 교민에게 방독면 등 물자를 제공하고, 특별기 파견 등으로 비상시 대피할 수 있도록 지원했다. 비록 전쟁 부담금과 유가 상승 등 어려움도 있었지만, 걸프전 파병과 군사 외교를 통해 한국은 유엔 가입에 박차를 가할 수 있었고 미국 등 선진 우방국, 아랍권 국가 등과 밀접한 외교 관계를 유지하며 여러 국익을 창출할 수 있었다.

　본 총서는 외교부에서 작성하여 30여 년간 유지한 걸프 사태 관련 자료를 담고 있다. 미국을 비롯한 여러 국가와의 군사 외교 과정, 일일 보고 자료와 기타 정부의 대응 및 조치, 재외동포 철수와 보호, 의료지원단과 수송단 파견 및 지원 과정, 유엔을 포함해 세계 각국에서 수집한 관련 동향 자료, 주변국 지원과 전후복구사업 참여 등 총 48권으로 구성되었다. 전체 분량은 약 2만 4천여 쪽에 이른다.

2024년 3월

한국학술정보(주)

| 일러두기

· 본 총서에 실린 자료는 2022년 4월과 2023년 4월에 각각 공개한 외교문서 4,827권, 76만 여 쪽 가운데 일부를 발췌한 것이다.

· 각 권의 제목과 순서는 공개된 원본을 최대한 반영하였으나, 주제에 따라 일부는 적절히 변경하였다.

· 원본 자료는 A4 판형에 맞게 축소하거나 원본 비율을 유지한 채 A4 페이지 안에 삽입 하였다. 또한 현재 시점에선 공개되지 않아 '공란'이란 표기만 있는 페이지 역시 그대로 실었다.

· 외교부가 공개한 문서 각 권의 첫 페이지에는 '정리 보존 문서 목록'이란 이름으로 기록물 종류, 일자, 명칭, 간단한 내용 등의 정보가 수록되어 있으며, 이를 기준으로 0001번부터 번호가 매겨져 있다. 이는 삭제하지 않고 총서에 그대로 수록하였다.

· 보고서 내용에 관한 더 자세한 정보가 필요하다면, 외교부가 온라인상에 제공하는 『대한 민국 외교사료요약집』 1991년과 1992년 자료를 참조할 수 있다.

| 차례

정 리 보 존 문 서 목 록					
기록물종류	일반공문서철	등록번호	2017060006	등록일자	2017-06-05
분류번호	731.33	국가코드	XF	보존기간	30년
명 칭	걸프사태 관련 유엔안전보장이사회 동향, 1990-91. 전5권				
생 산 과	국제연합과/중동1과	생산년도	1990~1991	담당그룹	
권 차 명	V.4 1991.3월				

내용목차	* 1991.3.2 대이라크 휴전 조건 결의 채택 (미국측 결의안, 686호)
	  3.5 이라크측, 쿠웨이트 재산 (1990.8.2 이후 취득) 반환 결정 유엔 통보
	  3.22 안보리 제재위원회, 인도적 목적의 대이라크 군수 해제 조치 결정				

0001

외 무 부

종 별 :

번 호 : UNW-0488　　　　　　　　일 시 : 91 0301 2040

수 신 : 장 관(국연,중근동,해기,기정)(사본:노창희대사)

발 신 : 주 유엔 대사

제 목 : 걸프사태(안보리)

　　안보리는 3.1.20:40 현재 상임 이사국들간에 별첨 미측 결의안 초안에 관한 협의를 계속중인바, 관련 동향 추보위계임.

　　첨부:미측결의안: UNW(F)-094

　　끝

　　(대사대리 신기복-국장)

국기국	1차보	2차보	중아국	국기국	정와대	안기부	공보처	대사실

The Security Council,

Recalling and reaffirming its resolutions 660 (1990), 661 (1990), 662 (1990), 664 (1990), 665 (1990), 666 (1990), 667 (1990), 669 (1990), 670 (1990), 674 (1990), 677 (1990), and 678 (1990),

Taking note of the letters of the Foreign Minister of Iraq confirming Iraq's acceptance of all of the resolutions noted above, and stating its intentions to release prisoners of war after a ceasefire,

Taking note of the suspension of offensive combat operations by the forces of the Member States cooperating with the Government of Kuwait pursuant to Resolution 678 (1990),

Bearing in mind the world's need to be assured of Iraq's peaceful intentions, and the requirement in Resolution 678 (1990) to restore international peace and security in the region,

Acting under Chapter VII of the Charter,

1. Affirms that all twelve resolutions noted above continue to have full force and effect, except as modified in paragraph 6 below.

2. Demands that Iraq, in order to implement its acceptance of all twelve resolutions noted above, immediately take all actions necessary to fulfill its obligations arising from these resolutions, and in particular that Iraq:

    (a) rescind immediately its actions purporting to annex Kuwait;

    (b) accept in principle its liability for any loss, damage, or injury arising in regard to Kuwait and third states, and their nationals and corporations, as a result of the invasion and illegal occupation of Kuwait by Iraq;

    (c) immediately release under the auspices of the International Committee of the Red Cross, Red Cross Societies, or Red Crescent Societies, all Kuwaiti and third country nationals detained by Iraq;

    (d) immediately return the remains of any deceased Kuwaiti and third country nationals detained by Iraq; and

    (e) immediately return all Kuwaiti property seized by Iraq;

3—1

0003

3. Further demands:

   (a)   the permanent cessation of hostile or provocative actions by Iraqi forces against all Member States and other parties, including missile attacks and combat aircraft flights;

   (b)   the immediate designation by Iraq of military commanders to meet with counterparts from the forces of Member States cooperating with Kuwait pursuant to Resolution 678 (1990) by 0001 hours Eastern Standard Time 2 March 1991 to arrange for the military aspects of a cessation of hostilities;

   (c)   the immediate release by Iraq, under the auspices of the International Committee of the Red Cross, of all prisoners of war;

   (d)   the immediate return of the remains of any deceased personnel of the forces of the Member States cooperating with Kuwait pursuant to Resolution 678; and

   (e)   that Iraq provide all information and assistance in identifying Iraqi mines, booby traps and other explosives as well as any chemical and biological weapons and materiel in Kuwait, in areas of Iraq presently under the temporary control of forces of Member States cooperating with the Government of Kuwait pursuant to Resolution 678 (1990), and in the Gulf.

4. Affirms the right of the Member States cooperating with the Government of Kuwait pursuant to Resolution 678 (1990) to resume offensive combat operations if Iraq does not comply with all demands set forth in paragraphs 1, 2 and 3 above;

5. Calls on Member States cooperating with the Government of Kuwait pursuant to Resolution 678 (1990) to commence the orderly repatriation of Iraqi prisoners of war as required by the terms of the Third Geneva Convention of 1949, under the auspices of the International Committee of the Red Cross;

3—2

0004

6. Decides that, upon and pursuant to the request of the legitimate government of Kuwait, the economic sanctions and other measures imposed or authorized by Resolutions 661 (1990), 665 (1990), 666 (1990) and 670 (1990) shall have no further force and effect with respect to Kuwait; and

7. Requests all Member States, as well as the United Nations Organization, the specialized agencies and other international organizations in the United Nations system, to take all appropriate action to assist the Government and people of Kuwait in the reconstruction of their country.

TOTAL P.04

0005

3-3

유엔 안보리 동향

91. 3. 2.
국제연합과

(다음 사항은 3.2.(토) 14:10 주유엔대표부에서 전화로 통보한 사항임.)

개   요

o 현지시각 3.1(금) 오전부터 23:00까지 하루종일 결의안 추진 노력이 있었
  으나,

o 미측 제시 결의안(초안)에 대한 안보리 상임이사국 및 비 비동맹국 비상임
  이사국의 동조에도 불구,

o 7개 비동맹이사국(인도, 예멘, 쿠바, 코트디브와르, 자이르, 에쿠아돌,
  짐바브웨)의 반대로 채택추진 불가

결   론 : 본국과의 협의 목적으로 토의 24시간 연기에 합의

* 단, 미측은 가능한한 빨리 채택되도록 추진하고 있음.

진행상황

o PERM-5 (상임이사국)회의

  - 오전부터 19:00까지 미측결의안(초안) 중심으로 비공식 협의 계속

  - 수차례 수정을 거쳐 합의

o PERM 5 + 비 비동맹이사국 (벨지움, 오지리, 루마니아)

  - 2시간이상 토의후 상기 PERM 5 합의안에 동의

o 상기 "P-5+ 비 비동맹 합의안"에 대하여 비동맹이사국은 신중 또는
  반대의사 표명

앙고재고	년 월 일	담 당	과 장	국 장
	91 3 2			

0006

* 비동맹이사국의 불동의 이유

    1. 결의안(초안)에 <u>공식휴전</u> 내용 없음.

    2. 다국적국측에 <u>전투행위 재개 권한</u>을 부여하고 있음.

    3. <u>평화유지군 파견</u>에 관한 규정이 없음.

<u>기   타</u>

o 피커링 미대사는 공식 휴전개념 불사용 사유에 관한 질문에 대하여

    - 동 결의안(초안)은 군사적 측면을 마무리 하는데 있으며,

    - 공식휴전 또는 평화유지군 파견 문제는 그 이후에 검토될 사항이라고
      답변

* 미측 결의안 초안은 UNW-0488 참조

0007

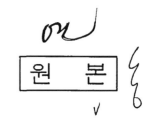

외 무 부

종 별 :

번 호 : UNW-0489 일 시 : 91 0302 0700

수 신 : 장관 (국연,중근동,해기,기정) 사본:노창희대사

발 신 : 주유엔대사대리

제 목 : 걸프 사태 (안보리)

연: UNW-0488

1. 안보리는 다국적군의 대 이락 전투행위 정지에 따른 후속조치와 관련, 3.1.(금) 11시경부터 22:00 경 까지 일련의 그룹별 협의를 가진바, 주요경과는 아래와 같음.

2. 상임이사국들은 오전부터 19:00 경까지 미국이 제시한 결의안 초안을 중점 협의한바, 4차에 걸친 수정을 거쳐 별첨 (FAX) 문안에 최종 합의하였으며, 이를 토대로 곧이어 상임이사국들을 대표하여 미국과 영국이 비동맹이 아닌 비상임이사국들 (오지리, 벨지움, 루마니아) 들과 협의를 가진후 20:00-22:00 간 미국, 영, 소련과 안보리내 비동맹 CAUCUS (7 개국)간의 연석협의를 가짐.

3. 미국은 별첨 결의안 초안을 제시하면서 여타 이사국들의 반응을 감안, 3.2.(토)중 안보리 공식회의를 소집하고자 하는 의도를 강력히 표명한것으로 알려짐.

4. 상기 미측 초안에 대해 안보리 비동맹 이사국중 쿠바, 예멘, 짐바브웨가 강력히 반대하고, 인도와 에콰돌도 매우 신중한 반응을 보인것으로 알려진바, 비동맹측은동 초안이 1) 공식 휴전 (FORMAL CEASEFIRE) 조치에 관한것이 아니며 2)다국적군의전투행위 재개 권한을 그대로 유지시키고 있으며 3) 평화유지국 파견에 관한 규정이없다는 점 등을 주요 반대 내지 유보 이유로 제시하고, 본국정부 청훈을 위해 24시간협의 연기를 요청하였다고함. (이상 미,영,코트디브와르, 루마니아, 자이르등 대표부관계관으로 부터 탐문)

5. 금일 협의 종료직후 PICKERING 미국대사는 미측 결의안에 공식휴전 및 평화유지군 파견 문제가 언급되지 않은 이유를 묻는 기자들의 질문에 대하여 공식휴전 (결의안 초안에는 DEFINITIVE END TO HOSTILITIES) 은 이락이 필요한 조치를 이행한후의다음 단계 조치이며, 현재로서는 결의안 초안에 있드시 적대행위 중지의 군사적 측면마무리에 역점을 두고 있음과 평화유지군은 이다음 단계에서 검토할수

국기국	장관	차관	1차보	2차보	미주국	중아국	정문국	대사실
정와대	총리실	안기부	공보처					

PAGE 1

91.03.03 00:35 DQ

외신 1과 통제관

0008

있을것 이라는취지로 답변함.

6.안보리 주변 소식통 들에 의하면 상기 협의결과에 비추어 빠르면 금주 주말중늦어도 내주초에는 결의안 채택을 위한 안보리 공식회의가 열릴 가능성이 크다고 전망하고 있음.

7.3.1. 부터 오지리가 안보리 3월 의장직을 수행함.끝

(대사대리 신기복-국장)

첨부: FAX (UNW(F)-095)

UNW(F) --05 1301 2230
(국연, 중요용, 여기 기업 > C사본: 노창희 대사)

Draft Resolution

as of 3/01   17:00

The Security Council,

A   Recalling and reaffirming its resolutions 660 (1990), 661
(1990), 662 (1990), 664 (1990), 665 (1990), 666 (1990), 667
(1990), 669 (1990), 670 (1990), 674 (1990), 677 (1990), and
678 (1990),

B   Recalling the obligations of Member States under Article
25 of the Charter,

C   Recalling paragraph 9 of Resolution 661 (1990) regarding
assistance to the Government of Kuwait and paragraph 3(c) of
that resolution regarding supplies strictly for medical
purposes and, in humanitarian circumstances, foodstuffs,

D   Taking note of the letters of the Foreign Minister of
Iraq confirming Iraq's agreement to comply fully with all of
the resolutions noted above, and stating its intention to
release prisoners of war immediately,

E   Taking note of the suspension of offensive combat
operations by the forces of Kuwait and the Member States
cooperating with Kuwait pursuant to Resolution 678 (1990),

F   Bearing in mind the need to be assured of Iraq's peaceful
intentions, and the objective in Resolution 678 (1990) of
restoring international peace and security in the region,

G   Underlining the importance of Iraq taking the necessary
measures which would permit a definitive end to the
hostilities,

H   Affirming the commitment of all Member States to the
independence, sovereignty and territorial integrity of Iraq
and Kuwait, and noting the intention expressed by the Member
States cooperating under paragraph 2 of Security Council
Resolution 678 (1990) to bring their military presence in
Iraq to an end as soon as possible consistent with achieving
the objectives of the resolution,

I   Acting under Chapter VII of the Charter,

13매

0010

191 P01   LENINPROTOCOL   '91-03-02 14:07

- 2 -

1. Affirms that all twelve resolutions noted above continue to have full force and effect;

2. Demands that Iraq implement its acceptance of all twelve resolutions noted above and in particular that Iraq:

    (a)   rescind immediately its actions purporting to annex Kuwait;

    (b)   accept in principle its liability for any loss, damage, or injury arising in regard to Kuwait and third states, and their nationals and corporations, as a result of the invasion and illegal occupation of Kuwait by Iraq;

    (c)   immediately release under the auspices of the International Committee of the Red Cross, Red Cross Societies, or Red Crescent Societies, all Kuwaiti and third country nationals detained by Iraq and return the remains of any deceased Kuwaiti and third country nationals so detained; and

    (d)   immediately begin to return all Kuwaiti property seized by Iraq, to be completed in the shortest possible period;

3. Further demands that Iraq:

    (a)   cease hostile or provocative actions by its forces against all Member States and other parties, including missile attacks and flights of combat aircraft;

    (b)   designate military commanders to meet with counterparts from the forces of Kuwait and the Member States cooperating with Kuwait pursuant to Resolution 678 (1990) to arrange for the military aspects of a cessation of hostilities at the earliest possible time;

    (c)   arrange for immediate access to and release of all prisoners of war under the auspices of the International Committee of the Red Cross and return the remains of any deceased personnel of the forces of Kuwait and the Member States cooperating with Kuwait pursuant to Resolution 678 (1990); and

- 3 -

(d) provide all information and assistance in
     identifying Iraqi mines, booby traps and other
     explosives as well as any chemical and biological
     weapons and material in Kuwait, in areas of Iraq
     where forces of Member States cooperating with
     Kuwait pursuant to Resolution 678 (1990) are present
     temporarily, and in the Gulf;

4. Recognizes that during the period required for Iraq to
comply with paragraphs 2 and 3 above, the provisions of
paragraph 2 of Resolution 678 (1990) remain valid;

5. Welcomes the decision of Kuwait and the Member States
cooperating with Kuwait pursuant to Resolution 678 (1990) to
provide access and to commence the release of Iraqi prisoners
of war as required by the terms of the Third Geneva
Convention of 1949, under the auspices of the International
Committee of the Red Cross;

6. Requests all Members States, as well as the United
Nations, the specialized agencies and other international
organizations in the United Nations system, to take all
appropriate action to cooperate with the Government and
people of Kuwait in the reconstruction of their country.

7. Decides that) in order to secure the rapid achievement of
a definitive end to the hostilities, Iraq shall notify the
Secretary General and the Security Council when it has taken
the actions set out above;

8. Decides that in order to secure the rapid establishment
of a definitive end to the hostilities, the Security Council
remains actively seized of the matter.

외 무 부

종 별 : 지 급

번 호 : UNW-0490   일 시 : 91 0303 0230

수 신 : 장관(국연,중근동,해기,기정)

발 신 : 주 유엔대사

제 목 : 걸프사태 (안보리)

연: UNW-0489

1. 연호, 안보리는 미국 요청에 의거 금 3.2.(토) 오후 안보리 전체 비공식 회의를 가진데 이어, 19:30-24:00간 안보리공식(공개) 회의를 개최하였음.

2. 금일 안보리 공식회의에는 연호 미국 결의안이 안보리문서 S/22298 (첨부 1)로 정식제출 되었으며, 이와함께 동 결의안에 대한 쿠바의 18개 수정안이 각각 3.1.자로 제출되었음.

또한 쿠바가 즉각적인 휴전 선포등에 관한 결의안 (S/22232/REV.2) 과 유엔사무총장의 중동평화 중재역할 강화결의안 (S/22233/REV.2) 을, 인도등 비동맹 안보리 이사국 5개국 (쿠바, 에쿠아돌, 인도, 예멘, 짐바브웨) 이 이락및 쿠웨이트에 대한 인도적 지원 관련 결의안(S/22318) 을 금 3.2.자로 각각 제출함.

3. 금일 회의에서는 미국 결의안과 쿠바 수정안만을 토의한바, 안보리 의사규칙에 따라 18개 쿠바 수정안을 먼저 표결에 부친결과 모두 부결 되었으며, 이어 미국이 여타 6 개 이사국 (벨지움, 불란서, 루마니아, 소련, 영국, 자이르) 들과 공동으로 제안한 연호 결의안 (첨부 1) 이 일부 구두 수정을 거쳐 표결에 회부됨.

4. 상기 미국측 결의안이 찬성 11, 반대 1, 기권 3으로 3.2. 22:00 경 채택된바, 국별 표결태도는 아래와같음.

가. 찬성: 오지리, 벨지움, 코트디브와르, 에쿠아돌, 불란서, 루마니아, 소련, 영국, 미국, 자이르, 짐바브웨 (11개국)

나. 반대:쿠바 (1)

다. 기권:중국, 예멘, 인도 (3)

5. 금일 통과된 미국측 결의안 (수정부분 포함), 쿠바측 18개 수정안 (표결현황 포함) 및 회의 의제를 별첨 FAX 송부하며, 회의 진행경과는 별전 보고함.

국기국	장관	차관	1차보	2차보	미주국	중아국	정문국	정와대
종리실	안기부	공보처	대책반					

PAGE 1

91.03.03 19:01 DA

외신 1과 통제관

0013

첨부 FAX:1. 미국측 결의안,
2. 쿠바수정안 (18개):UN₩(F)-096
끝
(대사대리 신기복-국장)

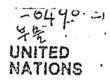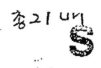
 Security Council

PROVISIONAL

S/22298
1 March 1991

ORIGINAL: ENGLISH

<u>United States of America: draft resolution</u>

<u>The Security Council</u>,

<u>Recalling</u> and <u>reaffirming</u> its resolutions 660 (1990), 661 (1990), 662 (1990), 664 (1990), 665 (1990), 666 (1990), 667 (1990), 669 (1990), 670 (1990), 674 (1990), 677 (1990), and 678 (1990),

<u>Recalling</u> the obligations of Member States under Article 25 of the Charter,

<u>Recalling</u> paragraph 9 of resolution 661 (1990) regarding assistance to the Government of Kuwait and paragraph 3 (c) of that resolution regarding supplies strictly for medical purposes and, in humanitarian circumstances, foodstuffs,

<u>Taking note</u> of the letters of the Foreign Minister of Iraq confirming Iraq's agreement to comply fully with all of the resolutions noted above (S/22275), and stating its intention to release prisoners of war immediately (S/22273),

<u>Taking note</u> of the suspension of offensive combat operations by the forces of Kuwait and the Member States cooperating with Kuwait pursuant to resolution 678 (1990),

<u>Bearing in mind</u> the need to be assured of Iraq's peaceful intentions, and the objective in resolution 678 (1990) of restoring international peace and security in the region,

<u>Underlining</u> the importance of Iraq taking the necessary measures which would permit a definitive end to the hostilities,

<u>Affirming</u> the commitment of all Member States to the independence, sovereignty and territorial integrity of Iraq and Kuwait, and <u>noting</u> the intention expressed by the Member States cooperating under paragraph 2 of Security Council resolution 678 (1990) to bring their military presence in Iraq to an end as soon as possible consistent with achieving the objectives of the resolution,

<u>Acting</u> under Chapter VII of the Charter,

2882E

21 — 1

1. **Affirms** that all twelve resolutions noted above continue to have full force and effect;

2. **Demands** that Iraq implement its acceptance of all twelve resolutions noted above and in particular that Iraq:

   (a) Rescind immediately its actions purporting to annex Kuwait;

   (b) Accept in principle its liability *under international law* for any loss, damage, or injury arising in regard to Kuwait and third States, and their nationals and corporations, as a result of the invasion and illegal occupation of Kuwait by Iraq;

   (c) Immediately release under the auspices of the International Committee of the Red Cross, Red Cross Societies, or Red Crescent Societies, all Kuwaiti and third country nationals detained by Iraq and return the remains of any deceased Kuwaiti and third country nationals so detained; and

   (d) Immediately begin to return all Kuwaiti property seized by Iraq, to be completed in the shortest possible period;

3. **Further demands** that Iraq:

   (a) Cease hostile or provocative actions by its forces against all Member States ~~and other parties~~, including missile attacks and flights of combat aircraft;

   (b) Designate military commanders to meet with counterparts from the forces of Kuwait and the Member States cooperating with Kuwait pursuant to resolution 678 (1990) to arrange for the military aspects of a cessation of hostilities at the earliest possible time;

   (c) Arrange for immediate access to and release of all prisoners of war under the auspices of the International Committee of the Red Cross and return the remains of any deceased personnel of the forces of Kuwait and the Member States cooperating with Kuwait pursuant to resolution 678 (1990); and

   (d) Provide all information and assistance in identifying Iraqi mines, booby traps and other explosives as well as any chemical and biological weapons and material in Kuwait, in areas of Iraq where forces of Member States cooperating with Kuwait pursuant to resolution 678 (1990) are present temporarily, and in the ~~Gulf~~ *adjacent waters*;

4. **Recognizes** that during the period required for Iraq to comply with paragraphs 2 and 3 above, the provisions of paragraph 2 of resolution 678 (1990) remain valid;

21 — 2   0016

S/22298
English
Page 3

immediately

5.   **Welcomes** the decision of Kuwait and the Member States cooperating with Kuwait pursuant to resolution 678 (1990) to provide access and to commence the release of Iraqi prisoners of war as required by the terms of the Third Geneva Convention of 1949, under the auspices of the International Committee of the Red Cross;

6.   **Requests** all Member States, as well as the United Nations, the specialized agencies and other international organizations in the United Nations system, to take all appropriate action to cooperate with the Government and people of Kuwait in the reconstruction of their country;

7.   **Decides** that Iraq shall notify the Secretary-General and the Security Council when it has taken the actions set out above;

8.   **Decides** that in order to secure the rapid establishment of a definitive end to the hostilities, the Security Council remains actively seized of the matter.

21-3

0017

UNITED NATIONS

(첨부2)　　　　　　　　　투표순서 ①

Security Council

PROVISIONAL

S/22300
2 March 1991

ORIGINAL:　ENGLISH

<u>Cuba:　amendment to the draft resolution contained in
document S/22298</u>

<u>Preambular paragraph 1</u>:　<u>Delete</u> the words "and reaffirming".

찬 2 (쿠바, 예멘)7반1 (2차료)7개된12

2917E

21-4　　　　　　　　　　　　0018

**UNITED
NATIONS**

S

  Security Council

PROVISIONAL

S/22301
2 March 1991

ORIGINAL: ENGLISH

<u>Cuba: amendment to the draft resolution contained in
document S/22298</u>

<u>Preambular paragraph 2</u>: Delete the words "Article 25 of".

1 (쿠바) - 0 - 14

2915E

21-5   0019

UNITED NATIONS

Security Council

PROVISIONAL

S/22302
2 March 1991

ORIGINAL: ENGLISH

<u>Cuba: amendment to the draft resolution contained in
document S/22298</u>

<u>Preambular paragraph 5:</u> <u>Delete</u> the words "pursuant to resolution
678 (1990)".

2 (쿠바, 예멘) - 0 - 13

2937E

21-6

0020

UNITED NATIONS

Security Council

PROVISIONAL

S/22304
2 March 1991

ORIGINAL: ENGLISH

<u>Cuba: amendment to the draft resolution contained in document S/22298</u>

<u>Preambular paragraph 8:</u>   <u>delete</u> the whole paragraph.

((쿠바) - 0 - 14

2921E

2-1-7   0021

**UNITED
NATIONS**

S

Security Council

PROVISIONAL

S/22310
2 March 1991

ORIGINAL: ENGLISH

<u>Cuba: amendment to the draft resolution contained in document S/22298</u>

<u>Operative paragraph 3 (c)</u>: between the words "International Committee of the Red Cross" and "return the remains", <u>add</u> the following phrase "and in conformity with Article 118 of the Third Geneva Convention of 1949,".

찬 : 6 (쿠바. 예멘, 짐바브웨, 오스리, 불란서, 인도,
에콰돌)
반 : 6
기권 : 1

2944E

21-8   0022

**UNITED
NATIONS**

S

Security Council

PROVISIONAL

S/22311
2 March 1991

ORIGINAL: ENGLISH

<u>Cuba: amendment to the draft resolution contained in document S/22298</u>

<u>Operative paragraph 3 (d)</u>: <u>delete</u> the phrase starting with "in the areas of
Iraq where ..." up to the end of the paragraph.

2 (쿠바, 예멘) - 0 - 13

2950E

24-9

0023

S

UNITED NATIONS

 Security Council

PROVISIONAL

S/22312
2 March 1991

ORIGINAL: ENGLISH

<u>Cuba: amendment to the draft resolution contained in
document S/22298</u>

<u>Operative paragraph 4</u>: delete.

(전투재개 권한유보)   _____

찬 3 (쿠바. 예멘, 콜롬)
반 0
기: 12

2911E

21-10   0024

UNITED NATIONS

S

Security Council

PROVISIONAL

S/22317
2 March 1991

ORIGINAL: ENGLISH

Cuba: amendment to the draft resolution contained in
document S/22298

<u>Operative paragraph 7</u>: Delete.

----- 2 (쿠바.데멘)-0-13

2919B

21-11

UNITED NATIONS

 Security Council

PROVISIONAL

S/22305
2 March 1991

ORIGINAL: ENGLISH

<u>Cuba: amendment to the draft resolution contained in document S/22298</u>

<u>Operative paragraph 1</u>: <u>Replace</u> by the following "<u>Welcomes</u> the restoration of the independence, sovereignty and territorial integrity of Kuwait."

2 (국회.예민) - 6 - 13

2927E

21 - 12

0026

UNITED
NATIONS

   Security Council

PROVISIONAL

S/22315
2 March 1991

ORIGINAL: ENGLISH

<u>Cuba: amendment to the draft resolution contained in document S/22298</u>

<u>Insert a new operative paragraph that would read as follows</u>:   "<u>Decides</u> to declare
nul and void all provisions contained in the pertinent resolutions of the Security
Council regarding trade in foodstuffs and in all other products essential for the
health and well-being of the Iraqi people."

-----

2 (31. 세반) - 6 - 13

29138

21-13   0027

UNITED NATIONS

Security Council

PROVISIONAL

S/22306
2 March 1991

ORIGINAL: ENGLISH

<u>Cuba: amendment to the draft resolution contained in document S/22298</u>

    <u>Insert</u> a new operative paragraph with the following text: "<u>Decides</u> an immediate cease fire."

2 (국비. 배씬) - 0 - 13

2932E

21—14

0028

P.1

UNITED NATIONS

Security Council

PROVISIONAL

S/22307
2 March 1991

ORIGINAL: ENGLISH

<u>Cuba: amendment to the draft resolution contained in document S/22298</u>

<u>Insert</u> a new operative paragraph with the following text: "<u>Requests</u> the Secretary-General to immediately dispatch a military observer mission to the area with the aim of monitoring and supervising compliance with the cease fire decided above".

S/ 22306 부결에 따라 철회

2934V

0029

21-15

UNITED
NATIONS

Security Council

PROVISIONAL

S/22308
2 March 1991

ORIGINAL: ENGLISH

<u>Cuba: amendment to the draft resolution contained in
document S/22298</u>

   <u>Operative paragraph 2</u>: <u>Replace</u> the chapeau with the following: "<u>Notes</u> that
Iraq has committed itself to:"

찬 2 (3바.베베)- 0 - 13

2939E

24-16   0030

Security Council

PROVISIONAL

S/22309
2 March 1991

ORIGINAL: ENGLISH

<u>Cuba: amendment to the draft resolution contained in document S/22298</u>

<u>Operative paragraph 3</u>: <u>Replace</u> the chapeau with the following: "<u>Further notes</u> that Iraq is fully willing to:"

-----

2 (국바.베네)-0-13

2948E

21-17

UNITED NATIONS

Security Council

PROVISIONAL

S/22314
2 March 1991

ORIGINAL: ENGLISH

<u>Cuba: amendment to the draft resolution contained in document S/22298</u>

<u>Insert a new operative paragraph with the following text</u>: "Requests the Secretary-General to urgently draw-up plans for the deployment of a United Nations Peace Keeping Force in the area, in consultation with the countries where it would be deployed, and report back to the Security Council for consideration and approval."

찬: 5 (쿠바, 예멘, 인도, 에라돌, 짐비브웨)
반: 6
기: 10

2926E

21-18

0032

**UNITED
NATIONS**

S

Security Council

PROVISIONAL

S/22313
2 March 1991

ORIGINAL: ENGLISH

Cuba: amendment to the draft resolution contained in
document S/22298

Insert a new operative paragraph with the following wording:

"Affirms the obligation of all member States to fully respect the
independence, sovereignty and territorial integrity of Iraq and Kuwait and
notes the commitment of the member States cooperating with Kuwait under
paragraph 2 of Security Council resolution 678 (1990) to bring their military
presence in Iraq to an end as soon as possible."

2 (국비. 비제) - 0 - 13

2904E

2가-19

0033

UNITED NATIONS

   S

 ## Security Council

PROVISIONAL

S/22303
2 March 1991

ORIGINAL: ENGLISH

Cuba: amendment to the draft resolution contained in document S/22298

 Preambular paragraph 6: Replace the phrase starting with "and the objective in resolution ..." by the following: "and the role that the United Nations has to play in restoring and maintaining international peace and security in the region."

-----

4 (쿠바, 예멘, 인도, 에콰들)- 0 = 11,

UNITED NATIONS

Security Council

PROVISIONAL

S/22316
2 March 1991

ORIGINAL; ENGLISH

Cuba: amendment to the draft resolution contained in document S/22298

Insert a further operative paragraph as follows: **Requests** all Member States, the United Nations, the specialized agencies, as well as other international organizations to provide, on an urgent basis, humanitarian assistance, including foodstuffs and medical supplies to Iraq and Kuwait."

2908E

외 무 부

종 별 : 지급

번 호 : UNW-0491　　　　　　　　　　　일 시 : 91 0303 0345

수 신 : 장관(국연,중근동,해기,기정)(사본:노창희대사)

발 신 : 주 유엔대사대리

제 목 : 걸프사태(안보리)

　　　연: UNW-0490

　　　1. 연호로 채택된 미국측 결의안 표결 경과는 아래와 같음.

　　　가.표결전 발언

　　　0.예멘

　　　-동 결의안이 인도적, 군사적, 정치적 측면에서 걸프사태 해결에 긍정적 기여예상인식하나, (1)공식 휴전 선언 불언급, (2) 이락에 대한 식량금수 해제 불언급, (3)유엔, 특히 유엔사무총장의 역할 불거론, (4) 이락에서의 다국적군 철수불언급, (5)대 이락 적대 행위재개 가능성 상정(본문 4항)등은 주요한 문제점임.

　　　-특히, 유엔 (사무총장)의 역할 강화관련 쿠바 수정안에 대한 다수 지지 유념할것

　　　-안보리가 아랍.이스라엘 분쟁관련 제반 결의안에 대하여도 즉각 그리고 최대 역점을 두어그 이행을 촉구할것

　　　0.쿠바

　　　-즉각 휴전을 선언 안함으로써 오히려 긴장 조성

　　　-유엔및 유엔사무총장의 역할 배제등은 국제평화와 안전에 대한 안보리의 1차적역할을 방기하는것

　　　-다국적군의 이락 계속 주둔 근거 없음.

　　　-금번 결의안은 다국적군과 이락 군사령관들의 3.3. 군사적 측면의 휴전 협의지원을 위한것에 불과

　　　0.짐바브웨

　　　-전반적인 결의안 내용은 긍정적으로 평가

　　　-즉각적인 휴전이 바람직하나, 금번 조치는 그 전단계임을 인정

　　　-적대행위 재개권한 유보는 유감

국기국 총리실	장관 안기부	차관 공보처	1차보 대책반	2차보 국기국(대사)	미주국	중아국	정문국	정와대

외신 1과 롱제관

0036

-군사령관 회담시 유엔사무총장 대표 입회 희망

-안보리가 아랍.이스라엘 문제 해결에도 같은 성의와 속도로 임할것을 촉구 (불연시 DOUBLESTANDARD)

　나.표결후 발언

　0.미국

-금번 결의안은 걸프사태의 분수령 (WATERSHED) 이며, '적대 행위의 분명한 종결'을 위한 첫단계

-이락이 동 결의안 이행시까지 안보리 결의안 678호에 규정된 모든 필요한 수단사용중단 유보

-동 결의안은 향후 걸프사태 해결을 위한 BROADFRAMEWORK

- 미국은 중동평화를 위해 필요한 조치 검토예정이며 중동지역 국가들의 주도적 문제 해결노력 지원

-쿠웨이트 및 이락에대한 인도주의적 지원 필요성 인식

-금번 사태로 집단 안전보장 체제의 중요성 인식제고

　0.소련

-금번 이락의 쿠웨이트 철수는 걸프사태의 평화적 해결을 위한 고르바쵸프 대통령의 외교노력의 결실

-걸프사태 후속 안보강화 장치가 필요한바, 이를위해서는 지역국가들의 역할 제고, 유엔 역할강화, 무기이전 통제등 포함 필요

-특히 장기적인 중동평화를 위해서는 중동문제에 관한 국제회의를 개최, 아랍.이스라엘 문제등 해결 필요

-이를 위해 ' FRESH APPROACH ' 필요

　0.중국

-걸프사태 발생이래 계속 평화적 해결 희망

-쿠웨이트 정부 회복및 적대행위 정지 환영

-안보리가 공식휴전 성립에 적극 역할 촉구

-비공식 협의시 제시한 중국측 의견이 충분히 반영되지 않아, 결의안에는 기권(678호에도 기권)

　0.불란서

-금번 결의안은 공식 휴전위한 선결조치

PAGE 2

0037

-중동지역의 여타 분쟁도 공평하게 처리 필요

0.벨지움

-향후 중동평화를 위해 동 지역국가의 주도적역할 긴요

-이와관련 (1) 이락.쿠웨이트 국경준수, (2)이락의 대량파괴 무기 보유능력 제거,(3)아랍- 이스라엘 분쟁해결 노력 가속화등이 주요 고려 사항임.

0.자이르

-아랍.이스라엘 문제 적극 해결 촉구

0.코트디브와르.루마니아

-쿠웨이트 정부 회복 환영, 국제법과 집단안보의 중요성 강조

0.영국

-금번 결의안은 걸프사태 처리에 있어 3단계의시작임.

(1단계는 12개 결의안 채택, 2단계는 군사행동, 3단계는 중동평화 장치강구)

-이락은 (1)적십자 요원들의 전쟁포로 접근제한, (2)전쟁 억류자 불석방, (3)기뢰등 위험수단 정보 불제공, (4)쿠웨이트에 대한 손해배상 불수락 중인바, 이에 대한 분명한 이행 약속필요

-금번 걸프사태 해결후 기타 중동문제 협의 가능시

인도

-공식휴전 불언급, 휴전감시 장치불명확, 사무총장 역할부재, 적대행위 재개권한 유보, 대이락 제재 계속등의 이유로 결의안에 기권함.

-특히 안보리가 제재조치 해제문제 조기협의 요망

-중동평화 회복 과정에 있어서도 유엔의 역할제고 필요

-이락및 쿠웨이트에 대한 인도적 지원 촉구

0.에쿠아돌

-공식휴전 선포및 동 감시과정에 있어 안보리 및사무총장 역할 강화

-이락및 쿠웨이트에 대한 인도적 지원 지지

-다국적군의 대 이락 적대 행위 재개없기를 희망

-여타 중동지역문제 조기 해결 노력 강화 촉구

0.오지리

-금번 사태는 분쟁의 정치적 해결의 중요성을 일깨워줌.

-중동지역 문제 해결에 있어 CBM, 군비축소, 대량 파괴무기 핵 불확산,

PAGE 3

0038

아랍.이스라엘 분쟁등을 포괄적으로 검토필요

　　0.쿠웨이트

　-미국.소련 및 기타 안보리 이사국, 다국적군 참가국, 유엔사무총장, 비동맹국들의 지원에 감사

　　0.사우디아라비아

　-팔레스타인 문제등 기타 중동 문제 해결 노력강화 촉구

　2.안보리는 3.3.(일) 16:30 공식회의를 재개, 잔여 결의안 토의를 계속 예정이며, 이에 앞서 비공식협의를 가질예정임.

　　첨부 FAX: UNW(F)-097:

　1. 쿠바 결의안(S/22232),

　2. 쿠바결의안(S/22233),

　3. 비동맹 5개국 결의안,

　4. 대쿠웨이트 .이락 인도적 지원관련 사무총장 발언. 끝

　(대사대리 신기복-국장)

UNITED NATIONS

Security Council

PROVISIONAL

S/22232/Rev.2
2 March 1991
ENGLISH
ORIGINAL: SPANISH

Cuba: draft resolution

The Security Council,

Deeply concerned at the loss of human life, the material destruction, the tension and the instability caused by the situation in the Gulf region,

Committed to restoring the independence, sovereignty and territorial integrity of Kuwait,

Recalling the Geneva Conventions of 1949,

Considering its primary responsibility for the maintenance of international peace and security, as established in Article 24 of the Charter of the United Nations,

Convinced that it is its duty to use all peaceful means for the settlement of international conflicts and differences in order to maintain international peace and security and "save succeeding generations from the scourge of war", as proclaimed in the Preamble to the Charter of the United Nations,

Noting the suspension of offensive combat operations in the Gulf region,

1. Decides to declare a cease-fire immediately;

2. Requests the Secretary-General to dispatch immediately a United Nations military observer mission to supervise the cease-fire declared in paragraph 1 above;

3. Requests also the Secretary-General to submit to it a plan for the urgent establishment of a United Nations peace-keeping force, in consultation with the countries in which the peace-keeping force will be stationed, for the purpose of re-establishing international peace and security in the Gulf region.

2896E

4 —1

0040

Security Council

PROVISIONAL

S/22233/Rev.2
2 March 1991
ENGLISH
ORIGINAL: SPANISH

Cuba: draft resolution

The Security Council,

Recalling its resolution 674 B (1990),

Reaffirming the need to take steps with a view to reaching a permanent peaceful solution to the situation in the Gulf region.

Committed to restoring the independence, sovereignty and territorial integrity of Kuwait and to avoiding further losses of life and material property,

Considering the role which the Secretary-General has played in the elimination and avoidance of situations of conflict and the role he has to play in achieving a permanent peaceful solution in the situation,

Considering also the efforts which the Secretary-General made to that end before hostilities erupted on 16 January 1991,

Expressing its support for the statement to the press by the Secretary-General on 15 January 1991,

1.   Reiterates its confidence in the Secretary-General in the exercise of his good offices and requests him to take diplomatic initiatives to re-establish and guarantee the maintenance of peace and security in the region on the basis of the relevant elements of his statement to the press of 15 January 1991 and of any other subsequent element he may consider appropriate;

2.   Requests the Secretary-General to inform the Security Council of the outcome of his good offices and diplomatic efforts dedicated to the objectives specified in paragraph 1 above.

2898E

4 - 2

0041

Security Council

PROVISIONAL

S/22318
2 March 1991

ORIGINAL: ENGLISH

Cuba, Ecuador, India, Yemen and Zimbabwe: draft resolution

The Security Council,

Recalling its relevant resolutions, particularly resolutions 660 (1990), 661 (1990), 665 (1990), 666 (1990) and 670 (1990),

Welcoming Kuwait's liberation following total withdrawal of Iraq's forces from Kuwait in compliance with paragraph 2 of resolution 660 (1990),

Noting the urgent humanitarian circumstances in both Iraq and Kuwait,

1. Determines that humanitarian circumstances have arisen in Iraq and Kuwait, including for the purposes of paragraphs 3 (c) and 4 of resolution 661 (1990);

2. Decides that none of the provisions of resolution 661 (1990) and other relevant provisions of subsequent resolutions, in regard to supplies for medical purposes, foodstuffs, water, fuel and electricity, shall have any further force and effect;

3. Requests the United Nations specialized agencies, the International Committee of the Red Cross and other humanitarian agencies to extend assistance in implementing this resolution, particularly for supplies and distribution of foodstuffs.

2952E

4-3

0042

Press Release

Department of Public Information • News Coverage Service • New York

SG/SM/4548
IK/2
1 March 1991

SECRETARY-GENERAL TO SEND MARTTI AHTISAARI TO KUWAIT-IRAQ AREA TO DETERMINE UNITED NATIONS ROLE IN PROVIDING URGENT HELP TO PEOPLE IN NEED

Following is the text of a statement by Secretary-General Javier Perez de Cuellar, delivered this morning at a press briefing given by the heads of the World Health Organization (WHO) and the United Nations Children's Fund (UNICEF), who reported on a joint WHO/UNICEF mission to Iraq:

I met yesterday afternoon with a group of my senior colleagues concerning various aspects of the situation in Kuwait and Iraq, including of course emergency assistance relating to their peoples. The people of Kuwait have suffered greatly since August of last year and those of Iraq have recently endured immense hardship.

It was evident to us that the United Nations system must react with all due speed in order to provide help urgently to those in need. Every effort must be made to avoid further human suffering and to prevent catastrophes from occurring, notably in the fields of health and nutrition.

Having this in mind, and in light of my discussions with my colleagues, I have decided to ask Under-Secretary-General Martti Ahtisaari to travel to the area on my behalf on a short mission, at the earliest appropriate moment, and to report back to me on the various actions that the United Nations can take.

As far as emergency assistance is concerned, there has been considerable prior planning and various stocks have been pre-positioned in the vicinity of the areas most affected by recent events. These stocks can be moved speedily to those in need.

Furthermore a joint mission, undertaken by the World Health Organization (WHO) and the United Nations Children's Fund (UNICEF) has just returned from Iraq, having sought to ascertain essential health needs there, especially among mothers and children. I am confident that action can be taken expeditiously on the basis of the findings of that mission.

I wish the peoples of the area to know that the United Nations system stands ready in the period ahead, to be of all possible help to them.

* *** *

2128p

4—4

0043

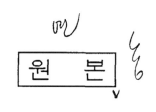

외 무 부

종 별 :

번 호 : UNW-0493　　　　　　　　　일 시 : 91 0304 0700

수 신 : 장 관(국연,중근동,해기,기정) 사본:노창희대사

발 신 : 주유엔대사

제 목 : 걸프사태 (안보리)

연: UNW-0489,0490

1. 안보리는 연호 3.2.(토) 미국 결의안 (S/RES/686) 을 채택한데 이어 3.3.(일)20:30 공식회의를 개최한바, 인도적 원조 문제에관한 의장의 별첨 성명 발표만을 청취 하고 약5분만에 종료되었음.

2. 금일 공식회의에 앞서 오후 6시부터 약 2시간반 동안 이사국간 비공식 협의가있었는바, 동협의에서는 제 686호 결의안을 수락하는 이락 외상명의 3.3.자. 서한, 상기 의장 성명문안, 연호비동맹 및 쿠바 결의안 초안 (S/22318, 22232,22233) 처리문제가 토의된 것으로 알려짐.

3. 상임이사국 들은 인도적 원조에 관한 연호 비동맹 5개국 결의안 초안 (S/22318)을 의식하여 상기 의장 성명을 적극 추진한것으로 관측되며, 비공식 협의과정에서동 초안 제안국들은 금일 공식회의 에서는 의장 성명만을 발표하고 동 초안 처리는일단 미루기로 양해 하였다고 함.

4. 또한 쿠바 결의안 초안 (S/22232/REV.3,S/22233/REV.2) 도 쿠바가 금일 회의에서의 처리를 고집하지 않기로하여 연기된것으로 알려짐.

5. 안보리 차기회의 일시는 이사국간 협의를 거쳐 추후발표될 예정임. 끝

(대사대 리 신기복-국장)

첨부: FAX (UNW(F)-098)

국기국	차관	1차보	2차보	중아국	국기국(대사)	청와대	안기부	장관	공보관

PAGE 1　　　　　　　　　　　　　　　　　91.03.05　00:57 CT

외신 1과 통제관

0044

DRAFT PRESIDENTIAL STATEMENT

The Council welcomes the decisions taken to date relating to food and medical needs by the Committee established under resolution 661 including those just taken to facilitate the provision of humanitarian assistance including infant formula and water purification material.

It calls upon the Committee to continue to act promptly on requests submitted to it for humanitarian assistance.

It urges the Committee to pay particular attention to the findings and recommendations on critical medical/public health and nutritional conditions in Iraq which have been and will continue to be submitted to it by the World Health Organization, UNICEF, the International Committee of the Red Cross and other relevant organizations, consistent with the relevant resolutions, and urges these humanitarian agencies to play an active role in this process and co-operate closely with the Committee in its work.

The Council welcomes the Secretary-General's announcement that he plans to send urgently a mission led by Under-Secretary-General Martti Ahtisaari comprising representatives of the appropriate United Nations agencies to Iraq and Kuwait to assess the humanitarian needs arising in the immediate post crisis environment. The Council invites the Secretary-General to keep it informed in the shortest possible time on the progress of his mission on which it pledges to take immediate action.

4 - 1

Sir,

I have the honour to inform you that the Iraqi Government has taken note of the text of Security Council resolution 686 (1991) and that it has agreed to fulfil its obligations under the said resolution. We hope that the Council, in its turn, will interact in an objective and honourable manner, pursuant to the provisions of international law and the principles of equity and justice, with our faithful and - to the extent that we are able - speedy fulfilment of those obligations.

You and the members of the Security Council are well aware of the manner in which the American forces and their partners in the military operations against Iraq have implemented Security Council resolution 678 (1990), and of the major losses which Iraq has suffered to its infrastructure, economic, civilian, cultural and religious property, basic public services such as electricity, water, telephones, transport, fuel and other essential requirements of everyday life.

Despite these facts, resolution 686 (1991) has ignored the Iraqi people's suffering and the imposition on Iraq alone of a long series of obligations. A number of members of the Security Council referred to this fact, leading one of them (Cuba) to vote against the resolution, while three States - India, Yemen and China, the latter being a permanent member of the Council - abstained.

We record these facts for history and for the attention of those members of the Security Council and the international Organization - and those elements of international public opinion - who have a conscience. Our agreement to fulfil our obligations under this resolution stems from our determination to refute the pretexts which some may employ in order to persist in their aggression against Iraq and to inflict further harm on its people.

Iraq hopes that the Security Council will ensure the adoption of a resolution proclaiming an official cease-fire and the cessation of all military operations on land, at sea and in the air, as well as the immediate withdrawal of the foreign military forces stationed without any justification in various regions of Iraq. Iraq also hopes that the Security Council will proceed to declare, with all possible speed, the bases for its adoption of Security Council resolutions 661 (1990), 665 (1990) and 670 (1990) as having elapsed, with the result that the resolutions become null and void.

Accept, Sir, the assurances of my highest consideration.

The President of the Security Council; and
The Secretary-General of the United Nations

4 - 2

0046

(Signed)   Tariq AZIZ
                Deputy Prime Minister
           Minister for Foreign Affairs

Baghdad, 3 March 1991

4-3

0047

Security Council

PROVISIONAL

S/22232/Rev.3
3 March 1991
ENGLISH
ORIGINAL: SPANISH

Cuba: draft resolution

The Security Council,

Deeply concerned at the loss of human life, the material destruction, the tension and the instability caused by the situation in the Gulf region,

Committed to restoring the independence, sovereignty and territorial integrity of Kuwait,

Recalling the Geneva Conventions of 1949,

Considering its primary responsibility for the maintenance of international peace and security, as established in Article 24 of the Charter of the United Nations,

Convinced that it is its duty to use all peaceful means for the settlement of international conflicts and differences in order to maintain international peace and security and "save succeeding generations from the scourge of war", as proclaimed in the Preamble to the Charter of the United Nations,

Resolved to work assiduously in favour of the full restoration of peace in the Gulf region and of the role the United Nations should play in that process,

1. Notes the suspension of offensive combat operations in the Gulf region;

2. Requests the Secretary-General to dispatch immediately a United Nations military observer mission to supervise the suspension of offensive combat operations in the Gulf region and contribute to the speedy and effective conclusion of a definitive cease-fire;

3. Requests also the Secretary-General to submit to it a plan for the urgent establishment of a United Nations peace-keeping force, in consultation with the countries in which the peace-keeping force will be stationed, for the purpose of re-establishing international peace and security in the Gulf region.

2971E

4-4

0048

외　무　부

종　별 :

번　호 : UNW-0500　　　　　　　　　　　일　시 : 91 0304 1800

수　신 : 장 관(국연,중근동,해기,기정)(사본:노창희대사)

발　신 : 주 유엔 대사

제　목 : 걸프사태(안보리)

연: UNW-0493

1. 연호 3.3. 회의 이후 3.4. 오후 현재 안보리는 공식회의 또는 비공식협의 일정이 잡혀있지 않고있으며 3.5. 개별협의가 있을 것으로 보임.

2. 연호 비동맹 5개국 결의안 초안은 공식 철회되지는 않았으나 3.3. 의장 성명발표에 따라 동 제안국들이 더이상 채택을 추진하지않을 것으로 보이며, 쿠바의 2개 결의안 초안도 현재호응을 받지 못하고 있는것으로 알려짐.끝

(대사대리 신기복-국장)

국기국　　1차보　　중아국　국가국(대사)　안기부　　공보처　2차인　차관　중관　대화반

외 무 부

종 별 :

번 호 : UNW-0509 일 시 : 91 0305 1810

수 신 : 장 관(국연,중근동,해기,기정) 사본:노창희대사

발 신 : 주 유엔 대사

제 목 : 걸프사태 (안보리)

연: UNW-0500

1. 안보리는 3.5.현재 표제사태, 서부 사하라, 사이프러스 문제를 포함한 주요 현안들에 관해 의장이 이사국들과 개별 협의를 진행중임.

2. 지난 3.2. SAFWAN 군사회담시 합의와 관련, 미측의 위반 사례를 항의하는 이락 외상 명의 3.4.자 별첨 서한이 안보리 문서로 배포되었음.

3. 3.5. 국제적십자위원회 (ICRC) 는 이락측으로부터 다국적군 포로 35명 (미군 15명 포함)을 인수하였음을 발표함.

4. 한편 2.27. 전투중지 조치와 관련 3.4.까지 다음국가들이 자국의 관련 성명을 안보리 문서로 배포한바, 모두 전투 중지와 쿠웨이트 해방을 환영하는 내용으로서 다수국가들이 팔레스타인 문제를 포함한 중동문제 해결 필요성을 아울러 지적하였음.

다음

싱가폴 (2.28.외상), 인니 (2.28.외상), 말련 (2.28.외상), 알제리아 (2.28. 외무부대변인), 룩셈불그 (2.28. EC 12 개국 성명), 파라과이 (2.28. 외무부), 네팔 (3.1.정 부), 몽고 (3.1.외무부대변인), 유고 (3.1.외무부: 비동맹 의장국), 체코(3.4.외무부)

(대사대리 신기복-국장)

첨부: FAX (UNW(F)-0101)

국기국   1차보   중아국   국기국(대사)정문국   안기부   공보처   으자선   차관   장관

PAGE 1

UNITED
NATIONS

UNW(FI)-0101   10305 1810   첨부물 UNW-0509   S

Security Council

Distr.   총 3매
GENERAL

S/22324
4 March 1991
ENGLISH
ORIGINAL: ARABIC

IDENTICAL LETTERS DATED 4 MARCH 1991 FROM THE PERMANENT
REPRESENTATIVE OF IRAQ TO THE UNITED NATIONS ADDRESSED
RESPECTIVELY TO THE SECRETARY-GENERAL AND THE PRESIDENT
OF THE SECURITY COUNCIL

    On instructions from my Government, I have the honour to transmit a letter addressed to you from Mr. Tariq Aziz, Deputy Prime Minister and Minister for Foreign Affairs of the Republic of Iraq, dated 4 March 1991.

    I should be grateful if you would kindly have this letter and its annex circulated as a document of the Security Council.

                            (Signed)   Abdul Amir A. AL-ANBARI
                                         Ambassador
                                Permanent Representative

배부처	장관실	차관실	일차보	이차보	기획실	의전장	아주국	미주국	구주국	중아국	국가국	경제국	통상국	정문국	영교국	총무피	감사관	공보관	외연원	청외대	총리실	안기부	문공부
									이														2098

91-07312   2098c (E)   /...

3-1

0051

S/22324
English
Page 2

<u>Annex</u>

<u>Identical letters dated 4 March 1991 from the Deputy Prime Minister
and Minister for Foreign Affairs of Iraq addressed respectively to
the Secretary-General and the President of the Security Council</u>

I have the honour to inform you that, between yesterday and the time of
writing, American aircraft have deliberately broken the sound barrier over Baghdad
four times. This has also been done in other Governorates. You are not unaware of
the terror this causes to civilians, particularly children, as a result of the loud
noise produced and the shaking of buildings and houses.

At 2155 hours (local time) yesterday, 2 March, the American forces discharged
armed troops from six helicopters near kilometre 160 on the Baghdad-Amman road.
This area is very distant from the theatre of operations.

These two acts are inconsistent with the bases and foundations of the
agreement reached at the military meeting at Safwan on the afternoon of
2 March 1991.

These acts constitute flagrant and unjustified provocations. In expressing
its condemnation of these acts, the Iraqi Government registers its vigorous protest
against them and appeals to you to endeavour to halt them.

(Signed) Tariq AZIZ
Deputy Prime Minister
Minister for Foreign Affairs
of the Republic of Iraq

3-2

0052

INTERNATIONAL COMMITTEE OF THE RED CROSS
Information Department

19, avenue de la Paix
1202 Geneva
Switzerland
Tel. 41 22 734-6001
Fax 41 22 734-8280

Delegation to the United Nations
780 Third Avenue - Suite 2802
New York, N.Y. 10017
Tel: (212) 371-0770
Fax (212) 838-5397

PRESS RELEASE

Communication to the press No. 91/13
5 March 1991

THIRTY-FIVE POWS HANDED OVER TO THE ICRC

Geneva (ICRC) - The International Committee of the Red Cross
(ICRC) confirms that 35 POWs, members of the coalition armed
forces, were handed over this morning to its delegation in
Baghdad.

The 35 POWs - 15 Americans, nine British, nine Saudi Arabians,
one Italian and one Kuwaiti - will be flown to Riyadh on an ICRC
aircraft as soon as weather conditions permit. They will be
accompanied by a delegate and a doctor from the ICRC and will be
met in Riyadh by representatives of their respective countries.

++++

3-3

0053

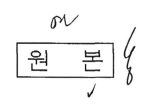

외 무 부

종 별 :

번 호 : UNW-0518　　　　　　　　　일 시 : 91 0306 1820

수 신 : 장 관 (국연,중근동,해기,기정) 사본:노창희대사

발 신 : 주 유엔 대사

제 목 : 걸프사태 (안보리)

　　연: UNW-0509

　　1. 안보리 제686호 결의 관련 이락은 자국이 90.8.2.이후 취득한 쿠웨이트 재산의 반환 결정을 유엔측에 3.5.자로 통보해 온바, 동내용은 별첨서한 (S/22330) 참조바람.

　　2.쿠웨이트 측은 동국 거주 팔레스타인인을 쿠웨이트 당국이 탄압하고 있다는 주장과 관련 이를 부인하는 자국 외상 성명을 3.5. 안보리 문서 (S/22331) 로 배포하였음. 한편 이스라엘은 이락의 쿠웨이트 침공후 PLO 의 이락 지원언동을 비난하는 대표부 명의 서한 (S/22295) 을 안보리 문서로 배포함.

　　3. 3.6. NYT 지는 유엔발 기사에서 이락에 억류중인 쿠웨이트 민간인 석방문제가 정식휴전의 조기타결에 주요 장애요인이 될 가능성이 있다고 언급함. 또한 동지는 90.2 월 중순경 국제적십자사 측 추정에 의하면 상기 억류민간인이 7,000명 수준이었으나 이락군 철수시 다수민간인이 납치되었으므로 그후 숫자가 훨씬늘은 것으로 보고있다고 보도함. (단, 일부 쿠웨이트 관리들의 2-3만명선 주장은 가능성이 크지않은 것으로 알려짐) 끝

　　(대사대리 신기복-국장)

　　첨부: 이락측 서한(S/22330) FAX(UNW(F)-0104)

UNW(f)-0104   10306 1820   첨부료 UNW-0518

UNITED
NATIONS

Security Council

총 2매

Distr.
GENERAL

S/22330
5 March 1991
ENGLISH
ORIGINAL: ARABIC

IDENTICAL LETTERS DATED 5 MARCH 1991 FROM THE PERMANENT
REPRESENTATIVE OF IRAQ TO THE UNITED NATIONS ADDRESSED
RESPECTIVELY TO THE SECRETARY-GENERAL AND THE PRESIDENT
OF THE SECURITY COUNCIL

On instructions from my Government, I have the honour to transmit a letter
addressed to you from Mr. Tariq Aziz, Deputy Prime Minister and Minister for
Foreign Affairs of the Republic of Iraq, dated 5 March 1991, concerning the return
of property seized by Iraq after 2 August 1990.

I should be grateful if you would kindly have this letter and its annex
circulated as a document of the Security Council.

(Signed) Abdul Amir A. AL-ANBARI
Ambassador
Permanent Representative

91-07474 2211e (E)   /...

2-1

0055

S/22330
English
Page 2

<u>Annex</u>

<u>Identical letters dated 5 March 1991 from the Deputy Prime
Minister and Minister for Foreign Affairs of Iraq addressed
respectively to the Secretary-General and the President of
the Security Council</u>

I have the honour to inform you that the Iraqi Government has decided,
pursuant to its acceptance of Security Council resolution 686 (1991), as
communicated in my letter to you dated 3 March 1991, to return the following
property seized by the Iraqi authorities after 2 August 1990:

1.   Quantities of gold

2.   Quantities of Kuwaiti paper currency

3.   Museum objects

4.   Civilian aircraft

The competent Iraqi authorities are prepared to hand over this property as
soon as possible. Please be so kind as to inform us of the procedures for carrying
out the hand-over.

> (Signed) Tariq AZIZ
> Deputy Prime Minister
> Minister for Foreign Affairs
> of the Republic of Iraq

2-2

0056

주 국 련 대 표 부

주국련 20313211-
　　　　　144

수신 장관　　　　　　　　　　　1991.　3.　7.

참조 국제기구조약국장, 중동아프리카국장

제목 걸프사태 (안보리)

　　표제사태 관련 안보리 문서를 별첨과 같이 송부합니다.

첨 부 : 상기 문서. 끝.

주　　　국　　　련　　　대

0057

13367

**UNITED
NATIONS**

Security Council

Distr.
GENERAL

S/22282
28 February 1991

ORIGINAL: ENGLISH

LETTER DATED 28 FEBRUARY 1991 FROM THE PERMANENT REPRESENTATIVE OF
MALAYSIA TO THE UNITED NATIONS ADDRESSED TO THE SECRETARY-GENERAL

I have the honour to transmit herewith the text of the statement by
H.E. Dato' Haji Abu Hassan bin Haji Omar, Minister of Foreign Affairs of Malaysia
dated 28 February 1991 on the situation in the Persian Gulf.

I should be grateful if the text of the statement could be circulated as a
document of the Security Council.

(Signed) RAZALI Ismail
Ambassador

91-06620 2764a (E)   /...

0058

Annex

Statement dated 28 February 1991 by the Minister for
Foreign Affairs of Malaysia

Malaysia shares in the happiness of the people of Kuwait over the liberation
of their country and looks forward to the re-establishment of the legitimate
Government of Kuwait. With the accomplishment of the task in fulfilment of
resolution 678, all efforts must now be directed towards bringing an urgent
cessation of hostilities to minimize further destruction and loss of lives.

Malaysia welcomes today's announcement by President Bush of the suspension of
all offensive combat operations. Malaysia welcomes Iraq's declaration accepting
all 12 Security Council resolutions on the Iraq-Kuwait situation and commends its
earlier decision to withdraw from Kuwait in response to the Soviet Union's peace
proposals. Given Iraq's acceptance, the Security Council should move immediately
to arrange for a cease-fire and the cessation of hostilities. Governments of the
allied forces must cooperate with the Security Council to bring about an immediate
end to hostilities now that Kuwait has been liberated.

Malaysia calls upon the Arab States to begin the process of reconciliation
amongst themselves and to agree on the necessary security arrangements to prevent
the occurrence of a similar crisis in the future.

Malaysia believes it is now incumbent upon the Security Council to work
towards a framework for a political settlement to the Gulf crisis and the broader
issue of the Arab-Israeli conflict, including the Palestine problem. Malaysia
strongly urges all parties concerned, including Iraq, to extend their fullest
cooperation to the Security Council in this urgent task to restore international
peace and security in the region.

Ministry of Foreign Affairs
Kuala Lumpur

0059

UNITED NATIONS

Security Council

S

Distr.
GENERAL

S/22284
28 February 1991
ENGLISH
ORIGINAL: FRENCH

LETTER DATED 28 FEBRUARY 1991 FROM THE CHARGE D'AFFAIRES A.I. OF
THE PERMANENT MISSION OF ALGERIA TO THE UNITED NATIONS ADDRESSED
TO THE SECRETARY-GENERAL

I have the honour to transmit herewith the text of the statement, dated
28 February 1991, by the spokesman for the Ministry of Foreign Affairs concerning
the latest developments in the Gulf situation. I would request that you arrange
for the text of this letter and its annex to be circulated as a document of the
Security Council.

(Signed) Amar BENDJAMA
Chargé d'affaires a.i.

91-06653 2323d (E)

/...

0060

<u>Annex</u>

STATEMENT BY THE SPOKESMAN FOR THE MINISTRY OF FOREIGN AFFAIRS

Following its withdrawal from Kuwait, Iraq informed the Security Council of its decision to comply with the resolutions of the United Nations. Since that time a suspension of hostilities has been observed.

The Security Council must consequently declare an immediate cease-fire and order the immediate withdrawal of all foreign forces from Iraqi territory.

It is also incumbent upon the Security Council to give the Secretary-General a mandate to act quickly to establish appropriate machinery with respect to peace-keeping operations for the consolidation of the cease-fire, the withdrawal of foreign forces from Iraqi territory and an exchange of prisoners.

It is Algeria's understanding that once the withdrawal of Iraq's forces from Kuwait has been completed, the rationale for some of the measures which the Council has taken against Iraq will no longer exist.

The lifting of these measures and the commitment on the part of the Security Council to guarantee respect for the sovereignty and territorial integrity of Iraq and Kuwait are needed to promote calm and a climate conducive to the reconstruction of Iraq and Kuwait.

Algeria maintains that future security concerns are the responsibility of the countries of the region alone.

It reminds the members of the Security Council and the entire international community of their commitment to seek an urgent and definitive solution to all the problems in the Middle East and to the Palestinian question in particular.

The promotion of stability that is lasting and genuine also requires that all nuclear weapons and weapons of mass destruction be eliminated from every part of the region.

Acting in the framework of the Arab Maghreb Union, Algeria calls for a rigorous and uncompromising appraisal of the consequences of the tragedy that has been thrust upon the Arab nation and expresses its readiness to unite its efforts with the efforts of those who are concerned with drawing the true lessons from this tragedy in order to find anew reasons for believing in their common destiny and in the abiding worth of the values embodied in their civilization.

Algiers, 28 February 1991

0061

UNITED NATIONS

A S

General Assembly   Security Council

Distr.
GENERAL

A/45/967
S/22289
1 March 1991

ORIGINAL: ENGLISH

GENERAL ASSEMBLY
Forty-fifth session
Agenda item 153
IRAQI AGGRESSION AND THE CONTINUED
  OCCUPATION OF KUWAIT IN FLAGRANT
  VIOLATION OF THE CHARTER OF THE
  UNITED NATIONS

SECURITY COUNCIL
Forty-sixth year

Letter dated 1 March 1991 from the Permanent Representative
of Mongolia to the United Nations addressed to the
Secretary-General

On instructions received from my Government, I have the honour to transmit herewith the statement made by the spokesman of the Ministry of Foreign Relations on the situation in the Persian Gulf (see annex).

I should be grateful if you would kindly have the present letter and its annex circulated as an official document of the General Assembly, under agenda item 153, and of the Security Council.

(Signed) M. DUGERSUREN
Permanent Representative

91-06858 2106i (E)

/...

ANNEX

Statement made at Ulaanbaatar on 1 March 1991 by the spokesman
of the Ministry of Foreign Relations of Mongolia

As a result of the liberation by the multinational forces of the State of Kuwait pursuant to United Nations Security Council resolution 678 (1990), the independence and sovereignty of Kuwait have been restored and the combat operations in the Persian Gulf have been halted. The Government of the Mongolian People's Republic deems it as a triumph of justice and a victory of the United Nations and of the world community.

From the very beginning, the Mongolian People's Republic denounced firmly Iraqi annexation of the sovereign State of Kuwait by force. Mongolia's principled position was clearly set forth, _inter alia_, in the statement issued by the Government of the Mongolian People's Republic on 17 January 1991.*

Had the successive resolutions of the United Nations Security Council on the immediate and unconditional withdrawal of Iraqi troops from Kuwait and on restoration of this country's independence and sovereignty through political means, as well as the world community's legitimate demands, been implemented from the very beginning, the events would not have escalated into the armed conflict and would not have brought about numerous human casualties and extensive material losses. The Persian Gulf war has become a unique lesson in the history of mankind.

The Government of the Mongolian People's Republic considers that this event once again demonstrates the vital importance of the strict observance of the fundamental principles of international law and inter-State relations, and respect for sovereignty and independence of all States, large and small alike.

-----

* S/22112.

0063

Security Council

Distr.
GENERAL

S/22291
1 March 1991

ORIGINAL: ENGLISH

LETTER DATED 1 MARCH 1991 FROM THE PERMANENT REPRESENTATIVE OF NEPAL
TO THE UNITED NATIONS ADDRESSED TO THE SECRETARY-GENERAL

I have the honour to enclose herewith a statement issued by His Majesty's Government of Nepal on the cessation of armed hostilities in the Persian Gulf region.

I have the further honour to request that the statement be circulated as a document of the Security Council.

(Signed) Jai Pratap RANA
Ambassador
Permanent Representative

Annex

Statement of His Majesty's Government of Nepal on
the end of the Gulf war

With the cessation of armed hostilities and the acceptance by Iraq of the resolutions of the Security Council, the war in the Persian Gulf has come to an end, which His Majesty's Government of Nepal heartily welcomes. We particularly welcome the withdrawal of Iraqi forces from Kuwait and the restoration of that small non-aligned country's independence and sovereignty. His Majesty's Government of Nepal supported the efforts of the United Nations and its Secretary-General as well as other nations whose moral and material contributions helped achieve these noble goals.

Now that the war has ended, His Majesty's Government of Nepal looks forward to the peaceful works of reconstruction in the Gulf and the political settlement of the entangled problems of the Middle East, including the Palestinian problem.

UNITED NATIONS

Security Council

S

Distr.
GENERAL

S/22293
1 March 1991

ORIGINAL: ENGLISH

LETTER DATED 1 MARCH 1991 FROM THE PERMANENT REPRESENTATIVE OF
YUGOSLAVIA TO THE UNITED NATIONS ADDRESSED TO THE PRESIDENT
OF THE SECURITY COUNCIL

I have the honour to transmit the text of the statement by the Federal
Secretariat for Foreign Affairs of the SFR of Yugoslavia dated 1 March 1991
concerning the ending of the hostilities in the Persian Gulf.

I would be grateful if the text of the statement would be circulated as a
document of the Security Council.

(Signed) Darko SILOVIC
Ambassador

91-06827 2173g (E)

/...

0066

Annex

Statement by the Federal Secretariat for Foreign Affairs of the SFR of Yugoslavia concerning the ending of the hostilities in the Persian Gulf, 1 March 1991

It was with greatest satisfaction and relief that Yugoslavia received news on the ending of the war in the Persian Gulf, on the liberation of Kuwait and the restoration of its sovereignty and legitimate Government. This historic moment for the Kuwaiti people represents at the same time the triumph of all the peoples and countries in the world in their quest for freedom and peace.

In times of building new and more just relations in the world, the international community through its decisive action, reaffirmed the unacceptability of the policy of aggression and fait accompli, which strengthened the possibilities and perspectives for achieving stable peace and security in the interest of all.

Ever since the outbreak of the crisis in the Persian Gulf, non-aligned countries and Yugoslavia, as the Chairman of the Movement, in a principled and decisive manner declared against the aggression, occupation and annexation of independent and non-aligned Kuwait and engaged themselves in seeking peaceful and just solution to the crisis on the basis of the Security Council resolutions and the basic principles of the policy of non-alignment. Such positions and activities were fully expressed at the Ministerial Meeting of Non-Aligned Countries, held in New York on 4 October 1990.

Acting within the mandate given to it at this meeting, Yugoslavia has made intensive and numerous contacts both with the parties directly involved in this conflict and with the major international factors, particularly with the permanent members of the Security Council, the European Community and the United Nations Secretary-General, putting forward the proposals and initiatives for the political solution of this dangerous crisis.

Regrettably, the efforts exerted by the Movement and the international community as a whole have not been met with favourable response and acceptance by the Iraqi leadership which resulted in unnecessary continuation of the war and further destruction, bloodshed and sufferings of the Kuwaiti and Iraqi people.

Yugoslavia particularly emphasizes the important and irreplaceable role of the United Nations in working out the uniform position of the entire international community in renouncing and condemning the policy of force and aggression and in seeking just solutions to the acute international problems, based on the United Nations Charter.

The countries of the region and the international community as a whole, and the Movement of Non-Aligned Countries accordingly, are now faced with a great responsibility and obligations to eliminate the grievous consequences of the war as soon as possible, and to consolidate peace, security and create durable stability

0067　/...

in this area. This would provide the necessary conditions for the opening up of the process of speedy resolution of the Middle East crisis in its integrity, the Palestinian question in particular.

Yugoslavia will exert efforts to have non-aligned countries engage in rebuilding trust and cooperation among the peoples of non-aligned Kuwait and Iraq and all other countries of the region. Yugoslavia views this as a proper way for the realization of interests of the entire international community, as well as of the principles and goals of the United Nations Charter and the policy of non-alignment.

0068

UNITED
NATIONS

S

Security Council

Distr.
GENERAL

S/22295
1 March 1991

ORIGINAL: ENGLISH

LETTER DATED 1 MARCH 1991 FROM THE PERMANENT REPRESENTATIVE
OF ISRAEL TO THE UNITED NATIONS ADDRESSED TO THE
SECRETARY-GENERAL

I wish to draw your attention to the role played by the Palestine Liberation Organization (PLO) in Iraq's unprovoked acts of aggression against various States in the Middle East, including Israel.

PLO officials have repeatedly backed Iraq's aggression and its defiance of binding Security Council resolutions, having hailed it as "the battle for Palestine". They have added their voice and arms to Iraqi efforts aimed at undermining other Arab States in the region, urging Iraq to cross the brink of war.

Casting itself as an unabashed supporter of Iraqi aggression, with renewed fervour since the start of the Gulf crisis, the PLO has exhorted Saddam Hussein to resort to the illegal use of force and to employ his arsenal of weapons of mass destruction against the civilian population of Israel.

Since 18 January 1991 Iraq has launched 39 Scud missiles at Israeli cities, causing scores of casualties and considerable damage to property.

While the international community has reacted with revulsion to these unprovoked acts of aggression against the civilian population of a country not involved in the hostilities, the PLO has responded with exuberance. This attitude, which applauds aggression, should be a cause of serious concern for States Members of the United Nations.

PLO verbal plaudits have been accompanied by action. Arafat has instructed his followers to support Saddam Hussein against the international coalition and has attempted to draw Israel into the war by calling for acts of terrorism both within Israel and throughout the world. As part of that effort, the PLO has fired scores of Katyusha rockets from Southern Lebanon and has attempted to infiltrate armed groups across Israel's boundaries. The PLO has sought to gather information on potential targets and on missile landing-sites for Iraqi intelligence. Moreover, it has contributed to the Iraqi disinformation campaign by alleging Israeli participation in the Gulf War.

91-06920 2775a (E)

/...

0069

The above constitutes clear evidence as to the true character of the PLO. It is time for Governments and international organizations to draw the inevitable conclusions regarding this organization. Attached is an annex containing a selection of statements by PLO officials supporting Iraq's aggression and terrorism on its behalf.

I should be grateful if you would have this letter and its annex circulated as a document of the Security Council.

(Signed) Yoram ARIDOR
Ambassador
Permanent Representative

0070

/...

Annex

PLO statements in support of Iraq

I. SUPPORT FOR IRAQI AGGRESSION

Arafat:

"We now ask this question to those who inquire about the Palestinian
position. We ask: Where does Israel stand in this confrontation? ... We can only
be in the trench hostile to zionism and its imperialist allies." (Sawt al-Sha'b,
4 September 1990)

"I say welcome, welcome, welcome to war ... Iraq and Palestine represent a
common will. We will be side by side and after the great battle, God willing, we
will pray together in Jerusalem ... The Iraqi fighters and the Palestinian
stone-throwers have an appointment with victory together." (The Associated Press,
7 January 1991)

Speaking of Saddam: "I am not his ally. He is my ally, he is the strongest
ally to my people and their occupation." (Canadian Broadcasting Service,
7 January 1991)

"Yasir Arafat expressed the support of the Palestinian Arab people and their
leadership in the face of the imperialist-Zionist aggression. He asserted that
Palestine and Iraq are standing in the same trench to regain Arab rights." (Baghdad
INA, 14 January 1991)

Speaking of Saddam: "Mountain, O mountain, the wind will not move you."
(Monte Carlo, 30 January 1991)

"We stand alongside the Iraqi people since our struggle against the Americans
and their allies is the Palestinian struggle." (Agence France Presse,
9 February 1991)

"These are fabulous days for our Arab nation, as we are witnessing the
mythical steadfastness of the Iraqi people and its heroic army commanded by my
knightly brother Saddam ... This is the mother of battles, waged for the mother of
causes, our beloved Palestine." (Algiers, Voice of Palestine, 11 February 1991)

On 25 February Arafat sent a message of support to Saddam Hussein following
the launching of the ground offensive against Iraq.

In it, Arafat pays tribute to "the fight of the people and the army of Iraq
against American hegemony and dictatorship."

"In this historic and crucial moment for our nation," declares the chief of
the PLO, "I pray for your victory and promise you the support of our people, who
fight the same war to protect the honour, nobility, security and existence of our
nation." (Agence France Presse, 25 February 1991)

0071   /...

<u>Farouk Kaddoumi</u> ("Foreign Minister"):

"We Palestinians are 100 per cent behind Iraq against the American aggression." (<u>Die Presse</u>, Vienna, 31 January 1991)

<u>Hani al-Hassan</u> (Arafat's chief political adviser):

"We have coordinated our plans to fight with Iraq in one trench." (The Associated Press, 12 December 1990)

<u>Excerpts from PLO Executive Council statement</u>:

"We call today for a firm stand ... on the side of the steadfast and combatant Iraq in the confrontation of the American-Zionist-Atlantic aggression ... The PLO calls on all the peoples of our nation and its dynamic forces to participate in the battle of confronting the American and allied aggression ... The PLO extends a salute of military brotherhood to the steadfast people of Iraq and its militant President Saddam Hussein and the valiant Iraqi army ..." (Algiers, Voice of Palestine, 29 January 1991)

II. SUPPORT FOR IRAQI MISSILE ATTACKS AGAINST ISRAEL

<u>Arafat</u>:

Addressing a public rally in Baghdad on 29 March 1990, while standing beside Saddam Hussein, Arafat declared that both leaders would enter Jerusalem victoriously, with Saddam mounted on a white horse, fighting Israel with stones, rifles and the "El-Abed" - Iraq's long-range missiles. (The Associated Press, 29 March 1990)

"The Iraqi military will resort to its chemical and biological weapons and the first missile will be directed at Israel." (Reuters, 5 November 1990)

"The Palestinian stone in Jerusalem has turned into that binary missile in Baghdad." (Algiers, Voice of Palestine, 31 December 1990)

"The Palestinian stones in Jerusalem would become chemical missiles from Baghdad." (Baghdad, Voice of Palestine, 31 December 1990)

"We will answer the Zionist enemy and say to him in 1991: a land without the Israeli or Zionist people. This land is Arab, Arab, Arab, Palestinian in her face and Arab in her heart ... The holy Palestinian stone in the hand of the Palestinian child will turn into the binary missile - this is a symphony." (Baghdad Television, 31 December 1990)

The Iraqi missiles "took the air out of the Israeli balloon." (<u>Al-Houriyyah</u>, Reuters, 23 January 1991)

0072

/...

<u>Abu Iyad</u> (Arafat's second in command):

"What they need is a missile that will put them in their place." (<u>Al-Dustur</u>, 2 January 1991)

<u>Farouk Kaddoumi</u>:

"Kaddoumi does not regret Iraqi missile attacks against Israel: 'When someone fights our enemy, we are pleased'" (Vienna Domestic Service, 31 January 1991)

<u>Hawatimah</u> (Democratic Front for the Liberation of Palestine (DFLP)):

"The Iraqi bombardment of Israel is a real wedding and the punishment for Zionist aggression." (Arab Voice of Lebanon, 20 January 1991)

"DFLP today hailed the Iraqi missile attack on Israel. <u>Hawatimah</u> said that this action calls for celebration by the Palestinians." (Radio Monte Carlo, 20 January 1991)

"<u>Hawatimah</u> described the launching of the Iraqi missiles at Tel Aviv as a cause of 'real rejoicing' for the Palestinians." (<u>Al-Ahali</u>, Egypt, 22 January 1991)

"When they say that the missiles that fall on Israeli towns fall on populated areas, we would say: it is a tit for tat ... We all must have seen ... how the Algerian youth called out in one voice: 'O beloved Iraq, strike, strike Tel Aviv'. In saying this, they speak for all peoples ..." (Algiers Radio, 29 January 1991)

<u>Habash</u> (Popular Front for the Liberation of Palestine (PFLP)):

"Iraq has restored its credibility by launching missiles against Israel, causing great satisfaction among the ranks of the Palestinian people." (Voice of the Mountain, 20 January 1991)

"PFLP said that by pounding Tel Aviv and other Zionist colonialist gatherings, Iraq has carried out the promises it issued before the war. This resulted in great relief among the Palestinian people's ranks." (Baghdad Domestic Service, 20 January 1991)

<u>Abu al-Abbas</u> (PFLP):

"Our masses in the occupied homeland have seen the enemy's forces trembling with fear and rushing to shelters to escape the Iraqi missiles, which crushed the heads of the Zionist occupiers ... Palestine will, God willing, be liberated. Today, the missiles of Iraq reached Tel Aviv. Tomorrow, the march of the believers will reach holy Jerusalem." (Baghdad Domestic Service, 19 January 1991)

0073

/...

<u>Abbas Zaki Mazid</u> (PLO Central Committee member):

"For the first time in history Tel Aviv has been bombarded and an Arab leadership has proven by a premeditated action that al-Hussein missiles reach Tel Aviv and all strategic targets in the Zionist entity. Shamir and all the arrogant forces were struck with fear and are totally impotent in the face of the fabulous steadfastness and tremendous combat capability of the secret Iraqi cavalry ... You have given the Palestinian people the most beautiful gifts ... The al-Hussein missiles constitute the most important gift in this dark era." (Baghdad Radio, 8 February 1991)

<u>Muhammad Jihad</u> (PLO official responsible for military affairs in Jordan):

"We are happy about the Scud missile attacks on Israel." (Berlin, <u>Der Morgen</u>, 30 January 1991)

<u>Yasser Abd Rabbo</u> (PLO Executive Committee member):

"... said Iraq has the right to attack Israel, as it is one of the parties in the confrontation. When asked about the firing of Iraqi missiles against Israel he praised the action." (French, British news agencies, 20 January 1991)

"The missiles have toppled the myth of the Israeli security barrier." (Baghdad Radio, 8 February 1991)

"Palestinian sources in South Lebanon said the purpose of the Katyusha attack was to do 'what the Iraqi Scuds had not yet succeeded in doing: to drag Israel into the Gulf war. When the Israelis react with fire, we shall turn this into an Israeli-Arab war'. The sources reported that Arafat has ordered the attack 'to defend innocent people in Iraq.'" (Agence France Presse, 29 January 1991)

III. FALSE ALLEGATIONS AS TO ISRAEL'S PARTICIPATION IN THE WAR

<u>Arafat</u>:

"I have information that Israel has been totally implicated in the war from the start ... Some of their planes participate in the attacks ... Moreover, there are missiles used by the Israeli Army from the Negev desert near Dimona against the western part of Iraq." (Paris Antenne-2 Television Network, 29 January 1991)

"Who said that Israel is not participating? Israel is taking part with its aircraft, its aircraft are deployed alongside United States aircraft at a number of bases ... there is now shelling from the Negev. The United States is covering this up and saying that submarines deployed in the Red Sea are doing the shelling. This is not correct. The shelling is originating from surface-to-surface missile launchers in the Negev." (Radio Monte Carlo, 30 January 1991)

<u>Yasser Abd Rabbo</u>:

Claimed that Israel, since the beginning of the war, has deployed aircraft in Turkish bases. (Agence France Presse, Reuters, 20 January 1991)

<u>PLO representative in Mexico</u>:

"Israel brought hundreds of Palestinians to the Israeli nuclear centre in the Negev so that they can serve as 'human shields' against a possible Iraqi missile attack." (<u>Uno Más Uno</u>, 1 February 1991)

<u>Bassam Abu-Sharif</u> (adviser to Yasser Arafat):

"The B-52 bombers are being drawn from bases in Britain, Spain, Diego Garcia and Israel." (Reuters, 4 February)

"Abu-Sharif said the stationing of Patriot missiles in Israel was proof that Israel is now 'part of the war'." (Monte Carlo, 21 January 1991)

IV. TERRORISM IN SUPPORT OF IRAQ

Yasser Arafat is supplying the Iraqi intelligence services with hundreds of Tunisian, Algerian and Moroccan passports to assist the Iraqis in attacking American and other targets. (<u>Rhein-Pfalz</u>, 22 January 1991)

<u>Hawatimah</u>:

Each and every Arab people is called upon to besiege and strike at United States, British, and French interests wherever their hands can reach." (Algiers Radio, 29 January 1991)

<u>George Habash</u>:

"The Palestinian fedayeen will strike Western targets hostile to Iraq." (Radio Monte Carlo, 31 January 1991)

<u>Muhammad Jihad</u>:

"The PLO has stated that it will support Iraq all it can in order to face the United States-Israeli aggression. This means an armed fight against our enemy Israel, with guns, bombs and knives." (Berlin, <u>Der Morgen</u>, 30 January 1991)

<u>Yasser Abd Rabbo</u>:

"The Palestinian fighters who launched an attack today against a convoy of the Israeli enemy in the heart of the Negev near the Dimona reactor are not only brothers-in-arms to the Iraqi fighters on the front, but share one destiny with her. Together, the Palestinian and Iraqi rifles are conducting the battle for the national destiny." (Baghdad Radio, 8 February 1991)

0075   /...

<u>Abd al-Rahim Ahmad</u> (PLO Executive Committee member):

"We urge the masses of our Arab nation and the Muslims to expand the theater of confrontations over the whole world. They must strike violently all United States interests and institutions everywhere." (INA, 22 January 1991)

<u>Zayid Wahbah</u> (PLO representative in Lebanon):

"When the shooting begins on Iraqi forces, the Palestinian forces will attack American interests in Palestine, outside Palestine and around the world." (Voice of the People, 14 January 1991)

"We'll act from Lebanon, Amman, Cairo and Damascus and orders have been given to fighters to prepare to attack United States and British interests around the world." (Agence France Presse, 16 January 1991)

"Zayid Wahbah called for attacking the interests of the coalition members and fighting the United States and Israel under the leadership of the president of Iraq." (Reuters, 27 January 1991)

V.   THE PLO IN LEBANON: OPENING A SECOND MISSILE
FRONT AGAINST ISRAEL

"Palestinian sources have said that Palestinian leader Yasir Arafat has called on the Palestinians in Lebanon to fight on the side of Iraq if a war breaks out in the Gulf. Palestinian sources also said that approximately 6,000 Palestinian fighters in the Sidon area have been placed on high alert." (Voice of Lebanon, 14 January 1991)

<u>Arafat</u>:

Concerning firing rockets at Israel, Arafat said, "It is our legal right" (Radio Monte Carlo, 30 January 1991)

<u>Hawatimah</u>:

"I call upon all PLO detachments to join the national Lebanese forces in the carrying out of fedayeen operations against the Zionist occupation forces in Southern Lebanon so that we can divert the largest possible power of the Israeli Army away from the battlefront with Iraq. I call on all PLO detachments ... to join in the fedayeen operations in Southern Lebanon and in the heart of Israel so that we prevent the Israeli forces from having a free hand ..." (Algiers Radio, 28 January 1991)

"DFLP ... called for clashing with and using arms against the Israeli enemy whenever possible and urged all the Palestinian fighters in Southern Lebanon to ... confront the Israeli enemy with arms and fire in order to open a new front with the enemy forces and zionism." (Amman, <u>Al-Ra'y</u>, 29 January 1991)

0076 /...

<u>Zayid Wahbah</u>:

"Zayid Wahbah has threatened that the PLO will shell deep inside Israel if the international alliance continues its raids on Iraqi civilians and installations. Wahbah said: Do not forget that we are struggling alongside Iraq, and that Southern Lebanon is an open front to contribute to the defence of Iraq." (Voice of Lebanon, 28 January 1991)

"Wahbah told AFP on 28 January that the PLO military forces are ready to launch attacks and bombardments deep inside Israel, if the bombardment of Iraqi civilians and institutions continues ... He added that one should not forget the PLO is fighting on the side of Iraq, and South Lebanon is an open front ... He called on the other Arab States bordering on Israel to fulfil their obligation and strike the Israeli enemy in order to thwart the destruction of Iraq ... these countries should enable Palestinian and Arab fighters to join in the battle from their own fronts." (Agence France Presse, 28 January 1991)

"We will respond to the attacks against Iraq by hitting targets inside Israel ... we view ourselves as part of the campaign in the Gulf." (Reuters, 29 and 30 January 1991)

<u>Saher Habash</u> (PLO Executive Committee member):

"The Fatah bases, the Palestinian resistance and the Lebanese national resistance front in Southern Lebanon have opened a front in South Lebanon against the Zionist enemy, in support of the just Arab front which Iraq is defending. This front will be an effective armed front in support of Iraq. He called for the opening of another front against the Zionist enemy from the Syrian-Palestinian border." (<u>Al-Jumhuriya</u>, Iraqi News Agency, 1 February 1991)

"In Sidon in Southern Lebanon, a PLO spokesman affirmed that Palestinian fighters shelled four settlements in northern Israel at dawn today. He indicated that 80 Grad projectiles were fired at the settlements of Metulla, Misgav Am, Kefar Gil'adi, and Nahariya." (Radio Monte Carlo, 29 January 1991)

"Palestinian sources in South Lebanon have announced the establishment of a unified military command embracing all Palestinian organizations to coordinate military action and open a front against Israel in South Lebanon to support Iraq." (Voice of Lebanon, 5 February 1991)

"A member of the PLO military leadership in Lebanon, Lt. Cl. Amran, said that Arafat and the PLO command gave instructions to increase the struggle against Israel in response to her military cooperation in the Gulf ... He said: 'The implementation of the instructions has already begun with the bombardment of a number of Zionist settlements in the Galilee ...'" (Agence France Presse, 29 January 1991)

"The PLO spokesman said the PLO has decided to carry out qualitative operations and escalate the armed struggle against Israel in solidarity with Iraq." (Free Lebanon Radio, 4 February 1991)

0077

UNITED NATIONS

S

 Security Council

Distr.
GENERAL

S/22299
1 March 1991

ORIGINAL: ENGLISH

LETTER DATED 1 MARCH 1991 FROM THE CHARGE D'AFFAIRES A.I. OF THE
PERMANENT MISSION OF INDONESIA TO THE UNITED NATIONS ADDRESSED
TO THE SECRETARY-GENERAL

I have the honour to transmit herewith the text of the statement by
H.E. Mr. Ali Alatas, Minister for Foreign Affairs of the Republic of Indonesia
dated 28 February 1991 on the situation in the Persian Gulf.

I would be grateful if the text of the statement could be circulated as a
document of the Security Council.

(Signed) Nugroho WISNUMURTI
Ambassador
Chargé d'affaires a.i.

91-06903   2326d (E)

/...

0078

Annex

Statement by H.E. Mr. Ali Alatas, Foreign Minister of the Republic
of Indonesia, dated 28 February 1991 on the situation in the
Persian Gulf

The Government of Indonesia welcomes the announcement by the United States, on
behalf of the Coalition Forces, of the suspension of offensive combat operations
starting at noon of 28 February 1991. We are also pleased to learn that the
Security Council will convene a meeting in which Iraq will convey its decision to
comply fully with all the relevant resolutions of the United Nations Security
Council.

We therefore fervently hope that steps will be taken towards a cease-fire and
that a comprehensive cessation of hostilities will take place. Furthermore we
would like to express our hope that the Council will immediately initiate the
consideration of the political aspects of the settlement to the Gulf war and
appropriate actions to be taken.

Finally, Indonesia shares in the happiness of the people of Kuwait as they
regain their freedom and independence in conformity with the United Nations
Security Council resolutions.

0079

UNITED NATIONS

 General Assembly   Security Council

Distr.
GENERAL

A/45/969
S/22323
1 March 1991
ENGLISH
ORIGINAL: ENGLISH/FRENCH

GENERAL ASSEMBLY
Forty-fifth session
Agenda items 35 and 153
THE SITUATION IN THE MIDDLE EAST
IRAQI AGGRESSION AND THE CONTINUED
  OCCUPATION OF KUWAIT IN FLAGRANT
  VIOLATION OF THE CHARTER OF THE
  UNITED NATIONS

SECURITY COUNCIL
Forty-sixth year

Letter dated 1 March 1991 from the Permanent Representative
of Luxembourg to the United Nations addressed to the
Secretary-General

    I have the honour to transmit herewith the French and English texts of the statement on the Gulf issued on 28 February 1991 by the European Community and its 12 member States.

    I should be grateful if you would have this letter and its annex circulated as a document of the General Assembly, under agenda items 35 and 153, and of the Security Council.

(Signed)   Jean FEYDER
Ambassador
Permanent Representative

91-07232   2097c (E)   /...

0080

ANNEX

Statement on the Gulf issued on 28 February 1991 by the European Community

The Community and its member States welcome the suspension of military operations in the Gulf.

The Community and its member States are greatly satisfied that Kuwait has recovered its freedom and that international legality has been restored. They express their gratitude to all States that committed forces to the cause of ensuring respect for the resolutions of the Security Council of the United Nations.

They pay their respects to all those who have lost their lives in this conflict.

They note Iraq's acceptance of the 12 resolutions of the Security Council of the United Nations and express the hope that its Government will rapidly accept the conditions put forth by the coalition.

It is now the task of the Security Council of the United Nations to define the necessary arrangements to put an end to the conflict.

As they stated on the day on which military operations began, the Community and its member States reaffirm their commitment to contribute to bringing about for all the peoples of the region, in dignity and security, a future of peace, stability and development in a context of social justice and regional economic solidarity.

To this end, they will make a major effort to develop an overall approach with regard to the region, bearing at one and the same time on security questions, political problems and economic cooperation.

0081

UNITED NATIONS

Security Council

S

Distr.
GENERAL

S/22325
4 March 1991

ORIGINAL: ENGLISH

LETTER DATED 4 MARCH 1991 FROM THE PERMANENT REPRESENTATIVE
OF CZECHOSLOVAKIA TO THE UNITED NATIONS ADDRESSED TO THE
PRESIDENT OF THE SECURITY COUNCIL

I have the honour to transmit to you herewith the text of the Statement of the Federal Ministry of Foreign Affairs of the Czech and Slovak Federal Republic of 1 March 1991, on the suspension of military operations in the Persian Gulf.

Text follows:

"The Federal Ministry of Foreign Affairs of the Czech and Slovak Federal Republic was fully satisfied and pleased to receive reports on the suspension of military operations in the Persian Gulf and on the restoration of the independence and sovereignty of the State of Kuwait. Thus, the months-long unceasing efforts by the international community, expressed also in twelve United Nations Security Council resolutions, to eliminate the Iraqi aggression against and illegal annexation of the neighbouring Kuwait has been crowned with success. One can only regret that this outcome had to be achieved through the force of weapons and at the cost of human and material casualties due to the intransigence and stubbornness of the Iraqi leadership to comply with the relevant Security Council resolutions. The consequences of the military operations, that have affected so heavily Iraq itself and its people, fall solely and fully on the Iraqi leadership.

The Federal Ministry of Foreign Affairs of the Czech and Slovak Federal Republic appreciates the unity, resolve and determination with which the international community has come forward to protect and liberate Kuwait, and with which it has adopted unambiguously the principle that the aggressor must not be allowed to benefit from its malevolent way of action. This is a result of the hopefully unfolding process of shaping the international relations on the principles of respect for national and human rights, friendship and cooperation.

91-07295   2194f (E)

/...

0082

The crisis in the Persian Gulf has shown that the accumulation of unresolved problems between States, ethnic strife, and religious intolerance, combined with excessive armament and stockpiling of weaponry, are no guarantee for the security of nations and for the stability in the whole region. The Ministry expresses its conviction that the international community shall exert equal efforts not only to eliminate the political, economic and moral consequences of the Persian Gulf war but also to settle all long-standing and unresolved problems of the Middle East region. For its part, it is determined to contribute to such a settlement through a well-balanced policy and relations with all countries of the region, as well as through its diplomatic activities."

End of text.

I would be most grateful if you could have the text of this letter, including the Statement of the Federal Ministry of Foreign Affairs of the Czech and Slovak Federal Republic, circulated as a document of the Security Council.

(Signed) Eduard KUKAN
Ambassador
Permanent Representative

0083

UNITED NATIONS

Security Council

S

Distr.
GENERAL

S/22326
4 March 1991
ENGLISH
ORIGINAL: SPANISH

LETTER DATED 4 MARCH 1991 FROM THE CHARGE D'AFFAIRES A.I. OF THE
PERMANENT MISSION OF PARAGUAY TO THE UNITED NATIONS ADDRESSED TO
THE SECRETARY-GENERAL

I have the honour to transmit herewith the communiqué dated 28 February 1991 from the Ministry of Foreign Affairs of Paraguay concerning the cease-fire in the Persian Gulf and the liberation of Kuwait.

I should be grateful if you would have this letter and its annex circulated as a document of the Security Council.

(Signed) Genaro V. PAPPALARDO
Chargé d'affaires a.i.

91-07324   2208e (E)

/...

0084

Annex

Communiqué dated 28 February 1991 from the
Ministry of Foreign Affairs of Paraguay

The Ministry of Foreign Affairs of Paraguay expresses the satisfaction of that country's Government with respect to the cease-fire in the Persian Gulf and the liberation of Kuwait. It at the same time affirms its support for all the Security Council resolutions relating to that conflict which have made it possible to restore Kuwait's sovereignty and territorial integrity. It expresses its conviction that an effort must be made, in the framework of the United Nations and in accordance with the Charter and the principles of international law, to bring about a just and lasting peace in the region.

UNITED NATIONS

 General Assembly   Security Council

Distr.
GENERAL

A/45/970
S/22327
4 March 1991
ENGLISH
ORIGINAL: ARABIC AND
ENGLISH

GENERAL ASSEMBLY
Forty-fifth session
Agenda item 153
IRAQI AGGRESSION AND THE CONTINUED
  OCCUPATION OF KUWAIT IN FLAGRANT
  VIOLATION OF THE CHARTER OF THE
  UNITED NATIONS

SECURITY COUNCIL
Forty-sixth year

<u>Letter dated 4 March 1991 from the Permanent Representative
of Saudi Arabia to the United Nations addressed to the
Secretary-General</u>

I have the honour to transmit to you the text of a letter from
His Royal Highness Prince Saud Al-Faisal, the Foreign Minister, addressed to you.

I should be grateful if you would kindly have the present letter and the
attached text circulated as a document of the General Assembly, under agenda item
153, and of the Security Council.

(<u>Signed</u>) Samir S. SHIHABI
Ambassador
Permanent Representative

91-07330 2785a (E)   /...

0086

ANNEX

Letter dated 4 March 1991 from the Foreign Minister of
Saudi Arabia addressed to the Secretary-General

As you are aware, the Iraqi régime has spilled more than 10 million barrels of crude oil into the waters of the Gulf, thus creating an environmental disaster that is considered the worst of its kind in history, and has waged an environmental war without regard for its neighbouring countries or for the lives of animals and plants in the region.

I do not need to mention to you that this oil pollution caused by the Iraqi régime is premeditated and intentional and is considered an irresponsible act of aggression against humans and natural resources with all the related living organisms and unique natural heritage; this, in addition to the great harm that befell many civilians who live on the coast of the Gulf, many of whom make their living from fishing or from the other resources of the sea.

This damage was reflected in particular in many human activities that are related to the waters of the Gulf, such as fisheries, desalination and other human activities, whose effect could extend to the next generation, as the Gulf is a shallow body of water and the rate of water renewal with the Indian Ocean is extremely slow because of the natural impediment presented by the Strait of Hormuz.

I would like to mention to you on this occasion some of the important natural resources that were actually exposed to danger as a result of the pollution that resulted from this environmental catastrophe and was caused by the Iraqi régime:

- Coral reefs;

- Sandy beaches;

- Al-shora plant (manjaroof);

- Seaweed;

- Lagoons;

- Tortoises and sea turtles;

- Sea and shore birds;

- The coastal environment;

- Fish and non-vertebrates.

Because the danger of crude oil leakage into the waters of the Gulf is continuing and its destructive effects have not become fully apparent, the Government of the Kingdom of Saudi Arabia will continue to monitor the environmental developments that will undoubtedly occur and keep you informed in this regard.

0087

/...

At the same time, I would like to communicate the Government of Saudi Arabia's willingness to receive technical assistance to face the expected dangers, whether from the Member States of the United Nations or from concerned specialized agencies.

May I request you kindly to distribute the present message as a document of the General Assembly and the Security Council.

Saud AL-FAISAL
Foreign Minister of the
Kingdom of Saudi Arabia

0088

UNITED NATIONS

I

S

Security Council

Distr.
GENERAL

S/22329
5 March 1991
ENGLISH
ORIGINAL: FRENCH

LETTER DATED 4 MARCH 1991 FROM THE PERMANENT REPRESENTATIVE OF
GUINEA TO THE UNITED NATIONS ADDRESSED TO THE SECRETARY-GENERAL

I have the honour to transmit herewith the French text of the communiqué
concerning the Gulf crisis issued by the Government of the Republic of Guinea on
28 February 1991.

I should be grateful if you would have the text of this communiqué circulated
as a document of the Security Council.

(Signed)   Zaïnoul Abidine SANOUSSI
Ambassador
Permanent Representative

Annex

Communiqué from the Government of the Republic of Guinea concerning the Gulf crisis

The Government of the Republic of Guinea is gladdened by the news of the suspension of hostilities following Iraq's withdrawal from Kuwait and unconditional acceptance of all the twelve (12) Security Council resolutions relating to the Gulf crisis.

The people of Guinea is deeply hopeful that all hotbeds of tension in that part of the world will be eliminated and is greatly heartened by the termination of this crisis, which has produced so many innocent victims and caused incalculable material losses.

With the help of courageous political will on the part of all the parties involved and with support from all countries which seek peace and social justice, everything must be done to facilitate the achievement of a permanent cease-fire, this being an essential precondition for the creation of an atmosphere of lasting and just peace in the region.

Such an attitude will then permit the peoples who have been reconciled to confront the many challenges facing them after this unfortunate crisis.

0090

**UNITED
NATIONS**

General Assembly　　**Security Council** Distr.
GENERAL

A/45/971
S/22331
5 March 1991
ENGLISH
ORIGINAL: ARABIC AND ENGLISH

GENERAL ASSEMBLY
Forty-fifth session
Agenda item 153
IRAQI AGGRESSION AND THE CONTINUED
  OCCUPATION OF KUWAIT IN FLAGRANT
  VIOLATION OF THE CHARTER OF THE
  UNITED NATIONS

SECURITY COUNCIL
Forty-sixth year

Letter dated 5 March 1991 from the Permanent Representative
of Kuwait to the United Nations addressed to the
Secretary-General

I have the honour to forward herewith the text of the statement made today by His Excellency Sheikh Sabah Al Ahmad Al Jaber Al Sabah, Deputy Prime Minister and Minister for Foreign Affairs of the State of Kuwait (see annex).

I should appreciate it if you would arrange for the present letter and its annex to be circulated as an official document of the General Assembly, under agenda item 153, and of the Security Council.

(Signed)　Mohammad A. ABULHASAN
Ambassador
Permanent Representative

91-07497　2180h (E)

/...

ANNEX

Statement made on 5 March 1991 by the Deputy Prime Minister and Minister for Foreign Affairs of Kuwait

Some irresponsible parties in Palestinian circles have been deliberately circulating false allegations and slanders to the effect that the official authorities in Kuwait have initiated certain practices against the Palestinian community residing in Kuwait. In doing so, those parties aim only to spread a spirit of resentment and disunity in a blatant attempt to cast themselves as the defenders of the fraternal Palestinian people.

As all are aware, the State of Kuwait has embraced expatriates from all parts of the world, including the fraternal Palestinian community, and provided them with the means to make a decent and comfortable living. It has done so on the basis of its belief in its Arab, Islamic and humanitarian obligations and its constant keen commitment to noble Arab values and principles.

Following the wicked occupation of Kuwait's land and people by the Iraqi forces for more than six months, the Kuwaiti authorities resumed - immediately the hated Iraqi occupation was ended - their normal duties of maintaining security in Kuwait. The criminal Iraqi occupiers had destroyed all the country's assets and set up a gang of conspirators and collaborators with a view to achieving their aim of perpetuating the occupation. In order to perform their duty of establishing security and stability in the country, the Kuwaiti authorities are obliged relentlessly to pursue any criminal elements, from whatever community they may come, and to show them no leniency, because those elements have not treated Kuwait and the security of its people in a manner consistent with the dictates of their position as expatriates and guests.

In categorically rejecting these allegations, Kuwait draws attention to its honourable record in its dealings with all those living in its territory and affirms that allegations by diseased minds such as these are false and utterly untruthful. The right of Kuwait to ensure and enhance its security can in no way be interpreted as being directed against any honourable person in the territory of Kuwait - the land of love and peace and the community of building and giving.

0092

Security Council

Distr.
GENERAL

S/22335
6 March 1991

ORIGINAL: ENGLISH

NOTE VERBALE DATED 6 MARCH 1991 FROM THE PERMANENT MISSION OF NIGERIA
TO THE UNITED NATIONS ADDRESSED TO THE SECRETARY-GENERAL

The Permanent Mission of the Federal Republic of Nigeria to the United Nations Organization presents its compliments to the Secretary-General of the United Nations and has the honour to forward herewith, the text of a statement, issued 1 March 1991 by the Federal Military Government of Nigeria on the Gulf crisis.

The Permanent Mission of Nigeria to the United Nations will greatly appreciate it if the attached statement is published as a Security Council document.

91-07599 2305j (E) ·

/...

<u>Annex</u>

<u>Federal Government's statement on the Gulf crisis</u>

The Federal Government welcomes the announcement by President Bush of the suspension of fighting in the Gulf, following Iraq's unconditional acceptance of all the United Nations resolutions. Nigeria believes this will lead to a speedy arrangement of a permanent cease-fire and an end to the conflict.

Nigeria is further convinced that this offers opportunity for the international community to address itself to the issue of bringing a durable peace to the Middle East.

In the attainment of this objective, Nigeria stands ready to assist the United Nations in ensuring peace and security in that region.

0094

UNITED
NATIONS

A S

 General Assembly   Security Council

Distr.
GENERAL

A/45/972
S/22337
6 March 1991

ORIGINAL: ENGLISH

GENERAL ASSEMBLY
Forty-fifth session
Agenda items 23 and 153
QUESTION OF PALESTINE
IRAQI AGGRESSION AND THE CONTINUED
  OCCUPATION OF KUWAIT IN FLAGRANT
  VIOLATION OF THE CHARTER OF THE
  UNITED NATIONS

SECURITY COUNCIL
Forty-sixth year

<u>Letter dated 6 March 1991 from the Chargé d'affaires a.i. of the</u>
<u>Permanent Observer Mission of Palestine to the United Nations</u>
<u>addressed to the Secretary-General</u>

I am instructed by the Executive Committee of the Palestine Liberation
Organization, which has the powers and responsibilities of the Provisional
Government of Palestine, to bring the following to your immediate attention.

The violent and hostile actions against the Palestinian people living in
Kuwait continues at the hands of the armed vigilantes and some elements from the
Kuwaiti army in an illegal manner. This includes terror and harassment campaigns
launched in the regions of Al Noukra, Hawali, Khitan and Al Salmieh in Kuwait City,
resulting in the arrests of great numbers of Palestinians; many of these actions
have been covered by several media networks and news agencies. Noting further that
the issue of the safety and security of the Palestinians living in Kuwait has been
raised on my part with the President of the Security Council, who in turn informed
the members of the Council, during the informal consultation of 3 March 1991, of my
grave concern expressed to him in this regard.

The Palestine Liberation Organization believes that the Kuwaiti Government and
the Arab forces, as well as the foreign forces present in Kuwait, are responsible
for the safety and security of our people. At the same time, and as a result of
the special existing situation, the international community and the Security
Council, in particular, cannot be exempted from this responsibility.

The Palestine Liberation Organization would like to recall that the majority
of Palestinians living in Kuwait are long-time residents of the country, and

91-07581 2357b (E)

/...

0095

expresses its hope that the Kuwaiti Government will take the initiative in presenting a clear-cut position on this situation, as well as taking action towards a concrete and immediate solution to the problem.

I should be grateful if you would arrange to have the text of the present letter circulated as an official document of the General Assembly, under agenda items 23 and 153, and of the Security Council.

(Signed) Dr. Nasser AL-KIDWA
Alternate Permanent Observer of
Palestine to the United Nations
Chargé d'affaires a.i.

0096

Security Council

Distr.
GENERAL

S/22338
6 March 1991

ORIGINAL: ENGLISH

LETTER DATED 6 MARCH 1991 FROM THE CHARGE D'AFFAIRES A.I. OF THE
PERMANENT MISSION OF KUWAIT TO THE UNITED NATIONS ADDRESSED TO
THE SECRETARY-GENERAL

I have the honour to transmit herewith a message from His Excellency
Sheikh Sabah Al-Ahmad Al-Jaber Al Sabah, Deputy Prime Minister and Minister of
Foreign Affairs, addressed to Your Excellency.

I should appreciate it if you would arrange for this message to be circulated
as a document of the Security Council.

(Signed) Nabeela AL-MULLA
Chargé d'affaires a.i.

91-07623   2338d (E)   /...

<u>Annex</u>

[Original: Arabic/English]

<u>Letter dated 4 March 1991 from the Deputy Prime Minister
and Minister for Foreign Affairs of Kuwait addressed to
the Secretary-General</u>

I have the honour and pleasure to inform you that the Government of Kuwait is resuming the functions of the State and directing the affairs of the nation from Kuwait City.

I should like to seize this opportunity to express our gratitude and appreciation to you personally and to the United Nations system as a whole for the indispensable role played to reverse the Iraqi aggression and to end the occupation of Kuwait.

The contribution of the United Nations system to the restoration of Kuwait's territorial integrity, and the return of the legitimate government to the country has reconfirmed the purposes and objectives of the Charter and the importance of the Organization in maintaining international peace and security.

Sabah Al-Ahmad Al-Jaber AL SABAH
Deputy Prime Minister
and Minister of Foreign Affairs

0098

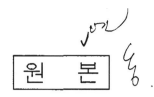

외 무 부

종 별 :

번 호 : UNW-0526　　　　　　　　　일 시 : 91 0307 1800

수 신 : 장 관(국연,중동일,해기,기정)(사본:노창희대사)

발 신 : 주 유엔 대사

제 목 : 걸프사태(안보리)

　　1. J.PEREZ DE CUELLAR 사무총장은 쿠웨이트요청에 의거, 이락 침공으로 인한 쿠웨이트의 인명손실과 재산 피해등을 조사하기 위해 유엔대표단 (단장: A. FARAH 전사무차장)을 곧현지에 파견예정인 것으로 알려졌음. (별첨 안보리문서참조)

　　2.쿠웨이트 수도의 정부기능 재개를 알리는 3.4.자 쿠웨이트 외상 명의 서한이 안보리 문서로 배포되었으며, 한편 쿠웨이트내 팔레스타인인 탄압을 항의하는 PLO 측 서한도 3.6. 자로 배포됨.

　　첨부:상기 안보리문서 (S/22333,22334):UNW(F)-0106

　　끝

　　(대사대리 신기복-국장)

총기국 총리실	장관 안기부	차관 공보처	1차보	2차보	국기국(대사)	정문국	대사실	청와대

PAGE 1　　　　　　　　　　　　　　　　　　　　　　　91.03.08　　08:53 WG

　　　　　　　　　　　　　　　　　　　　　　　　　외신 1과 통제관

　　　　　　　　　　　　　　　　　　　　　　　　　　　0099

UNITED
NATIONS

Security Council

Distr.
GENERAL

S/22333
6 March 1991

ORIGINAL: ENGLISH

**LETTER DATED 1 MARCH 1991 FROM THE SECRETARY-GENERAL
ADDRESSED TO THE PRESIDENT OF THE SECURITY COUNCIL**

I have the honour to inform you that the Permanent Representative of Kuwait addressed a letter to me on 27 February 1991, in which, on behalf of his Government, he requested that I authorize the immediate dispatch of a mission to Kuwait. A copy of the letter is attached.

In view of the fact that this request has direct bearing on Security Council resolution 674 (1990), I would appreciate it if you would bring this letter to the attention of the members of the Council so that I may receive their guidance on how to respond.

(Signed) Javier PEREZ de CUELLAR

91-07558 2117i (E)   /...

3 — 1

0100

Annex

Letter dated 27 February 1991 from the Permanent Representative of Kuwait to the United Nations addressed to the Secretary-General

Upon instructions from my Government, I should like to request that a mission, authorized by Your Excellency, be immediately dispatched to Kuwait to assess the losses in life incurred during the Iraqi occupation of Kuwait, and to examine the practices by the Iraqi occupation forces against the civilian population in Kuwait. It is requested that the team assesses, as well, the damages inflicted on the general infrastructures in Kuwait. In this regard we propose that the team includes representatives from UNEP, UNESCO, UNICEF and WHO. A report by such a team shall, among other things, guide us in drawing up the requirements for the reconstruction of the country.

(Signed) Mohammad A. ABULHASAN
Ambassador
Permanent Representative

3-2

0101

UNITED
NATIONS

Security Council

S

Distr.
GENERAL

S/22334
6 March 1991

ORIGINAL: ENGLISH

LETTER DATED 6 MARCH 1991 FROM THE PRESIDENT OF THE
SECURITY COUNCIL ADDRESSED TO THE SECRETARY-GENERAL

I have the honour to inform you that I have brought your letter dated
1 March 1991 and its enclosure to the attention of the Council members (S/22333).
They have considered the matter and they would welcome your responding positively
to the request contained in the letter dated 27 February from the Permanent
Representative of Kuwait to send a mission to Kuwait, recognizing the importance of
taking all actions possible to facilitate Kuwait's reconstruction and
re-integration into the international economic system.

(Signed) Peter HOHENFELLNER
President of the Security Council

91-07564 2214e (E)

3-3

0102

외 무 부

종 별 :

번 호 : UNW-0532   일 시 : 91 0308 1200

수 신 : 장관 (중동일,법규,국연,기정)

발 신 : 주 유엔 대사

제 목 : 걸프사태 (손해배상 청구)

대: WUN-0434, 0468

대호 손해배상 청구문제 관련 당관에서 유엔사무국 및 관련 대표부들에 탐문한바,
동 반응을 아래 보고함.

1. 사무국 (B.BLENMAN 안보리 담당관, N.SCHRIJVER 법률담당관)

가. 안보리 결의 674, 686 호는 국제법상의 이락의 배상책임을 재확인하고 있고,
특히 674 호는 (본문 9 항) 각국에게 자국의 청구사항을 수집토록 권유 (INVITE) 하고
있음.

나. 그러나 동 결의는 본건 관련 사무국에 어떤 권한이나 임무를 부여하고 있지
않은바, 사무국측이 현재 취하고 있거나 검토중인 조치는 없음.

다. 본건은 안보리 제재위원회 (661 호 결의에 의거 설치) 에서도 다루어지고 있지
않으며 각 관련국이 개별적으로 자국의 청구사항을 수집하고 있다고 듣고 있음. (미,
영, 쿠웨이트 예시)

2. 관련국 대표부

가. 쿠웨이트 (M.AL SALLAL 참사관)

1) 현 단계에서 자국 청구사항 수집은 관련국들이 각자 조치할 문제이며,
쿠웨이트가 어떤 주도적인 역할을 하고있지 않음. (대호 배상 신청 안내문 배부사실
부인)

2) 실제적인 청구와 관련한 절차문제는 추후 유엔에서 토의가 있을것으로 봄.

나. 영국 (I.CLIFF 서기관)

1) 본국에서 자국의 청구내용을 정리중에 있으나, 추후의 청구절차 (안보리의장,
사무총장을 통한 방법 또는 이락에 대한 직접 청구방법)에 관해서는 영국으로서나
주요 관련국간에 방침이 아직 서있지 않은것으로 알고있음.

중아국	장관	차관	1차보	2차보	국기국	국기국	청와대	안기부

2) 불, 독을 비롯한 서구제국, 인도등도 자국의 배상청구 관련 자료를 정리중이며 미국의 경우 정리작업이 완료되었다고 들었음.

다. 미국 (D.RUSSEL 담당관)

1) 미국도 청구할것이 적지않으나 현단계에서 구체적인 조치를 취하고 있지는 않음.

2) 앞으로 적절한 시기에 유엔 (안보리)에서 청구 절차에 관한 후속 논의가 있을것으로 봄.

라. 일본 (S.SUMI 서기관)

1) 개별적으로 자국의 청구내용을 수집하고 있는 나라들 (카나다 예시) 이 있다고 듣고있으나, 일본으로서는 아직 구체적 조치를 취하고 있지 않음.

2) 향후 안보리에서 청구절차 문제에 관한 토의가 있을것으로 기대하나, 현재로서는 본건 청구문제에 관한 어떤 전망을 하기에는 이른감이 있음. 우선은 유엔 조사단 쿠웨이트 방문 (UNW-0526) 결과, 대 이락 경제제재조치 해제문제 추이를 지켜보아야 할것으로 봄. 끝 (대사대리 신기복-국장)

예고 91.6.30. 일반 예고문에 의거 일반문서로 재분류됨

외   무   부

종   별 :

번   호 : UNW-0539   일   시 : 91 0308 1900

수   신 : 장 관(국연,중동일,해기,기정)(사본:노창희대사)

발   신 : 주 유엔 대사

제   목 : 걸프사태

　　　　연: UNW-0526

　　1. 연호 쿠웨이트 인명및 재산피해 조사를 위한 유엔대표단은 3.11. 쿠웨이트 향발 예정이며 동대표단은 A. FARAH 단장 포함 26명으로 구성된바, 2.28까지 쿠웨이트에 체류함.

　　2. 한편 이락및 쿠웨이트의 인도적 원조수요 파악을 위한 유엔조사단 (단장: M.AHTISAARI 사무차장) 은 3.9. 이락 도착예정인바, 관련상세는 별첨참조바람.

　　3. 이락측은 안보리결의 686 호 표결시 반대 또는기권한 4개국 (중, 쿠바, 인도, 예멘) 외상앞으로 보내는 T.AZIZ 외상명의 서한을 3.6 자로 안보리문서 (S/22332)로 배포한 바, 동 서한은 4개국에 대한 사의표명, 대미비난, 팔레스타인 문제해결을 촉구하는 내용임.

　　4. 금 3.8 국제적십자사 (ICRC) 는 이락측으로 부터 미군 포로 2명및 서방언론인 40명의 신병을 인수하였음을 발표함.

　　첨부:1. 상기 유엔조사단관련 발표내용

　　2. 3월6일자 이락안보리문서 중 중국외상앞 서한내용:UNW(F)-108

　　끝

　　(대사대리 신기복-국장)

국기국　　1차보　　중아국　　국기국　　정문국　　안기부　　공보처

#UNW-0539
첨부

UNW(A)-108   103일 1900
(국연. 중동일. 해기. 기타) (사본: 노창희 〈대사〉)

총3대

SECRETARY-GENERAL'S HUMANITARIAN MISSION TO IRAQ AND KUWAIT
TO DEPART FROM GENEVA

On behalf of the United Nations Secretary-General, Under-Secretary-General Martti Ahtisaari, will leave Geneva, on Saturday 9 March, for an on-the-spot assessment of the humanitarian assistance needs of Iraq and Kuwait, following the end of the recent war. Mr. Ahtisaari will be leading a mission comprised of representatives of the United Nations agencies concerned, following a day of consultations with senior representatives of the humanitarian agencies in Geneva.

The mission will be composed of delegates from UNDP, UNICEF, UNDRO, UNHCR, FAO, WFP and WHO. They will be flying to Baghdad, via Amman, Jordan, aboard a Boeing 707 aircraft placed at the disposal of UNDRO by the Government of Argentina, as a contribution to the international relief effort.

In addition to the UN officials, the aircraft will carry over 28̸ 20 tons of relief items to Iraq, in accordance with a decision taken yesterday by the Sanctions Committee of the Security Council. Prior to this mission, the Argentinian aircraft had been used since the end of January for the transport of emergency relief goods from UNDRO's warehouse in Pisa, Italy, to various destinations in the Gulf area.

The mission was decided upon by Secretary-General Javier Pérez de Cuéllar on 28 February, following a meeting in New York with Executive Heads of UN agencies. After his visit in Iraq, Mr. Ahtisaari will proceed to Kuwait.

3-1

0106

S/22332
English
Page 2

Annex I

Letter dated 4 March 1991 from the Deputy Prime Minister and
Minister for Foreign Affairs of Iraq addressed to the Minister
for Foreign Affairs of China

    The people and leadership of Iraq have followed the positions adopted by China in the Security Council during discussion of aspects relating to the Gulf crisis and, in particular, China's abstention from the vote on Security Council resolutions 678 (1990) and 686 (1991).

    History will speak of a significant distinction whereby China abstained from the vote on the unjust resolution 686 (1991), at a time when Iraq agreed to fulfil its obligations under that resolution. History will provide the proper interpretation of that fact. We are pleased that China is able to speak the truth and to adopt the position which it deems fit in accordance with its assessments. Iraq, for its part, has aquiesced in its acceptance because of circumstances which are well known.

    Another of the distinctions which history will record is that distortion of the truth has extended even to the formulation of resolutions by the highest international organization. Such resolutions are supposed to maintain at least a minimum level of credibility. The provisions of resolution 686 (1991) make frequent reference to "the forces of Kuwait and the Member States cooperating with Kuwait", implying that it is those forces which fought the war against Iraq. As everyone in the world is aware, the war plan is an American plan. It was the American President who declared war and it was he who announced the cessation of military operations. It was the American forces, together with much more limited forces from other Western countries, particularly Britain and France, which fought the war. As everyone in the world knows, it is the American political machine which dictates, directs and applies pressure in order to fashion the political position on this subject, and thus the resolutions of the Security Council.

    These distinctions will not pass without being seen as signs of a dark age which the human race is now entering ... an age of domination by a brutal super-Power over the resources of the world and the international establishment, imposing its will on them with impunity ... distorting the truth as it distorts history. The free peoples of the world, their national Governments and all those with a clear conscience must draw the pertinent conclusions from these facts. They must also expose the premeditated designs against Iraq which lie behind everything that has happened in the past. The principal truth of the matter is that the fundamental issue, regardless of differences of opinion on one side or another, which are natural and legitimate, was not that of respect for international legitimacy and international law but the imposition of hegemony over the resources of the Gulf region and the Middle East and thereby over the world.

    Events prove once again that peace, stability, security and justice cannot be secured in the Middle East region and that this region will not enjoy security and tranquillity until the question of the Palestinian Arab people is solved on a just

/...

3－2　　　　　　　　　　0107

basis which guarantees that people its legitimate rights to recover its territory
and to establish its own free independent State in that territory, including its
capital, Jerusalem.

(Signed) Tariq AZIZ
Deputy Prime Minister
Minister for Foreign Affairs
of the Republic of Iraq

/...

3-3

0108

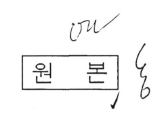

외 무 부

종 별 :

번 호 : UNW-0546　　　　　　　　　일 시 : 91 0311 1600

수 신 : 장 관(국연,중동일,해기,기정)(사본:노창희대사)

발 신 : 주 유엔 대사

제 목 : 걸프사태

　　연: UNW-0526

　　1. 연호 유엔조사단 (단장: M.AHTISAARI사무차장)의 이락체류 활동에 관한 금 3.11유엔사무총장 대변인 발표내용을 별첨송부함.

　　2.한편, E.BRUNNER 현 주미 스위스 대사가 사무총장중 동담당 특사로 곧 임명될것으로 알려짐. (금주중 발표가능성)

　　3.이락의 혁명위 (RCC) 쿠웨이트 병합 무효화결정 (S. HUSSEIN 서명)을 알리는 3.8.자 이락대표부 서한이 안보리 문서로 배포됨.

　　첨부:1.유엔조사단활동발표내용

　　2.이락안보리문서(S/22342):UNW(F)-0109

　　끝

　　(대사대리 신기복-국장)

국기국　　1차보　　중아국　　　　정문국　　안기부　　공보처　　대사실

PAGE 1

91.03.12　　08:52 WG

외신 1과 통제관

0109

UN 입도사업자료

UNW(F)-0109 103111000 첨부 UNW-0546 총 3매

THE FOLLOWING IS ATTRIBUTABLE TO THE SPOKESWOMAN FOR THE SECRETARY-GENERAL

THE MISSION LED BY MR. MARTTI AHTISAARI TO IRAQ AND KUWAIT ARRIVED YESTERDAY AFTERNOON IN BAGHDAD FROM AMMAN (WHERE MR. AHTISAARI HAD MEETINGS WITH CROWN PRINCE HASSAN AND JORDANIAN FOREIGN MINISTER MR. TAHER AL-MASRI).

THE MISSION WAS MET AT BAGHDAD AIRPORT BY A REPRESENTATIVE OF THE IRAQI FOREIGN MINISTRY, AND BY SENIOR UN PERSONNEL FROM UNDP, UNICEF AND ESCWA.

APART FROM MEMBERS OF THE SECRETARIAT, THE 20 PERSON MISSION HAS REPRESENTATIVES FROM UNDP, UNICEF, WFP, UNHCR, UNDRO, FAO AND WHO.

YESTERDAY EVENING MR. AHTISAARI AND THE MISSION MET WITH MR. MOHAMMAD SAID AL-SAHAF, MINISTER OF STATE AT THE FOREIGN MINISTRY, AND REPRESENTATIVES OF VARIOUS GOVERNMENT DEPARTMENTS. WORKING GROUPS WERE ESTABLISHED TO ASSIST WITH THE MANDATE'S TASK OF ASSESSING EMERGENCY HUMANITARIAN NEEDS. THE WORKING GROUPS HAD THEIR FIRST MEETNGS LAST NIGHT.

THE MISSION TRAVELLED TO BAGHDAD IN AN AIRCRAFT SUPPLIED TO UNDRO BY THE ARGENTINE GOVERNMENT. IT ALSO CARRIED TWENTY TONS OF URGENT MEDICAL SUPPLIES AS AUTHORISED ON 7 MARCH BY THE SECURITY COUNCIL'S SANCTIONS COMMITTEE.

MR. AHTISAARI EXPECTS TO REMAIN IN IRAQ UNTIL 18 MARCH, AFTER WHICH HE ANTICIPATES TRAVELLING TO KUWAIT. ENDALL.

II MARCH 1991

3-1

0110

UNITED NATIONS

  S

Security Council

Distr.
GENERAL

S/22342
8 March 1991
ENGLISH
ORIGINAL: ARABIC

IDENTICAL LETTERS DATED 8 MARCH 1991 FROM THE PERMANENT
REPRESENTATIVE OF IRAQ TO THE UNITED NATIONS ADDRESSED
RESPECTIVELY TO THE SECRETARY-GENERAL AND THE PRESIDENT
OF THE SECURITY COUNCIL

On instructions from my Government, and further to its acceptance of Security
Council resolution 686 (1991), as indicated in the letter addressed to you by the
Minister for Foreign Affairs of my Government, dated 3 March 1991, I have the
honour to transmit to you a copy of Revolution Command Council decision No. 55 of
5 March 1991 concerning the application of paragraph 2 (a) of resolution 686 (1991).

I should be grateful if you would have this letter and its annex circulated as
a document of the Security Council.

                                        (Signed) Abdul Amir A. AL-ANBARI
                                                  Ambassador
                                                  Permanent Representative

3-2

91-07853 2340d (E)   /...

0111

<u>Annex</u>

<u>Revolution Command Council decision No. 55 dated
17 Sha'ban A.H. 1411 (5 March A.D. 1991)</u>

In accordance with the acceptance by the Iraqi Government of Security Council resolution 686 (1991) and with its previous declarations regarding acceptance of the other Security Council resolutions, and pursuant to the provisions of article 42, paragraph (a) of the Constitution,

The Revolution Command Council has decided as follows:

1.   All Revolution Command Council decisions subsequent to 2 August 1990 regarding Kuwait are null and void.

2.   All laws, decisions, regulations, instructions, directives and measures issued by virtue of the decisions of the Council referred to in paragraph 1 above are abrogated and all the effects arising therefrom are nullified.

3.   No text which is contradictory to the provisions of this decision shall have any effect.

4.   This decision shall be published in the Official Gazette and shall take effect from 3 March 1991.

5.   The competent ministries and authorities shall undertake the implementation of this decision.

(<u>Signed</u>) Saddam HUSSEIN
Chairman of the Revolution
Command Council

3-3

0112

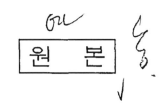

외 무 부

종   별 :

번   호 : UNW-0572   일   시 : 91 0313 1900

수   신 : 장 관(국연,중동일)

발   신 : 주 유엔 대사

제   목 : 걸프사태(유엔대표단)

1. 이락및 쿠웨이트의 인도적 원조수요 파악을 위한 유엔대표단 (단장: M.AHTISAARI 사무차장)의 이락체류 활동에 관해서는 별첨 3.13.자 유엔측 발표내용을 참조바람.

2. 한편, 쿠웨이트 인명및 재산피해 상황 조사를 위한 유엔대표단 (단장: A.FARAH 전사무차장)일행은 현재 바레인 체류중이며 3.16쿠웨이트 도착예정이라고함.

첨부:상기 유엔측 발표내용: UNW(F)-113

끝

(대사대리 신기복-국장)

국기국   1차보   2차보   중아국   정문국   안기부   차관   장관   검안대

JW-0572

P.1

United Nations

UNW(R)-113 10313 1900
(국연.중동일)

Press Release

Department of Public Information • News Coverage Service • New York

IK/5
13 March 1991

SECRETARY-GENERAL'S MISSION TO IRAQ AND KUWAIT TO ASSESS
HUMANITARIAN RELIEF NEEDS CONTINUES WORK

(Received from a UN official accompanying the mission.)

BAGHDAD, 13 March —— The mission sent by the Secretary-General to Iraq and Kuwait to assess the need for urgent humanitarian relief continued its work in Baghdad yesterday and again this morning.

All joint working groups, consisting of senior Iraqi government officials and members of the mission, made further analyses of available data. They are continuing their work today in the context of plans to make inspection visits to a number of locations in various parts of Iraq outside Baghdad during the rest of the week.

Mr. Ahtisaari met with senior Iraqi and foreign diplomatic representatives yesterday. This morning, he inspected several power stations in Baghdad.

Yesterday evening, members of the mission had a working dinner at the headquarters of the International Committee of the Red Cross. Also invited were senior government officials.

Apart from members of the Secretariat, the mission also comprises senior personnel from the United Nations Development Programme (UNDP), the Food and Agriculture Organization (FAO), the World Health Organization (WHO), the Office of the United Nations Disaster Relief Coordinator (UNDRO), the United Nations Children's Fund (UNICEF), the World Food Programme (WFP) and the United Nations High Commissioner for Refugees (UNHCR).

* *** *

/ — /

2294P

0114

주 국 련 대 표 부

주국련 20313- **161**   1991. 3. 13.

수신 장관

참조 국제기구조약국장, 중동아프리카국장

제목 걸프사태 (안보리)

표제 관련 안보리 문서를 별첨과 같이 송부합니다.

첨 부 : 상기 문서. 끝.

주   국   련   대

선결			결재	1:5052
1991. 18				
汎				

0115

UNITED NATIONS

Security Council

S

Distr.
GENERAL

S/22328
4 March 1991

ORIGINAL: ENGLISH

NOTE BY THE SECRETARY-GENERAL

At the request of the Chairman of the Security Council Committee established by resolution 661 (1990) concerning the situation between Iraq and Kuwait, I have the honour to bring to the attention of all States the attached report of the WHO/UNICEF Special Mission to Iraq.

91-07341   2351b (E)

/...

0116

WHO/UNICEF SPECIAL MISSION

TO IRAQ

February 1991

/...

0117

CONTENTS

JOINT WHO/UNICEF TEAM REPORT

A VISIT TO IRAQ, FEB 16-21 1991

/...

0118

<u>IRAQ MISSION TEAM MEMBERS</u>

Dr. Ali Khogali, WHO/EMRO, co-leader.

Mr. Richard Reid, UNICEF/MENA, co-leader.

Dr. Abdullah Dirya, WHO/EMRO

Dr. El-Fateh El-Samani, UNICEF/MENA

Dr. Gianni Murzi, UNICEF/MENA

Mr. Raymond Naimy, UNICEF/MENA

Dr. Annette Verster, WHO/EMRO

0119 /...

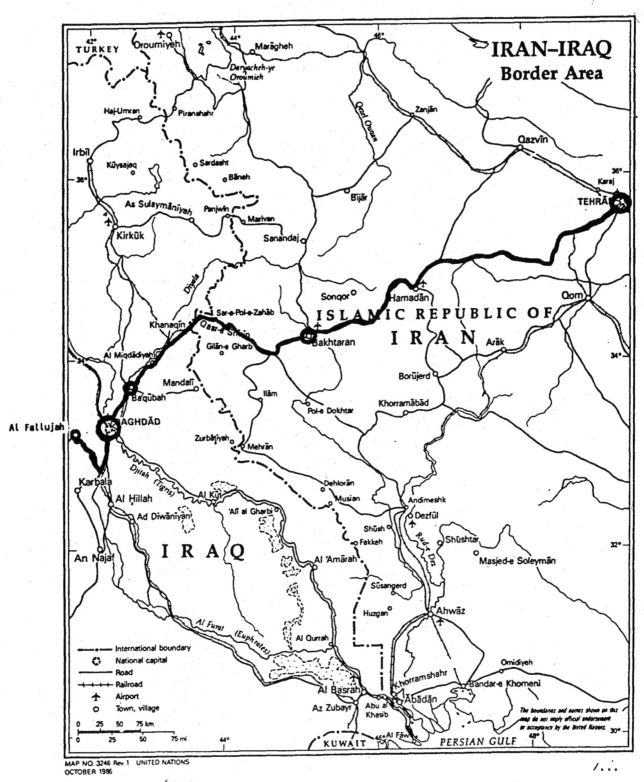

JOINT WHO/UNICEF TEAM REPORT
A VISIT TO IRAQ, FEB 16-21, 1991

I. Background & Overview

On Saturday morning, 16 Feb 1991, a seven-person joint WHO/UNICEF mission to Iraq crossed the border at Khosravi/Munzaria by road from Tehran, bringing with it a 12-truck convoy carrying 54 tons of basic medical and health supplies.
The mission's broad mandate, set out by the UN Secretary General in his press statement Feb. 6, was "to deliver a shipment of emergency medical supplies to assist in the care of children and mothers, and to ascertain essential health needs". Under this mandate, the joint mission was to look at immediate needs for further medical supplies; for protection against communicable diseases; at the status of supplies and sanitation; and at other health needs for children and mothers. The team's conclusions and recommendations were to be delivered, respectively, to the Director General of WHO and the Executive Director of UNICEF.

Prior to the mission, the Secretary-General had informed the Security Council Committee Established by Resolution 661 (1990), which took note of his intention to send the team without objection. The mission's mandate fell fell within the spirit of the provision of the Geneva Convention of 1949, the UN Convention on the Rights of the Child and the World Summit for Children.

This report emerges from that mandate, and is the joint product of the mission's four UNICEF and three WHO team members. It covers the five days that the team spent in Iraq, and summarizes the observations and recommendations of its members.

After crossing and clearing Iranian/Iraqi border formalities at Khosravi/Munzaria on Feb. 16, the team left the truck convoy for off-loading on the Iraqi side and travelled southward on the main Baghdad highway to Baquba together with a welcoming delegation of Ministry of Health officials, who had brought a small bus to the border for the trip. In Baquba the group lunched with the district health director and discussed storage arrangements with him, since it was at Baquba, 55 kilometers from Baghdad and out of the line of bombardment, that the Ministry of Health had planned to store the supplies brought in. Baquba appears to be the Iraqi government's main health supply distribution point. ICRC's medical materials are also stored there.

From Baquba, the group travelled directly to Baghdad, dropping the Ministry of Health officials at their homes and arriving at 4.00 p.m. at the Al-Rasheed Hotel, which was to be the home base of the WHO/UNICEF team through its visit.   /...

0121

The methodology used by the team from the start was observation- oriented and pragmatic. Daylight hours were used for field trips, meetings, and visits, since the lack of electricity put a blackout on virtually all movements between 5.00 p.m and 6.00 a.m. To maximize coverage, the team divided itself most days into three units -- one of three persons, covering medical supplies and vaccine needs; a second of three persons, covering communicable diseases, nutrition, the operation of the public health system, and the situation of children and mothers; and the third, a one-person unit, covering drinking water and sanitation. All seven team members participated in broad-purpose meetings and visits. The full team also came together for sharing and de-briefing twice a day.

Throughout the mission, the team was in regular contact with three ministries--Health, Labor and Social Welfare, and External Affairs -- as well as the Mayor of Baghdad. The government gave the mission broad latitude in its movements, and set no substantive restrictions. Officials accompanied mission members on most of their visits. Trips and visits were allowed to continue despite daylight bombardments. The team members basically set their own schedules and itineraries.

The days' activities tended to be an interweave of visits to ministry offices, large and small health facilities (urban, peri-urban and rural), homes, informal water-collection points (the Tigris river, ditches, irrigation canals), markets, water and sewage installations, and medical and vaccine stores. One day was spent outside Baghdad, on a trip to Falluja and points along the way.

Aside from daily coordination meetings in ministry offices, there were meetings with four high Government officials -- the Minister of Health, the Minister of Labor and Social Welfare, the Deputy Minister of Foreign Affairs (H.E. Nizar Hamdoon), and the Mayor of Baghdad.

The mission found in Baghdad that normal life had come almost to a halt. The city's citizens now spend much of their time in family support preoccupations, searching for food, trying to find water, and improvising cooking and heating amidst an acute shortage of all kinds of fuel. Baghdad has no public electricity, no telephones, no gasoline for civilian vehicles, and less than 5% of its normal water supply. None of its water treatment plants are functioning. Toilets go unflushed, and unpumped raw sewage is backing up and overflowing in residential areas. Basic food items are scarce; rice and sugar are increasingly difficult to find. Most basic food items that are available are expensive. Meat is $ 36 per kilo -- this in a society where $ 300 is an   /...

0122

average monthly urban wage. Homes have no refrigeration for
the preservation of food. Bottled gas for cooking and
heating is so hard to come by that sales of it set off near
stampedes.

A lack of heating fuel has left homes and public
buildings so cold that the writers of this report have worn
overcoats, sweaters, and scarves to all visits and meetings.
Conditions in rural areas and other cities -- where
electricity, water and fuel are also absent -- are said to be
equally bad, and Basra is reported to be worse.

These conditions appear to have had a heavy impact on
public health and the quality of life of children and mothers
in Baghdad, whose population is a quarter of that of all of
Iraq, and in which a single large popular quarter, Saddam
City, has 40,000 inhabitants per square kilometer.

At this writing, the single most urgent health threat,
to Baghdad and the country, is that of waterborne epidemics
that could soon result from increasingly widespread public
use of the Tigris river and other heavily polluted bodies of
water for drinking. Free-lance tank trunks are already
selling water taken straight from the Tigris in urban
neighborhoods. Radio warnings to boil water (there is no
television) are largely unheeded, since the hard-pressed
population is using scarce fuel for other purposes.

A main concern of the team was the need to assure that
the supplies it delivered would be distributed evenly, and
according to need, to all civilian populations under Iraqi
Government administration -- including Kuwait. A plan to
guide this distribution was agreed upon with the MOH, and is
being monitored on the ground by UNICEF team members who
remained in Baghdad after the mission completed its stay .

In another distribution-related context, the team was
aware that the timing of shipment of a number of the supply
items recommended in this report may need to be delayed until
the overall situation permits.

The drinking water and sanitation threat spelled out
above is one of several central problems that the remainder
of this report will take up. The following sections will
address 1) The Situation of Women & Children in Baghdad, 2)
The Situation of the Health Services, 3) Communicable
Diseases, 4) Essential Drug and Vaccine Needs, and 5) Water &
Sanitation. Each section will present a summary sectoral
picture, outline problems and needs, and suggest actions to
be taken.

0123   /...

II The Situation of Women and Children in Baghdad

The situation of women and children is severely affected by the general conditions described above. The lack of fuel and electricity at the household level has caused great strains, especially on food preparation. The team visited families at home, observed the improvised stoves, and saw firewood collected on the streets of Baghdad. Bread is baked at home on improvised ovens. Food preparation is much more time-consuming than before the crisis, and food preservation is impossible due to lack of electricity for refrigeration.

Sufficient water for basic needs is not available in most homes, and when available it is in short supply. The collection of water from rivers and the search for fuel put a great strain on women.

All children are at home, as schools have been closed since the start of the bombardment. The team was repeatedly informed about, and observed, children's fear of being left alone. Women bear the burden of these additional care needs.

Essential commodities are rationed. An official ration of rice, flour, sugar, cooking oil, tea and soap is provided at low cost. The present ration provides an estimated 750 to 1000 calories per day, irrespective of age. Children under one year of age receive, in addition, two tins of 450 grams of powdered milk per month. This is 30 grams per day.

It was noted that due to limited supplies of infant formula, the milk ration consists often of full cream milk powder, which is unsuitable for babies. Diarrhoea in small children was reported as a consequence.

The ration of 750-1,000 calories available at present is less than half the daily requirement of a five-year old child, or less than one-third of the requirement of a pregnant woman. This is obviously not enough for subsistence. The diet must be supplemented by purchases from the market.

The team visited local markets and shops to ascertain what kinds of food are available and at which cost. Families were interviewed about their food intake, both from rations and purchases. At present, fruits, vegetables, potatoes, dates, dried beans and meat are available. Families report that they rely heavily on potatoes and such vegetables as tomatoes to supplement their rations. Prices are, however, prohibitive.

/...

0124

The only high-energy food source is dates. Cooking oil is unavailable on the open market. The official ration contains 7-10 grams of cooking fat per person per day.

The quality of the foods now available on the market is low and deteriorating. Transport problems limit availability. In the near future the season for vegetable will be over. Storage is not possible.

At present, it appears that the amount of food the average family is able to purchase, combined with the government's ration, may give each person something close to the daily minimum calorie requirement.

The team is convinced that in the near future, that is a month or less from now, the gap will widen as purchasable goods will rapidly become unavailable. The team saw strong indications of this decrease in availability during the five days it was in Baghdad.

Nutrition of Children

The general food situation has particularly severe consequences in the case of children. Children are at present receiving a diet that is very different from what they are used to, both in quality and in quantity. The available rations are bulky staples such as rice and wheat, as are the foods available on the market, such as potatoes. Energy-dense foods like oil and sugar are scarce. Iraqi infants are traditionally kept on a milk diet for several months, with the introduction of solid foods late in the first year.

Reports from before the war give evidence that most Iraqi mothers have customarily breastfed for a very short time. Artificial feeding is introduced right from the start. The team was repeatedly told that small babies are now given rice and water and orange juice when milk is unavailable. Mothers do not have the knowledge to prepare the necessary and proper diet with the ration and other foods available. Breasfeeding failure was reported by many health staff interviewed, due to the stress and anxiety caused by the bombing.

0125   /...

The current high incidence of diarrhoea and upper respiratory tract infections result in an increased need for food. At the same time, the child's appetite is reduced by these illnesses, and depressed further by the anxiety and fear noticeable in many children. Bed-wetting and sleeplessness were reported. All these mechanisms together lay the foundation for malnutrition, sooner rather than later.

Iraq has no evidence of malnutrition from past records, although accurate data is scarce. The team did not yet see malnutrition, but prodromal symptoms like listless behaviour was observed in some children seen by the team, suggesting conservation of energy. Weight-loss was reported by health staff interviewed and by mothers. This could not be substantiated by records, as no growth monitoring is carried out at present. The increased incidence of diarrhoea, coupled with food shortages, will certainly result in outright malnutrition, specially among one-to-three-year-olds, in the near future.

Given the difficulty of assessing present food intake or supplies, it is not easy to make a reliable estimate of additional needs for young children and pregnant women. A very rough estimate on the immediate needs was made by the team on the basis of the following assumptions:

-    The present population of Iraq is 18 million. Of these 4%, (770,000) are children below one year of age. Infant formula will be needed for the children under 4-6 months only.

-    Pregnant women will also number an estimated 770,000.

-    Children aged 0-5 years will be an estimated 20% of total population, and of those the 1-3 year age group can be estimated to number 2,500,000.

-    A period of 30 days is arbitrarily chosen for the first phase. Within this period it will be necessary to undertake a more detailed assessment of the situation in the country.

-    Quantities are expressed for infant formula and in rations for other supplements. The kind of supplements available will determine costs.

0126   /...

The mission recommends that an appropriate high energy/protein food ration be provided to these vulnerable groups for an initial period of 30 days. During this time it will be necessary to reassess the situation in order to determine any changes in the food availability and the nutritional status of the population.

Growing from these needs, the recommended short term programmatic actions are:

(1) A resumed supply of infant formula for children under four months, as detailed above.

(2) The promotion of breastfeeding.

(3) The development and promotion of a weaning food, based on the commodities presently available. A cereal-legume mixture mixed with dates could be envisaged.

(4) Social mobilization of all population groups and religious and political leaders, to support the promotion of breastfeeding and appropriate weaning foods.

(5) Resumed growth and monitoring of all children visiting health facilities, so as to monitor the nutrition situation.

0127

/...

III The Situation of the Health Services

Disruption of routine health services was observed by the team at all levels. A main cause of this is the lack of private or public transport, tied to the non-availability of vehicle fuel; professional and para-medical staff regularly fail to come to work because there is no way to get there. Those who do come often arrive by foot or bicycle. On average, the health centers visited by the team operate at a third of their total manpower, with each doctor coming to the center once every three days.

As a result, several of the usual services have been stopped or severely curtailed. Primary care and preventive activities have suffered the most. Antenatal care, MCH clinics, and growth monitoring have ceased. Laboratory services in Baghdad health centers are closed, including those for pregnant women such as blood sugar and albumine, as well as haemoglobin tests. The team was told that the same conditions obtained throughout the country.

Before the war, the majority of urban women delivered in hospitals. In today's war circumstances, hospital deliveries are growing more and more improbable, especially at night. The great majority of deliveries now take place at home, aided by traditional birth attendants wherever possible. In a visit to a rural health center catering to 65,000 people, the team learned that more than 70 per cent of deliveries now take place at home, compared to 47 per cent before the war.

At the center of the health system, further disarray has come from the dispersal of all staff, including the Minister, from the Health Ministry after the building was put out of operation. Staff from the Ministry have now been reassigned to several improvised locations in Baghdad. This has cut contact among Ministry departments and services to a minimum, and has created constant difficulties in communication and coordination.

The immunization of children stopped completely at the start of the war when electricity was cut. All vaccines were sent back to generator-operated central stores and hospitals. Only in the few days prior to the mission's visit had some centers resumed immunization one day per week, using cold boxes and vaccine carriers. However, not enough vaccines are available. The team observed up to 20 children in one health center who were sent away for lack of vaccines. Booster doses and the third shots of DPT and polio have been stopped in order to conserve supplies.

0128

/...

The team observed a serious shortage of syringes. It
was reported that syringes were being reused after boiling,
if fuel was available, or were cleaned with spirit,
introducing a new dimension of risk of hepatitis B and other
infections.

The team looked into prescription practices, and
observed that only a day's dose of the doctor's prescription
is issued at a time. Many women and children are not able to
come back every day to complete the treatment. The danger of
introducing resistance to antibiotics due to this non-
compliance cannot be over emphasized. Treatment cannot be
effective under these circumstances.

The shortage of medical staff and medicine, the lack of
continuity of care, and the fear of going outside all
combined to reduce attendance and render the primary health
care system ineffectual.

IV. Communicable Diseases

All the technical services of the Ministry of Health
have been disrupted, but none more severely than
epidemiological surveillance and the reporting of
communicable diseases. These have practically ceased.
Laboratory services in Baghdad have been cut back almost to
zero. No information has been available since September, 1990
on communicable diseases that were routinely reported by the
health services up to that date.

However, as the team reviewed the registers of health
facilities visited during the mission, it became clear that
the incidence of diarrhoeal diseases reported in these
centres had increased fourfold over expected levels since the
war began, and that the incidence of acute respiratory
infections has shown a very similar upward trend.

Since such communicable diseases as typhoid, meningitis,
measles, poliomyelitis, hepatitis A, and malaria are endemic
in Iraq, the present conditions of contaminated main water
supply and untreated, backed-up sewage have set the stage for
the onset of some of these diseases in epidemic proportions.
No cases of cholera, typhoid, or meningitis have been
officially reported to date, but the danger is real and
increasingly present. This situation is compounded by the
fact that the MOH is not at present in a position to respond
to any epidemic.

0129   /...

The team urged the Ministry to resume immediately some form of monitoring, sentinel on otherwise, of the more serious communicable diseases, and accepted a list of laboratory reagents submitted by the Ministry.

It is recommended that supplies for the control of cholera and meningococcal meningitis be procured and prepositioned in Iran for immediate shipment to Iraq.

V. Essential Drugs and Vaccine Needs

Essential Drugs

Iraq's health situation has been exacerbated by a critical shortage of essential drugs and medical supplies. The stoppage of industrial production, the absence of raw materials, and the lack of electricity have also knocked out the 25 per cent of national drug and medical needs that were met by local production before the crisis. A further loss has been the cutting off of the five per cent of national needs that were met by imports from Jordan.

Visits by the team to the national drug and medical warehouses in Baghdad, along with reports and statistics provided by procurement officials of the Ministry of Health, show that Iraq's civilian reserves have been reduced to one-sixth their normal level-- that is, to a point at which an unevenly depleted three-month supply of basic drugs exists at this writing.

During its mission, the team visited a number of health centers whose pharmacies lacked virtually all essential drugs, including antibiotics.

The production of disposable plastic bags for intravenous infusions, as well as disposable syringes, has been brought to a halt. These are even more needed at a time when sterilization cannot be done for lack of fuel and electricity.

Recommendation for proposed supplies of essential drugs have been prepared by the team and will be reviewed at their respective headquarters.

Vaccines (EPI)

The Iraqi national vaccination programme has been essentially stopped by the lack of electricity needed to protect vaccines, and the inability to import them.

0130   /...

Added to this, the lack of fuel for transportation greatly limits the possibility of carrying vaccines from the central vaccine store to the peripheral health centres, while the production of ice appears to be limited and does not suffice.

Due to the pre-crisis success of the Iraqi EPI, there is still a great demand for vaccination. But the number of vaccination days has been reduced from a daily schedule to one day a week, due to shortages.

A new vaccine supply system was discussed by the team and MOH officials. Under this radical alternative plan, vaccines would be flown to Tehran and transported to Baghdad by road, possibly using UNICEF drivers and some of the seven refrigerated trucks ordered last year by UNICEF for the MOH, but held back by the embargo.

The new plan would see three or four new vehicles supplementing the present available MOH vehicles, to take vaccines in cold boxes from the Baquba stores to outlying governorates and districts. There, cold storage facilities, based on small generator-powered ice-lining refrigerators and freezers, would hold the vaccines for administration in carefully-monitored batches.

UNICEF Baghdad has on order 250 cold boxes that could not be delivered due to the situation. These cold boxes would be most useful in the new system, and it is suggested they be shipped to Baghdad to be used under UNICEF supervision. Ice making capacity has to be evaluated. At this stage it is estimated that at least 18-20 ice making freezers should be supplied for running the cold chain.

0131

/...

VI. Water and Sanitation

The mission gave high priority to its inspection of
Baghdad's water and sanitation situation, and saw a grim
picture. If quick intervention does not take place, the Iraqi
population faces the prospect of epidemics. Diarrhoeal rates
are already four times their normal level.

An in-depth assessment was carried out for Baghdad city.
Interviews and discussion took place at the MOH Department of
Communicable Diseases, from which two doctors and two
engineers accompanied us to the Water Authority Directorate.
Here the team discussed with the Director the obstacles now
confronting water supply and sanitation. Field trips took
place to the April 7 water treatment station, where the full
current process of treatment was followed and observed. There
was then a tour with network maintenance engineers to observe
damages to pipes. Further visits took place to the banks of
the Tigris river, to see and discuss with people their own
water supply improvisations.

For the affected parts of the country, outside Baghdad,
information is not yet fully available. Time did not permit
visits to those areas. But all reports indicate that the
situation faced by Baghdad is similar in other areas, with
the most severe conditions in Basra. Wherever the team went,
in meetings with the Director of the Baghdad Water Authority,
the Directorate of the Ministry of Local Government, and
otherwise, there were detailed reports that the whole of the
Iraqi drinking water system is in or near collapse.

General Situation

Most of Iraq's population of 18 million enjoyed, before
the crisis, an average of over 250 litres per head daily.
Baghdad city, with 4.5 million, received up to 500 litres per
head. Over 95 percent of this water was the product of
river water treatment provided by seven electro mechanical
plants, all of which operated with electric power and
required chemicals for treatment.

All significant electrical power generating plants in
Iraq have now been destroyed, and similarly the refineries
and main fuel storage facilities, leaving water treatment
plants dead for all but six hours per day of operation on
stand-by diesel generators. This necessitates a careful
rationing of the systems remaining fuel supply, which will
not last more than five more weeks.

/...

0132

The chemical plants which used to supply the main
treatment elements, aluminium sulphate (alum) and chlorine,
have been destroyed by bombing . Small quantities of alum
and chlorine are still stored at treatment plants, and
minimal amounts of these dwindling supplies are used for
treating the water that is still sent out. On February 21,
the chlorine residue in the water was measured at the plant
in the team's presence. The level was found to be only 0.75
mg/litres. Double this figure should have been expected even
at the end of the water network, where chlorine levels should
be diffused to their lowest strength.

Water quality tests, which are usually carried out at
the treatment plant laboratories, are much less frequent than
before the crisis. There are shortages of the reagents used
to carry out chemical tests. Bacteriological tests are not
being carried out at all, because the available equipment
that performs these tests requires 24 hours of electricity.
Hence the water is distributed without knowing its
bacteriological characteristics, at a time when treatment
levels are markedly sub-standard.

Baghdad City

The city of Baghdad is served by the seven treatment
stations mentioned above, each pumping directly into a
network of over 6,000 kilometers of pipes. At present, the
water supply to the inhabitants is between zero and 15 litres
per person daily, with minimum treatment specifications at
the stations and insufficient disinfection. The distribution
is rationed in an uneven manner, since the rationing
operation requires the manual maneuvering of over 20,000
valves. This cannot be performed adequately by the
available personnel, who have no fuel to travel about in
their few vehicles.

In no sector of the city can water reach higher than the
ground level of buildings, due to the weak pressure in the
pipes. Some districts of the city receive 3-4 hours of water
every three to four days, other districts 3-4 hours every two
weeks. During the team's presence at the Water Authority
Director's office, people came complaining that they had not
received water for 20 days. About one million people receive
almost nothing, since their main water feeder pipes have been
severely damaged and cannot be repaired for lack of parts.
These areas are fed from other ends of the system, with
pressure which is barely enough to drive water.

0133

/...

Interrupted pumping inevitably leaves stagnant water in the pipes. This causes further degradation of the originally poor quality of the water.

Intervention

In order to limit the on-going health threats and prevent epidemics, it is proposed to supply the city with 40 liters of water per head per day. In order to achieve that, the following intervention is urgently recommended for Baghdad city. It must be understood that some of the supply items listed below can be provided only when circumstances permit.

. Supply of the necessary fuel to operate stand-by generators for a period of three months.
   Qty for 3 months = 1800 tons
   Est. cost for 3 months = US $ 540,000

. Supply of alum for three months
   Qty for 3 months = 1500 m. tons
   Est. cost for 3 months = US $ 525,000

. Supply of chlorine for 3 months
   Qty for 3 months = 45 m. tons
   Est. cost for 3 months = US $ 22,500

. Supply of necessary collars to repair broken mains. (List attached under Appendix no. 1)
   Est. cost US $ 52,920

. Supply of material and laboratory items (List attached under Appendix no. 2)
   Est. cost US $ 49,240

. Supply of spare parts for treatment station equipment.
   Est. cost US $ 150,000
   (List attached Appendix no. 3)

. Estimated Total Cost to support the water supply of Baghdad city for 3 months = US $ 1,339,660

Considering the situation of the whole country, an additional budget of US $ 4,000,000 should be kept in mind as an initial step for three months, until more accurate figures are obtained.

/...

0134

Sanitation

During our five days' stay in Baghdad, members of the team saw that the sanitation status of the city is critically deteriorating. The three main sectors of concern are the following:

- . Shortage of water;
- . Stoppage of the sewer system;
- . Acute decrease of garbage disposal.

The water shortage has been discussed earlier. The garbage disposal system, which depends on a large equipment fleet and labour force, is not addressed in this report. The proposed focus of sanitary intervention at this stage is the sewerage system. Baghdad is a flat city. The sewerage system cannot operate by gravity; therefore sewerage is passed through to the treatment plants by pumping stations (lifting stations) at intervals. There are 252 of these stations, which are electrically operated, about 192 of which have stand-by generators.

If those lifting stations do not operate, the sewage pipes fill up and houses flood with sewage. This is occurring in Baghdad now. Additionally, large pools of sewage are forming due to the overflow of sewage at the pumping pits, creating other health hazards.

Three main problems face the sewerage system.
1. Lack of fuel to operate the stand-by generators.
2. Stoppage of generators due to lack of spare parts.
3. Absence of stand-by generators in 60 stations, meaning that half a million homes cannot flush out their sewage.

The above matter was discussed with the directors of both the Baghdad Water Authority and the Baghdad Sewerage Authority. Visits took place to sites. The team observed the manual operation of the lifting pumps, which requires the constant presence of staff at a time when they are frequently unavailable and have very little transport.

In order to partially contain this problem and keep up operation at a minimum safety level, the following are required:

Enough diesel fuel to operate the lifting pumps, generator, and sewage treatment stations for three months.

/...

0135

Quantity required for three months: 900 m. tons
Estimated cost of diesel for 3 months: US $ 270,000

. A supply of essential spare parts sufficient to repair stopped generators. The list is being prepared and will be ready within a week of this writing.

Estimated figure for this activity: US $ 100,000.

. The supply of four 110 kva generators for mobile use, in order to supply power to the 60 lift pumps which have no stand-by power.

Estimated cost for 4 generators: US $ 150,000.

. Estimated total budget for sanitation for three months: US $ 520,000.

In short, the children and mothers of Iraq are living in a very acute water supply situation and in dangerous sanitation conditions, in weather which is now favourably cold, but which will warm to more than 40 degrees in another five or six weeks. Few public services whatsoever are available. Fuel is not existent. Transport services do not function. If nothing is done to remedy water supply and improve sanitation, a catastrophe could beset Iraq.

0136

UNITED NATIONS

 Security Council

S

Distr.
GENERAL

S/22332
6 March 1991
ENGLISH
ORIGINAL: ARABIC

LETTER DATED 5 MARCH 1991 FROM THE PERMANENT REPRESENTATIVE OF
IRAQ TO THE UNITED NATIONS ADDRESSED TO THE SECRETARY-GENERAL

On instructions from my Government, I have the honour to transmit herewith
letters dated 4 March 1991 from Mr. Tariq Aziz, Deputy Prime Minister and Minister
for Foreign Affairs of the Republic of Iraq, addressed to the Ministers for Foreign
Affairs of China, Cuba, India and Yemen.

I should be grateful if you would have this letter and its annexes circulated
as a document of the Security Council.

(Signed) Abdul Amir A. AL-ANBARI
Ambassador
Permanent Representative

Annex I

Letter dated 4 March 1991 from the Deputy Prime Minister and Minister for Foreign Affairs of Iraq addressed to the Minister for Foreign Affairs of China

The people and leadership of Iraq have followed the positions adopted by China in the Security Council during discussion of aspects relating to the Gulf crisis and, in particular, China's abstention from the vote on Security Council resolutions 678 (1990) and 686 (1991).

History will speak of a significant distinction whereby China abstained from the vote on the unjust resolution 686 (1991), at a time when Iraq agreed to fulfil its obligations under that resolution. History will provide the proper interpretation of that fact. We are pleased that China is able to speak the truth and to adopt the position which it deems fit in accordance with its assessments. Iraq, for its part, has aquiesced in its acceptance because of circumstances which are well known.

Another of the distinctions which history will record is that distortion of the truth has extended even to the formulation of resolutions by the highest international organization. Such resolutions are supposed to maintain at least a minimum level of credibility. The provisions of resolution 686 (1991) make frequent reference to "the forces of Kuwait and the Member States cooperating with Kuwait", implying that it is those forces which fought the war against Iraq. As everyone in the world is aware, the war plan is an American plan. It was the American President who declared war and it was he who announced the cessation of military operations. It was the American forces, together with much more limited forces from other Western countries, particularly Britain and France, which fought the war. As everyone in the world knows, it is the American political machine which dictates, directs and applies pressure in order to fashion the political position on this subject, and thus the resolutions of the Security Council.

These distinctions will not pass without being seen as signs of a dark age which the human race is now entering ... an age of domination by a brutal super-Power over the resources of the world and the international establishment, imposing its will on them with impunity ... distorting the truth as it distorts history. The free peoples of the world, their national Governments and all those with a clear conscience must draw the pertinent conclusions from these facts. They must also expose the premeditated designs against Iraq which lie behind everything that has happened in the past. The principal truth of the matter is that the fundamental issue, regardless of differences of opinion on one side or another, which are natural and legitimate, was not that of respect for international legitimacy and international law but the imposition of hegemony over the resources of the Gulf region and the Middle East and thereby over the world.

Events prove once again that peace, stability, security and justice cannot be secured in the Middle East region and that this region will not enjoy security and tranquillity until the question of the Palestinian Arab people is solved on a just

0138   /...

basis which guarantees that people its legitimate rights to recover its territory
and to establish its own free independent State in that territory, including its
capital, Jerusalem.

(<u>Signed</u>) Tariq AZIZ
Deputy Prime Minister
Minister for Foreign Affairs
of the Republic of Iraq

0139

/...

Annex II

Letter dated 4 March 1991 from the Deputy Prime Minister and
Minister for Foreign Affairs of Iraq addressed to the Minister
for Foreign Affairs of Cuba

The people and leadership of Iraq have followed the bold and principled positions adopted by Cuba in the Security Council during discussion of aspects relating to the Gulf crisis, the latest example being Cuba's vote against Security Council resolution 686 (1991). The people and leadership welcome those positions.

History will speak of a significant distinction whereby Cuba rejected the unjust resolution 686 (1991) at a time when Iraq agreed to fulfil its obligations under that resolution. History will provide the proper interpretation of that fact. We are pleased that Cuba is able to speak the absolute truth and to adopt the position dictated by its principles. Iraq, for its part, has acquiesced in its acceptance because of circumstances which are well known.

Another of the distinctions which history will record is that distortion of the truth has extended even to the formulation of resolutions by the highest international organization. Such resolutions are supposed to maintain at least a minimum level of credibility. The provisions of resolution 686 (1991) make frequent reference to "the forces of Kuwait and the Member States cooperating with Kuwait", implying that it is those forces which fought the war against Iraq. As everyone in the world is aware, the war plan is an American plan. It was the American President who declared war and it was he who announced the cessation of military operations. It was the American forces, together with much more limited forces from other Western countries, particularly Britain and France, which fought the war. As everyone in the world knows, it is the American political machine which dictates, directs and applies pressure in order to fashion the political position on this subject, and thus the resolutions of the Security Council.

These distinctions will not pass without being seen as signs of a dark age which the human race is now entering ... an age of domination by a brutal super-Power over the resources of the world and the international establishment, imposing its will on them with impunity ... distorting the truth as it distorts history. The free peoples of the world, their national Governments and all those with a clear conscience must draw the pertinent conclusions from these facts. They must also expose the premeditated designs against Iraq which lie behind everything that has happened in the past. The principal truth of the matter is that the fundamental issue, regardless of differences of opinion on one side or another, which are natural and legitimate, was not that of respect for international legitimacy and international law but the imposition of hegemony over the resources of the Gulf region and the Middle East and thereby over the world.

Events prove once again that peace, stability, security and justice cannot be secured in the Middle East region and that this region will not enjoy security and

0140   /...

tranquillity until the question of the Palestinian Arab people is solved on a just basis which guarantees that people its legitimate rights to recover its territory and to establish its own free independent State in that territory, including its capital, Jerusalem.

(Signed) Tariq AZIZ
Deputy Prime Minister
Minister for Foreign Affairs
of the Republic of Iraq

0141   /...

Annex III

Letter dated 4 March 1991 from the Deputy Prime Minister and
Minister for Foreign Affairs of Iraq addressed to the Minister
for Foreign Affairs of India

The people and leadership of Iraq have followed the position adopted by India in the Security Council when it abstained from the vote on Security Council resolution 686 (1991).

History will speak of a significant distinction whereby India abstained from the vote on the unjust resolution 686 (1991) at a time when Iraq agreed to fulfil its obligations under that resolution. History will provide the proper interpretation of that fact. We are pleased that India is able to speak the truth and to adopt the position which it deems fit in accordance with its assessments. Iraq, for its part, has acquiesced in its acceptance because of circumstances which are well known.

Another of the distinctions which history will record is that distortion of the truth has extended even to the formulation of resolutions by the highest international organization. Such resolutions are supposed to maintain at least a minimum level of credibility. The provisions of resolution 686 (1991) make frequent reference to "the forces of Kuwait and the Member States cooperating with Kuwait", implying that it is those forces which fought the war against Iraq. As everyone in the world is aware, the war plan is an American plan. It was the American President who declared war and it was he who announced the cessation of military operations. It was the American forces, together with much more limited forces from other Western countries, particularly Britain and France, which fought the war. As everyone in the world knows, it is the American political machine which dictates, directs and applies pressure in order to fashion the political position on this subject, and thus the resolutions of the Security Council.

These distinctions will not pass without being seen as signs of a dark age which the human race is now entering ... an age of domination by a brutal super-Power over the resources of the world and the international establishment, imposing its will on them with impunity ... distorting the truth as it distorts history. The free peoples of the world, their national Governments and all those with a clear conscience must draw the pertinent conclusions from these facts. They must also expose the premeditated designs against Iraq which lie behind everything that has happened in the past. The principal truth of the matter is that the fundamental issue, regardless of differences of opinion on one side or another, which are natural and legitimate, was not that of respect for international legitimacy and international law but the imposition of hegemony over the resources of the Gulf region and the Middle East and thereby over the world.

Events prove once again that peace, stability, security and justice cannot be secured in the Middle East region and that this region will not enjoy security and tranquillity until the question of the Palestinian Arab people is solved on a just

0142

/...

basis which guarantees that people its legitimate rights to recover its territory
and to establish its own free independent State in that territory, including its
capital, Jerusalem.

(Signed) Tariq AZIZ
Deputy Prime Minister
Minister for Foreign Affairs
of the Republic of Iraq

0143 /...

<u>Annex IV</u>

<u>Letter dated 4 March 1991 from the Deputy Prime Minister and
Minister for Foreign Affairs of Iraq addressed to the Minister
for Foreign Affairs of Yemen</u>

The people and leadership of Iraq have followed the positions adopted by Yemen in the Security Council during discussion of aspects relating to the Gulf crisis, its decision to vote against Security Council resolution 678 (1990) and its recent decision to abstain from the vote on resolution 686 (1991), which we had hoped would be a vote against the resolution rather than an abstention.

History will speak of a significant distinction whereby Yemen abstained from the vote on the unjust resolution 686 (1991) at a time when Iraq agreed to fulfil its obligations under that resolution. History will provide the proper interpretation of that fact. We are pleased that Yemen is able to speak the truth and to adopt the position which it deems fit in accordance with its assessments. Iraq, for its part, has acquiesced in its acceptance because of circumstances which are well known.

Another of the distinctions which history will record is that distortion of the truth has extended even to the formulation of resolutions by the highest international organization. Such resolutions are supposed to maintain at least a minimum level of credibility. The provisions of resolution 686 (1991) make frequent reference to "the forces of Kuwait and the Member States cooperating with Kuwait", implying that it is those forces which fought the war against Iraq. As everyone in the world is aware, the war plan is an American plan. It was the American President who declared war and it was he who announced the cessation of military operations. It was the American forces, together with much more limited forces from other Western countries, particularly Britain and France, which fought the war. As everyone in the world knows, it is the American political machine which dictates, directs and applies pressure in order to fashion the political position on this subject, and thus the resolutions of the Security Council.

These distinctions will not pass without being seen as signs of a dark age which the human race is now entering ... an age of domination by a brutal super-Power over the resources of the world and the international establishment, imposing its will on them with impunity ... distorting the truth as it distorts history. The free peoples of the world, their national Governments and all those with a clear conscience must draw the pertinent conclusions from these facts. They must also expose the premeditated designs against Iraq which lie behind everything that has happened in the past. The principal truth of the matter is that the fundamental issue, regardless of differences of opinion on one side or another, which are natural and legitimate, was not that of respect for international legitimacy and international law but the imposition of hegemony over the resources of the Gulf region and the Middle East and thereby over the world.

Events prove once again that peace, stability, security and justice cannot be secured in the Middle East region and that this region will not enjoy security and

/...

0144

tranquillity until the question of the Palestinian Arab people is solved on a just basis which guarantees that people its legitimate rights to recover its territory and to establish its own free independent State in that territory, including its capital, Jerusalem.

(Signed) Tariq AZIZ
Deputy Prime Minister
Minister for Foreign Affairs
of the Republic of Iraq

0145

UNITED
NATIONS

A S

 General Assembly   Security Council

Distr.
GENERAL

A/46/111
S/22336
6 March 1991
ENGLISH
ORIGINAL: ARABIC

GENERAL ASSEMBLY
Forty-sixth session
Items 33, 35 and 46 of the
  preliminary list*
QUESTION OF PALESTINE
THE SITUATION IN THE MIDDLE EAST
IRAQI AGGRESSION AND THE CONTINUED
  OCCUPATION OF KUWAIT IN FLAGRANT
  VIOLATION OF THE CHARTER OF THE
  UNITED NATIONS

SECURITY COUNCIL
Forty-sixth year

Letter dated 5 March 1991 from the Permanent Representative of
Egypt to the United Nations addressed to the Secretary-General

   I have the honour to transmit herewith the text of the statement made by
President Muhammad Hosni Mubarak, President of the Arab Republic of Egypt, at the
joint meeting of the People's Assembly and the Advisory Council on 3 March 1991.

   I would be grateful if you would kindly have this letter and its annex
circulated as an official document of the General Assembly, under items 33, 35
and 46 of the preliminary list for its forty-sixth session, and as an official
document of the Security Council.

(Signed) Amre MOUSSA
Permanent Representative

_____

   *   A/46/50.

<u>Annex</u>

Ladies and gentlemen,

Members of the People's Assembly and the Advisory Council,

In these historic days, in which a distinction is being drawn between light and darkness, between hopes and sufferings, and between the announcement of liberation and victory, on the one hand, and the horrors of war and the signs of devastation, on the other, ...

I have come to you mainly in order to present my second testimony, for the historical record, concerning all the circumstances surrounding the sanguinary disaster that has afflicted our Arab nation.

I have also come in order to launch a pan-Arab appeal, from the Egyptian people's Parliament, to all fraternal Arab peoples, calling upon them to strive towards a path of action and a new future; a future of peace and security, work and development.

I tell you frankly; in these last few weeks, I have faced my roughest and most difficult days in office and the most severe and overwhelming distress, in which my heart has been weighed down with anxiety and grief and I have asked myself in bewildered astonishment: Did we not caution the ruler of Iraq against all that has happened? Did we not give him sincere advice and tell him the truth from the very first day of his occupation of the State of Kuwait? Did we not diligently endeavour, by various means, to make him aware of the true situation, the real state of affairs and the proper course of action, since there was every indication that the international consensus would not condone that crime and would not permit it to continue? Did we not overlook all his insults, abuse and insolence? Did we not constantly warn him of his miscalculations and his erroneous assumptions, which inevitably led, as we had expected and warned, to ruin, destruction, death and collapse?

May God curse arrogance and self-delusion! May God curse the decision of an individual when that individual is deified!

Self-delusion, hypocrites, conspirators, self-interested persons and buffoons gave him the false impression that the world would be divided in the face of his arguments, his wisdom and his courage, that Kuwait would become an easy prey, and that its annexation to Iraq would be a fictitious crowning achievement of his misguided leadership.

However, it became clearly evident, from the outset, that his judgement was naive and capricious and that he had deluded himself, once again, into believing that, by maintaining his stubborn attitude and remaining entrenched in his fortified bunker, he would be able to bring down governments, overthrow systems and redraw the map of the world.

0147   /...

It then became unquestionably evident that his judgement was based on advice received from ignorant and dim-witted persons and adepts in the art of creating slogans and catchwords.

He subsequently deluded himself into thinking that the international community would not adopt a resolution calling for the use of armed force to ensure withdrawal. I warned him about this in a long letter - I repeat, I warned him about this in a long letter - in which I assured him that the resolution would be adopted in the very near future. He responded, as usual, with further abuse, vituperation and frivolity.

It then became increasingly evident that he had acted on blind impulse and that he was unaware of, or unable to understand, the most fundamental facts concerning the international community.

Yet again, he deluded himself into thinking that the Arab and friendly allied forces feared confrontation in a land battle and were terrified of his mythical overwhelming power capable of transforming vast territories into a huge cemetery and a sea of blood that would not be deep enough to cover the corpses of the tens of thousands of victims. He mistakenly believed that, if this happened, peoples would revolt against their leaders and governments, thrones would be toppled and presidents would be overthrown, leaving his misguided leadership to reign supreme and strut imperiously on the world stage.

Accordingly, he warned of ruin, death and calamity and announced, in an extremely confident, arrogant and boastful manner, that the odds against his overwhelming victory were less than one in a million!

He then announced that the damage suffered by military installations inside Iraq as a result of the air raids was much less than he had estimated on the basis of a careful calculation and that he would be able to wage a victorious war for a period of six years. He ridiculed those who had referred only to a period of three years!

There was also a constantly mounting deluge of statements, declarations and communiqués from four radio stations, concerning fabulous secret weapons that would cause the world to tremble, ingenious military strategies that would astound military leaders for all time, and frightful prospects of slaughter in which the combatants would be sent home in hundreds of thousands of shrouds.

The truth must be told! Whenever a head of State expressed a view contrary to his own, this man accused him of being ignorant, degenerate, contemptible, cowardly, irreligious, etc. All these shameful, vulgar and abusive epithets were heaped on a large number of world leaders, whom he expected to grovel at his feet pleading for mercy and forgiveness after the annihilation of their armies and the collapse of their regimes and governments!

0148   /...

He therefore believed that, when the leaders of the major Powers had been overthrown, his glorious historic victory would place the leadership of the world in his hands.

Believe me, ladies and gentlemen,

I am still bewildered and confused.

Even now, I am still bewildered and confused.

How could any intelligent, logical or perceptive student of military history imagine that he would be able to wage a battle, even on a very limited scale, when he did not possess a single aircraft, not even a single defensive missile, after the air war and before the air battle!

Even the aircraft that escaped destruction were surreptitiously flown to Iran.

Is this the heroic steadfastness of which he boasted and which was reiterated by some deceitful or gullible voices?

Does steadfastness imply that all military installations, armament factories and command and control centres in Iraqi territory should be left exposed to bombardment and destruction without the slightest resistance and without a single fighter aircraft capable of protecting a position?

Does steadfastness imply that civilian locations should be used as military centres or that military hardware should be placed in schools, in hospitals, in civilian shelters, in the vicinity of places of worship and in hotels, which would therefore be subject to bombardment, and that one should subsequently bewail the civilian victims?

There is a big difference between steadfastness and suicide ... a very big difference between steadfastness and suicide.

Steadfastness means that a person fights, while still in possession of his weapons, with the least possible losses.

Suicide means sacrificing thousands of men to fight for a lost cause. This is a decision to be taken by a leader.

A courageous leader is one who is the most steadfast of all and who assiduously protects the safety of his army and his people.

It is insanity and a betrayal of the honourable and responsible position of leadership for a leader to order his forces to commit suicide, while he himself remains safely in his bunker, out of a crazy desire to be hailed as a steadfast leader in mass demonstrations.

0149

/...

Gullible and other persons who took part in noisy demonstrations, raised banners and shouted slogans in a number of Arab countries sought to mislead the public and exploit the situation in order to achieve internal party political objectives designed to arouse and mislead the masses.

They tried to convince the world that he was the hero who would liberate Jerusalem.

They tried to convince the world that he would vanquish colonialism and smash imperialism.

They tried to convince the world that he was the audacious leader who would annihilate Israel.

They even tried to convince the world, as he tried to convince himself, that he was the messenger of divine providence who would raise the banner of Islam, propagate justice and rescue the poor. Of this and other things they tried to convince the world.

And while they tried to convince the world and he tried to convince himself of these things, he knew better than anyone that all these falsehoods and lies sprang from the trumpets of his own propaganda, on which billions had been spent in order to mask the crime of the occupation of an Arab country, a friendly and weak neighbour which had long given generously to him. He reckoned with his sick imagination and his even sicker calculations that these demonstrations were his path to the leadership of which he dreamt and that, since he had become a leader, any Arab force which liberated Kuwait was an infidel, treacherous force and that any international force which, with the Arab forces, implemented the Security Council resolution to liberate Kuwait were forces that had crossed the oceans to bring down his leadership, to destroy his military force and to obliterate Iraq from the map of the world.

Such is the game played by some who are still living with the mentality of the 1940s and 1950s, which sold out the cause of the Palestinian people and deceived the Arab masses with spurious slogans on the part of Israel and assertions that they would cast Israel into the sea.

In the meantime, it was Egypt that was fighting and Egypt that was sacrificing thousands of the lives of its purest sons and Egypt that was losing billions in its wars for the Palestinian cause and for the security of the Arab world.

Where is the Jerusalem which he has liberated?

Where is the Israel which he has annihilated and demolished?

Where is the Islam which this tyrant transformed into killing, plunder, rape and barbarous forms of torture whereby women are killed in front of their fathers and sons, eyes are gouged out with red-hot skewers and heads are cleft open with axes?

0150

/...

Where is justice for the poor in the destruction and burning of oil wells and the poisoning of the seas?

Who has brought the American, British, French and other allied forces to our land?

Who has sent the Iraqi army to its destruction and collapse?

Did not the ruler of Iraq have the opportunity over a long period of six months to accept the Security Council resolutions and withdraw within the period laid down by the Security Council, after which there would have been no war, no destruction or devastation?

Would it not have been nobler and more honourable for him to withdraw, as all the world's leaders were begging him and advising him to do, using every means to convince him and bring him to reason, rather than to be forced finally into a humiliating and ignominious withdrawal, with his forces surrendering, his military equipment destroyed and his army suffering tens of thousands of casualties?

Did we not warn him 30 times in letters and appeals on behalf of every man, woman and child, with the greatest respect and desire to see him save face; did we not warn him of the dreadful and terrifying consequences and did we not say at that time that those consequences would be humiliating and ignominious?

Even after the ground war began, which he in his innermost (if not inane) calculations had reckoned would not happen for fear of his false and empty threats, did we halt our efforts to advise him to announce a withdrawal and accept the Security Council resolutions? That is what we did. I say clearly that, even a few hours before the battle began, the international efforts from all capitals were not halted.

The Soviet Union intervened, advising him, indeed warning him, to weigh matters carefully and to accept the international resolutions. But he tried to prevaricate and accused the Soviet leader Gorbachev of being subservient! (He too was subservient - everyone is under some form of subservience nowadays.) Moscow did not succeed, after 10 days of efforts, in obtaining the necessary decision from him. He set impossible conditions, one of which was that he should be rewarded for what he had done and that Iraq should not forfeit its right to annex Kuwait.

Did he not propose, inter alia, that the withdrawal should take place within 21 days?

Did he not finally withdraw within hours?

Ladies and gentlemen, I tried my utmost, with all sincerity and perseverance, together with our brothers, the leaders of the Arab nation and our friends, the leaders of the major Powers of both West and East, I tried, they tried, we all tried together first to avoid this war, which was imposed by international legality, and then to avoid pursuing it. Yet we have found in this tyrant nothing

0151

/...

but obstinacy, persistence, tortuous promises, deceitful undertakings and puerile manoeuvres which mock fate and destiny.

He says one thing and its opposite at the same time!

His promises carry within themselves confirmation of his clear intention not to carry them out.

And then there are vainglorious speeches, delivered in heroic tones, in which he deceives himself even more than he deceives the masses of the Arab nation with lies, delusions and distortions of the truth.

In the midst of all this, there is a sanguinary and evil insistence on the heedless sacrifice of thousands of innocent lives among the Iraqi army and the Iraqi people. There is an even more evil aberration in wanting to be surrounded by devastation and corpses, burning oil wells and a sea which is being poisoned. He destroyed Kuwait's facilities before withdrawing and plundered its coffers in the dark of night.

The future will soon reveal the hideous nature of these vile crimes, which are without historical precedent, even in the worst ages of oppression and tyranny; crimes committed and ordered by the ruler of Iraq.

In his first declarations, he was intent on laying down fanciful conditions, to which he added the guarantee that his rule should be safeguarded and that his life should not be endangered. He continued to equivocate with his conditions, hoping to gain time and prevent the continuation of the war, due to a change in the weather, which would give him an excuse not to withdraw. Then he became two-faced: one face announced that he would agree to withdraw, at the same time as the other face was destroying and burning the oil wells; one face was showing a desire for peace, while the other face was trying to avoid implementing the Security Council resolutions. It was therefore natural that the Soviet Union should declare its solidarity with the other countries of the coalition and the absolute necessity of unconditional withdrawal and compliance with all the Security Council resolutions, which the ruler of Iraq had lost four days in agreeing to one after the other!

Ladies and gentlemen, members of the People's Assembly and the Advisory Council,

The page has been turned and a new page has begun.

The days of darkness have passed and the dawn of a new day has broken.

The terrible tragedy has ended and Kuwait has been liberated. Our armed forces, in collaboration with the Arab and coalition forces, have played their heroic role in the battle for liberation. All the military leaders have praised the coalition. Through their military correspondents in the theatre of war, the greatest newspapers in the world have celebrated the valour of the Egyptian fighting man, his magnificent performance and the force of his onslaught. They

0152   /...

have also commended the fact that the Egyptian armed forces completed all their combat missions in a shorter time than that envisaged in the planning of military operations.

It was another illustrious role performed, and one to be added to the distinctions achieved by our armed forces in protecting Arab security. They fought with faith and conviction. They attacked with courage, manliness and daring. They achieved their objectives with military expertise and superior execution. Each fighting man was an honour to Egypt and conferred honour and distinction on every family in Egypt.

Egypt will not forget, the people of Kuwait will not forget and free people everywhere will not forget our righteous martyrs who gave their lives in the most honourable of battles. I should like us, ladies and gentlemen, to stand for two minutes in salute to the departed spirits of our martyrs and of all the martyrs of the victory achieved in the liberation of Kuwait.

Ladies and gentlemen,

The flag of Kuwait has been raised over the land of Kuwait. The flag of Egypt has been raised over the Embassy of Egypt in the free, independent and sovereign State of Kuwait.

It is no secret that we had no desire that the obduracy, self-delusion and arrogance of the ruler of Iraq should lead to hostilities with the army of Arab Iraq. It is he who made the decision, it is he who sought the conflict, and it is he who insisted and acted with intransigence and contempt. It is he who declared, in the closed meeting of the Arab Summit Conference held at Casablanca and in a meeting with the Arab Lawyers Union, that the Arabs would be entitled to mobilize their armies against the army of Iraq if it were to violate the sovereignty of an Arab State.

From this podium, ladies and gentlemen, I address each individual member of our armed forces in the theatre of war, and I say to them with full pride: glory belongs to those who achieve glory; and honour is due to those who have fought with honour for their people and for their Arab nation. The banners of Egypt are deserving of manly arms.

From this podium, I also address the fraternal people of Iraq, the army of Iraq and all those on whom this war was forcibly imposed in the land of Kuwait and the land of Iraq. I say to them: the people of Egypt is a brother to the people of Iraq. The decision of a single individual cannot destroy this brotherliness. The people of Egypt will not stint in contributing to the reconstruction of Iraq. The people of Iraq is an inseparable part of the Arab nation, and it must play its own political, cultural and social role in days to come.

I say to Baghdad's broadcasting services: we have had enough of the ignominy of mendacity, deception and deceit. Do not make of noble, Arab Iraq, which has a civilization and a history, an object of ridicule to the people of the world with reports of fables about imaginary battles in which every day you exterminate

0153 /...

thousands down to the last man! We have had enough of frustrating mockery, after you have done such things to Iraq, to the army of Iraq and to the people of Iraq as have filled the hearts of the Arab nation with sorrows that will not be effaced for decades to come and have done such things as relegate all of those responsible for this catastrophe to the darkest corner of our contemporary history. It saddens me, ladies and gentlemen, to have heard just recently one trying, with enviable boldness, to shed with honeyed words this grave responsibility, imagining to himself that history can be deceived by ignominious guises donned for every occasion without shame or embarrassment.

From this podium, I speak to the people of Kuwait in the land of Kuwait, a people that has borne the most heinous cruelties of a brutal occupation with forbearance and which has been subjected to the greatest crimes of repression, torture, plunder and looting. The most recent of these crimes have been the burning of the major hotels and the seizure of their stocks and the arrest of hundreds and their removal to Iraq, all in the last hours before the withdrawal. The forces of popular resistance, however, never hesitated in their defiance and opposition.

I also speak to those of the people of Kuwait in Egypt and in every Arab land. I say to all of them: warm congratulations on the liberation of your country, Kuwait, and it is a matter of pride and glory enough to you that there appeared among you none who broke faith and collaborated with usurpation, tyranny and aggression. Once again, I say to all of them: warm congratulations on the liberation of your country, and it is a matter of pride and glory enough to you that there appeared among you none who broke faith and collaborated with usurpation, tyranny and aggression.

Ladies and gentlemen, members of the People's Assembly and of the Advisory Council,

We do not gloat at the distress of others; rather do we commiserate with them. We do not rejoice at a shocking defeat and at abiding destruction. Rather do we hope for a speedy recovery and a wakeful vigilance that will draw all eyes and minds towards the future. We are not proponents of settling for the bloody present and dwelling on pains and sorrows; our call is for a forward-looking outlook that will address the inter-Arab situation seriously and realistically and for the building of the new international order so that we may salvage what has been lost in terms of lives, infrastructure and progress.

It would be wise to profit from the lessons of this ordeal and from all the bitter consequences that it has brought with it for the Arab world at a time when we had come close to interlinkage, solidarity and integrated planning for the present and the future and then calamity struck. If the catastrophe has set us back into remote and gloomy depths, the primary responsibility of the Arab leaders and of the Arab peoples is that they should, through remedial action, correct this grave situation. Then, all may lend a helping hand and work together to agree on a basis from which to set out towards a better future and a new life in which wounds are healed, mutual recriminations cease and new and rejuvenated blood is infused after the enormous bloodshed that has afflicted the Arab nation in battle.

/...

0154

The cruel experience that confronts us all in the entire Arab world is a moral lesson. The future will be harsher and more bitter if Arab forces, governmental or popular, proceed in the self same manner with regard to conflicts. Such conflicts may be compounded if we abandon our destiny to the rule of whims and exaggerations, factions may multiply, the trade in slogans and incantation may flourish, and policies for the deception of peoples may continue under clashing banners. The most pertinent example to that effect is the statement made only recently, as I have told you, in lofty contempt for the consciousness of the masses and their honour, by an Arab leader.

A moment for soul-searching, O nation of the Arabs ...

A moment for soul-searching, O nation of the Arabs ...

A moment for deep study, penetrating to the depths, speaking truly and frankly and proceeding in purity of word and deed.

We do not intend to settle accounts or to exacerbate differences. The doors must be closed on all those who wish to augment the catastrophe: what we have undergone is already enough.

We are confronted with fundamental, topical and urgent issues. While the ruler of Iraq forced us to bring in foreign forces to help us defend the sovereignty of another Arab State, we should be aware that the vast expanses of the Arab nation have the political, economic and social capacities and resources to enable us alone to establish the new basis for progress towards a better future.

We must not squander these vast resources. It is already enough that we should have been afflicted by the greatest and most dangerous wastage of our material and spiritual resources ever to have been seen in the history of the Arab nation.

We do not seek a division between East and West. We do not look for a continuation of campaigns of resentment, deceptive allegations, slogans which take cheap advantage of events or the machinations of poisonous intrigues and multiple hypocrisies.

We have no wish to see the Arab nation divided into two. We have no wish to see the Arab nation divided into two, and we do not want the single Arab people to be scattered as separate peoples and deceived by wicked objectives which drive them to internecine strife within a single country. It is neither the undercurrents nor the currents on the surface which dominate the consciousness of peoples, their true path, their just and legitimate right to a future of peace, safety, co-operation, solidarity and unity - with all honour and probity - in support of their principles.

The Arab world is confronted with crucial issues. Agreement must be reached on ways to address them in order to ensure that the correct path is followed.

0155

/...

We have before us the question of the Palestinian people. It is a question of a people and not a question of leaderships, exaggerations, intrigues and conspiracies. I repeat: it is a question of a people and not a question of leaderships, not a question of exaggerations, intrigues or conspiracies.

The Palestinian people has the paramount right to self-determination after all these years of suffering, of the folly of slogans and of conflict between leaderships, the result being dissipation of the major issue and its conversion into a question of differences between individuals and the exchange of accusations.

No one will deny that the solution of the question of Palestine is the prime key to a just and lasting peace in the Arab region.

We do not treat this question as a commercial proposition. Sufficient offence has been dealt to our Arab history by this absurd and misleading assertion that the occupation of Kuwait represented the path to Jerusalem.

We must tear up all these rotten pages. We must tear them up in order to begin a clean and serious page which restores the freshness and integrity of this just and topical question, in order that banners of peace may be raised with faithful hearts, with open minds, with desires to attain solutions and without discourses of intrigue.

The Palestinian people represents a trust which is borne by all of us, and we shall not betray that trust. We have before us the question of the Golan and the question of the single united Arab people of Lebanon. All these questions are interrelated. The time has come for us to proceed, by solving them rapidly and decisively, towards stability and peace.

We have before us the question of Arab security.

This is an extremely important question. It warrants priority treatment following the exposure of the existence and destiny of the Arab nation to the most serious threat as a result of the Iraqi invasion of Kuwait and all the distresses and horrors which that has entailed.

Arab security shall be Arab and Arab alone, ensuring full immunity and protection for this region of the world.

We have before us the questions of economic and social development and the integration required for planned comprehensive development such as will ensure social justice and draw upon the enormous Arab capacities in terms of resources, manpower and scientific evolution. In so doing, we shall construct a solid, strong, proud and upstanding Arab nation, which will have its eminent place in interaction with the new international order based on peace, technological and economic competition and consolidation of political democracy.

We have before us the questions of disputed boundaries with their long-standing conflicts.

We have before us the question of cooperation with the people of Iraq, which shall not be separated from the Arab nation. The people of Iraq is the master of its own fate and has the paramount right to determine its future. It is that people which is now experiencing the bloody tragedy brought upon it by the tyranny of falsehood over that which is right and the ambitions of one individual at the expense of the freedom of millions.

Ladies and gentlemen, members of the People's Assembly and the Advisory Council,

All these crucial and weighty issues require from us innovative thinking which relates to reality from a premise of strength and solidarity, as well as statements of fact from hearts which are free of caprice and arbitrary views.

My call is not one for Arab reconciliation by means of the declarations, statements and slogans which we have learned by heart. How easily those words flow in our political dictionary and in our Arab region.

My call is one for Arab candour, pledged to sincerity and to a deep conviction that the downfalls and collapses by which we have been beset can lead us only to a yet more severe and bitter fate, unless we all face up to the full dangers of the situation.

Candour which is constructive and not destructive.

Candour which brings protection and not disunity.

It is my belief that Egypt was the first to display such candour at the Arab Summit Conference held in Casablanca - the first summit meeting which it attended following the reconciliation between Egypt and the League of Arab States.

As you may remember, I raised some specific points at that Conference which I considered appropriate in order to enrich united progress as one nation. I wish to add the following points in the wake of the bloody events which began with the Iraqi invasion of Kuwait:

1. We must neither lose any time nor waste any effort in giving thought to reprisals, revenge or the settling of accounts. We must turn this sad page in our history and direct our hearts and eyes towards the future, with all the hope and aspiration which it bears for our peoples.

2. We must exert our utmost efforts to restore faith in the domain of the Arab family at the earliest opportunity, in order that doubts should not grow deeper and divisions spread in our ranks. No nation is capable of any joint action if doubt and suspicion hold sway over the minds of its members.

3. The events of the calamitous invasion and its aftermath make it necessary that every one of us should state his vision of objectives for both his nation and his country, as well as the means which he believes should be used in order to attain those objectives. In this way, each Arab country will have knowledge in advance of what the other countries intend to strive to implement and achieve.

/...

0157

4. We must also redouble our efforts in the months and years to come to settle the outstanding differences between all Arab countries, first and foremost among these being differences over boundaries, even if this means that new machinery must be invented in order to enhance our ability to overcome the difficulties and problems which cast gloom on Arab relations.

5. We must hasten to complete our concept of the situation in the region after the war, concentrating on two essential points - namely, security and development - which are complementary, interrelated and interdependent elements. They cannot be separated, nor can one be considered in isolation from the other. In order for this to come about, there must be collective thought and continuous consultation, because the future of all of us depends on our success in formulating a joint and integrated vision.

6. Events have proved how right we were to have urged, for more than two years, that the Middle East region - meaning the region as a whole, including Israel - should be kept free of weapons of mass destruction. When we urged that, the ruler of Iraq and the Iraqi leadership objected to making it free of nuclear, chemical and biological weapons of mass destruction. We should also consider other means of preventing the accumulation of weapons in the region and the race to acquire and make use of them.

7. If we are to bring about security and stability in the region, we must all devote our utmost efforts to settling the Arab-Israeli conflict, and particularly its Palestinian element, because this conflict is the principal source of anxiety and tension in the region and plunges it into a vicious circle of violence and counter-violence.

8. In order to consolidate comprehensive reconstruction in the phase to come, we must endeavour to extend opportunities for cooperation to every Arab citizen in public work and to strengthen the march of democracy in the manner which each Arab country determines in accordance with its circumstances and experiences.

9. We must become conscious of the falsehood of words spoken in the miasma of events over a period of seven sad months, which attempted to portray what happened as a battle between East and West, between Muslims and non-Muslims or as a return to the Crusades. All this was bogus, a sham. The battle was between legitimacy and anarchy, between right and wrong, between that which is lawful and that which is unlawful. We praise God that Arab legitimacy matched international legitimacy and that the victory - in the end - lay with the forces of right and good and not with the forces of aggression and injustice.

This, then, is my pan-Arab appeal, on your behalf and on behalf of the people of Egypt, which I direct to the Arab people at this decisive and crucial time when, if we are properly heedful, we may proceed to advance and to march upward and onward.

The downfalls of dispersal could sweep us away, and the exaggerations of slogans could lead us to a yet more wretched fate, a fate which we must not accept.

0158

/...

History will not forgive us ... nor will any generation forgive us ... nor will the blood of a free and noble life course once again through our Arab nation ... if we remain aloof and if we continue to chase our own tails in vicious circles which never end or fall still.

Ladies and gentlemen,

I know that you are expecting some words from me about our economic situation. We have been dealt major blows by the disaster of the invasion, over and above the crushing difficulties from which we already suffered, which have their obvious negative effects on our daily life. I know that you are waiting for me to speak on this subject, which is a matter of concern for every family in Egypt.

I shall say only this, on this vitally significant matter: our brothers in Saudi Arabia, Kuwait, the United Arab Emirates and the other Gulf States fully understand the realities of our economic situation and believe - with the best of possible intentions - that an Egypt with a strong foundation and economy means an Egypt committed to the principle and honour of its position and an Egypt which never abandons its pioneering role, whatever hardships that may entail. Important messages have been exchanged in this regard, and I hope that their effects will become apparent in the near future. In addition, steps were taken from the outset of the events of the invasion.

Egypt will play its constructive role in measures to rebuild Kuwait, and our brothers will welcome Egyptian workers in all matters relating to development. These workers will be treated with all due consideration and reverence: agreements to this effect ensure that the rights of every entitled person will be respected.

Ladies and gentlemen,

I am fully confident of my vision of the immediate and distant future. Our path stretches out, blazing and aglow, to horizons radiant with development and peace. This confidence is not unfounded.

It stems from the inspiration of the great and noble people of Egypt ... the great and noble people of Egypt which has stood as one man and whose heart has beat as one since the crime of the invasion began and which showed - as a matter of spontaneous civilized awareness - that the people knows how to make the right decision at the right time ...

The great and noble people of Egypt, which with all its vigour and strength brushed aside tendentious and arbitrary assertions that endeavoured to falsify the facts before its eyes, to distort the image in its mind or to stir up its feelings with superficial provocations and misleading appeals ...

The great and noble people of Egypt, which, massed in its millions, formed a mighty shield that swept aside spurious assertions and rose up in pride and glory above the provocations of those consumed by convulsions and the lies of those who deliberately incite trouble ...

0159

/...

The great and noble people of Egypt, which with historic heedfulness, refused to be an instrument of deception, a victim of events or a trumpet for the voices of untruth and slander ...

The great and noble people of Egypt, which scoffed at those who wished to belittle its intelligence and awareness and prevailed over those who thought they could deceive it ...

The great and noble people of Egypt, which raised the banner of great an1 noble Egypt and before which all the slogans of untruth and deception and all the propaganda of terror and intimidation bowed down in submission and exhaustion ...

The great and noble people of Egypt ... the people of principle, glory and honour which stood by its armed forces in the battle for Arab dignity as a solid and united front under a single flag, the flag of Egypt.

Egypt ... peace which does not betray. Egypt ... the shield which protects and preserves. Egypt ... which may not be sold or bought at any time.

Egypt ... which has suffered and continues to suffer but does not neglect its dignity or indulge in trading of its position and words.

Egypt, in looking forward to a new Arab world, believes that time is golden if we base our endeavours on candour and sincerity; gold, however, turns to dust if we fall behind the march of growth and development or if we turn our backs on a society bound by ties of veracity, loyalty and the rule of humans who respect human rights.

Ladies and gentlemen, we are marching and advancing in the procession of honour ... In constructing the present for the sake of the future, we represent an unshakeable example, an inextinguishable flame and an unbending determination.

O Lord, deepen our faith and grant us, by Your good grace, strength, charity and reason.

"God singles out for His mercy whom He will; God is of bounty abounding."

"God is powerful over everything."

May God grant success to us and to you.

Peace be upon you and the mercy of God.

0160

**UNITED
NATIONS**

Security Council

S

Distr.
GENERAL

S/22339
7 March 1991

ORIGINAL: ENGLISH

LETTER DATED 1 MARCH 1991 FROM THE PERMANENT REPRESENTATIVE OF
THAILAND TO THE UNITED NATIONS ADDRESSED TO THE PRESIDENT OF
THE SECURITY COUNCIL

I have the honour to transmit herewith the text of the statement by the
Ministry of Foreign Affairs of Thailand issued on 1 March 1991 concerning the
developments in the Persian Gulf.

I should be grateful if Your Excellency could have the text of this letter and
its annex circulated as a document of the Security Council.

(Signed) Nitya PIBULSONGGRAM
Ambassador
Permanent Representative

Annex

Statement issued on 1 March 1991 by the Ministry of
Foreign Affairs of Thailand

1.   Thailand warmly welcomes the agreement by Iraq to comply fully with Security Council resolution 660 (1990) and all the other Security Council resolutions on the Gulf crisis, as well as the agreement on the cease-fire of 28 February 1991.

2.   Thailand has taken a firm position in opposing the invasion and occupation of Kuwait and has given its strong support to all the Security Council resolutions concerning the Gulf crisis. For these reasons, Thailand congratulates the coalition forces for their successful liberation of the State of Kuwait and the restoration of full independence and sovereignty of Kuwait to its nation and people.

3.   In this connection, the spokesman of the Ministry of Foreign Affairs of Thailand also indicated that the maintenance of peace in the Gulf is a matter of great concern to Thailand. He said that if a United Nations peace-keeping operation should be required and should Thailand be requested to participate in it, Thailand would be willing to do so.

0162

UNITED NATIONS

 Security Council

S

Distr.
GENERAL

S/22340
7 March 1991

ORIGINAL: ENGLISH

LETTER DATED 7 MARCH 1991 FROM THE CHARGE D'AFFAIRES A.I. OF THE
PERMANENT MISSION OF BRUNEI DARUSSALAM TO THE UNITED NATIONS
ADDRESSED TO THE SECRETARY-GENERAL

I have the honour to transmit herewith the text of the statement of the Government of Brunei Darussalam dated 1 March 1991 on the Liberation of Kuwait and the Suspension of War.

I would be grateful if the text of the statement could be circulated as a document of the Security Council.

(Signed) SUYOI Haji Osman
Chargé d'affaires a.i.

91-07802   2105c (E)

/...

0163

<u>Annex</u>

<u>Statement of Brunei Darussalam on the liberation</u>
<u>of Kuwait and the suspension of the war</u>

Brunei Darussalam joins the people of Kuwait in their happiness on the liberation of their country. Brunei Darussalam has consistently supported all the twelve United Nations Security Council resolutions towards the restoration of the sovereignty of Kuwait and the re-establishment of its legitimate Government.

Brunei Darussalam welcomes the announcement of President Bush in suspending all military operations against Iraq. Brunei Darussalam also welcomes Iraq's decision to accept all the twelve Security Council resolutions.

Brunei Darussalam urges the Security Council to arrange for an immediate cease-fire and cessation of hostilities. Brunei Darussalam also calls on the United Nations to address and resolve the many outstanding issues including the Palestinian problem to ensure lasting peace and stability in the region.

0164

Security Council

Distr.
GENERAL

S/22341
8 March 1991

ORIGINAL: ENGLISH

LETTER DATED 5 MARCH 1991 FROM THE PERMANENT REPRESENTATIVE OF THE
UNITED STATES OF AMERICA TO THE UNITED NATIONS ADDRESSED TO THE
PRESIDENT OF THE SECURITY COUNCIL

In accordance with paragraph 4 of resolution 678 (1990), I wish, on behalf of
my Government, to submit the following report on actions undertaken pursuant to
paragraphs 2 and 3 of that resolution up to the time of the suspension of offensive
military operations against Iraq by coalition military forces at midnight (eastern
standard time) on 27 February.

On the night of 23 February (eastern standard time), the military forces of
the coalition, including United States' military forces, acting in accordance with
Security Council resolution 678 (1990), launched ground operations to obtain full
Iraqi compliance with all 12 relevant Security Council resolutions, and
particularly to ensure the full withdrawal of Iraqi forces from Kuwait.

This move by the combined surface, naval and air units of the coalition forces
came about following intensive diplomatic efforts aimed at achieving peaceful Iraqi
withdrawal and after provocative actions by the Government of Iraq, including the
continued indiscriminate launching of surface-to-surface missiles at civilian
targets, commencement of a "scorched earth" policy, including large-scale
destruction of oil facilities and public and private buildings in Kuwait, and
evidence of increased atrocities against the Kuwaiti civilian population.

At least 600 oil installations were set on fire prior to 23 February.
Coalition forces have physical evidence that these fires were deliberately set by
Iraqi forces and have in their possession captured Iraqi documents giving orders to
destroy oil installations. In the last few days of their occupation of Kuwait,
Iraqi forces deliberately set about destroying major public buildings and hotels
and some private residences.

Members of the Kuwaiti resistance report that in addition to cases of torture,
rape and murder committed by the Iraqi forces during the period of control of
Kuwait (currently being documented by the international media), large numbers of
Kuwaiti civilians were rounded up and detained during the last days of Iraqi
occupation. It is believed that these detainees were transferred to Iraq.

91-07828   2122i (E)   /...

In response to these actions and in accordance with Security Council resolution 678 (1990), United States and other coalition ground forces attacked on several fronts on the night of 23 February. The operation included an outflanking movement to prevent the Iraqi forces in southern Iraq from moving into Kuwait. At no time did the coalition forces have any intention of destroying Iraq or of attacking Baghdad.

In a briefing on the last day of the military action, General Norman Schwarzkopf gave a description of the planning and execution of the ground campaign. He explained that a key purpose of the extensive coalition air campaign in the weeks leading up to 23 February was to isolate the Kuwaiti theatre of operations by destroying all the bridges and supply lines that ran between the northern and southern parts of Iraq. He said this action was taken to prevent the reinforcement and supply of forces in southern Iraq and Kuwait. Heavy bombing was necessary, he explained, to weaken Iraqi forces, particularly along the front line barrier that coalition forces would have to go through. He explained that once Iraqi air reconnaissance was deterred by coalition control of the air, in a massive move to the west, coalition personnel, equipment and supplies were positioned to outflank the Iraqi forces.

Coalition forces rapidly achieved their objectives of defeating the Iraqi forces that had carried out the invasion and occupation of Kuwait, and of permitting the return of the territory of Kuwait to its legitimate Government. This success constitutes a significant milestone towards the goal of restoring international peace and security to the area as set forth in Security Council resolution 678 (1990).

In the course of the engagement, coalition forces captured more than 50,000 Iraqi soldiers. These prisoners of war (POWs) have been treated in accordance with the Third Geneva Convention Relative to the Treatment of Prisoners of War, which has included the provision of medical care, shelter, food and water.

The Iraqi Government continues to hold United States POWs, other coalition POWs, an undetermined number of Kuwaiti civilians and military personnel, and other civilians of different nationalities. The Iraqi authorities have refused representatives of the International Committee of the Red Cross (ICRC) access to coalition POWs and have refused to enter into discussions with ICRC on those listed as missing in action.

The Iraqi forces continued to fire surface-to-surface missiles until the last days of the military engagement. The total number of such missiles fired since 16 January was 81 - 41 against Saudi Arabia, 38 against Israel, one against Bahrain and one against Qatar.

Coalition air attacks against military and strategic targets in Iraq and Kuwait continued until the suspension of military operations. Coalition forces took every precaution to minimize collateral damage to civilian facilities. The Iraqi Government, however, intentionally placed civilians at risk through its behaviour. Following are a few concrete examples of such behaviour:

/...

0166

(a)   The Iraqi Government moved significant amounts of military weapons and equipment into civilian areas with the deliberate purpose of using innocent civilians and their homes as shields against attacks on legitimate military targets;

(b)   Iraqi fighter and bomber aircraft were dispersed into villages near military airfields where they were parked between civilian houses and even placed immediately adjacent to important archaeological sites and historic treasures;

(c)   Coalition aircraft were fired upon by anti-aircraft weapons in residential neighbourhoods in various cities. In Baghdad, anti-aircraft sites were located on hotel roofs;

(d)   In one case, military engineering equipment used to traverse rivers, including mobile bridge sections, was located in several villages near an important crossing point. The Iraqis parked each vehicle adjacent to a civilian house.

Total casualties reported as of 1 March for United States forces participating in military actions in accordance with Security Council resolution 678 (1990) are 79 killed in action, 241 wounded in action and at least 44 missing or captured in action.

On 27 February, in an address to the nation, President Bush reported coalition action against Iraq had been successful and thus the coalition would suspend offensive combat operations as of midnight (eastern standard time) on that day.

In conclusion, I would like to quote from that address, in which President Bush said: "no one country can claim this victory as its own. It was not only a victory for Kuwait, but a victory for all the coalition partners. This is a victory for the United Nations, for all mankind, for the rule of law and for what is right."

I should be grateful if you would circulate this letter as a document of the Security Council.

(Signed)   Thomas R. PICKERING

0167

UNITED NATIONS

S

Security Council

Distr.
GENERAL

S/22343
8 March 1991

ORIGINAL: ENGLISH

LETTER DATED 5 MARCH 1991 FROM THE PERMANENT REPRESENTATIVE
OF BOTSWANA TO THE UNITED NATIONS ADDRESSED TO THE
SECRETARY-GENERAL

I have the honour to transmit herewith a Press Release issued by the
Government of Botswana on the liberation of Kuwait and the cessation of hostilities
in the Gulf.

I should be most grateful if the Press Release could be circulated as a
document of the Security Council.

(Signed) Legwaila J. M. J. LEGWAILA
Ambassador/Permanent Representative

91-07859 2310j (E)

0168　　/...

<u>Annex</u>

<u>Press statement issued by the Department of External Affairs
of Botswana on 4 March 1991 in Gaborone</u>

The Government of Botswana welcomes the liberation of Kuwait and shares in the happiness of its people as they celebrate the restoration of their country's sovereignty and freedom.

Botswana also welcomes the outcome of the meeting of the military commanders representing the allied forces and the Iraqi forces aimed at establishing the modalities for a permanent cease-fire so that the arduous task of building a durable peace in the Gulf area can begin in earnest.

Botswana urges all parties to the Gulf conflict and the international community as a whole to renew their efforts to address the broader problems of the Middle East, including, in particular, the Palestinian problem. A comprehensive process of reconciliation among the countries and peoples of the Middle East must begin if that vital area of the world is to be rid of the cycle of violence that has wreaked so much destruction and inflicted so much pain and sorrow on its peoples over the years.

0169

UNITED NATIONS

 General Assembly   Security Council

Distr.
GENERAL

A/46/113
S/22345
8 March 1991
ENGLISH
ORIGINAL: ARABIC

GENERAL ASSEMBLY
Forty-sixth session
Items 29, 33, 35 and 37 of the
  preliminary list*
THE SITUATION IN AFGHANISTAN AND ITS
  IMPLICATIONS FOR INTERNATIONAL
  PEACE AND SECURITY
QUESTION OF PALESTINE
THE SITUATION IN THE MIDDLE EAST
POLICIES OF APARTHEID OF THE
  GOVERNMENT OF SOUTH AFRICA

SECURITY COUNCIL
Forty-sixth year

        Letter dated 7 March 1991 from the Permanent Representative of
        Egypt to the United Nations addressed to the Secretary-General

     I have the honour to transmit herewith the text of the communiqué issued by
the meeting of Ministers for Foreign Affairs of the member States of the
Organization of the Islamic Conference, held in New York on 1 October 1990.

     I should be grateful if you would kindly have this letter and its annex
circulated as an official document of the General Assembly, under items 29, 33, 35
and 37 of the preliminary list, and of the Security Council.

                                         (Signed) Amre MOUSSA
                                                   Ambassador
                                         Permanent Representative

     *   A/46/50.

91-07903   2344d (E)   /...

                                                              0170

ANNEX

Final communiqué of the annual meeting of Ministers for Foreign Affairs of the member States of the Organization of the Islamic Conference, held at United Nations Headquarters, New York, on 12 Rabi' I A.H. 1411 (1 October 1990)

1.   The Ministers for Foreign Affairs of the member States of the Organization of the Islamic Conference held their annual coordinating meeting on 1 October 1990 at United Nations Headquarters in New York under the chairmanship of His Excellency Dr. Boutros Ghali, Minister of State for Foreign Affairs of the Arab Republic of Egypt, representing the President of the Nineteenth Islamic Conference of Foreign Ministers.

2.   The meeting listened with feelings of profound respect and esteem to the important opening address delivered by His Highness Sheikh Jaber Al-Ahmad Al-Jaber Al-Sabah, Amir of the State of Kuwait and President of the Fifth Islamic Summit Conference, concerning the questions preoccupying the Islamic nation, and particularly the grave situation resulting from the invasion and occupation of Kuwait by Iraq.

3.   The meeting adopted the proposed agenda.

4.   The reports of the Secretary-General concerning the matters included on the agenda were submitted to the meeting, as were the reports prepared by the OIC Committees on Palestine, Afghanistan, Namibia and South Africa.

5.   The meeting expressed its appreciation for the Secretary-General's report on Iraq's invasion of Kuwait and its consequences for regional security, peace and stability. The meeting strongly condemned Iraq's invasion and occupation of Kuwait and deemed Iraq's annexation of Kuwait to be null and void. The meeting expressed its full support and appreciation for the endeavours that were being made by the United Nations, and particularly by the Security Council. It emphasized the member States' determination to seek the full implementation of all the Security Council resolutions concerning the Iraq-Kuwait crisis. The meeting also emphasized the provisions contained in the communiqué issued by the Nineteenth Islamic Conference of Foreign Ministers, concerning the situation between Iraq and Kuwait, and urged Iraq to comply with the provisions of that communiqué and the relevant Security Council resolutions. The meeting called upon Iraq to withdraw its forces fully and immediately from Kuwait and to refrain from the use or threatened use of force against other Islamic States.

The meeting expressed its full support for, and solidarity with, the Amir, Government and people of the State of Kuwait and affirmed its determination to seek the restoration of the authority of the legitimate Government in Kuwait, headed by His Highness Sheikh Jaber Al-Ahmad Al-Jaber Al-Sabah, Amir of the State of Kuwait and President of the Fifth Islamic Summit Conference.

/...

0171

The meeting called upon Iraq to immediately cease the campaign of ill-treatment that it was pursuing in the occupied territory of Kuwait, to promptly release the nationals and hostages of third countries whom it was holding, and to facilitate their return to their countries in safety and dignity. The meeting also called upon Iraq to fulfil its international obligations, to respect the immunity of diplomatic and consular premises and to afford protection to all diplomatic and consular staff in Kuwait.

The meeting confirmed the urgent need to provide humanitarian assistance for refugees from Iraq and Kuwait and invited the international community in general, and the member States in particular, to intensify their endeavours in this regard. The meeting also called upon the donor countries and international financial institutions to assist the States that had suffered severe detriment as a result of the Gulf crisis.

The meeting affirmed its full support for, and solidarity with, the Kingdom of Saudi Arabia and other member States in the region in their individual and joint endeavours to protect their security, sovereignty and territorial integrity against the use or threatened use of force by Iraq or any other party.

6.   The meeting discussed the situation in the occupied Palestinian territories and adopted the report of the six-member Committee on Palestine. The meeting reaffirmed its support for, and total solidarity with, the struggle of the valiant Palestinian people and its glorious intifadah. The meeting called upon the member States to continue providing the Palestinian people with various forms of material and moral support and assistance in order to alleviate its sufferings, mitigate the tragic circumstances in which it was living and strengthen its heroic steadfastness in the face of the tyrannical Israeli occupation forces.

The meeting urged the international community and the States concerned to prevent the enforced mass emigration of Soviet and other Jews to occupied Palestine, since that would be incompatible with international law and conventions and would pose a threat to peace and security in the region.

The meeting called for the early convening of the international peace conference on the Middle East under the auspices of the United Nations and with the participation of the permanent members of the Security Council and all the parties to the dispute, on a footing of equality, including the Palestine Liberation Organization, the sole legitimate representative of the Palestinian people, in order to establish a just and lasting peace in the region which would ensure the withdrawal of the Israeli forces from Palestinian territory, including Holy Jerusalem, the Syrian Arab Golan and the other occupied Arab territories, and enable the Palestinian people to exercise its right of return, its right to self-determination and its right to establish its independent Palestinian State on its national soil, with Holy Jerusalem as its capital.

The meeting stressed the need for the Islamic Group to pursue its endeavours in the General Assembly of the United Nations, and also in the Security Council, with a view to the adoption of a resolution placing the Palestinian territories occupied in 1967, including Holy Jerusalem, under the supervision of the United Nations and

/...

0172

ensuring international protection for the civilian population in accordance with the provisions of the Fourth Geneva Convention of 1949.

The meeting expressed its gratitude and appreciation for the positive and fruitful positions adopted by all States and international organizations, including the United Nations, as well as the European Community, the Non-Aligned Movement, the Organization of African Unity, the Holy See and other peace-loving forces throughout the world, which were supporting the legitimate national rights of the Palestinian people.

7.   The meeting adopted the recommendations contained in the report of the Committee on Afghanistan, as well as the draft resolution submitted by Pakistan for adoption by the General Assembly of the United Nations at its forty-fifth session, and urged the member States to coordinate their endeavours with a view to mobilizing international support for the just cause of the Afghan people. The meeting also expressed its hope that the draft resolution would be adopted by consensus.

8.   The meeting adopted the recommendations contained in the report of the Committee on Namibia and South Africa, reaffirmed the provisions of the resolutions adopted by the Nineteenth Islamic Conference in that connection, and renewed its full support for the people of South Africa in its heroic struggle against racial discrimination and apartheid.

9.   The meeting discussed the critical economic situation in Africa and urged the member States to coordinate their endeavours with a view to the mobilization of further international support to deal with that situation and to secure the adoption of the appropriate resolutions by the General Assembly of the United Nations.

10.   The meeting reaffirmed the provisions of resolution 21/19-S, which was adopted at the Nineteenth Islamic Conference of Foreign Ministers, and called for a peaceful settlement of the dispute concerning Jammu and Kashmir in accordance with the relevant United Nations resolutions and the provisions of the Simla Agreement.

The meeting called upon India and Pakistan to redeploy their forces to their peace-time positions.

The meeting expressed its concern at the situation in Kashmir and affirmed its readiness to send a mission, by way of good offices on the part of the President of the Islamic Conference of Foreign Ministers, with a view to defusing tension between the two countries and promoting a peaceful settlement.

11.   The meeting called upon the member States to concert their endeavours during the forty-fifth session of the General Assembly of the United Nations and to endeavour to secure the adoption of appropriate resolutions on all the questions of concern to it, particularly those relating to peace, security, progress and development in the Islamic world.

0173

UNITED NATIONS

A S

General Assembly   Security Council

Distr.
GENERAL

A/46/114
S/22346
11 March 1991

ORIGINAL: ENGLISH

GENERAL ASSEMBLY
Forty-sixth session
Items 33 and 35 of the preliminary list*
QUESTION OF PALESTINE
THE SITUATION IN THE MIDDLE EAST

SECURITY COUNCIL
Forty-sixth year

Note verbale dated 8 March 1991 from the Permanent Representative of
Ghana to the United Nations addressed to the Secretary-General

The Permanent Representative of Ghana to the United Nations presents his compliments to the Secretary-General of the United Nations and has the honour, upon instruction, to quote hereunder, for circulation as an official document of the forty-sixth session of the General Assembly, under agenda items 33 and 35, and of the Security Council, the text of a statement by the Government of Ghana on the suspension of military hostilities in the Gulf, issued on 28 February 1991:

The Government of Ghana welcomes the suspension of military hostilities in the Gulf by the coalition forces following Iraq's acceptance to comply with all United Nations Security Council resolutions.

The Government seizes this opportunity to address an urgent appeal to all concerned, particularly the Security Council, to take immediate steps to transform the suspension of hostilities into a durable cease-fire.

The Gulf war has brought into sharp relief the paramount and urgent need for a lasting peace in the Middle East. The Government of Ghana accordingly calls on the international community to redouble its efforts, in the post-Gulf war period, to work relentlessly towards a comprehensive and long-term settlement of all the problems, including the Palestinian question in particular, which have been the source of perennial instability in the Middle East and the Gulf region as a whole.

-----

* A/46/50.

91-08024   2224e (E)

0174

UNITED NATIONS

 General Assembly   Security Council

Distr.
GENERAL

A/46/116
S/22348
12 March 1991
ENGLISH
ORIGINAL: ARABIC

GENERAL ASSEMBLY
Forty-sixth session
Items 33, 35 and 73 of the
  preliminary list*
QUESTION OF PALESTINE
THE SITUATION IN THE MIDDLE EAST
REPORT OF THE SPECIAL COMMITTEE TO
  INVESTIGATE ISRAELI PRACTICES
  AFFECTING THE HUMAN RIGHTS OF
  THE PALESTINIAN PEOPLE AND OTHER
  ARABS OF THE OCCUPIED TERRITORIES

SECURITY COUNCIL
Forty-sixth year

<u>Letter dated 12 March 1991 from the Permanent Representative of
Jordan to the United Nations addressed to the Secretary-General</u>

On instructions from my Government, I have the honour to inform you that, in January 1991, the Israeli occupation authorities arrested two Muslim theologians and placed them in administrative detention for a period of one year. The persons concerned are:

1.   His Reverence Sheikh Hamid al-Beitawi, preacher at the Al-Aqsa Mosque, member of the Council for Awqaf and Islamic Affairs at Jerusalem, and judge of the Shari'a Court at Tulkarm.

2.   His Reverence Sheikh Muhammad Fuad Abu Zaid, preacher at the Al-Aqsa Mosque and Director of Awqaf at Jenin.

It is self-evident that such arbitrary acts violate the relevant international instruments and challenge the pertinent resolutions adopted by the Security Council, the General Assembly and other organs of the United Nations. Consequently, it is essential that the United Nations should take the measures needed to induce the Israeli occupation authorities to refrain from committing such inhuman acts and to rescind their decisions in this respect, including the decision to detain the two above-mentioned theologians.

---

*   A/46/50.

91-08220   2805a (E)

0175   /...

I would be grateful if the present letter were circulated as an official document of the General Assembly, under items 33, 35 and 73 of the preliminary list, and of the Security Council.

(Signed) Abdullah SALAH
Ambassador
Permanent Representative

0176

Security Council

Distr.
GENERAL

S/AC.25/1991/22
4 March 1991

ORIGINAL: ENGLISH

SECURITY COUNCIL COMMITTEE ESTABLISHED BY
 RESOLUTION 661 (1990) CONCERNING THE
 SITUATION BETWEEN IRAQ AMD KUWAIT

NOTE VERBALE DATED 22 FEBRUARY 1991 FROM THE PERMANENT MISSION OF
BARBADOS TO THE UNITED NATIONS ADDRESSED TO THE SECRETARY-GENERAL

The Permanent Mission of Barbados to the United Nations presents its
compliments to the Secretary-General and, with reference to note SCPC/7/90 (3-2) of
20 December 1990, has the honour to provide the following information on measures
taken by the Government of Barbados in accordance with the provisions of Security
Council resolution 661 (1990).

Questions 2 and 3

The Miscellaneous Controls Act, 1970 - The Importation and Exportation of
Goods (Prohibition) Regulations, 1971, was amended by the Minister responsible for
Trade on 24 October 1990.

This order allows Barbados to comply with the provisions of resolution
661 (1990) relating to the import and export or transshipment of goods from Iraq
and Kuwait.

Question 4

The Ministry of Foreign Affairs of Barbados has been advised by the competent
government authorities that the Exchange Control Act, CAP 71, Laws of Barbados, is
sufficient to prevent any breach of Security Council resolution 661 (1990). Under
this act, prior approval is required for transactions between residents and
non-residents and for the movement of economic resources into and out of Barbados.

Question 5

The relevant order is expected to be laid before Parliament during its current
session, which began on 6 February 1991.

Copies of the above-mentioned legislation are enclosed for the information of the Secretary-General.

Enclosures*

The Miscellaneous Controls Act, CAP 329

The Importation and Exportation of Goods (Prohibition) (Amendment) Regulations, 1971

The Importation and Exportation of Goods (Prohibition) (Amendment) Regulations, 1990

The Exchange Control Act, CAP 71, Laws of Barbados

---

* Copies of the legislation may be consulted in Room S-3520.

0178

UNITED
NATIONS

A S

General Assembly   Security Council

Distr.
GENERAL

A/45/974
S/22349
13 March 1991

ORIGINAL: ENGLISH

GENERAL ASSEMBLY
Forty-fifth session
Agenda item 153
IRAQI AGGRESSION AND THE CONTINUED
  OCCUPATION OF KUWAIT IN FLAGRANT
  VIOLATION OF THE CHARTER OF THE
  UNITED NATIONS

SECURITY COUNCIL
Forty-sixth year

<u>Letter dated 13 March 1991 from the Permanent Representative of
Japan to the United Nations addressed to the Secretary-General</u>

    I have the honour to transmit herewith the text of a statement issued on
13 March 1991 by a spokesman of the Ministry of Foreign Affairs of Japan on an
additional contribution to the Gulf Peace Fund (see annex).

    I should be grateful if you would arrange to have the text of the present
letter and its annex circulated as an official document of the General Assembly,
under agenda item 153, and of the Security Council.

                              (<u>Signed</u>) Yoshio HATANO
                                     Ambassador Extraordinary
                                        and Plenipotentiary
                                  Permanent Representative of
                                  Japan to the United Nations

91-08331 2366b (E)

ANNEX

Statement issued on 13 March 1991 by a spokesman of the Ministry
of Foreign Affairs of Japan on an additional contribution to the
Gulf Peace Fund

On Wednesday, 13 March, the Government of Japan extended an additional
contribution of 1.17 trillion yen to the Gulf Peace Fund, which was set up by the
Co-operation Council for the Arab States of the Gulf (GCC) in order to support
countries undertaking activities to restore peace and stability in the Gulf region
in accordance with relevant resolutions of the United Nations Security Council.
This additional contribution is based on notes exchanged on 12 March between the
Government of Japan and the GCC, and follows the contributions of
122.88 billion yen in September 1990 and 130 billion yen in December 1990.

The liberation of Kuwait has been realized, but the burden of the countries
working for the restoration of peace and stability in the Gulf region is
exceedingly heavy. The Government of Japan has extended this contribution,
recognizing that it is indispensable for Japan to assume responsibility
commensurate with its status in the international community and within the
framework of its Constitution and that it should continue to contribute actively to
international efforts for restoring peace and stability in the region.

0180

외 무 부

종 별 :

번 호 : UNW-0582

수 신 : 장 관(국연,중동일,법규)

발 신 : 주 유엔 대사

제 목 : 걸프사태

일 시 : 91 0314 2400

연: UNW-0572

1.3.13. 일시귀국을 마치고 돌아온 M.ABULHASAN주유엔 쿠웨이트 대사는 동일 유엔 출입기자단과 회견을 갖고 포로 및 억류자 석방, 쿠웨이트 재산반환, 이락 배상책임 문제등에 관해 언급한바, 동회견 내용을 별첨송부함.

2.3.14. 사무총장 대변인에 의하면, 연호 1항 유엔대표단은 금주말경 이락에서 쿠웨이트로이 동예정이라고함.

3.표제관련 일본은 걸프평화기금 (GPF 기여금1.17 조엉 추가공여에 관한 3.13.자 외무성 성명을 안보리문서로 배포함.

4.한편 금 14일자 NYT 지는 안보리의 정식휴전 결의에 앞서 안보리가 이락의 생화학무기 제거를 요구하는 문제를 영국이 제기하고 있다고 보도한바, 동 문제와 관련 안보리에서 구체적인움 직임은 현재 없는 것으로 보임. 걸프사태에 관한 안보리 논의는 베이커 미 국무장관 순방이 끝난후 다음주 후반부부터나 재개 가능성이 있는 것으로 알려 짐.

첨부:1.쿠웨이트 회견내용

2. NYT 지 기사:UNW(F)-114

끝

(대사 대리 신기복-국장)

국기국   1차보   중아국   국기국   정문국   안기부

PAGE 1

#UNW-7582
정리

총609

UNW(カ)- 0114 10314 2400

(국연, 중동적, 법규) PRESS CONFERENCE BY KUWAIT

13 March 1991

At a press conference held today at Headquarters, Mohammmad A. Abulhasan, Permanent Representative of Kuwait, expressed gratitude to the people and States "who stood with us in our darkest days" and particularly to the United Nations system, the Security Council, and to representatives of the media for their reporting of the crisis.

The Kuwaiti people were now living the aftermath of 209 days of brutal Iraqi occupation, he said. He had just returned from Kuwait, where he had seen the effects of destruction and devastation on the people, their economy and environment. It was "indescribable and unimaginable", he said, while the human tragedies resulting from crimes and atrocities perpetuated by the Iraqi forces on the Kuwaiti people were beyond description.

He said that the Kuwaiti people were worried and disturbed by the lack of progress in exchanging prisoners and captives. His country was extremely alarmed to see the Iraqi regime delaying its implementation of all the provisions of the relevant Security Council resolutions, particularly those relating to prisoners of war. That was a matter governed by the Geneva Conventions, of which Iraq was a signatory.

"It is worth noting", he continued, "that Iraq released a group of detained civilians without handing them over to the International Committee of the Red Cross (ICRC). Instead, it just left them out in the cold, roaming and straying in the desert. That was a clear violation of the provisions of the Fourth Geneva Convention. On the other hand, Iraq, under false pretexts, is not taking back its prisoners of war."

Asked what his country's policy would be regarding non-Arabs in Kuwait, Mr. Abulhasan said that his country had declared its policy of respect for all non-Kuwaitis living peacefully in Kuwait and participating in its development, particularly now when a wide-scale rebuilding of its economy was beginning. However, those who had helped the occupying Power would be brought to justice.

What was the bottom line to putting a definitive end to hostilities, according to his Government? a correspondent asked. Was there a list of things left undone by Iraq, and were they moving fast enough? Mr. Abulhasan said that Iraq had not tackled seriously the list contained in Security Council resolution 686, which addressed such questions as the rescindment of annexation, the return of properties and the release of prisoners.

Continuing, Mr. Abulhasan said that the National Assembly of Iraq had not yet acted on the decision of its Revolutionary Council. The word annexation had not been used by the Iraqi Government, its Revolutionary Council or in its official gazette. Rather, reference had been made to nullifying "legislation concerning Kuwait".

(more)

3090B

6 -- 1.

0182

Kuwait Briefing   - 2 -   13 March 1991

Regarding the return of properties, a letter from the Foreign Minister of
Iraq spoke of quantities of gold, currency, commercial airplanes and museum
objects. However, it did not refer to quantities stolen or confiscated. It
did not mention military airplanes and equipment, valued at $2.3 billion,
which had been moved. It did not mention materials looted from the libraries
of Kuwait, the University of Kuwait, the Institute of Scientific Research of
Kuwait. It did not mention factories which had been dismantled and moved to
Iraq. It did not mention the International Centre for Telecommunication,
which cost more than $1 billion.

His country wanted to see Iraq make a clear declaration of intent to
accept the principle of compensation under international law. Kuwait also
wanted to see selection of a juridical board to consider specific claims, as
well as the establishment of a fund, to be financed in a manner to be agreed
upon beforehand.

Regarding prisoners of war, he said that only 1,200 civilians had been
released, and that "in a very shameful manner".

A correspondent asked how Iraq could be expected to begin paying
reparations while the United Nations economic embargo remained in place.
Mr. Abulhasan said he wanted to see Iraq accept the principle concerned and to
agree on the format to be employed to consider claims. How could the matter
be addressed at a later stage unless those theoretical questions were settled.

Do you foresee a role of Iran in the aftermath of the present struggle in
Iraq? a correspondent asked. Also, should Iran "give up those planes that
belong to Iraq" before reparations were paid to Kuwait? Mr. Abulhasan said
that no country should interfere in the internal affairs of Iraq or any other
sovereign country. The question about the return of military planes should be
addressed to the Mission of Iran. However, any Kuwaiti airplanes that might
be in Iran should be given only to the legitimate Government of Kuwait.

Mr. Abulhasan was asked if he had an actual list for the President of the
Security Council of items stolen from Kuwait and whether he was suggesting to
the President the ways that Iraq should return that property to Kuwait. "Yes,
we have a list", he said; it was not exhaustive, however, since many
government buildings had not yet been cleared militarily of mines and booby
traps. The Ministries of Defence, Justice and Education had so far been
cleared and had provided relevant lists. His country was now forming a
liaison with the Secretariat to determine the manner of the return of stolen
property.

Asked why he thought the Iraqis were "stalling like this", Mr. Abulhasan
said they were not serious about tackling the problem. Following the war with
Iran, Iraq took two and half years to release the prisoners. "Unfortunately,
they are still not learning the lessons of the defeat which they have
subjected their people to", he said. Iraq should be made to understand that
the use of all means available to the Security Council remained valid and
would be used against them if they did not abide by all Security Council
resolutions.

(more)

0183

3090B   /一2

How many Iraqi soldiers are presently being held in Kuwait? a
correspondent asked. Did the Government of Kuwait intend to try them for war
crimes? How many Kuwaitis were now being held by Iraq?

Mr. Abulhasan said that the number of Kuwaitis being held by Iraq was
33,000 minus the 1,200 which had been returned. Kuwait definitely was not in
a position to try them as war criminals, as that matter was governed by the
Geneva Conventions. The issue was that the Iraqis were not ready to receive
their own people. The ICRC had arranged a schedule for transferring war
prisoners to the central command in Iraq, but the Iraqis had refused under
false pretexts. The reason for that was clear, he said: "they don't want
them to go to tell the truth of what happened to the Iraqi army or to side by
the rebels and the popular uprising which is taking place now".

Did Kuwait intend to hand back people who had committed atrocities
against Kuwaiti citizens? the correspondent continued. Would Kuwait hand them
over to ICRC? Mr. Abulhasan said Kuwait would honour the Fourth Geneva
Convention. It was for ICRC to handle and register them; Kuwait would not
intervene at the current stage.

A correspondent asked a comment on "consistent reports" of indiscriminate
reprisals by Kuwaiti authorities against perceived Palestinian supporters or
supporters of the Iraqi Government and that they were not even being given
medical attention. Mr. Abulhasan said there was "no discrimination whatsoever
between Kuwaitis and non-Kuwaitis". He had just returned from Kuwait, where
"on the top of the list are the Palestinians, benefiting from the free access
to everything in Kuwait". That included free access to food, water, oil and
supermarkets. The United Nations team in Kuwait would be able to report on
the impartial manner in which the Palestinians were living. However, certain
individuals who were "culprits" and had been involved with the Iraqi aggressor
would be brought to justice under the laws of Kuwait.

Asked about complaints from Kuwaiti citizens that the Government was not
dealing with the food shortage very well, Mr. Abulhasan said that there had
been a popular expectation that the supermarkets would be filled immediately
after the liberation of his country. However, it took between 24 and 36 hours
to obtain military clearance to assure that those areas were free of mines and
booby traps. "The supplies are abundant now", he said.

Do you have a priority list of issues before you will discuss border
questions with Iraq? a correspondent asked. When is it appropriate for such
negotiations to begin? Mr. Abulhasan said there should first be full
implementation of Security Council resolution 686, which dealt with such
humanitarian matters as return of prisoners, innocent Kuwaitis and properties.

A correspondent asked for comment on a report by the British Information
Service that said there were Kuwaiti-born people "stranded, marooned on the
border and being denied entry to Kuwait" on the grounds that they had been
denied citizenship because their ancestors were born elsewhere. "I am
surprised about this statement", Mr. Abulhasan said. Even the 450,000
Kuwaitis who had been forced to leave were not being permitted to return until
the infrastructure could support them. Very shortly, all Kuwaitis carrying
national passports and authentic documentation would be allowed to return in

(more)

3090B   0184

412 P03   LENINPROTOCOL   '91- 3-15 12: 7

Kuwait Briefing — 4 — 13 March 1991

an organized manner. Kuwaitis born outside Kuwait during that period would also be considered Kuwaiti people.

Asked why Sheikh Jaber Al-Ahmad Al-Jaber Al-Sabah, Emir of the State of Kuwait, was not yet back in the country, Mr. Abulhasan said he would be back this week. "You expect the Emir of Kuwait, when he is there, to be able to communicate with the world leaders, to start his official duties in a manner which does not prevent him from reaching the outside world." Until now, the devastation in Kuwait was of such magnitude that even minimal repair had taken some time.

If one could prosecute Iraqi collaborators, why was it incompatible to charge Iraqi officers with war crimes under the Geneva Conventions? a correspondent asked. Mr. Abulhasan said that, at present, the best course was to hand those prisoners over to ICRC. Asked if he was keeping the option open to prosecute for war crimes, he said that not only was Kuwait keeping it open; the Security Council was keeping it open also, under its resolution 674.

A correspondent asked if it was possible that Iraq was being vague about "annexation" because it wanted to have negotiations on the border issue. Mr. Abulhasan said that, just as Iraq had abrogated an officially signed treaty with Algeria, no one should be surprised that they would "return to the same method as they have done with the Algerian treaty". It was therefore essential that there be international guarantees for the nullification of their annexation.

Was Saddam Hussein's retention of power in Iraq "a deficient factor in all this"? a correspondent asked. Mr. Abulhasan said it was not only a deficient factor "in this only", but was also a deficient factor for the stability of the region. He should draw a lesson from his isolation in the region and the popular uprising of his own people.

Asked if Kuwait would close its borders to Iraqis fleeing from Basra, Mr. Abulhasan said that Kuwait was closing its border for the time being, as that border was now a strictly military zone.

The Iraqis had stated that they would return "quantities of gold and quantities of currency", a correspondent said. "What figures do you put on those two items?" Mr. Abulhasan said that those figures would be submitted to the President of the Security Council, "maybe tonight or tomorrow morning". Asked for a ballpark figure, he said he would first give them to the President of the Council and later to the media.

Asked if the list he would be presenting to the Council just concerned currency, Mr. Abulhasan said "we have several lists, actually", concerning gold, aircraft, military equipment and other important property stolen from the Ministries of Justice and Higher Education; and more lists were coming.

In response to another question, Mr. Abulhasan said his country did not, for the time being, envisage action against President Hussein in terms of a trial for war crimes.

(more)

3090B   0185

Kuwait Briefing   - 5 -   13 March 1991

A correspondent asked whether Kuwait would like to see a United Nations peace-keeping force dispatched "rather quickly" to monitor the border situation. Mr. Abulhasan said his country had informed the Secretary-General and the President of the Council that it would be ready to receive such a force at an appropriate time, once matters covered by the existing Security Council resolutions were solved in a manner that was satisfactory to both the Council and the Kuwaiti Government.

Asked when that appropriate time would be, Mr. Abulhasan said "it depends on the Iraqis".

* *** *

3090B

0186

0187

United Nations

Destruction of Iraqi Chemical Arms Urged in U.N.

By PAUL LEWIS
Special to The New York Times

UNITED NATIONS, March 13 — Britain is pressing the Security Council to demand that President Saddam Hussein destroy all his chemical and biological weapon stocks under international inspection and publicly renounce terrorism before a formal cease-fire in the Persian Gulf war is put into place, diplomats said today.

The British argument is that the Council is now in a position to impose such further conditions on President Hussein as part of an obligation under previous resolutions to restore "international peace and security in the area."

The British and other diplomats said Britain believed that Iraq was likely to go along with such a demand because it had already shown itself eager to see the Council's economic sanctions lifted by agreeing in principle to other conditions for a cease-fire. Baghdad has agreed in principle, for example, to pay damages to Kuwait and return abducted people and property, even if though it might be slow to carry these out in practice.

So far, the United States and the other countries with forces in the gulf say they have not captured any Iraqi chemical or biological weapons, suggesting that the Iraqi Government has somehow managed to preserve its known stocks intact.

The Bush Administration has apparently come to the conclusion that Iraq still has ample stocks of chemical or biological weapons, since Washington has threatened to resume air strikes against Iraq if such weapons are used against rebel groups now trying to overthrow President Hussein.

Other members of the Security Council, however, want to refrain from imposing further conditions on Baghdad, moving instead to enact a formal end to hostilities and lift economic sanctions so Iraq can start earning some of the money it will need to compensate Kuwait for losses suffered during its occupation.

The Bush Administration is not expected to decide where it stands on the British proposal until Secretary of State James A. Baker 3d. returns from the Middle East over the weekend.

Comment From Kuwait

Today the Kuwaiti United Nations representative, Mohammad A. Abulhassan, who has just returned from Kuwait, told a news conference that Iraq was still showing no readiness to comply with the Security Council's existing terms for a cease-fire in practical ways, even though it claims it has accepted them in principle.

He said Iraq's National Assembly has still not specifically rescinded the law it passed formally annexing Kuwait and officially published that decision, although the Revolutionary Command Council, the country's supreme decision making body, invalidated all laws concerning Kuwait.

Mr. Abulhassan stressed the point that Iraq had freed only about 1,200 of the estimated 33,000 Kuwaiti civilians he claims were abducted and has failed even to provide the names of the prisoners of war it is holding, while refusing to take back any of its own P.O.W.'s when the Red Cross tried to send them home.

Finally, Mr. Abulhassan said Iraq should show its readiness to pay compensation for damage caused in Kuwait by agreeing to accept the adjudication of the World Court or some other international tribunal and by creating a fund it would pay money into when sanctions are lifted and it can start selling oil again.

He said Iraq's total liability for such damage could reach $100 billion.

Meanwhile, the United Nations Security Council authorized the largest emergency food shipment to war-torn Iraq today-20,000 tons of wheat flour sent by Yemen, which sided with Baghdad in the gulf crisis.

P.6

발 신 전 보

번 호 : WUN-0538   910315 2033 FG 종별 : 지급

수 신 : 주 유엔   대사. /총영사 (오윤경 공사님)

발 신 : 장 관 (중동일 김의기)

제 목 : 업연

1. 유엔 안보리 결의 661호에 의거, 각국이 쿠웨이트에 대해 취한
경제 제재 조치를 안보리 결의 686호 제 6항에 따라 해제해도 무방한지 또는
대 쿠웨이트 경제 제재 해제를 위한 유엔 안보리의 별도 조치가 있을지 여부를
확인 알려주시면 도움이 되겠읍니다.

2. 영국은 3.13. 쿠웨이트 자산 동결 해제 조치를 취했으며, 일본도
3.18. 대 쿠웨이트 경제 제재 조치를 해제할 예정이라 합니다.   끝.

예 고 : 독후 파기

보 안 통 제	2t

앙 고 재	91 년 월 일	중동 아 과	기안자 성 명		과 장		국 장		차 관	장 관
					2h					

외신과통제

0188

#UNW-0490 의
첨부문
**UNITED
NATIONS**

UNW(표)-096 10303 0330
(국연. 중근동. 해기. 기점) 사본: 노창회 댓사   〈 첨부 1 〉

총21 대

Security Council

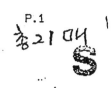

PROVISIONAL

S/22298
1 March 1991

ORIGINAL: ENGLISH

<u>United States of America: draft resolution</u>

The Security Council,

<u>Recalling</u> and <u>reaffirming</u> its resolutions 660 (1990), 661 (1990), 662 (1990), 664 (1990), 665 (1990), 666 (1990), 667 (1990), 669 (1990), 670 (1990), 674 (1990), 677 (1990), and 678 (1990),

<u>Recalling</u> the obligations of Member States under Article 25 of the Charter,

<u>Recalling</u> paragraph 9 of resolution 661 (1990) regarding assistance to the Government of Kuwait and paragraph 3 (c) of that resolution regarding supplies strictly for medical purposes and, in humanitarian circumstances, foodstuffs,

<u>Taking note</u> of the letters of the Foreign Minister of Iraq confirming Iraq's agreement to comply fully with all of the resolutions noted above (S/22275), and stating its intention to release prisoners of war immediately (S/22273),

<u>Taking note</u> of the suspension of offensive combat operations by the forces of Kuwait and the Member States cooperating with Kuwait pursuant to resolution 678 (1990),

<u>Bearing in mind</u> the need to be assured of Iraq's peaceful intentions, and the objective in resolution 678 (1990) of restoring international peace and security in the region,

<u>Underlining</u> the importance of Iraq taking the necessary measures which would permit a definitive end to the hostilities,

<u>Affirming</u> the commitment of all Member States to the independence, sovereignty and territorial integrity of Iraq and Kuwait, and <u>noting</u> the intention expressed by the Member States cooperating under paragraph 2 of Security Council resolution 678 (1990) to bring their military presence in Iraq to an end as soon as possible consistent with achieving the objectives of the resolution,

<u>Acting</u> under Chapter VII of the Charter,

2882E

21 — 1

1.   **Affirms** that all twelve resolutions noted above continue to have full force and effect;

2.   **Demands** that Iraq implement its acceptance of all twelve resolutions noted above and in particular that Iraq:

(a) Rescind immediately its actions purporting to annex Kuwait;

(b) Accept in principle its liability *under international law* for any loss, damage, or injury arising in regard to Kuwait and third States, and their nationals and corporations, as a result of the invasion and illegal occupation of Kuwait by Iraq;

(c) Immediately release under the auspices of the International Committee of the Red Cross, Red Cross Societies, or Red Crescent Societies, all Kuwaiti and third country nationals detained by Iraq and return the remains of any deceased Kuwaiti and third country nationals so detained; and

(d) Immediately begin to return all Kuwaiti property seized by Iraq, to be completed in the shortest possible period;

3.   **Further demands** that Iraq:

(a) Cease hostile or provocative actions by its forces against all Member States ~~and other parties~~, including missile attacks and flights of combat aircraft;

(b) Designate military commanders to meet with counterparts from the forces of Kuwait and the Member States cooperating with Kuwait pursuant to resolution 678 (1990) to arrange for the military aspects of a cessation of hostilities at the earliest possible time;

(c) Arrange for immediate access to and release of all prisoners of war under the auspices of the International Committee of the Red Cross and return the remains of any deceased personnel of the forces of Kuwait and the Member States cooperating with Kuwait pursuant to resolution 678 (1990); and

(d) Provide all information and assistance in identifying Iraqi mines, booby traps and other explosives as well as any chemical and biological weapons and material in Kuwait, in areas of Iraq where forces of Member States cooperating with Kuwait pursuant to resolution 678 (1990) are present temporarily, and in the *adjacent waters*;

4.   **Recognizes** that during the period required for Iraq to comply with paragraphs 2 and 3 above, the provisions of paragraph 2 of resolution 678 (1990) remain valid;

0190

21 — 2

immediately

5.   <u>Welcomes</u> the decision of Kuwait and the Member States cooperating with Kuwait pursuant to resolution 678 (1990) to provide access and to commence the release of Iraqi prisoners of war as required by the terms of the Third Geneva Convention of 1949, under the auspices of the International Committee of the Red Cross;

6.   <u>Requests</u> all Member States, as well as the United Nations, the specialized agencies and other international organizations in the United Nations system, to take all appropriate action to cooperate with the Government and people of Kuwait in the reconstruction of their country;

7.   <u>Decides</u> that Iraq shall notify the Secretary-General and the Security Council when it has taken the actions set out above;

8.   <u>Decides</u> that in order to secure the rapid establishment of a definitive end to the hostilities, the Security Council remains actively seized of the matter.

0191

21-3

199 P03   LENINPROTOCOL   '91-03-03 16:35

주 영 대 사 관

UKW (F) -   0158   DATE: 10314 1700

수 신 : 장   관 (기협, 중근동)

발 신 : 주 영 국 대 사

제 목 : 쿠웨이트 재산 동결 해제

10174 21

THE FINANCIAL TIMES (1991. 3. 14)

UK lifts freeze on Kuwaiti assets

By Stephen Fidler,
Euromarkets
Correspondent

THE UK Treasury yesterday lifted the order freezing Kuwaiti assets in Britain, imposed on August 2 to prevent the Iraqi seizure of Kuwaiti assets following its invasion of Kuwait.

The freeze of Iraqi assets imposed by the government at the same time and designed as a punitive rather than protective measure, remains in place.

Britain is thought to be the second main western government to unfreeze Kuwaiti assets, after France.

Since its imposition, the Bank of England, which has been responsible for administering the freeze, agreed a number of relaxations. It allowed the Kuwait Investment Office, which is based in London, and the Kuwait Petroleum Corporation to operate, although under some restrictions. It also freed accounts to allow Kuwaiti individuals access to funds.

In the last two weeks, the UK and the US have allowed Kuwait's domestic banks access to their accounts to settle outstanding liabilities.

The total amount affected by the UK freeze is not known, but the gross sum on deposit with banks in Britain at the end of last year was $12.46bn.

According to the Treasury, there were no known breaches of the freeze, which was intended to cover gold, securities, payments and credits.

0192

외 무 부

종 별 :

번 호 : UNW-0587

일 시 : 91 0315 1520

수 신 : 장관 (김의기 중근동과장)

발 신 : 주 유엔 대사 (원종찬 배상)

제 목 : 업연

대: WUN-0538

1. 대호 유엔사무국 및 관련국 대표부에 문의한 결과는 아래와 같음.

가. 안보리의 명시적 조치는 없었으나, 쿠웨이트 점령 종결 및 686 호 결의(6항)에 비추어 661 호에 의한 대 쿠웨이트 제재조치는 이미 해제되었다고 보는것이 일치된 해석임. (동 해제기점을 사실상의 점령종결 시점 또는 686 결의 채택 시점으로 할것인지에 대해서는 논의가 있으나 3.2. 686 결의 채택을 기준으로 하는것이 다수의견 이라고함)

나. 대 쿠웨이트 해제를 위한 안보리의 별도 조치 필요 문제에 관해 제재위원회에서 논의가 있었으나 동 제재조치의 실효가 자명하다고 보고, 별도의 조치는 취하지 않기로 양해되었다고 함. (다만 추후 안보리의 후속결의 채택 과정에서 본건 해제의 재확인 언급 가능성은 있다고함)

다. 이와 관련 EC 는 회원국들이 각자 필요한 조치를 취하기로 하였으며 미,일 등도 필요한 국내절차를 밟고 있다함.

2. 건승 기원함. 끝

중아국

협조문용지

지급

분류기호 문서번호	통일 2065- 283 (2193, 2194)	결재	담당	과장	심의관
시행일자	1991. 3. 18.				
수 신	국제기구조약국장	발신	통상국장		(서명)
제 목	대쿠웨이트 경제제재 해제				

　　1. 이라크 및 쿠웨이트에 대하여 90.8.9부터 실시중인

경제제재조치중 쿠웨이트 지역에 대한 경제제재조치를 3.8부로

해제하는 것에 대해 별첨과 같이 장관님 결재를 득하였는 바,

대유엔 통보등 필요한 조치를 취하여 주시기 바랍니다.

　　2. 상금 이라크 지역에 대해서는 유엔의 경제제재

해제 결의가 없음에 비추어 상황진전을 보아 추후 경제제재조치

해제를 검토할 예정인 바, 참고하시기 바랍니다.

　　첨부 : 동 재가문서 사본 1부.　끝.

1981. 6. 30. 에 예고문에
의거 일반문서로 재분류됨

기 안 용 지

분류기호 문서번호	통일 2065-	기 안 용 지 (전화 :)	시 행 상 특별취급	
보존기간	영구. 준영구 10. 5. 3. 1.	차 관		장 관
수 신 처 보존기간				
시행일자	1991. 3. 16.			
보조 기 관	국 장		협 조 기 관	제 1 차관보	서 통 제
	심의관			제 2 차관보	
	과 장			아중동국장	
기안책임자	김 상 윤				발 송 인
경수 참조	유신 내부결재		발신명의		
제 목	대쿠웨이트 경제제재 해제				

1. 정부는 지난 90.8.9 국무총리주재 관계부처 장관회의에서 유엔안보리

   결의 제661호 (대이라크 제재)를 지지하여 아래와 같이 이라크 및

   쿠웨이트 지역에 대한 경제제재 조치를 취한 바 있읍니다.

   - 아 래 -

   가. 이라크와 쿠웨이트 지역으로부터 오는 원유 수입은 금지한다.

   나. 이 지역과의 상품교역도 의약품등 인도적인 소요에 해당하는

      물품을 제외하고는 수입과 수출을 공히 금지한다.

      유엔 결의에는 특히 무기 수출 금지를 요청하고 있는 바,

/// 계 속

0195

한국은 무기를 수출한 적도 없고 앞으로도 수출하지 않는다.

다. 이 양 지역에 있어서 건설 공사는 수주하지 않는다.

라. 이라크와 쿠웨이트 정부 자산의 동결 요청에 대하여는 이러한

자산이 한국내에는 없음을 확인한다.

2. 현재 걸프전쟁 종결로 쿠웨이트 지역에 대한 경제제재 조치 계속

사유가 소멸되었을 뿐만 아니라 유엔안보리 결의 686호 제6항은

쿠웨이트 복구협조를 위해 모든 적절한 조치를 유엔회원국이 취할

것을 요청하고 있는바, 이에따라 쿠웨이트 지역에 대한 아국의

경제제재조치를 아래와 같이 해제할 것을 건의하오니 재가하여

주시기 바랍니다.(영국은 3.13 쿠웨이트 자산 동결해제 조치를

취했으며, 일본도 3.18, 대쿠웨이트 경제제재조치를 해제할 예정)

- 아 래 -

가. 해제조치 내용

(1) 쿠웨이트지역으로부터의 원유 수입금지 해제

(2) 쿠웨이트와의 상품교역금지 해제

(3) 쿠웨이트 지역에 대한 건설수주 중지 해제

/// 계 속

0196

- 3 -

나. 관계국 통보 및 대외발표

　ㅇ 미국 및 쿠웨이트에 대해서는 상기 조치계획을 사전에 통보

　ㅇ UN 에 대해 경제제재 해제 조치내용 통보

　ㅇ 대외발표문(안)

　- 정부는 쿠웨이트 지역에 대한 경제제재 조치

　　사유가 소멸되었으므로 동 지역에 대하여 90.8.9일부터

　　실시중인 경제제재 조치를 91.3.18부로 해제한다.

3. 상금 이라크 지역에 대해서는 UN 의 경제제재 해제 결의가 없음에

　비추어 상황진전을 보아 추후 경제제재조치 해제를 검토할 것을

　건의합니다.　끝.

0197

분류번호	보존기간

발 신 전 보

WUN-0562　　910319 1608 CT

번　　　호 :　　　　　　　　　　　　　　　　종별 : 지급

수　　　신 : 주 유연　　　대사 . 총영사 //

발　　　신 : 장 관　　(국연)

제　　　목 : 대쿠웨이트 경제제재 해제

　　　아국은 90.8.9.부터 이락 및 쿠웨이트에 대하여 실시한 바 있는 경제제재
조치중 쿠웨이트에 대한 제재를 91.3.8.부로 해제하고 동　해제조치를 유연에
통보할 것을 검토중인 바, 동일 내용의 조치를 유연에 통보한 국가가 있는지
파악·보고바라며 주요우방국의 해제통보가 안보리문서 또는 기타 유연문서로
회람되었을시 사본을 지급 FAX 송부바람.　　　끝.

(국제기구조약국장　문동석)

검 토 필 (1991. 6. 30.)

앙고재	91년 3월 19일	기안자	과장	국장	차관	장관	보안통제	외신과통지

0198

관리 9/
번호 -262

외 무 부

종 별 :

번 호 : UNW-0610   일 시 : 91 0319 1800

수 신 : 장관 (국연,중동일)

발 신 : 주 유엔 대사

제 목 : 대 쿠웨이트 경제제재 해제

대: WUN-0562

대호 해제조치 통보문제 관련, 유엔사무국 및 오스트리아 대표부 (제재위원회 의장국)에 문의한바, 표제 해제조치를 통보해온 국가는 없다고 하며 별도의 통보는 불필요할것으로 본다는 반응임을 참고바람. 끝

(대사 노창희-국장)

예고:91.6.30. 일반

1991. 6.30. 에 예고문에 의거 일반문서로 재분류됨

───────────────────────────────

국기국   차관   2차보   중아국

PAGE 1   91.03.20   09:26
                                          외신 2과 통제관 BW

0199

외 무 부

원 본

종 별 :

번 호 : UNW-0601   일 시 : 91 0318 1900

수 신 : 장 관(국연,중동일,기정)

발 신 : 주 유엔 대사

제 목 : 걸프사태(유엔조사단)

연: UNW-0582

1. 연호 쿠웨이트 인명및 재산 피해현황 파악을 위한 유엔조사단의 쿠웨이트 체류활동에 관한 3.18자 유엔측 발표내용을 별첨 송부함.

2. 한편 대이락 및 쿠웨이트 원조문제 관련 유엔대표단은 이락방문을 마치고 3.16 쿠웨이트에 도착하여 동국에서의 조사활동을 개시하였음.

첨부:상기 유엔측 발표내용 (IK/6):UNW(F)-116

끝

(대사 노창희-국장)

국기국   1차보   중아국   정문국   안기부

PAGE 1   91.03.19   09:59 WG
                                          외신 1과 통제관

0200

UNW(H) - 116

(국연. 중동일. 기261)

United Nations

Press Release

Department of Public Information • News Coverage Service • New York

IK/6
18 March 1991

UN MISSION, ARRIVING IN KUWAIT, DISCUSSES METHOD OF WORK AND DATA REQUIRED

(Received from the spokesman for the special mission to Kuwait.)

KUWAIT, 16 March -- The mission sent by the Secretary-General to Iraq and Kuwait to assess the need for urgent humanitarian relief arrived in Kuwait today at 1500 hours (local time) by a special aircraft provided by the Kuwaiti Government. The mission was received at the airport by the Kuwaiti Minister of State for Foreign Affairs, Nasser Mohamed Al-Sabah, and other senior officials.

Soon after arrival, a preliminary meeting took place between a multisectoral Kuwaiti team headed by Suleiman Al-Shahin, Under-Secretary for Foreign Affairs, and the United Nations mission, to discuss the modalities of work as well as data required. Tomorrow, the mission will be received by the Crown Prince, Sheikh Saad Al-Sabah

The mission has also been invited to survey areas of the capital, including private and public properties, where damage has been particularly heavy, and to meet a cross section of the affected population.

* **** *

2341P

1 - 1

0201

외 무 부

종 별 :

번 호 : UNW-0617　　　　　　　　　　　일 시 : 91 0319 1930

수 신 : 장 관 (국연,중동일,기정)

발 신 : 주 유엔 대사

제 목 : 걸프사태 (유엔 조사단)

　　연: UNW-0601

　　금 3.19. 유엔사무총장 대변인에 의하면 이락및 쿠웨이트에 대한 인도적 원조문제 관련 조사단은 현재 바레인 체류중 (연호 쿠웨이트 도착은 착오) 이며, 동 조사단장인 M. AHTISAARI 사무차장은 일시 귀임, 사무총장에게 이락 방문결과를 보고 예정이라고 함. 끝

　　(대사 노창희-국장)

국기국　　1차보　　　중아국　　　정문국　　　안기부

PAGE 1　　　　　　　　　　　　　　　　　　　　91.03.20　　10:54 WG

　　　　　　　　　　　　　　　　　　　　　　외신 1과 통제관

　　　　　　　　　　　　　　　　　　　　　　　　　　0202

외 무 부

종 별 :

번 호 : UNW-0619

일 시 : 91 0319 1930

수 신 : 장 관 (국연,중동일,기정)

발 신 : 주 유엔 대사

제 목 : 걸프사태 (안보리)

1. 금 3.19. NYT 지는 표제관련 새로운 안보리 결의안 골자에 관해 상임이사국들 간에 의견이 접근되어 가고 있다는 요지의 기사가 게재된바별첨 동기사 참조바람.

2. 당관에서 파악한바에 의하면 상임이사국 들은 지난 3.15. 상기 결의안 문제에 관해 초안없이 일차 의견을 교환한바 있으며 금 3.19. 재 협의예정이나 결의안 성안 및 채택까지에는 상당한 시일과 교섭이 필요할것 이라는 관측임.

3. 안보리는 3.21. 오후 사무총장 중독특사 (E.BRUNNER주미 스위스대사) 임명, UNFICYP 문제와 관련 비공식 협의 개최 예정이나, 동 협의시 걸프사태에 관한 실질적 논 의 가능성은 크지않은것으로 알려짐.

4. 한편 이락이 쿠웨이트로 부터 강취한 재산반환문제와 관련 이락측은 별첨 서한들을 3.18. 안보리 문서로 배포함. 끝

(대사 노창희-국장)

첨부: FAX (UNW(F)-0119)

국기국   1차보   중아국   정문국   안기부

PAGE 1

91.03.20   10:57 WG

외신 1과 통제관

0203

Security Council Reaches Broad Agreement on Terms of Cease-Fire

By PAUL LEWIS
Special to The New York Times

UNITED NATIONS, March 18 — The five permanent Security Council members have reached broad agreement on the main elements of a new resolution for ending the Persian Gulf war and allowing the withdrawal of United States and allied forces, diplomats say.

But significant details remain unresolved, the officials said.

The diplomats said the new resolution will set out again, but in greater detail, the cease-fire terms the Council approved on March 2 in Resolution 686. It is to make clear that once Baghdad has complied with the terms, a permanent cease-fire will take effect.

Iraq would not necessarily need to complete compliance with all conditions before the cease-fire occurred, diplomats said. The return of stolen Kuwaiti property and the payment of restitution, for instance, might continue after a formal end to hostilities.

But the five members envisage the Secretary General being given the task of monitoring Iraq's compliance and deciding when sufficient progress has been made to justify a cease-fire.

Diplomats said an important feature of the negotiations was a decision by President Bush and British Prime Minister John Major this weekend to add to the terms the destruction of President Saddam Hussein's remaining chemical and biological weapons and to seek a declaration from him renouncing terrorism.

While the new terms were never specified in previous Council resolutions, British and American officials say they can be justified by the Council's earlier decision to seek the "restoration of international peace and security in the area."

But the call for the destruction of chemical and biological weapons raises difficulties, diplomats admit. Iraq must cooperate with the destruction plan and allow monitoring of its stocks. And while the Soviet Union and France seem to support the demand, China, which also has a veto on decisions, says it would constitute interference in Iraq's internal affairs.

In addition, the United States and the Soviet Union are the only countries with the heavy-duty equipment needed for destroying the armaments.

There is broad agreement among the five Council members that Iraq must promise to establish some mechanism for committing future oil revenue to compensating Kuwait for war damages.

But how this would take place is unclear, since any agreement to pay compensation to Kuwait would eventually

require the Council to lift the commercial sanctions imposed on Iraq, so that it can start selling oil again. This might only happen when the cease-fire comes into effect.

The Council members plan to maintain the embargo on military deliveries indefinitely and perhaps impose special restrictions on the transfer of dangerous technologies used in chemical, bacteriological and nuclear weapons.

But plans for the Council to station some 250 United Nations military observers along Kuwait's border with Iraq have caused complications.

Kuwait wants the Council to place the troops along the frontier Iraq agreed to in 1963, but which it now disputes, and wants to require Baghdad to accept this boundary. But China appears unhappy with this arrangement, arguing that the Council has never previously claimed the right to settle this frontier dispute.

UNITED NATIONS

Security Council

Distr.
GENERAL

S/22355
18 March 1991
ENGLISH
ORIGINAL: ARABIC

IDENTICAL LETTERS DATED 18 MARCH 1991 FROM THE PERMANENT
REPRESENTATIVE OF IRAQ TO THE UNITED NATIONS ADDRESSED
RESPECTIVELY TO THE SECRETARY-GENERAL AND THE PRESIDENT
OF THE SECURITY COUNCIL

On instructions from my Government, I have the honour to inform you that the
Government of my country agrees that the Office of the Secretary-General shall be
entrusted with the receipt and delivery of Kuwaiti property and that it awaits the
machinery decided on in this matter.

I request you to have this letter circulated as a document of the Security
Council.

(Signed) Abdul Amir AL-ANBARI
Ambassador
Permanent Representative

91-08674 2233e (E)

4-2

0205

Security Council

Distr.
GENERAL

S/22356
18 March 1991
ENGLISH
ORIGINAL: ARABIC

IDENTICAL LETTERS DATED 18 MARCH 1991 FROM THE PERMANENT
REPRESENTATIVE OF IRAQ TO THE UNITED NATIONS ADDRESSED
RESPECTIVELY TO THE SECRETARY-GENERAL AND THE PRESIDENT
OF THE SECURITY COUNCIL

On instructions from my Government, I have the honour, with reference to the letter addressed to you by Mr. Tariq Aziz, Deputy Prime Minister and Minister for Foreign Affairs of the Government of my country, dated 5 March 1991, to confirm to you that the catalogues of the assets of the Islamic Museum and the National Museum that were brought to Iraq from Kuwait are ready for submission to the authority that may be designated.

I request you to have this letter circulated as a document of the Security Council.

(Signed) Abdul Amir AL-ANBARI
Ambassador
Permanent Representative

91-08663 .2352d (E)

4 - 3

0206

Security Council

Distr.
GENERAL

S/22357
18 March 1991
ENGLISH
ORIGINAL: ARABIC

IDENTICAL LETTERS DATED 18 MARCH 1991 FROM THE PERMANENT
REPRESENTATIVE OF IRAQ TO THE UNITED NATIONS ADDRESSED
RESPECTIVELY TO THE SECRETARY-GENERAL AND THE PRESIDENT
OF THE SECURITY COUNCIL

On instructions from my Government, I have the honour to inform you of the situation set forth below in the matter of Kuwaiti aircraft:

I.   Seven aircraft destroyed as a result of aerial bombardment by the Allied Forces, as follows:

   2 Airbus 300 aircraft;

   2 Boeing 767 aircraft;

   1 125 aircraft;

   2 G-3 aircraft.

II.   8 existing aircraft, as follows:

   1 Airbus 300 aircraft in Iran;

   5 Airbus 310 aircraft in Iran;

   1 Boeing 727 aircraft in Oman;

   1 125 aircraft in Iraq.

I request you to have this letter circulated as a document of the Security Council.

(Signed)   Abdul Amir AL-ANBARI
Ambassador
Permanent Representative

91-08680   2813a (E)

4 - 4

0207

외 무 부

종 별 :

번 호 : UNW-0630 일 시 : 91 0320 1830

수 신 : 장 관(국연,중동일,기정)

발 신 : 주 유엔 대사

제 목 : 걸프사태(안보리)

연: UNW-0619

1. 이락이 강취한 쿠웨이트 재산 반환절차 문제와 관련 안보리의장은 유엔사무총장실이 당사국과 협의하여 동 절차를 마련할것을 요망하는 이사국들의 의견을 3.19자로 사무총장에게 통보하였음. (S/22361)

2. 한편 상기 반환문제 관련 이락측은 연호통보에 이어 쿠웨이트 군용기 36대 현황에관해 3.19 유엔에 통보해 오면서 이락군의 쿠웨이트 철수시 회수치 못한 탱크를 비롯한 각종 이락군재산에 대한 권리를 주장하였음.(S/22360)

첨부:상기이락 안보리문서: UNW(F)-121 끝

(대사 노창희-국장)

국기국   1차보   중아국   정문국   안기부   2차보   차관   장관

PAGE 1

91.03.21   13:04 WG

외신 1과 통제관

0208

214 걸프 사태 유엔안전보장이사회 동향 3

UNITED
NATIONS

 Security Council

Distr.
GENERAL

S/22360
19 March 1991
ENGLISH
ORIGINAL: ARABIC

IDENTICAL LETTERS DATED 19 MARCH 1991 FROM THE PERMANENT
REPRESENTATIVE OF IRAQ TO THE UNITED NATIONS ADDRESSED
RESPECTIVELY TO THE SECRETARY-GENERAL AND THE PRESIDENT
OF THE SECURITY COUNCIL

On instructions from my Government, I have the honour to inform you of the situation set forth below in the matter of Kuwaiti military aircraft:

1. Mirages: 8 destroyed as a result of air raids.

2. Hawks: 6 in good condition.

3. Skyhawks: 5 in good condition.

                     2 damaged as a result of air raids.

                     3 destroyed as a result of air raids.

4. Transport aircraft:

   1 C 130:   Damaged as a result of air raids.

   2 aircraft: One in good condition and one damaged as a result of air raids.

5. Helicopters:

   2 Pumas: In good condition.

   1 Super Puma: Not in operating condition.

   1 Super Puma: Damaged as a result of air raids.

   2 Gazelles: Destroyed as a result of air raids.

   3 Gazelles: In good condition.

91-08822 2120c (E)   /...

S/22360
English
Page 2

    The Iraqi Government wishes on this occasion to reassert its right to the Iraqi military property, consisting of tanks, vehicles, artillery, equipment and materiel left on Kuwaiti soil owing to the disorderly withdrawal, lists of which, specifying numbers and types, will be presented at a later time.

    I request you to have this letter circulated as a document of the Security Council.

(Signed)   Abdul Amir AL-ANBARI
Ambassador
Permanent Representative

2 - 2

외 무 부

종 별 :

번 호 : UNW-0632

일 시 : 91 0320 1830

수 신 : 장 관(국연,중동일,기정)

발 신 : 주 유엔 대사

제 목 : 걸프사태(경제제재 조치)

1. 안보리결의 661호 (대이락 및 쿠웨이트 경제제재조치) 이행에 따른 자국의 특별한 경제난문제를 헌장 50조에 의거 안보리에 제기한 국가는 현재 총 21개국인바, 동 국가들은 본건 대책을 촉구하는 안보리앞 공동명의 각서를 현재준비중인 것으로 알려졌음.

2. 동 국가들은 상기 경제제재 조치로 인한 자국들의 전체 손실을 300억불로 추산하고 있으며, 본건 각서를 통해 다음 대책들을 요청할 예정이라고 함.

   ㉮ 주요 공여국들의 추가 재정지원 조치

   ㉯ 유엔관련 기구들의 특별원조계획 수립

   ㉰ 전후 경제복구 및 개발사업에의 참여지원

   ㉱ 자국산품 시장 회복문제

3. 상기 21개국 명단 및 본건 추진을 위한 대책위 결성현황은 다음과같음.

   가. 21개국: 방글라데쉬 불가리아 체코 지부티 인도 요르단 레바논 모리타니아 파키스탄 필리핀 폴랜드 루마니아 쉐이쉘 스리랑카 수단 시리아 뷔니지아 우루과이 베트남 예멘 유고 (단, 보츠와나도관심표명)

   나. 대책위: 루마니아(대표자격), 인도, 수단, 레바논, 우루과이. 끝

   (대사 노창

국기국   1차보   중아국   정문국   안기부

PAGE 1

외 무 부

종 별 :

번 호 : UNW-0641

일 시 : 91 0321 2030

수 신 : 장 관(국연,중동일,기정)

발 신 : 주 유엔 대사

제 목 : 걸프사태(안보리)

1. 안보리는 금 3.21. 오후 4시부터 약2시간 동안비공식협의를 갖고 중동특사임명, UNFICYP 및 표제사태에 관해 토의한바, 당관에서 탐문한 동토의 결과는 다음과같음.

　　가. 사무총장 중동특사 임명

　　E.BRUNNER (주미 스위스대사) 임명에 이의가 없었는바, 금일자로 사무총장의 동 특사임명 발표가 있었음.

　　나. UNFICYP 재정난

　　동 문제 검토를위해 작업반 (의장:에쿠아돌) 을설치키로함.

　　다. 걸프문제(대이락 구호)

　　1)인도적 원조수요 파악을 위한 유엔조사단 (단장:M.AHTISAARI 사무차장)이락 방문 (3.10-17)결과보고를 청취한다음, 인도적 품목에 대한 금수해제 문제가 논의됨.

　　2)상기 조사단보고서는 식량외에 연료 (유류), 농업장비에 대한 제재해제 필요성을 제기하고있는바, 식량문제는 3.22. 제재위원회에서 토의예정임.

　　3)여타 품목에 대해서도 쿠바, 예멘은 즉각적인 해제를 요구하였으며, 이와관련 동국들은 3월초 제출되어 계류중인 인도적 원조문제에 관한 비동맹 5개국 결의안의 표결문제를 제기하였으나 다른 국가들의 특기할 호응은 없었음.

　　4)본건 추가토의를 위해 명 3.22. 오후 비공식협의가 있을예정임.

2. 이락측은 3.20자 사무총장 및 안보리의장앞 서한을 통하여, 바스라를 비롯한자국 12개지역의 식량창고가 약탈되어 식량위기를 겪고있으며 이와관련 안보리의 자국에 대한 식량및 보급품금수 해제조치가 필요하다고 주장하였음.(S/22364).또한 이락은 미군용기의 이락영공 비행을 비난하는 안보리문서 (S/22365) 를 동일자로배포하였음.

3. 한편 상임이사국들은 정식휴전 (FORMALCEASE-FIRE) 을 위한 결의안 초안에 관해 계속협의를 진행중인 것으로 알려진바, 당관에서 입수한 미측초안을 별첨 송부함.

국기국	1차보	중아국	정문국	안기부	2차보

PAGE 1

91.03.22　　11:16 WG

외신 1과 통제관

0212

첨부:1. 유엔조사단보고서 (S/22366)

2. 이락측안보리문서(S/22364)

3. 미측 결의안초안:UNW(F)-122

끝

(대사 노창희-국장)

UNITED
NATIONS

 Security Council

Distr.
GENERAL

S/22364
20 March 1991
ENGLISH
ORIGINAL: ARABIC

IDENTICAL LETTERS DATED 20 MARCH 1991 FROM THE PERMANENT
REPRESENTATIVE OF IRAQ TO THE UNITED NATIONS ADDRESSED
RESPECTIVELY TO THE SECRETARY-GENERAL AND THE PRESIDENT
OF THE SECURITY COUNCIL

On instructions from my Government, I have the honour to inform you that, as a result of acts of sabotage carried out by bands which infiltrated from a neighbouring State, the contents of the people's food warehouses were plundered in the cities and villages of the governorates of Basra, Wasit, Maysan, Dhi Qar, Al-Qadisiyah, Al-Muthanna, Najaf, Karbala and Babil.

Similar acts were perpetrated in the governorates of Sulaymaniyah, Arbil and Dahuk by other bands which entered from the same neighbouring State.

The plundering of basic foodstuffs and the destruction of public and private warehouses by these bands has resulted in a severe food crisis that has the most dire consequences for these 12 governorates, which account for the majority of the population of Iraq.

This extremely grave crisis necessitates the adoption of immediate measures by the Security Council to remove any form of embargo on the import of foodstuffs and supplies to Iraq.

It is clear that measures taken by the Sanctions Committee cannot, owing to their slowness, provide an adequate solution to this grave problem affecting the humanitarian needs of the citizens.

I request you to take urgent measures with a view to the consideration of this question by the members of the Council.

I further request you to have this letter circulated as a document of the Security Council.

(Signed) Abdul Amir AL-ANBARI
Ambassador
Permanent Representative

91-08975 2215f (E)

27—14

0214

THE SECURITY COUNCIL,

A. RECALLING ITS RESOLUTIONS 660 (1990), 661 (1990) 662
(1990), 664 (1990), 665 (1990), 666 (1990), 667 (1990),
669 (1990), 670 (1990), 674 (1990), 677 (1990), 678 (1990)
AND 686 (1991),

B. REAFFIRMING THE NEED TO BE ASSURED OF IRAQ'S PEACEFUL
INTENTIONS, IN LIGHT OF ITS AGGRESSION AND USE OF MISSILES
AND WEAPONS OF MASS DESTRUCTION, AND THE OBJECTIVE IN
RESOLUTION 678 (1990) OF RESTORING INTERNATIONAL PEACE AND
SECURITY IN THE REGION,

C. TAKING NOTE OF THE LETTER SENT BY THE FOREIGN MINISTER

27-15

0215

OF IRAQ ON 27 FEBRUARY 1991 AND THOSE SENT PURSUANT TO
RESOLUTION 686 (1991), IN PARTICULAR THE LETTER
DATED   CONCERNING IRAQ'S FULFILLMENT OF THE
REQUIREMENTS IN RESOLUTION 686 (1991),

D. AFFIRMING THE COMMITMENT OF ALL MEMBER STATES TO THE
SOVEREIGNTY, TERRITORIAL INTEGRITY AND POLITICAL
INDEPENDENCE OF KUWAIT AND IRAQ, AND NOTING THE INTENTION
EXPRESSED BY THE MEMBER STATES COOPERATING UNDER PARAGRAPH
2 OF RESOLUTION 678 (1990) TO BRING THEIR MILITARY
PRESENCE IN IRAQ TO AN END AS SOON AS POSSIBLE CONSISTENT
WITH PARAGRAPH 8 OF RESOLUTION 686 (1991),

ACTING UNDER CHAPTER VII OF THE CHARTER,

1. AFFIRMS ALL THIRTEEN RESOLUTIONS NOTED ABOVE, EXCEPT
AS EXPRESSLY MODIFIED BELOW;

THE INTERNATIONAL BOUNDARY

2. DECIDES THAT THE BOUNDARY BETWEEN IRAQ AND KUWAIT AND
THE ALLOCATION OF ISLANDS SHALL BE AS AGREED TO BY THE
STATE OF KUWAIT AND THE REPUBLIC OF IRAQ IN THE MINUTE
SIGNED AT BAGHDAD, "REGARDING THE RESTORATION OF FRIENDLY
RELATIONS, RECOGNITION AND RELATED MATTERS ON 4 OCTOBER
1963," AND CALLS UPON IRAQ AND KUWAIT, IN ACCORDANCE WITH
THEIR CONSTITUTIONAL PROCESSES, TO ACCEPT THIS AS THE
INTERNATIONAL BOUNDARY AND ALLOCATION OF TERRITORY;

3. CALLS ON THE SECRETARY GENERAL, IN CONSULTATION WITH
IRAQ AND KUWAIT, TO DEMARCATE THE BOUNDARY BETWEEN IRAQ
AND KUWAIT AS DEFINED IN SERIES UNITED KINGDOM K7611
SERIES TOPOGRAPHIC MAPS AT SCALE 1:50,000;

4. CALLS UPON ALL STATES TO TREAT THE LINE DEMARCATED IN
ACCORDANCE WITH PARAGRAPH 3 ABOVE AS THE INTERNATIONAL
BOUNDARY BETWEEN IRAQ AND KUWAIT;

5. DECIDES THAT THE SECURITY COUNCIL GUARANTEES THE
INTERNATIONAL BOUNDARY AND THE ALLOCATION OF ISLANDS
REFERRED TO ABOVE, AND AUTHORIZES MEMBER STATES
COOPERATING WITH THE GOVERNMENT OF KUWAIT TO USE ALL
NECESSARY MEANS TOWARDS THAT END;

OBSERVER FORCE

6. REQUESTS THE SECRETARY GENERAL TO SUBMIT IMMEDIATELY
TO THE SECURITY COUNCIL A PLAN FOR THE DEPLOYMENT OF AN
OBSERVER FORCE TO: MONITOR THE KHOR 'ABDULLAH AND A ZONE
EXTENDING 10 KILOMETERS INTO IRAQ AND 5 KILOMETERS INTO
KUWAIT FROM THE BOUNDARY SPECIFIED PURSUANT TO PARAGRAPH 2
ABOVE; DETER ANY UNAUTHORIZED MILITARY OR PARAMILITARY
CROSSING OF THE INTERNATIONAL BOUNDARY; OBSERVE ANY
HOSTILE OR POTENTIALLY HOSTILE ACTION MOUNTED FROM THE
TERRITORY OF ONE STATE TO THE OTHER; AND TO REPORT
REGULARLY TO THE COUNCIL ON THE OPERATIONS OF THE FORCE,
AND IMMEDIATELY IF THERE ARE SERIOUS VIOLATIONS OR
POTENTIAL THREATS TO PEACE;

27-16

0216

WEAPONS OF MASS DESTRUCTION

7. REQUIRES THAT IRAQ UNCONDITIONALLY ACCEPT THE
DESTRUCTION, REMOVAL, OR RENDERING HARMLESS, UNDER
INTERNATIONAL SUPERVISION OF: ALL BALLISTIC MISSILE
SYSTEMS; ALL WEAPONS OF MASS DESTRUCTION (INCLUDING
CHEMICAL, BIOLOGICAL, AND NUCLEAR); ALL THEIR SUBSYSTEMS
AND COMPONENTS; ALL STOCKS OF CHEMICAL AND BIOLOGICAL
AGENTS; ALL NUCLEAR WEAPONS GRADE MATERIAL; AND ALL
RESEARCH DEVELOPMENT, SUPPORT, AND MANUFACTURING
FACILITIES RELATED TO THE ABOVE;

8. REQUIRES, FOR THE IMPLEMENTATION OF PARAGRAPH 7 ABOVE,
THE FOLLOWING.

A) IRAQ SHALL SUBMIT TO THE SECRETARY GENERAL, WITHIN
FIFTEEN DAYS OF THE PASSAGE OF THIS RESOLUTION, A
DECLARATION OF THE LOCATIONS, AMOUNTS AND TYPES OF ALL
ITEMS SPECIFIED IN PARAGRAPH 7 AND AGREE TO IMMEDIATE
ON-SITE INSPECTION AS SPECIFIED BELOW;

B) THE SECRETARY GENERAL, IN CONSULTATION WITH THE
GOVERNMENTS MENTIONED IN PARAGRAPH 2 OF RESOLUTION 678

(1990) AND, WHERE APPROPRIATE, WITH THE DIRECTORS GENERAL

27-17

0217

OF THE WORLD HEALTH ORGANIZATION (WHO) AND THE
INTERNATIONAL ATOMIC ENERGY AGENCY (IAEA), WITHIN 45 DAYS
OF THE PASSAGE OF THIS RESOLUTION SHALL DEVELOP, AND
SUBMIT TO THE COUNCIL FOR APPROVAL, A PLAN CALLING FOR THE
COMPLETION OF THE FOLLOWING ACTS WITHIN 45 DAYS OF SUCH
APPROVAL:

(I) A SPECIAL COMMISSION SHALL BE FORMED, WHICH SHALL
CARRY OUT IMMEDIATE ON-SITE INSPECTION OF IRAQ'S NUCLEAR,
BIOLOGICAL, CHEMICAL AND BALLISTIC MISSILE CAPABILITIES,
BASED ON IRAQ'S DECLARATION AND THE DESIGNATION OF ANY
ADDITIONAL LOCATIONS BY THE SPECIAL COMMISSION ITSELF;

(II) IRAQ SHALL, UNDER SUPERVISION OF THE SPECIAL
COMMISSION, DESTROY ALL ITS BALLISTIC MISSILES, INCLUDING
THEIR SUBSYSTEMS, COMPONENTS AND LAUNCHERS, AND YIELD
POSSESSION TO THE SPECIAL COMMISSION FOR DESTRUCTION,
REMOVAL OR RENDERING HARMLESS OF ALL OTHER ITEMS NOTIFIED
UNDER PARAGRAPH 8(A) ABOVE, OR OTHERWISE REQUIRED BY THE
SPECIAL COMMISSION;

(III) THE SPECIAL COMMISSION, IN CONSULTATION WITH THE
DIRECTOR GENERAL OF THE IAEA, SHALL ARRANGE FOR THE
REMOVAL AND SUBSEQUENT DISPOSAL OF ANY AND ALL
WEAPONS-GRADE NUCLEAR MATERIAL AND ANY EQUIPMENT
INAPPROPRIATE TO THE NEEDS OF IRAQ'S PEACEFUL NUCLEAR
RESEARCH PROGRAM;

9.   REQUIRES THAT IRAQ UNCONDITIONALLY UNDERTAKE NOT TO
DEVELOP CONSTRUCT OR ACQUIRE ANY OF THE ITEMS SPECIFIED
IN PARAGRAPH 7 ABOVE AND REQUESTS THE SECRETARY GENERAL
IN CONSULTATION WITH THE SPECIAL COMMISSION AND THE
DIRECTOR GENERAL OF THE IAEA (FOR NUCLEAR RELATED ITEMS),
TO DEVELOP A PLAN FOR THE FUTURE ONGOING MONITORING AND
VERIFICATION OF IRAQ'S COMPLIANCE WITH THIS PARAGRAPH, TO
BE SUBMITTED TO THE COUNCIL FOR APPROVAL WITHIN ONE
HUNDRED AND TWENTY DAYS OF THE PASSAGE OF THIS RESOLUTION;

COMPENSATION

10. REAFFIRMS THAT IRAQ, WITHOUT PREJUDICE TO THE DEBTS
AND OBLIGATIONS OF IRAQ ARISING PRIOR TO AUGUST 2, 1990
IS LIABLE FOR ANY LOSS, DAMAGE, OR INJURY TO FOREIGN
GOVERNMENTS, NATIONALS AND CORPORATIONS, AS A RESULT OF
IRAQ'S AGGRESSION, INCLUDING THE INVASION AND OCCUPATION
OF KUWAIT;

11. DECIDES TO CREATE A FUND TO PAY COMPENSATION FOR
CLAIMS THAT FALL WITHIN PARAGRAPH 10 ABOVE, INCLUDING:
INJURY AND DEATH; PROPERTY DAMAGE AND THEFT; DAMAGE TO AND
DEPLETION OF OIL RESOURCES; ACTIONS AFFECTING CONTRACT AND
PROPERTY RIGHTS; LOSSES OF DEPARTING PERSONS; VIOLATIONS
OF DIPLOMATIC PRIVILEGES AND IMMUNITIES; AND ENVIRONMENTAL
DAMAGE;

12. DECIDES THAT STATES WITH IRAQI ASSETS IN THEIR
TERRITORY, AS OF THE DATE OF PASSAGE OF THIS RESOLUTION
SHALL PREVENT THEIR REMOVAL, AND AUTHORIZES STATES, AFTER

27-18

0218

VALIDATION OF CLAIMS BY THE COMMISSION ESTABLISHED IN
PARAGRAPH 13, TO DISPOSE OF SUCH ASSETS TO COMPENSATE
THEMSELVES, AND THEIR NATIONALS AND CORPORATIONS, FOR
CLAIMS WHICH FALL UNDER PARAGRAPH 11 ABOVE, AND DECIDES
THAT ANY SUCH ASSETS USED SHALL BE REPORTED TO THE
COMMISSION ESTABLISHED PURSUANT TO PARAGRAPH 13, AND
ASSETS THAT ARE NOT NEEDED FOR SUCH COMPENSATION SHALL BE
MADE AVAILABLE TO THE FUND ESTABLISHED PURSUANT TO
PARAGRAPH 11 ABOVE;

13. DECIDES THAT A PERCENTAGE OF THE VALUE OF EXPORTS OF
PETROLEUM AND PETROLEUM PRODUCTS FROM IRAQ WILL BE
PROVIDED TO THE FUND ESTABLISHED IN ACCORDANCE WITH
PARAGRAPH 11 ABOVE, AND DECIDES TO ESTABLISH A COMMISSION
THAT WILL ADMINISTER THE FUND;

14. DIRECTS THE SECRETARY GENERAL TO DEVELOP AND PRESENT
TO THE COUNCIL, NO LATER THAN 30 DAYS FOLLOWING THE
ADOPTION OF THIS RESOLUTION, RECOMMENDATIONS FOR A PROGRAM
TO IMPLEMENT THE DECISIONS IN PARAGRAPHS 10-13, INCLUDING:
ADMINISTRATION OF THE FUND; MECHANISMS FOR DETERMINING
FROM TIME TO TIME WHAT PERCENTAGE OF THE VALUE OF THE
EXPORTS OF IRAQI PETROLEUM AND PETROLEUM PRODUCTS WILL BE
PROVIDED TO THE FUND, AND FOR ENSURING COMPLIANCE WITH
IRAQ'S REQUIREMENT TO CONTRIBUTE TO THE FUND; THE PROCESS
BY WHICH FUNDS WILL BE ALLOCATED AND CLAIMS PAID; AND THE

27-19

0219

COMPOSITION OF THE COMMISSION DESIGNATED ABOVE;

SANCTIONS

15. DECIDES, EFFECTIVE IMMEDIATELY, THAT THE PROHIBITIONS AGAINST THE SALE OR SUPPLY TO IRAQ OF COMMODITIES OR PRODUCTS AND PROHIBITIONS AGAINST FINANCIAL TRANSACTIONS RELATED THERETO (EXCEPT IN REGARD TO THE ASSETS DESCRIBED IN PARAGRAPH 12 ABOVE) CONTAINED IN RESOLUTION 661 (1990) SHALL NOT APPLY TO FOODSTUFFS AND MEDICAL SUPPLIES NOTIFIED TO THE COMMITTEE ESTABLISHED IN RESOLUTION 661

(1990) AND, WITH THE APPROVAL OF THAT COMMITTEE, MATERIALS AND SUPPLIES FOR ESSENTIAL CIVILIAN NEEDS;

16. DECIDES THAT THE COUNCIL SHALL REVIEW THE PROVISIONS OF PARAGRAPH 15 ABOVE EVERY SIXTY DAYS IN LIGHT OF THE POLICIES AND PRACTICES OF THE GOVERNMENT OF IRAQ FOR THE PURPOSE OF DETERMINING WHETHER TO MODIFY FURTHER OR LIFT THE PROHIBITIONS DESCRIBED THEREIN;

17. DECIDES THAT UPON THE APPROVAL BY THE SECURITY COUNCIL OF THE PROGRAM CALLED FOR IN PARAGRAPH 14 ABOVE AND OF THE COMPLETION OF ALL ACTIONS CONTEMPLATED IN PARAGRAPH 8 ABOVE, THE PROHIBITIONS AGAINST THE IMPORT OF COMMODITIES AND PRODUCTS ORIGINATING IN IRAQ AND THE PROHIBITIONS AGAINST FINANCIAL TRANSACTIONS RELATED THERETO (EXCEPT AS TO THE ASSETS DESCRIBED IN PARAGRAPH 12 CONTAINED IN RESOLUTION 661 (1990) SHALL HAVE NO FURTHER FORCE AND EFFECT;

18. DECIDES THAT ALL STATES SHALL PREVENT THE SALE OR SUPPLY (OR THE PROMOTION OR FACILITATION OF SUCH SALE OR SUPPLY) TO IRAQ BY THEIR NATIONALS, OR FROM THEIR TERRITORIES OR USING THEIR FLAG VESSELS OR AIRCRAFT, OF:

A) ARMS AND RELATED MATERIALS OF ALL TYPES, SPECIFICALLY INCLUDING THE SALE OR TRANSFER THROUGH OTHER MEANS OF ALL FORMS OF CONVENTIONAL MILITARY EQUIPMENT, INCLUDING FOR PARAMILITARY FORCES, AND SPARE PARTS AND COMPONENTS AND THEIR MEANS OF PRODUCTION, FOR SUCH EQUIPMENT;

B) ITEMS SPECIFIED AND DEFINED IN PARAGRAPH 7 ABOVE NOT OTHERWISE COVERED ABOVE;

C) TECHNOLOGY UNDER LICENSING OR OTHER TRANSFER ARRANGEMENTS USED IN THE PRODUCTION, UTILIZATION OR STOCKPILING OF ITEMS SPECIFIED IN PARAGRAPHS A AND B ABOVE;

D) PERSONNEL OR MATERIALS FOR TRAINING OR TECHNICAL SUPPORT SERVICES RELATING TO THE DESIGN, DEVELOPMENT, MANUFACTURE, USE, MAINTENANCE OR SUPPORT OF ITEMS SPECIFIED IN PARAGRAPHS A AND B ABOVE;

19. CALLS UPON ALL STATES AND INTERNATIONAL ORGANIZATIONS TO ACT STRICTLY IN ACCORDANCE WITH PARAGRAPH 18, NOTWITHSTANDING ANY CONTRACTS OR AGREEMENTS ENTERED INTO, LICENSES GRANTED OR OTHER ARRANGEMENTS MADE BEFORE THE

27-20

0220

DATE OF THE PRESENT RESOLUTION;

20. CALLS UPON ALL STATES TO IMPLEMENT SUCH NATIONAL
CONTROLS AND PROCEDURES AND TO TAKE OTHER SUCH ACTIONS AS
MAY BE NECESSARY TO ENSURE COMPLIANCE WITH THE TERMS OF
PARAGRAPH 18 ABOVE, AND CALLS UPON INTERNATIONAL
ORGANIZATIONS TO TAKE ALL APPROPRIATE STEPS TO ASSIST IN
ENSURING SUCH FULL COMPLIANCE;

21. REQUESTS THE SECRETARY GENERAL, IN COORDINATION WITH
THE ABOVE DESCRIBED GOVERNMENTS COOPERATING WITH KUWAIT,
TO DEVELOP WITHIN 60 DAYS GUIDELINES TO FACILITATE FULL
INTERNATIONAL IMPLEMENTATION OF PARAGRAPHS 18-20 ABOVE,
AND TO DEVELOP AND SUBMIT TO THE COMMITTEE ESTABLISHED IN
RESOLUTION 661 (1990) SUCH GUIDELINES AND FOR THE
COMMITTEE TO MAKE THEM AVAILABLE TO ALL NATIONS, AND TO
ESTABLISH A PROCEDURE FOR UPDATING THESE GUIDELINES
PERIODICALLY;

CEASEFIRE

22. DECLARES THAT, UPON FORMAL IRAQI ACCEPTANCE OF THE
PROVISIONS ABOVE, A CEASEFIRE IS EFFECTIVE BETWEEN IRAQ
AND KUWAIT AND THE ABOVE DESCRIBED GOVERNMENTS COOPERATING
WITH KUWAIT;

27-21

0221

23. DECIDES TO REMAIN SEIZED WITH IMPLEMENTATION OF THIS
RESOLUTION AND EFFORTS TO SECURE PEACE AND SECURITY IN THE
AREA.

END TEXT

27-22

0222

```
----------------,------,-,---,,--
      IMPLEMENTATION TIME LINE
-----,--------------------------
```

1. DAY ONE:

A. RESOLUTION ADOPTED BY THE SECURITY COUNCIL.

C. SANCTIONS NO LONGER APPLY TO FOODSTUFFS AND MEDICAL
SUPPLIES NOTIFIED TO THE SANCTIONS COMMITTEE, OR TO
MATERIALS FOR ESSENTIAL CIVILIAN NEEDS APPROVED BY
THE COMMITTEE (PARAGRAPH 16). SANCTIONS ON WEAPONS AND
RELATED MATERIALS CONTINUE (PARAGRAPH 18).

2. DAY TWO (OR LATER):

A. SYG BEGINS CONSULTATIONS WITH IRAQ AND KUWAIT TO
DEMARCATE THE BOUNDARY (PARAGRAPH 3).

B. SYG BEGINS PREPARATION OF A PLAN FOR AN OBSERVER FORCE,
FOR IMMEDIATE SUBMISSION TO THE SECURITY COUNCIL
(PARAGRAPH 6).

3. DAY FIFTEEN (OR EARLIER):

A. IRAQ SUBMITS TO THE SYG A DECLARATION OF WMD, AND
AGREES TO IMMEDIATE ON-SITE INSPECTION (PARAGRAPH 8(A)).

4. DAY THIRTY (OR EARLIER):

A. SYG SUBMITS RECOMMENDATIONS FOR A PROGRAM TO IMPLEMENT
THE COUNCIL'S DECISIONS IN PARAGRAPHS 10,13 RELATING TO
COMPENSATION, INCLUDING, INTER ALIA, THE ADMINISTRATION OF
THE FUND AND THE COMPOSITION OF THE COMMISSION
(PARAGRAPH 14).

5. DAY FORTY-FIVE (OR EARLIER):

A. SYG SUBMITS A PLAN FOR SECURITY COUNCIL APPROVAL,
CALLING FOR (I) CREATION OF A SPECIAL COMMISSION TO
CONDUCT ON-SITE INSPECTIONS; (II) IRAQ TO DESTROY ALL
BALLISTIC MISSILES AND TURN OVER TO THE SPECIAL COMMISSION
ALL WMD FOR DESTRUCTION; AND (III) THE SPECIAL COMMISSION
TO ARRANGE TO DISPOSE OF WEAPONS-RELATED NUCLEAR ITEMS
(PARAGRAPH 8(B)).

6. DAY SIXTY:

A. SECURITY COUNCIL CONDUCTS ITS FIRST REVIEW OF PARAGRAPH
15 IN LIGHT OF IRAQI POLICIES AND PRACTICES TO DETERMINE
WHETHER FURTHER MODIFICATIONS ARE IN ORDER; THIS REVIEW
WILL OCCUR IN FURTHER SIXTY DAY INTERVALS INDEFINITELY

27-23

(PARAGRAPH 16).

B. SYG TO DEVELOP GUIDELINES FOR IMPLEMENTATION OF THE WEAPO)
SANCTIONS IN PARAGRAPH 18-20, AND TO SUBMITTHEM TO THE
SANCTIONS COMMITTEE, WHICH IN TURN WILL MAKE THEM AVAILABLE
ALL STATES (PARAGRAPH 21).

7. DAY NINETY (OR EARLIER):

A. THE ACTS SPECIFIED IN ITEM 5.A. SHALL HAVE BEEN COMPLETED
(PARAGRAPH 8(F)).

B. ASSUMING THAT THE SECURITY COUNCIL SHALL HAVE APPROVED THE
SYG'S PLAN FOR COMPENSATION BY THIS DATE, AND ASSUMING THAT
ACTS SPECIFIED IN ITEM 5.A. SHALL HAVE BEEN COMPLETED, THE
SECURITY COUNCIL COULD APPROVE THE LIFTING OF ALL REMAINING
SANCTIONS ON IRAQI EXPORTS (EXCEPT AS TO FROZEN ASSETS
DESCRIBED IN PARAGRAPH 12) (PARAGRAPH 19). (FYI: BROAD
SANCTIONS ON IMPORTS INTO IRAQ COULD REMAIN IN EFFECT PER IT
6.A., ABOVE. END FYI.)

8. DAY ONE HUNDRED-TWENTY:

A. SYG TO DEVELOP A PLAN FOR LONG-TERM MONITORING TO AVOID
NEW WMD RESEARCH (PARAGRAPH 9).

27-24

0224

9. WFEN IRAQ FORMAILY ACCEPTS PROVISIONS OF THE RESOLUTION:

A. CEASEFIRE BECOMES EFFECTIVE (PARAGRAPH 22).

27-25

(PARAGRAPH 16).

B. SYG TO DEVELOP GUIDELINES FOR IMPLEMENTATION OF THE WEAPO)
SANCTIONS IN PARAGRAPH 18-20, AND TO SUBMITTHEM TO THE
SANCTIONS COMMITTEE, WHICH IN TURN WILL MAKE THEM AVAILABLE
ALL STATES (PARAGRAPH 21).

7. DAY NINETY (OR EARLIER):

A. THE ACTS SPECIFIED IN ITEM 5.A. SHALL HAVE BEEN COMPLETED
(PARAGRAPH 8(B)).

B. ASSUMING THAT THE SECURITY COUNCIL SHALL HAVE APPROVED THE
SYG'S PLAN FOR COMPENSATION BY THIS DATE, AND ASSUMING THAT
ACTS SPECIFIED IN ITEM 5.A. SHALL HAVE BEEN COMPLETED, THE
SECURITY COUNCIL COULD APPROVE THE LIFTING OF ALL REMAINING
SANCTIONS ON IRAQI EXPORTS (EXCEPT AS TO FROZEN ASSETS
DESCRIBED IN PARAGRAPH 12) (PARAGRAPH 17). (FYI: BROAD
SANCTIONS ON IMPORTS INTO IRAQ COULD REMAIN IN EFFECT PER IT
6.A., ABOVE. END FYI.)

8. DAY ONE HUNDRED-TWENTY:

A. SYG TO DEVELOP A PLAN FOR LONG-TERM MONITORING TO AVOID
NEW WMD RESEARCH (PARAGRAPH 9).

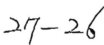

9. WHEN IRAQ FORMALLY ACCEPTS PROVISIONS OF THE RESOLUTION:

A. CEASEFIRE BECOMES EFFECTIVE (PARAGRAPH 22).

27-27/

0227

a1903ALL r
u i BC-GULF-UN   03-21 0464
BC-GULF-UN
FIVE U.N. COUNCIL POWERS STUDY FIRST DRAFT OF CEASEFIRE PACT
    By Evelyn Leopold
    UNITED NATIONS, March 20, Reuter - The United States late
on Wednesday distributed the first draft of a resolution
establishing a permanent ceasefire in the Gulf war to the
permanent members of the U.N. Security Council.
    Foremost among the conditions was a demand proposed by
Britain that Iraq submit to the supervised destruction of its
ballistic missiles and chemical and biological weapons,
diplomats said.
    Other provisions were reported to include a U.N. observer
force, a timetable for lifting trade sanctions against Iraq, a
system for paying war damages and proper demarcation of the
border between Kuwait and Iraq.
    Diplomats at the meeting said the Soviet Union, Britain,
France and China -- with the United States the five permanent
Council members -- would send the draft back to their capitals
to determine if there was enough agreement to present it to
the other 10 Council members.
    One envoy said the new resolution was to be "more
substantive in size and complexity" but that Washington hoped
it could be adopted by the end of next week. The draft was
said to number 12 pages.
    "We are working on a draft resolution which the United
States has presented which is now in the course of being
discussed by the permanent five," U.S. Ambassador Thomas
Pickering told reporters.
    The document was expected to specify a definitive end to
hostilities in the Gulf War.
    But still unclear in the draft is the sequence of events
necessary to attain a permanent ceasefire, diplomats said. The
new draft sets terms for a ceasefire as well as conditions for
the lifting of sanctions.
    However, one objective in the resolution was to accelerate
the withdrawal of U.S. and allied troops from southern Iraq
and to set up a U.N. observer force in a demilitarised zone on
the Kuwait-Iraq border as soon as possible.
    At the insistence of Kuwait the draft also included
provisions for Iraq to recognise 1963 borders it agreed on
with Kuwait and for the United Nations or another body to
clearly demarcate them.
    The five permament members were also working on a system
to commit Iraq to binding arbitration for war damages and to
determine how best to tap Iraq's oil revenues to pay for them.
    To that end some economic sanctions will be removed so
Iraq can sell oil abroad.
    France is pushing for a quick lifting of sanctions on
foodstuffs which currently must be approved on a case by case
basis by the council's sanctions committee and then
distributed by international organisations.
    Also under consideration was a suggestion by Austria that
the resolution be adopted at foreign minister level by the end
of the month, diplomats said. Pickering told reporters no
decision had yet been made on that.
    REUTER EL JWO LD
Reut02:54 03-21

                              12

                                                    0228

GLGL

유엔 제재위선희, 대이라크제재완화
검토 (3.2.)

00007 ASI/AFP-BA30-----
r i Gulf-U.N.-relief   03-21 0384
   U.N. Sanctions Committee considers easing rules for altering embargo on Iraq

   NEW YORK, United Nations, March 20 (AFP) - Health and food supply
conditions in Iraq have pushed the United Nations Sanctions Committee
implementing the international embargo on that country to consider easing
restrictions on altering the embargo's reach, diplomats said Wednesday.
   Meeting here Wednesday, the committee weighed the possibility of asking
U.N. agencies such as UNICEF and the World Health Organization (WHO) to handle
all long term humanitarian work as the International Committee of the Red
Cross (ICRC) said it was unable to do so according to its mandate.
   The committee also considered approving humanitarian aid shipments of
goods deemed necessary after they have been sent to Iraq in order to speed up
the current procedure.
   Since the total trade embargo on Iraq was put in place August 6 according
to U.N. Security Council instructions, the committee has been authorized only
to allow embargo exceptions for humanitarian reasons.
   The sanctions committee now apparently has decided to alter its form of
operation, faced with the ICRC's position, ICRC reports of conditions in Iraq,
and information passed on by special U.N. envoy to Iraq Martti Ahtisaari who
evaluated pressing humanitarian needs there.
   But the committee was awaiting Mr. Ahtisaari's full report, set to be
given to the Security Council Thursday. The committee was slated to meet again
on Friday.
   On Wednesday, however, the committee pressed ahead and approved a small
shipment of food products from Germany, India and Denmark.
   Meanwhile it refused to give final approval to a Turkish request to ship
25,000 tonnes of flour, as it had done one week earlier with a supply of
11,500 tonnes of wheat paid for by Yemen.
   Early information relayed by Mr. Ahtisaari corroborates a recent ICRC
report which said Iraq's 18 million citizens were on the brink of a public
health catastrophe due to allied bombing of the country's infrastructure.
   Diplomats said the Security Council was considering a draft resolution
adding new conditions to the formal cease fire, and appeared unlikely to lift
the sanctions on Iraq even partially in the immediate future.
   bfr/mla/hfw

   AFP 210017 GMT MAR 91
AFP 210019 GMT MAR 91

15

0229

걸프사태 관련 유엔안전보장이사회 동향, 1990-91. 전5권 (V.4 1991.3월) 235

주 국 련 대 표 부

주국련 203132- **182**   1991. 3. 21.

수신 장관

참조 국제기구조약국장, 중동아프리카국장

제목 걸프사태(안보리)

　　　　표제 사태 관련 안보리 문서를 별첨과 같이 송부합니다.

　　　　첨부 : 상기 안보리 문서.　끝.

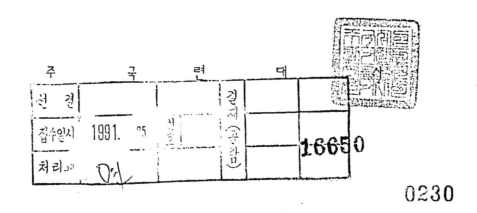

Security Council

Distr.
GENERAL

S/22021/Add.2
19 March 1991

ORIGINAL: ENGLISH

LETTER DATED 19 DECEMBER 1990 FROM THE CHAIRMAN OF THE SECURITY
COUNCIL COMMITTEE ESTABLISHED BY RESOLUTION 661 (1990) CONCERNING
THE SITUATION BETWEEN IRAQ AND KUWAIT ADDRESSED TO THE PRESIDENT
OF THE SECURITY COUNCIL

Addendum

Letter dated 18 March 1991 from the Chairman of the Security Council
Committee established by resolution 661 (1990) concerning the
situation between Iraq and Kuwait addressed to the President of the
Security Council

I have the honour to refer to the letters dated 19 and 21 December 1990,
respectively (S/22021 and Add.1), by which the Chairman of the Security Council
Committee established by resolution 661 (1990) concerning the situation between
Iraq and Kuwait transmitted to the Security Council the recommendations adopted by
the Committee in response to requests for assistance under the provisions of
Article 50 of the Charter of the United Nations.

At its 34th meeting, on 13 March 1991, the Committee adopted without objection
as further recommendations to be made to the President of the Security Council in
pursuance of Security Council resolution 669 (1990) the draft decisions submitted
by the Working Group with regard to the Syrian Arab Republic and Djibouti. In
accordance with the decision taken at the Committee's 21st meeting and at the
request of applicant States, the Committee is transmitting with the relevant
recommendation any additional explanatory material provided by those States.

(Signed) Peter HOHENFELLNER
Chairman
Security Council Committee established
by resolution 661 (1990) concerning the
situation between Iraq and Kuwait

91-08698 2139i (E)

/...

0231

<u>Annex I</u>

<u>Recommendation by the Security Council Committee established by
resolution 661 (1990) concerning the situation between Iraq and
Kuwait with regard to the Syrian Arab Republic</u>

<u>The Security Council Committee established by resolution 661 (1990) concerning
the situation between Iraq and Kuwait</u>,

<u>Having dealt</u> with the communication received from the Syrian Arab Republic
under Article 50 of the Charter of the United Nations, <u>a</u>/

<u>Recalling</u> Security Council resolution 661 (1990) of 6 August 1990, in which
the Council decided to impose sanctions in accordance with Chapter VII of the
Charter, as well as Security Council resolutions 660 (1990) of 2 August 1990,
662 (1990) of 9 August 1990, 664 (1990) of 18 August 1990, 665 (1990) of
25 August 1990, 666 (1990) of 13 September 1990, 667 (1990) of 16 September 1990,
669 (1990) of 24 September 1990, 670 (1990) of 25 September 1990, 674 (1990) of
29 October 1990 and 686 (1991) of 2 March 1991,

<u>Recalling also</u> the provisions of Articles 25, 49 and 50 of the Charter,

<u>Noting</u> the information given by the Syrian Arab Republic <u>a</u>/ regarding the
measures taken to give full effect to the sanctions as laid down in Security
Council resolution 661 (1990), and concerning the special economic problems it has
been confronted with as a result of the implementation of those measures,

<u>Having heard</u> the statement of the representative of the Syrian Arab Republic,

<u>Expressing concern</u> at the special economic problems confronting the Syrian
Arab Republic as a result of the severance of its economic relations with Iraq and
occupied Kuwait, as required by Security Council resolution 661 (1990), which are
particularly difficult in terms of commercial and financial losses incurred by the
Syrian Arab Republic,

<u>Recognizing</u> that the continued full implementation of Security Council
resolution 661 (1990) by the Syrian Arab Republic, as well as other States, will
support the measures to ensure compliance with paragraph 2 of that resolution,

1. <u>Commends</u> the Government of the Syrian Arab Republic for the measures it
has taken to comply with Security Council resolution 661 (1990);

2. <u>Recognizes</u> the urgent need to assist the Syrian Arab Republic in coping
with its special economic problems resulting from the severance of its economic
relations with Iraq and occupied Kuwait, as required by Security Council resolution
661 (1990), especially those losses resulting from undelivered Syrian products to

_____

<u>a</u>/ S/22193.

0232   /...

Iraq and occupied Kuwait, and undelivered Iraqi oil shipments to the Syrian Arab Republic, as well as commercial and financial losses incurred by the Syrian community in Kuwait;

3.   Appeals to all States on an urgent basis to provide immediate technical, financial and material assistance to the Syrian Arab Republic to mitigate the adverse impact on its economy of the application by the Syrian Arab Republic of sanctions against Iraq pursuant to Security Council resolution 661 (1990);

4.   Invites the competent organs and specialized agencies of the United Nations system, including the international financial institutions, and the regional development banks, to review their programmes of assistance to the Syrian Arab Republic with a view to alleviating its special economic problems arising from the application of sanctions against Iraq pursuant to Security Council resolution 661 (1990);

5.   Requests the Secretary-General, on a regular basis, to seek information from States and the concerned organs and agencies of the United Nations system on action taken to alleviate the special economic problems of the Syrian Arab Republic and to report thereon to the Security Council.

0233   /...

<u>Enclosure</u>

STUDY ON THE ECONOMIC DAMAGES AND LOSSES SUFFERED BY THE
SYRIAN ARAB REPUBLIC AS A RESULT OF THE GULF CRISIS <u>a</u>/

[Original: Arabic]

INTRODUCTION

The Gulf crisis has had far-reaching effects on the economic and social situation of numerous countries in the region of western Asia and elsewhere in the world. The Syrian Arab Republic is one of the countries of the region which has been adversely affected by this crisis. In addition to the disastrous losses suffered by the members of the Syrian community in Kuwait in regard to their property, business interests and bank balances, the Gulf crisis has entailed substantial losses that have directly affected the State Treasury and a number of industrial institutions and individuals in the Syrian Arab Republic. These overall losses have had direct adverse consequences on the Syrian economy and, by their very nature, will probably have detrimental repercussions in the foreseeable future on a number of the country's production and service sectors.

The purpose of this study, which was prepared by a team of researchers from the United Nations Economic and Social Commission for Western Asia (ESCWA), is to make an objective assessment of the economic losses and damages resulting directly from the Gulf crisis and to evaluate their effects and repercussions.

The research team wishes to express its deep gratitude and appreciation to all the officials and other persons whom it met during the preparation of the study for their sincere cooperation and help, which were highly instrumental in facilitating the completion of the study. The team is particularly grateful to Dr. Muhammad al-Imadi, the Minister of Economy and Foreign Trade, and Mr. Fathi al-Jabban, the Deputy Minister of Economy and Foreign Trade.

<u>Sources of information</u>

An objective assessment of the losses and damages suffered by the Syrian economy as a result of the Gulf crisis basically requires accurate statistics and reliable information. Although this principle has been respected to the greatest possible extent, in some cases the requisite estimates were obtained by indirect means based on deduction and inference. In other cases, hypotheses were adopted as unavoidable options in studies of this type.

With regard to the sources of information needed for purposes of assessment, the team relied on the publications of the Syrian Central Bureau of Statistics, particularly the Statistical Abstract published in 1990. Information was also derived from a number of official authorities in the Syrian Arab Republic,

_____

<u>a</u>/   S/22193, annex.

0234   /...

particularly the Ministries of Economy and the Interior, the Central Bank and the General Directorate of Customs. In order to obtain supplementary information, meetings were held with the head of the Syrian community in Kuwait, as well as a number of its members in various occupational categories.

<u>Profile of the Syrian community in Kuwait</u>

A certain degree of familiarity with the distinctive characteristics of the Syrian community in Kuwait is essential for an understanding of many of the fundamental concepts on which some of the estimates are based, particularly those derived from hypotheses. This is one of the oldest communities, which first arrived in Kuwait to further that country's development and progress when it began to invest its petroleum resources. Although the Syrian community was neither the numerically largest community in Kuwait nor the largest Syrian expatriate community, it was always characterized by a degree of economic activity that transcended the proportional number of its members in the host State or in their home country. This is obviously due to a number of considerations such as, in particular:

(a) A large proportion of the members of this community were businessmen, large and wealthy contractors owning extensive business enterprises, and craftsmen;

(b) The vast majority of the wage-earners employed by government institutions and private enterprises were highly qualified and skilled workers earning incomes that were relatively high in comparison with those received by the members of other communities;

(c) The members of this community were more closely attached to their home country than Syrian expatriates living in other countries, particularly in Europe and America. This is largely attributable to the fact that many of them left all or some of the members of their family in their home country, in which they owned real estate and property and possibly also had business interests, in addition to Kuwait's proximity to the Syrian Arab Republic.

In fact, these considerations are influential factors that must be taken into account when assessing the losses suffered by the members of the Syrian community in Kuwait, as well as the volume of their transfers and other aspects.

I. LOSSES SUFFERED BY THE MEMBERS OF THE SYRIAN COMMUNITY
    IN KUWAIT

Information derived from numerous sources indicates that the Syrian community in Kuwait numbered more than 100,000 persons, of whom 50,000 were economically active, the remainder being family members who were not economically active. The losses suffered by these persons were estimated at about $US 9,174 million. This estimate was calculated by dividing the economically active persons into two categories:

0235

/...

Category 1

Comprising 20,000 businessmen, contractors, craftsmen and other self-employed persons. Their losses in respect of their business interests were estimated at about $6,317 million, broken down as follows:

	$ million
Key money and equipment of commercial premises	2 069
Stock	2 207
Commercial vehicles	276
Reduced rates of exchange for deposits and liquid assets	1 282
Debts and lost deposits	345
Miscellaneous (stocks and bonds, etc.)	138

Category 2

Comprising 30,000 persons working for a fixed wage in government institutions or private enterprises. The total losses of the persons included in this category were estimated at about $1,582 million, broken down as follows:

	$ million
Separation from service indemnities	517
Reduced rates of exchange for deposits and liquid assets	962
Lost deposits	103

With regard to residential property and related losses, the losses of both categories were estimated at about $1,275 million, broken down as follows:

	$ million
Furniture, domestic appliances and clothing	1 034
Valuables and jewellery	172
Private vehicles	69

0236

/...

The per capita losses in each category were first estimated in respect of the items listed above and the total was then multiplied by the estimated number of persons who suffered loss. The average estimated per capita value in respect of each type of property or rights was multiplied by the probable proportional loss in value, which was assumed to be in the region of 60-100 per cent (see appendix I).

II. ECONOMIC LOSSES

In addition to the substantial losses suffered by the members of the Syrian community in Kuwait, the crisis has entailed considerable direct losses to the State Treasury and a number of economic enterprises and individuals in the Syrian Arab Republic itself. These aggregate losses have been highly detrimental to the Syrian economy and, by their very nature, are likely to have adverse repercussions on a number of production and service sectors in the foreseeable future. These losses resulted from circumstances brought about by the crisis, particularly:

(a) The cessation of transfers and remittances from Syrians in Kuwait and the reduction in the customary levels of remittances from the other Gulf States;

(b) The non-arrival of summer visitors from Kuwait and the Gulf States and a reduction in the number of persons visiting the Syrian Arab Republic from other countries;

(c) The suspension of Syrian exports to Kuwait and a reduction, to varying degrees, in the volume of exports to the Gulf States and Jordan;

(d) A reduction in the rate of exchange of the Syrian pound against foreign currencies;

(e) A decrease in the volume of goods and passengers passing through the Syrian Arab Republic; the suspension of air traffic between the Syrian Arab Republic and Kuwait; and the resulting decline in the volume of activity at Syrian ports;

(f) The postponement of the implementation of a draft agreement that was to have been concluded between the Syrian Arab Republic and Iraq shortly before the crisis. This agreement provided for the resumption of the pumping of Iraqi oil through the Syrian pipeline to the export terminal at Banias, the supply of quantities of oil at reduced prices to the Syrian Arab Republic, and the reopening of the borders between the two countries. The implementation of this agreement was postponed in view of the Syrian Government's compliance with the United Nations resolutions concerning the embargo on Iraq;

(g) The Syrian Government granted numerous facilities to the Syrians and Kuwaitis arriving from Kuwait, in the form of customs exemptions, enrolment of their children in Syrian schools and universities, etc.

These circumstances have had numerous repercussions on the economic and social situation. Although they are interrelated, their end result can be summarized as follows:

/...

0237

(a)   A decline in the country's foreign exchange earnings resulting, as already indicated, from the decline in the transfers and remittances of Syrian expatriates, the reduced income in the tourist sector, the lower volume of exports, the decline in the volume of transit trade and the suspension of the implementation of the oil agreement with Iraq;

(b)   The increased cost of Syrian imports of goods and services due to the drop in the exchange rate for the Syrian pound in neighbouring markets;

(c)   The reduction in the volume of exports led to a decline in production levels in enterprises that are dependent on Kuwaiti and other Gulf markets for the sale of their products, particularly enterprises in the textile, furnishings and plastics industries;

(d)   The decline in the number of summer visitors and tourists led to a reduction in levels of employment in tourist enterprises, particularly restaurants, hotels, tourist resorts and tourist transport services, etc.;

(e)   Government service agencies, and particularly educational institutions, were faced with increased expenditure, in addition to the extra burdens placed on the State Treasury due to the exemptions and facilities granted to persons arriving from Kuwait;

(f)   The rise in the rates of overt and disguised unemployment, due to the arrival of large numbers of Syrians of working age and the decline in levels of economic activity in many production and service institutions affected by the crisis.

However, in order to study the consequent damages and evaluate their economic effects and repercussions, information is needed concerning the quantitative level of the direct losses. These are reviewed below.

A.   Reduction in the value of the transfers and remittances
     of Syrians abroad

It is difficult to make satisfactory estimates of the transfers received from Syrians abroad and of the extent to which they have declined as a result of the crisis, since these transfers, and particularly the monetary remittances, are routed through various channels. Although most of these channels are lawful, they are in no way subject to statistical monitoring by the official authorities. In accordance with the customary procedures, a Syrian or foreign national arriving in the Syrian Arab Republic has the right to bring into the country an unlimited quantity of national or foreign currency and is not required to declare the amount of Syrian currency that he is carrying, nor is he normally obliged to declare the foreign currency that he is bringing into the country, unless he intends to re-export it, in whole or in part, on his departure or to exchange it at approved State banks.

0238

/...

Consequently, one possible method to estimate the volume of transfers from Syrians abroad is to monitor them by type, use and final destination. With regard to type, transfers take three principal forms:

(a) Transfers in kind, namely the value of the various goods and commodities brought into the country for the personal use of the visitor or his family or as gifts for relatives and acquaintances. The value of this type of transfer can be easily estimated by adopting a hypothetical average value for the items brought into the country by each visiting Syrian expatriate;

(b) Official drafts channelled through approved banks. However, this type of transfer constitutes only a very small proportion of the total transfers and the foreign exchange proceeds normally go to the State agencies concerned;

(c) Monetary remittances brought into the country or sent through third parties. These account for the largest proportion of the total value of transfers. The expatriate normally changes part of these transfers into Syrian currency, usually in the host country or in the markets of neighbouring countries, while retaining the larger part in the form of savings in foreign currency, which he changes as and when needed.

However, regardless of the channels through which the monetary remittances enter the Syrian Arab Republic, it is a well-known fact that, in actual practice, these transfers constitute the basic source of funds to pay for the materials, commodities and equipment imported by the private sector, since the State's current foreign trade policy is based on the principle that the provision of the foreign exchange needed to pay for private-sector imports is the responsibility of the importers themselves. This foreign exchange is obtained from two sources: (a) the proportional foreign exchange value of exports which, under the regulations in force, private-sector exporters are permitted to retain in order to import the raw materials and other production requisites that they need; (b) the foreign exchange that they obtain from the transfers of Syrian expatriates.

Moreover, the monetary transfers and remittances of Syrian expatriates provide, in one way or another, a considerable proportion of the value of public-sector and State imports, since the public sector basically covers the value of its imports from the value of its exports and the State's foreign exchange resources. Part of these resources are derived, either directly or indirectly, from the transfers and remittances of Syrian expatriates, since some public-sector products are sold to the private sector for foreign currency. Various dues and taxes are levied on Syrian expatriates in foreign currency, in addition to the amounts of foreign currency which Syrian expatriates change at approved banks in the Syrian Arab Republic at preferential rates.

Quite apart from the above, reference must be made to the fact that some of the goods and commodities imported into the country are brought in by visitors in the form of transfers in kind from the markets of neighbouring countries and are therefore not covered by the official foreign trade statistics. The greater part of the value of these imports is undoubtedly covered, in one way or another, by the monetary remittances of Syrian expatriates.

/...

0239

Accordingly, the proportional decline in the volume of transfers and remittances from Syrians abroad as a result of the Gulf crisis was estimated on the basis of the following principles and hypotheses.

1. Estimated aggregate value of transfers

(a) If we assume that the proportion of the foreign exchange retained by Syrian exporters under the regulations in force is more or less equivalent to the value of the country's imports that are not covered by the foreign trade statistics, it can be affirmed, fairly reliably, that the volume of the remittances sent by expatriates and their families is equivalent to the total value of private-sector imports from all sources except Kuwait.

(b) Some 25 per cent of the total value of public-sector imports are covered by the foreign exchange derived from the transfers of Syrians abroad.

2. Transfers from Syrians in Kuwait

(a) The Syrian labour force in Kuwait constituted 15 per cent of the total Syrian expatriate labour force. However, the transfers received from the Syrian community in Kuwait amounted to approximately 30 per cent of the total transfers from Syrians abroad. This is attributable to the distinctive characteristics and special circumstances of that community, as already indicated.

(b) The Syrian community in Kuwait accounted for 60 per cent of the total value of the private-sector imports from Kuwait. This assumption is based on the special relationships between the importers and the members of that community.

(c) The expatriates (and their families) retain in their home country an average amount of about $5,600 (approximately KD 1,600) from their monetary remittances in foreign currency.

(d) The average expatriate visits his home country once every year and, on each visit, carries with him goods and commodities, for his own use or to be given as gifts to his family and relatives in the Syrian Arab Republic, amounting to an estimated value of about $2,400 (approximately KD 700).

(e) Transfers from Syrians in Kuwait have been totally suspended and the monetary remittances from the Syrian communities in other countries have declined by 10 per cent.

(f) There has been no change in any of the factors applicable prior to the crisis.

In the light of the above-mentioned principles and hypotheses, the overall decline in the transfers and remittances of Syrians abroad was estimated at about $848 million, broken down as follows:

0240

/...

	$ million
1. Value of transfers and remittances in cash and in kind from Kuwait	766
Transfers and remittances used to finance imports	366
From Kuwait = 15	
From outside Kuwait = 351	
Monetary remittances accumulated in the Syrian Arab Republic	280
Remittances in kind	120
2. Decline in the value of transfers from other Syrian communities	82

B. Impact of the crisis on the foreign trade sector

The Syrian Arab Republic has preferential trade relations with a number of Gulf States and also with Jordan. Like Iraq, these countries constitute traditional markets for various Syrian products, particularly textiles and foodstuffs. In 1989, the value of Syrian exports to the Gulf States and Jordan amounted to about $310 million. This amount constituted about 62 per cent of the Syrian Arab Republic's total exports to the Arab countries and 10 per cent of the value of its exports to all countries of the world. If we exclude exports to the Soviet Union, the latter figure increases to 16 per cent.

A time-series study of Syrian exports to the Gulf States and Jordan shows that the volume of these exports was increasing every year and was expected to reach a record volume in 1990, particularly after the restoration of normal relations with the Sultanate of Oman. This is substantiated by the fact that the value of Syrian exports to the Gulf States and Jordan had risen to $293 million during the first three quarters of 1990, in spite of the fact that the chronological period to which this figure relates extended two months beyond the commencement of the crisis. At all events, if matters had continued to follow their normal pre-crisis course, the value of Syrian exports to the above-mentioned States would have risen to at least $390 million, i.e., an increase of 26 per cent over and above the figure for 1989.

In fact, the importance of Syrian trade relations with the Gulf States and Jordan is not attributable solely to their relatively high volume: it is noteworthy that the Syrian trade balance with those countries was in the Syrian Arab Republic's favour in a ratio of 3.5 to 1, since the value of Syrian imports from them in 1989 amounted to no more than $91 million.

During the period 1981-1989, the volume of transit trade declined from more than 14 million tonnes to less than 600,000 tonnes as a result of the rupture of relations with Iraq. The volume of such trade had been expected to increase with the resumption of normal relations between the Syrian Arab Republic and Iraq, which were once again broken off due to the crisis.

/...

0241

The circumstances brought about by the Gulf crisis have given rise to damage from the first day of the crisis and will continue to have a detrimental impact on foreign trade. Exports to Kuwait have stopped and exports to Jordan and the Gulf countries have gradually been falling off. This has affected in particular a number of traditional Syrian industries such as textiles, clothing and furnishings, as well as plastics, and foodstuffs such as chicken, eggs, vegetables and fruit. Furthermore, it had been expected that the normalization of relations between the Syrian Arab Republic and Iraq would lead to a record volume of Syrian exports.

On the other hand, the material and psychological conditions arising from the crisis have led to a sudden drop in the exchange rate of the Syrian pound in neighbouring countries of no less than 10 per cent, the unavoidable consequence of which has been a rise in import costs.

Thus, the damage due to the crisis has affected the three components of the foreign trade sector, which are exports, imports and transit. In the following section we shall give estimates of the direct economic losses arising from that damage in each of the three components separately.

1. Losses from exports

(a) Syrian exports to Kuwait

The value of exports to Kuwait over the first seven months of 1990 was approximately $17 million. On the basis of their monthly average, these exports were expected to reach $30 million per year. The sudden halt in exports to Kuwait caused losses to the State, exporters and producers alike. The State Treasury has been deprived of that proportion of foreign currency which exporters are obliged to exchange at official rates, or 25 per cent of the value of the exports. The market value of this currency is approximately four times greater than its nominal value, which affords the State a net surplus of 19 per cent of the value of the exports. The halt in exports to Kuwait has also inflicted a loss on exporters resulting primarily from unpaid obligations and export profits estimated at approximately 25 per cent of the value of the exports. Damage to producers has taken the form of a drop in prices for commodities made for export and similarly a fall in production levels in their enterprises, which has added to various other losses. With regard to Kuwait in particular, losses resulting from the drop in export commodity prices and the fall-off in production are estimated at approximately 30 per cent. On the basis of the foregoing, the losses resulting from the halt in exports to Kuwait for a full year are estimated at approximately $32 million, apportioned as follows:

19 per cent - losses in foreign currency to the State Treasury = $5.7 million

25 per cent - losses to exporters = $7.5 million

30 per cent - losses to producers = $19.0 million

0242   /...

(b) Syrian exports to other Gulf countries and to Jordan

The value of Syrian exports to the Gulf countries and Jordan, as we have indicated, was expected to reach approximately $390 million per year, of which $30 million was the expected value of exports to Kuwait. The decrease in these exports is estimated at approximately 25 per cent or $90 million. Therefore, the resulting loss is estimated at approximately $58 million apportioned as follows:

19 per cent - losses in foreign currency to the State Treasury = $17.1 million

20 per cent - losses to exporters = $18.0 million

25 per cent - losses to producers = $22.5 million

It will be noted that the loss in the value of exports used in this estimate is lower than that estimated for Kuwait because it is expected that in these cases there will be gradual adjustment to the new situation.

(c) Exports to Iraq

It is well known that there have been contacts between the Syrian Arab Republic and Iraq aimed at normalizing relations between the two countries. All the indications were that the two sides had reached a draft agreement to reopen the border between them and to resume pumping Iraqi oil through the Syrian pipeline and provide the Syrian Arab Republic with certain quantities of oil at reduced prices. However, the Syrian Government's observance of the international resolutions imposing an economic embargo on Iraq has led to halting work on what had been agreed.

This observance has deprived the Syrian Arab Republic of considerable economic gains, which are now seen as economic losses. It had been expected that Syrian exports to Iraq would grow and that transit through Syrian ports would become active. Despite insufficient data with which to estimate the losses in exports resulting from the suspension of the agreement, the history of commercial relations between the two countries suggests that Iraq had always been one of the most important traditional markets for Syrian products, in particular, clothes, textiles and certain chemical industries such as soap, plastic products and foodstuffs. There is sufficient evidence to estimate the loss in exports at no less than $100 million per year.

2. Losses from imports

As we have indicated, the exchange rate of the Syrian pound has fallen by 10 per cent from its level before the crisis. This drop has had a double impact. On the one hand, it has raised the value of exports and remittances from Syrians abroad as calculated in Syrian currency. On the other hand, however, it has raised the cost of imports as calculated in Syrian currency. The consequence of these two tendencies has been a loss for the national economy estimated at approximately $150 million per year. This estimate has been arrived at on the following basis:

0243 /...

(a) The value of expected exports (given by the foreign trade statistics) was approximately $2,143 million. Assuming constant import levels for the year following the date on which the crisis began, the cost of imports as calculated in Syrian currency will rise by the equivalent of $214 million (an increase of 10 per cent);

(b) The value of remittances before the crisis has been estimated at approximately $1,085 million per year. It is expected that income from these remittances will fall because of the crisis by $448 million to around $637 million (see appendix II). In view of the fall in the exchange rate of the Syrian pound, the increase in the value of remittances expected after the crisis as calculated in Syrian currency will be around $64 million;

(c) Therefore, the burden resulting from the drop in the exchange rate of the Syrian pound will be approximately $150 million.

It should be noted that in making this estimate it has been assumed that foreign exchange earnings from exports which have been paid for is equivalent to the value of imports on which customs duty has not been paid.

3. Losses from transit

Economic losses in the field of transit are estimated at approximately $100 million per year. This figure represents the expected decrease in the volume of transport to Arab Gulf countries, the expected traffic of goods to Iraq through Syrian ports and territory and the halting of flights to Kuwait.

C. Losses of foreign currency from tourism

The losses incurred in the tourist sector are basically due to the sudden halt in arrivals of summer visitors from Kuwait and the other Gulf countries, which took place at the height of the summer season. It is expected that this halt will remain in effect for the whole year following the beginning of the crisis. A substantial decrease is also expected in the number of tourists coming to the Syrian Arab Republic from other countries as a result of the crisis. In addition to the direct impact of these changes, which will be a drop in the country's foreign currency income, there will be all sorts of damage to the various tourist installations and individuals connected to that sector.

Total foreign currency losses resulting from the fall off in numbers of visitors to the country are estimated at approximately $454 million per year. This figure has been arrived at on the basis of the following considerations:

(a) It has been assumed that the number of visitors to the country during the year under study would remain at the same level as before the crisis, i.e., the number recorded in 1989;

(b)   Despite the fact that some of the visitors to the country cannot be considered tourists in the generally accepted sense of the term, one should not neglect the amount of foreign currency such visitors spend during their stay in the country. Therefore, for the purposes of estimation, all visitors to the country have been considered as tourists;

(c)   The estimate of foreign currency losses is in fact the product of the expected drop in the number of tourist nights spent because of the crisis and the single visitor's average expenditure per night, estimated at $150. This average includes what the visitor spends on hotel rooms or furnished flats, food, drink, transport, commodity purchases and various services;

(d)   The decrease in the number of tourist nights has been estimated by assuming an average number of nights for each visitor before the crisis and the expected decrease in this number because of the crisis. A distinction has been made between nationalities in the hypothetical averages and the rates of decrease (see appendix III).

D. State Treasury losses from taxes and duties

The relevant authorities in the Syrian Arab Republic granted visitors from Kuwait (Syrians and Kuwaitis) numerous facilities in the form of customs exemptions and special exceptions from some of the customary rules and procedures in a number of domains. The government agencies, in particular public security, the customs and education authorities made exceptional efforts to absorb the sudden flow of visitors during the first days of the crisis. The following is a list of the facilities granted to those visitors:

(a)   Visitors' cars were exempted from the customs duty, payable in foreign currency, of 115 dollars for each car for a stay of no more than four months inside the country. Approximately 15,000 tourist cars have entered the country since the beginning of the crisis;

(b)   The period for which these cars are allowed to stay in the country was extended for a further year and their owners were exempted from the customs duties arising therefrom;

(c)   Baggage accompanying the visitors was exempted from customs duty;

(d)   Shipments of furniture and household effects were granted temporary entry and consequently no customs duty was levied on them. The number of such shipments is expected to reach approximately 2,000;

(e)   Children of visitors have been given places in Syrian schools and universities and accepted provisionally until such time as they can produce the required school certificates;

(f)   Kuwaiti hotel guests have been exempted from paying their hotel bills in foreign currency as an exception from the customary rules.

0245   /...

As a result of these exceptions and facilities, the State Treasury has been deprived of tax revenue estimated at $31 million.

Moreover, law No. 109 of 1989 required every Syrian working abroad to pay a yearly duty in foreign currency. The amount of this duty depends on the professional level of the expatriate in the country in which he works. The duty varies between $50 for an ordinary unskilled worker and $700 for a businessman, industrialist or professional. The annual revenue from this duty with regard to the Syrian workforce in Kuwait is estimated at approximately $18 million, of which the State Treasury has been deprived as a result of the crisis (see appendix IV).

E. Kuwaiti grant to the Syrian Arab Republic

As part of economic cooperation between the Syrian Arab Republic and Kuwait, the Government of Kuwait pays for Syrian imports of urea fertilizer from Kuwait, the value of which is $50 million per year. In view of current circumstances, the import of this product has stopped.

F. Revenue from the transit of Iraqi oil

As we have indicated, Syrian observance of international resolutions, which call for a halt of commercial transactions with Iraq, has led to a suspension of the agreement in principle which had been reached to resume pumping of Iraqi oil through the Syrian Arab Republic and to provide the Syrian Arab Republic with 4 million barrels of oil per year at under 50 per cent of the market price. The loss resulting from the halting of work under the agreement is estimated at approximately $360 million per year. This sum represents the expected revenue from the transit of the oil and the differential of the reduced price of Iraqi oil which the Syrian Arab Republic would have obtained.

III. INDIRECT ECONOMIC LOSSES

As is apparent from the foregoing, the total direct economic losses resulting from the Gulf crisis are approximately $2,179 million (see appendix V). However, this does not account for the true damage inflicted on the Syrian economy as a result of the crisis. The economic consequences of the direct losses and the ensuing complications and psychological factors has resulted in damage and losses which are greater in volume than the direct losses inflicted on the Syrian economy. It is expected that the impact of these complications will continue for a long time, giving rise to vicious circles and new losses before government efforts are able to contain them. In the absence of sufficient data, the enumeration of these complications and the estimation of the consequent losses is impractical. However, in the light of economic laws, it is legitimate to forecast some of what may happen. For example, the decrease in foreign exchange earnings will upset the balance of payments, for which severe austerity measures had been adopted in recent years. This decrease will also affect the capacity of the economy to cover the costs of a sufficient quantity of imports into the country of raw materials,

0246   /...

equipment and other production inputs, which in turn will have an adverse effect on production levels and employment.

One of the main inflationary effects of the crisis has been the fall in the exchange rate of the Syrian pound in neighbouring markets, which will raise the cost of imports and consequently the cost of commodities and services, in particular those which are not subject to government price controls. It will also lessen the true value of interest on bank deposits, which may affect the growth rates of the volume of deposits.

The decrease in exports will lead to a decrease in production levels in some sectors and a reduction in the growth of the gross national product. In addition to all this, the psychological impact of the crisis and the fear of not being able to contain it will curtail expansion and investment by the private sector in commodity production and service enterprises.

Appendix I

ESTIMATE OF THE LOSSES OF THE SYRIAN COMMUNITY IN KUWAIT

(Millions of Kuwaiti dinars) a/

Businessmen, contractors, craftsmen (20,000)

Key money and equipment of commercial premises (20,000 premises x KD 30,000 x 100%)	600
Stock (20,000 premises x 40,000 x 80%)	630
Commercial vehicles (20,000 x KD 5,000 x 80%)	80
Depreciation of deposits and liquid assets (20,000 x KD 20,000 x 93%)	372
Unpaid obligations and lost deposits (20,000 x KD 5,000 x 100%)	100
Miscellaneous losses (20,000 x KD 2,000 x 100%)	40
Subtotal	1 832

Employed persons (30,000)

Separation from service indemnities (30,000 workers x KD 500 x 10 years x 100%)	150
Depreciation of deposits and liquid assets (30,000 x KD 10,000 x 93%)	279
Lost deposits (30,000 x KD 1,000 x 100%)	30
Subtotal	459

Residential property and related losses for both categories (50,000)

Furniture, domestic appliances, clothing (50,000 x KD 10,000 x 60%)	300
Valuables and jewellery (50,000 x KD 2,000 x 50%)	50
Private vehicles (10,000 vehicles x KD 2,000 x 100%)	20
Subtotal	370
Total	2 661

---

a/ The value in United States dollars should be calculated on the basis of $1 = KD 0.29.

Appendix II

ESTIMATE OF THE DECREASE IN VALUE OF TRANSFERS

1.	Total value of private-sector imports except Kuwait (official statistics)	$868 million
2.	25 per cent of public-sector imports (official statistics)	$302 million
3.	Total value of exports financed by available transfers (1+2)	$1,170 million
4.	Contribution of the Syrian community in Kuwait to the above value (assumed)	30 per cent
5.	Estimated value of the contribution of the Syrian community in Kuwait to financing imports (3x4)	$351 million
6.	Total value of private-sector imports from Kuwait (official statistics)	$25 million
7.	Contribution of the Syrian community to financing these imports (assumed)	60 per cent
8.	Contribution of the Syrian community to financing imports from Kuwait (6x7)	$15 million
9.	Average individual foreign currency savings among the workforce at home (estimate)	$5,600
10.	Syrian workforce in Kuwait (estimate)	50 000 workers
11.	Value of remittances deposited at home in foreign currency (9x10)	$280 million
12.	Value of transfers in kind each year per worker in Kuwait (estimate)	$2,400
13.	Total value of transfers in kind (10x12)	$120 million
14.	Other contributions of the Syrian community to financing imports (3-5)	$819 million
15.	Decrease in remittances from other communities (assumed)	10 per cent
16.	Decrease in remittances from other communities (14x15)	$82 million

0249 /...

Appendix III

ESTIMATE OF FOREIGN CURRENCY LOSSES IN THE TOURIST SECTOR

Nationality	Number of visitors in 1989 (thousands of visitors)	Average number of tourist nights per visitor before the crisis	Percentage decrease in the number of tourist nights because of the crisis	Decrease in the number of tourist nights because of the crisis (thousands of tourist nights)
1	2	3	4	5 = 2 x 3 x 4
Kuwaitis	14	20	100	280
Gulf Arabs	102	20	100	2 040
Jordanians and Lebanese	701	1	20	140
Other Arabs	80	5	25	100
Iranians	208	10	15	312
Turks	140	3	25	105
Other	118	2	20	47
Total	1 363			3 024

The loss in foreign currency is: 3,024 tourist nights x $150 = $453.6 million.

Appendix IV

ESTIMATE OF THE LOSS TO THE STATE TREASURY FROM TAXES AND DUTIES

(Thousands of United States dollars)

Emigration duty

20,000 expatriates x $600 + 30,000 expatriates x $200	18 000

Entry duty on vehicles

15,000 cars x $115	1 725

Prolonged stay duty on vehicles

15,000 vehicles x $115 x 3	5 175

Customs duties on accompanying effects

15,000 vehicles x $1,000 x 25 per cent	3 750

Customs duties on furniture shipments

2,000 shipments x 10,000 x 75 per cent	15 000

Educational and other administrative services (rough estimate)	5 000
Total	48 650

Appendix V

TOTAL DIRECT ECONOMIC LOSSES

(Millions of United States dollars)

Decrease in transfers

Transfers from Kuwait

Money transfers (financing of imports)	366		
Money transfers (from savings at home)	280		
Transfers in kind (goods, presents)	<u>120</u>		
Subtotal		766	
Decrease in transfers from Syrians abroad elsewhere		<u>82</u>	
Total			848

Losses in foreign trade

Exports

To Kuwait	22		
To other Gulf countries and Jordan	58		
To Iraq	<u>100</u>		
Subtotal		180	
Imports		150	
Transit duties		<u>100</u>	
Total			415

Losses from tourism

Total	454

Losses from oil

Losses due to suspension of the Iraqi transit agreement	300	
Losses due to the differential of the reduced prices of Iraqi oil	<u>60</u>	
Total		360

0252   /...

<u>Loss of foreign grants and aids</u>

Grant from Kuwait (urea fertilizer)

    Total   50

<u>Losses to the State Treasury from taxes, duties and services</u>

Emigration duties	18	
Duties on importing vehicles into the country and prolonging their stay	7	
Customs duties on shipments of furniture and accompanying effects	19	
Administrative services and fees for visitors	5	
Educational services	3	
Total		52
Overall losses to the national economy		2 179

Annex II

Recommendation by the Security Council Committee established by resolution 661 (1990) concerning the situation between Iraq and Kuwait with regard to Djibouti

The Security Council Committee established by resolution 661 (1990) concerning the situation between Iraq and Kuwait,

Having dealt with the communication received from Djibouti under Article 50 of the Charter of the United Nations, a/

Recalling Security Council resolution 661 (1990) of 6 August 1990 in which the Council decided to impose sanctions in accordance with Chapter VII of the Charter, as well as Security Council resolutions 660 (1990) of 2 August 1990, 662 (1990) of 9 August 1990, 664 (1990) of 18 August 1990, 665 (1990) of 25 August 1990, 666 (1990) of 13 September 1990, 667 (1990) of 16 September 1990, 669 (1990) of 24 September 1990, 670 (1990) of 25 September 1990, 674 (1990) of 29 October 1990 and 686 (1991) of 2 March 1991,

Recalling also the provisions of Articles 25, 49 and 50 of the Charter,

Noting the information given by Djibouti a/ regarding the measures taken to give full effect to the sanctions as laid down in Security Council resolution 661 (1990), and concerning the special economic problems it has been confronted with as a result of the implementation of those measures,

Having heard the statement of the representative of Djibouti,

Expressing concern at the special economic problems confronting Djibouti, a least developed country, as a result of the severance of its economic relations with Iraq and occupied Kuwait, as required by Security Council resolution 661 (1990), which are particularly difficult in terms of commercial and financial losses incurred by Djibouti,

Recognizing that the continued full implementation of Security Council resolution 661 (1990) by Djibouti, as well as other States, will support the measures to ensure compliance with paragraph 2 of that resolution,

1.   Commends the Government of Djibouti for the measures it has taken to comply with Security Council resolution 661 (1990);

2.   Recognizes the urgent need to assist Djibouti in coping with its special economic problems resulting from the severance of its economic relations with Iraq and occupied Kuwait, as required by Security Council resolution 661 (1990),

---

a/   S/22209, annex.

0254   /...

especially those losses resulting from undelivered products and suspended capital flows from Kuwait and Iraq, as well as other commercial and financial losses incurred by Djibouti;

3.   Appeals to all States on an urgent basis to provide immediate technical, financial and material assistance to Djibouti to mitigate the adverse impact on its economy of the application by Djibouti of sanctions against Iraq pursuant to Security Council resolution 661 (1990);

4.   Invites the competent organs and specialized agencies of the United Nations system, including the international financial institutions, and the regional development banks, to review their programmes of assistance to Djibouti with a view to alleviating its special economic problems arising from the application of sanctions against Iraq pursuant to Security Council resolution 661 (1990);

5.   Requests the Secretary-General, on a regular basis, to seek information from States and the concerned organs and agencies of the United Nations system on action taken to alleviate the special economic problems of Djibouti and to report thereon to the Security Council.

Enclosure

Immediate consequences for Djibouti of the Persian Gulf conflict

Just as is the case with all the conflicts arising in the area, the Djiboutian economy is undergoing at the present time a series of changes in the aftermath of the crisis, which has simultaneously taken a toll on its budget and the working order of the structures in all sectors.

Short term

1. Cost of stabilization of oil product prices

The initial effect of the current crisis in the Gulf is an increase in the cost of oil prices. During the last five years, the "Etablissement public pour les hydrocarbures" (public establishment for hydrocarbons) (EPH), created to stabilize the prices of oil products, has consistently generated a financial surplus, which the Treasury often resorted to whenever in difficulty. Thus, 1.2 billion Djibouti francs (DF) ($6.8 million) have in practice been contributed to the Treasury annually from this source. The year 1990, expected to be a year for the refurbishing of the fragile budgetary resources through external sources, will experience, owing to the increase in the price of oil products, a shortfall of at least DF 1.8 billion ($10.2 million) merely for the stabilization measures. The overall cost to the State towards the stabilization of the prices of the oil products will therefore reach the amount of DF 3 billion ($17 million).

With the additional bill that the Electricity Generating Board of Djibouti (EDD) will have to pay and which represents the only energy source for the production of electricity in the country, the total induced economic cost is DF 3.7 billion ($21 million), which will add an extra DF 0.7 billion to the bill of the oil imports mentioned above.

2. Loss of fiscal revenues on trading business with neighbouring countries

Without taking into account for the moment the loss relative to the commercial activity with the neighbouring Gulf countries, which is estimated at more than DF 12 billion ($68 million) as a direct loss of revenue owing to the sharp fall in the volume of trade, the State budget will forgo a further DF 1.5 billion ($8.5 million).

Consequently, owing to the new situation in the Gulf, the State budget will undergo a serious strain in the current fiscal year:

(a) Loss of earnings by EPH: DF 1.5 billion ($8.5 million);

(b) Decrease in EPH reserve: DF 1.2 billion ($6.8 million);

0256   /...

(c) Replenishment of the EPH stabilization fund: DF 1.8 billion ($10.2 million);

(d) Compensation to EDD to maintain the current rate of electricity: DF 700 million ($4 million).

Total budgetary constraints under this category are DF 5.2 billion ($30 million).

3. Higher importation and transport costs

Without in any way minimizing the adverse impact of external and internal economic factors operating in Djibouti and taking into account the daily upswing in the general price, the rise in the air and maritime transport costs is just another sign of the abnormality of the international situation. We must admit that a rise of no less than 15 per cent will hit our total imports. The loss to our economy will be at least DF 5.25 billion ($30 million), which will affect our foreign reserves and will further disrupt the livelihood of the population. This is, of course, a direct corollary of the risks engulfing our region as a result of the conflict.

4. Activities of small businesses

The volume of transactions of small businesses with the countries of the Gulf region is estimated at DF 12 billion ($67.7 million) a year at least. A loss in the amount of nearly DF 4 billion ($22.6 million) has been estimated. This activity is usually carried out by families without fixed income that constitute the informal sector of our economy.

5. Suspension of implementation of externally funded projects by Kuwait

Taking into account only those projects that are now in the process of execution through financing from the Arab Fund for Economic and Social Development in Kuwait, Djibouti is definitely confronted with the indefinite suspension of two important projects:

(a) The second phase of the extension of the container terminal at the port. This hold-up will frustrate our development strategy for the next decade. The programme involved the extension of the platform of the container terminal plus civil engineering works, at a cost of DF 3,375 million ($19 million), of which half was to be provided by Kuwait and the remaining balance by Saudi Arabia;

(b) Rehabilitation and extension of the airport. Only recently a contractor was selected and is in the process of executing the project.

Together with Saudi Arabia and the United Arab Emirates, Kuwait is also a major financier of this project, putting in almost 50 per cent of the overall

/...

0257

requirements: DF 1,462 million ($8.25 million). The project covers the improvement of facilities, renovation of the runway and development studies.

6. Other projects fully funded by Kuwait

(a) Ministry of Education. A Junior high school planned to be constructed at Balbala at a total cost of DF 540 million ($3 million);

(b) Electricity Generating Board of Djibouti. A training centre under consideration for financing by the Arab Fund (in Kuwait) and the Kuwaiti Fund, estimated at DF 302 million ($1.7 million);

(c) Ministry of Interior, Posts and Telecommunications. A building annex scheduled to be constructed with financing from the Arab Fund (Kuwait) and the Kuwaiti Fund, estimated at DF 264 million ($1.5 million);

(d) Ministry of Agriculture and Rural Development. Institutional reinforcement estimated at DF 30 million ($170,000) was expected to be financed by the Arab Fund (in Kuwait).

7. Projects with Iraq

Several development projects on the basis of outright grants were under serious consideration by the Iraqi Government prior to the present crisis. These chiefly consisted of:

(a) Construction of 150 low-cost housing units, including civil engineering works, estimated at DF 4.5 billion ($25.5 million);

(b) Provision and plantation of 55,000 date palms for environmental reasons, and the estimate was DF 980 million ($5.5 million).

The total value of projects with Iraq now in jeopardy as a result of this conflict is DF 5,550 million ($31.3 million).

0258

/...

Summary of adverse economic impact

	(billions of Djibouti francs)	(millions of dollars)
1. Stabilization cost of oil product prices:		
Fall of contribution to the public Treasury by EPH	1.2	6.8
Shortfall in the stabilization fund	1.8	10.2
Additional cost to the Electricity Board	0.7	4.0
Subtotal	3.7	21.0
2. Budget loss on small businesses		
Loss of revenue in the budget	1.5	8.5
3. Increase in the price of imported goods		
15 per cent of the total amount of imports	5.250	30.0
4. Reduction of trading in the informal sector (small businesses)		
Loss of revenues	4.0	22.6
5. Suspension of projects with Kuwaiti Fund and the Arab Fund		
Second-phase of the Djibouti post development	1.6	9.0
- Restoration of Djibouti airport	1.5	8.5
- Junior secondary school	0.540	3.0
- Training Centre, EDD	0.300	1.7
- Institutional reinforcement in agriculture	0.030	0.170
Subtotal	4.010	22.370

/...

	(billions of Djibouti francs)	(millions of dollars)
6. **Suspension of projects with Iraq**		
Construction of 150 units subsidized housing	4.5	25.5
Programme for 55,000 date palms	<u>0.980</u>	<u>5.5</u>
Subtotal	<u>5.480</u>	<u>31.0</u>
GRAND TOTAL	23.940	<u>a</u>/

<u>a</u>/   Approximately $140 million.

0260

UNITED
NATIONS

S

Security Council

Distr.
GENERAL

S/22358
18 March 1991
ENGLISH
ORIGINAL: FRENCH

LETTER DATED 15 MARCH 1991 FROM THE PERMANENT REPRESENTATIVE
OF FRANCE TO THE UNITED NATIONS ADDRESSED TO THE PRESIDENT
OF THE SECURITY COUNCIL

Pursuant to paragraph 4 of Security Council resolution 678 (1990), I have the honour to present to you a summary report on all the military operations carried out by the French armed forces with a view to the liberation of Kuwait, within the framework of the plans established jointly with the members of the coalition of countries cooperating with Kuwait.

Concerning ground forces, a division stationed in Saudi Arabia from the end of September 1990 to 23 February 1991 participated in the land offensive from 24 to 28 February, effecting a breakthrough and an encircling movement over a distance of 150 km. Two lives were lost, and 25 persons were wounded due to mine explosions.

Since 28 February, it has continued to ensure the safety of all the coalition forces facing the north-west.

Also since 28 February, a French detachment has been stationed in Kuwait City, in the compound of the French Embassy, which was able to reopen on the same day. Since that time, this detachment has responded to numerous requests from Kuwaiti and allied forces for assistance with mine-clearing operations, notably on the Kuwait City beach.

The Air Force deployed 48 combat aircraft and 22 support craft.

Until 17 January, our aircraft took part in missions for the air defence of the countries of the region.

From 17 January to 23 February, all our airborne forces were engaged in operations aimed at destroying hostile logistic installations and depots on the ground and weakening combat means to the greatest possible extent, with efforts also aimed at intelligence.

91-08691 2372b (E)   /...

0261

During the latter two phases, our Air Force carried out more than 2,700 sorties, including 826 ground attacks (bombing), 63 reconnaissance (intelligence) missions, 379 air defence missions and 1,460 support missions (in-flight refuelling, logistic transport, liaison).

As for naval forces, a regiment of combat helicopters embarked on an aircraft-carrier was put in place in the area on about 20 August 1990.

In addition, 12 vessels are taking part, either within a national framework or as part of EWU naval groups, in the monitoring of the Tiran, Bab al Mandab and Hormuz Straits: 7,612 vessels have been identified, 158 searched and 4 turned back.

Within the framework of the EWU naval groups, our vessels have also been engaged in escort, mine-clearing and straits surveillance operations.

French military operations ceased one hour before the announcement of the suspension of hostilities on 28 February, 0600 hours, Paris time.

I request you to have this letter circulated as a document of the Security Council.

(Signed) Pierre-Louis BLANC

0262

UNITED NATIONS

Security Council

Distr.
GENERAL

S/22350
14 March 1991
ENGLISH
ORIGINAL: ARABIC

S

LETTER DATED 14 MARCH 1991 FROM THE PERMANENT REPRESENTATIVE OF
SAUDI ARABIA TO THE UNITED NATIONS ADDRESSED TO THE PRESIDENT
OF THE SECURITY COUNCIL

In accordance with paragraph 4 of Security Council resolution 678 (1990), and pursuant to paragraphs 2 and 3 of the said resolution, I have pleasure in transmitting to you herewith an additional report on the progress of the military operations undertaken by the armed forces operating under the command of General Khalid bin Sultan bin Abdul Aziz, commander of the joint forces and the theatre of operations, during the period 18-24 February 1991.

I should be grateful if you would kindly have this report circulated as a document of the Security Council.

(Signed) Samir SHIHABI
Permanent Representative

91-08387 2202h (E)

/...

0263

<u>Annex</u>

Sir,

As you are aware, each of the States concerned has been notifying the Security Council, separately and consecutively, of the extent of the progress achieved in the measures that they are taking pursuant to paragraph 4 of Security Council resolution 678 (1990).

However, given the fact that the allied forces are stationed in the Kingdom of Saudi Arabia under our command, and in view of the joint endeavours that they are undertaking to liberate the sister State of Kuwait from Iraqi occupation and to restore international peace and security in the region, we have deemed it appropriate to save time and simplify the formalities, while achieving the same objective, by confining ourselves to a single joint report on all the collective measures and on the progress of the military operations of those forces, which I shall prepare and transmit to you, on behalf of those forces, in my capacity as commander of the joint forces and the theatre of operations.

Since the allied forces have a duty to implement the Security Council resolutions, during the fifth week of the operations the High Command diligently continued to weaken the Iraqi military machine and prepare the way for the ground campaign to recover the State of Kuwait while, at the same time, urging the pilots to avoid civilian targets and populated areas with a view to preventing civilian casualties or damage to civilian institutions.

I have pleasure in submitting the following first joint report:

The operations from 4 Sha'ban A.H. 1411 (18 February 1991) to 10 Sha'ban A.H. 1411 (24 February 1991) were conducted as follows:

1. <u>Military operations</u>

<u>Air</u>

The Royal Saudi Air Force flew 1,147 sorties against targets inside Iraq and Kuwait.

<u>Sea</u>

The Royal Saudi Navy took part in the naval operations. The total number of naval aircraft sorties on rescue missions and patrols amounted to 730.

<u>Land</u>

1. A mechanized infantry division, an armoured division and a commando brigade belonging to the Egyptian armed forces participated in the artillery bombardments of the enemy and also took part in the overall offensive.

0264/...

2.   A division and a commando brigade belonging to the Syrian armed forces participated in engagements with enemy patrols and also took part in the overall offensive.

3.   Saudi ground forces carried out artillery bombardments, engaged a number of enemy patrols and opened several breaches in the enemy's positions. They joined in the overall offensive as part of the joint forces.

During the past week, there was a notable intensification of engagements on the Saudi-Kuwaiti border, and also inside Kuwait itself, with a view to inflicting maximum losses on the Iraqi ground forces stationed there. The aerial bombardments also continued inside Iraq and Kuwait, prior to the commencement of the ground campaign, with a view to minimizing human casualties.

2.   Human casualties

These casualties were caused primarily by six Scud missiles which the Iraqi aggressor launched into the territory of the Kingdom of Saudi Arabia. The human casualties resulting from the battles that took place from the beginning of the offensive to the time of preparation of this report amounted to four killed, five wounded and four personnel carriers destroyed.

3.   Material damage

This damage consisted mainly in the destruction of a school, as well as structural damage to neighbouring buildings in the city of Riyadh, caused by a Scud missile launched by the enemy at 4.45 a.m. on Sunday, 10 Sha'ban A.H. 1411 (24 February 1991).

4.   Prisoners of war

The total number of Iraqi prisoners amounted to 141 officers and 1,899 other ranks, all of whom are receiving full care and attention and are being treated in accordance with the precepts of Islamic law and the provisions of the Third Geneva Convention of 1949. This treatment was commended by the team of the International Committee of the Red Cross.

Wishing to satisfy myself that the prisoners were being treated in a humanitarian and dignified manner in keeping with our Islamic ideals and principles, I paid an inspection visit to them during which I reassured myself in regard to their situation and proper treatment and issued the necessary directives in that connection to the responsible officials.

I should be grateful if you would kindly have this letter circulated as a document of the Security Council.

(Signed)   General Khalid bin Sultan bin Abdul Aziz
Commander of the joint forces and the
theatre of operations

0265

UNITED
NATIONS

Security Council

S

Distr.
GENERAL

S/22359
18 March 1991

ORIGINAL: ENGLISH

LETTER DATED 18 MARCH 1991 FROM THE PERMANENT REPRESENTATIVE OF
KUWAIT TO THE UNITED NATIONS ADDRESSED TO THE SECRETARY-GENERAL

I have the honour to transmit herewith the letter from His Highness
Sheikh Jaber Al-Ahmad Al-Sabah, Amir of the State of Kuwait, addressed to
Your Excellency.

I should appreciate it if you would arrange for this message to be circulated
as a document of the Security Council.

(Signed) Mohammad A. ABULHASAN
Ambassador
Permanent Representative

91-08704   2234e (E)   /...

0266

<u>Annex</u>

[Original: Arabic]

<u>Letter dated 5 March 1991 from His Highness the Amir of the State
of Kuwait addressed to the Secretary-General</u>

Thank you for the kind letter which you sent on the occasion of the end of the ordeal suffered by my country and my people and for the friendly feelings expressed in it towards Kuwait and its people. The people of Kuwait join me in expressing profound appreciation and immense gratitude towards the international community, represented by the United Nations, for its noble stand on the side of right and law, for its rejection of aggression, and for the collective resolutions adopted repeatedly by the Organization through the Security Council to restore justice and repel the aggressor. Moreover, I must praise your untiring personal efforts and the noble and scrupulous stand taken by you for the application of those resolutions.

You have earned our admiration and the admiration of the entire world for your tireless, persevering efforts to achieve a peaceful solution to this crisis from the outset. The important thing is that you made every effort in this respect with sincerity and integrity; yet you ran up against a frustrating, immovable wall of obstinacy. Without a doubt, the fact that your efforts to achieve a peaceful solution to the crisis met with failure is the sole responsibility of the aggressor, for he persisted in his aggression and his defiance of the will of the international community. Yet despite the overwhelming disaster that has befallen Kuwait, we now find some comfort in the fact that the international unity that came into being to repel the aggression has strengthened the position of the United Nations as an effective international Organization. The measures taken to restore justice now constitute an international precedent on which one can count and to which one will turn in future crises; what is more, they will be a powerful deterrent to any overbearing regime that feels tempted to swoop down upon a smaller State in order to engulf and control it.

Lastly, I thank you for the offer by the international Organization and your own personal offer of assistance. We shall turn to you for help whenever circumstances so require. I also assure you that the State of Kuwait will continue its commitment to the Charter of the United Nations and its strict compliance with it, as has always been the case in the past.

I extend my best wishes to you personally, and express my appreciation to the Organization for the work which it performed quietly yet untiringly throughout this crisis.

Jaber Al-Ahmad AL-SABAH
Amir of the State of Kuwait

0267

UNITED NATIONS

Security Council

S

Distr.
GENERAL

S/22361
19 March 1991

ORIGINAL: ENGLISH

LETTER DATED 19 MARCH 1991 FROM THE PRESIDENT OF THE
SECURITY COUNCIL ADDRESSED TO THE SECRETARY-GENERAL

With reference to Security Council resolution 686 (1991) which demands
<u>inter alia</u>, that Iraq "immediately begin to return all Kuwaiti property seized by
Iraq, to be completed in the shortest possible period", and with reference to the
identical letters dated 5 March 1991 from the Deputy Prime Minister and Minister
for Foreign Affairs of Iraq addressed respectively to the Secretary-General and the
President of the Security Council (S/22330) requesting to be informed of the
procedure for carrying out the hand-over, I should like to inform you that the
members of the Security Council are of the view that the modalities for return of
property from Iraq should be arranged through your office in consultation with the
parties.

This procedure also has the agreement of Iraq and Kuwait.

(<u>Signed</u>) Peter HOHENFELLNER
President of the Security Council

91-08828 2142i (E)

0268

Security Council

Distr.
GENERAL

S/22365
20 March 1991
ENGLISH
ORIGINAL: ARABIC

IDENTICAL LETTERS DATED 20 MARCH 1991 FROM THE PERMANENT
REPRESENTATIVE OF IRAQ TO THE UNITED NATIONS ADDRESSED
RESPECTIVELY TO THE SECRETARY-GENERAL AND THE PRESIDENT
OF THE SECURITY COUNCIL

On instructions from my Government, I have the honour to transmit to you an
annex to the letter dated 4 March 1991, addressed to you by Mr. Tariq Aziz, Deputy
Prime Minister and Minister for Foreign Affairs, to the effect that aircraft of the
United States Air Force have continued, since the cessation of hostilities on
28 February, to carry out constant flight operations in Iraqi air space and over
the cities in particular, in the form of a continual air umbrella during both day
and night. The details are as follows:

Date	Details
5 March	17 sorties concentrated over the city of Baghdad and the area to the west of it.
6 March	5 sorties concentrated in the region between Nasiriyah and Kut.
8 March	3 sorties concentrated in the region between Al-Ramadi and Tikrit.
9 March	2 sorties concentrated in the region between eastern Baghdad and Nasiriyah.
10 March	9 sorties concentrated in the region of Al-Haditha, northern Al-Ramadi, southern Baghdad and northern Kut.
11 March	7 sorties concentrated in the southern region between Nasiriyah and southern Baghdad, with one formation that went as far as the region of Mandali and another, as far as Al-Ramadi.
12 March	9 sorties concentrated over the city of Baghdad and between the cities of Kut and Nasiriyah.
13 March	1 sortie concentrated in the area between southern Kut and Al-Diwaniyah.

91-08981   2379b (E)   /...

0269

Date	Details
14 March	1 sortie in the region of western Amara, then in the direction of the city of Kut and the region of Al-Samawah.
16 March	100 formations, including a group of 192 aircraft over the city of Baghdad, the region of Mandali, eastern Tikrit, the cities of Kut and Karbala and the region of kilometre 160.
17 March	162 sorties divided among 107 formations concentrated in the regions of Al-Nukhayb, Kut, kilometre 160, Nasiriyah, Al-Samawah, Al-Diwaniyah, Tikrit, Mandali, Al-Najaf and Kirkuk, breaking the sound barrier over the city of Kirkuk.
18 March	67 formations, including a group of 148 aircraft concentrated in the region of western Al-Razazah and between Al-Hayy, Kut, northwestern Khanaqin, kilometre 160, Al-Rutbah, Al-Qadisiyah, Al-Najaf, Tharthar, Karbala, Kirkuk and Al-Ramadi.
19 March	208 sorties divided among 108 formations concentrated in the region of Al-Ramadi, eastern Al-Nukhayb, Samarra, Kut, Al-Hashimiyah, Baghdad (repeated sorties), Mandali, Al-Diwaniyah, Nasiriyah and Kirkuk.
20 March	288 sorties divided among 143 formations concentrated in the region of Al-Miqdadiyah, Suwayrah, Kut, Al-Razazah, Samarra, Tikrit, Al-Hashimiyah, Al-Habbaniyah and Baghdad.

It should be pointed out that the aircraft which took part in these umbrella operations were F-14s, F-15s and F-16s and that they flew at speeds ranging from 600 to 1,000 kilometres per hour and at altitudes ranging from 100 metres to 21 kilometres.

This continual air umbrella over the cities obviously causes a great disturbance and considerable anxiety to their civilian inhabitants, especially children, women, the elderly and the sick, causing them to experience unjustified terror. This leads one to wonder about the aim of the United States armed forces in carrying out these continuous air sorties over Iraq after having inflicted upon the Iraqi people devastation and widespread suffering that have shaken the foundations of their existence and deprived them of many of the essentials of daily life. The truth of the matter is that this is a primitive form of behaviour in which advanced technology is used for vindictive purposes and for terrorizing the Iraqi people. Human consciousness must remain alert with respect to this behaviour directed against the people of Iraq. And there can be no excuse for passing over it in silence.

We trust that the Security Council and the Secretary-General will take a stand in keeping with the dictates of the human conscience to stop this continual injury to the people of Iraq.

0270 /...

I request you to have this letter circulated as a document of the Security Council.

(Signed) Abdul Amir AL-ANBARI
Ambassador
Permanent Representative

0271

외 무 부

종 별 :

번 호 : UNW-0651 　　　　　　　　　　　일 시 : 91 0322 1700

수 신 : 장 관(국연,중동일,기정)

발 신 : 주 유엔 대사

제 목 : 걸프사태

　　1.쿠웨이트 피해상황 파악을 위해 현재 동국방문중인 유엔조사단 (단장: A .FARAH전사무차장)활동에 관한 유엔측 발표내용을 별첨송부함.

　　2.금 3.22. 배포된 표제관련 주요 안보리 문서는 다음과같음.

　　가.이락 T.AZIZ 외상의 안보리 의장앞 3.20자서한 (S/22371): 이란으로 부터의 다수 무장인원 침부활동 비난

　　나.쿠웨이트측이 3.14. 안보리 의장에게 제출한 이락에 의한 강취재산 예비 명세서 (S/22367): 금 (약 127만 온스), 금.은화, 민간항공기 15대, 공문서 및 도서류.

　　첨부:상기 유엔조사단 활동내용: UNW(F)-126

끝

　　(대사 노창희-국장)

국기국	1차보	중아국	정문국	안기부	

0651   UNW(H)-126   10322 170   총1매
                       (국연 . 중동일 . 기정)

March 20, 1991

        Concerning the special mission of former Under-Secretary-General
Abdulrahim Farah to Kuwait, Mr. Giuliani said that today Mr. Farah had met
Kuwait's Crown Prince and Prime Minister Sheikh Saad Abdullah Al-Sabah.
During the meeting, they had discussed the mandate of the mission, its
progress of work and the difficulties it was encountering in discharging its
task. In addition, the Crown Prince had expressed his appreciation for the
United Nations and the mission and promised to provide all necessary
assistance to expedite its work, particularly logistical support. Mr. Farah
would also meet this evening with members of the diplomatic community in
Kuwait City to discuss issues relevant to the mandate of the mission.

        Yesterday, continued Mr. Giuliani, Mr. Farah had met with Sheikh Nasser
Al-Sabah to review the progress of work of the mission and to coordinate its
activities with the Kuwaiti Government. At the same time, members of the
special mission had meetings with their counterparts and visited a number of
damaged sites. Mr. Giuliani said further details were available in a press
release — in room 378, after the briefing — which would be on the third
floor racks later this afternoon

March 21, 1991

        As far as the special mission of former Under-Secretary-General
Abdulrahim A. Farah to Kuwait was concerned, said Mr. Giuliani, the mission
had met yesterday with members of the diplomatic community in Kuwait, at which
time Mr. Farah had briefed them on the terms of reference of the mission
in so far as they related to human rights and the environment. The diplomatic
community had promised its full support to the mission. Concerning the
environment, Michael Gwynne of the United Nations Environment Programme (UNEP)
had briefed the assembled group. He explained that the mission would examine
changes in the infrastructure of environment and environment-related sectors,
such as agriculture, fisheries and meteorology.

        Concerning human rights, Mr. Giuliani said that other members of the
Farah mission held meetings with non-governmental associations in Kuwait. At
a meeting at the Centre for the Registration of Missing Persons, the team had
been informed that the Centre had compiled a list of over 11,000 persons —
including Kuwaiti citizens and non-Kuwaitis — whose whereabouts were
unknown. Mr. Giuliani said additional details on the Farah mission would be
available in room 378 after the briefing and later this afternoon as a press
release

                        1 - 1   :   0273

외 무 부

종 별 :

번 호 : UNW-0667   일 시 : 91 0322 2200

수 신 : 장 관(국연,중동일,기정,해기)

발 신 : 주 유엔 대사

제 목 : 걸프사태(안보리)

연: UNW-0641

1. 금 3.22. 안보리 제재위원회는 연호 유엔조사단의 이락방문결과 보고서 (S/22366) 을 검토한바, 식품류를 비롯한 인도적 목적의 품목에 대하여 대이락 금수해제조치를 결정하였음.(상세 별첨참조).동 조치는 식품류외에 동 식품류, 의약품과 관련되는 민간용 및 인도적 목적의 수입품 (CIVILIAN ANDHUMANITARIAN IMPORTS) 에도 적용되는바, 이는 유엔조사단의 건의를 수용한것임.

2.안보리는 동일 5시부터 약2시간동안 비공식협의를 갖고, 상기 제재위원회의 결정을 이의없이 접수 (TAKE NOTE) 키로 하였으며, 동결정 이행과 관련되는 후속조치 및 추가해제조치 문제에 관하여는 2.25. 의장이 이사국들과 개별협의를 진행키로 합의하였음.

3.이락방문결과 보고를 위해 일시귀국한 M.AHTISAARI 조사단장은 금주말 쿠웨이트에서 단원들과 합류예정임.

4.한편 연호 정식휴전 결의안과 관련 현재상임 이사국들간에 문안 협의가 진행중이며, 동결과는 다음주중에나 나올 것으로 관측되고있음.

첨부:상기 제재위원회 결정내용: UNW(F)-129

끝

(대사 노창희-국장)

국기국	1차보	중아국	정문국	안기부	공보처	

PAGE 1

91.03.23   12:11 WG

외신 1과 통제관

0274

#UNW-0667
첨부

UNW(布)-129 1032L 2200
(국연.중동일.기정. 해기)

총 2DH
P.1

SECURITY COUNCIL COMMITTEE ESTABLISHED
BY RESOLUTION 661 (1990) CONCERNING THE
SITUATION BETWEEN IRAQ AND KUWAIT

S/AC.25/1991/WP.1
22 March 1991
ORIGINAL: ENGLISH

Decision taken by the Security Council Committee established by
resolution 661 (1990) concerning the situation between Iraq and
Kuwait at its 36th meeting, on 22 March 1991, with regard to
the determination of humanitarian needs in Iraq

1.   The Security Council Committee established by resolution 661
(1990) concerning the situation between Iraq and Kuwait has carefully
considered Under-Secretary-General Ahtisaari's report of 20 March 1991
on his recent visit to Iraq (S/22366), as well as the report of the
ICRC of 19 March 1991 (S/AC.25/1991/COMM.102) summarizing the
conclusions of its own delegation in Iraq.

2.   Under paragraph 5 of resolution 666 (1990), the Committee has
the power to determine, after receiving all relevant reports and
information, that circumstances have arisen in which there is an
urgent humanitarian need to supply foodstuffs to Iraq in order to
relieve human suffering; and in that event the Committee will report
promptly to the Council its decision as to how such needs will be met.

3.   In the light of the new information available to it, the
Committee has decided to make, with immediate effect, a general
determination that humanitarian circumstances apply with respect to
the entire civilian population of Iraq in all parts of Iraq's national
territory. The Committee has also concluded that civilian and
humanitarian imports to Iraq as identified in Mr. Ahtisaari's report
are integrally related to the supply of foodstuffs and supplies
intended strictly for medical purposes (which are exempt from
sanctions under the provisions of resolution 661 (1990)) and that such
imports should also be allowed with immediate effect.

/...

2-1

0275

-4-

4.   The Committee decides upon a simple notification procedure for foodstuffs supplied to Iraq and a no-objection procedure for those civilian and humanitarian imports (other than supplies intended strictly for medical purposes) described in the preceding paragraph.

5.   Subject to prior notification to the Committee of the flight and its contents, the Committee hereby gives general approval under paragraph 4 (b) of resolution 670 (1990) for all flights which carry only foodstuffs or supplies intended strictly for medical purposes. This procedure applies equally to the civilian and humanitarian imports referred to in paragraph 3 above, the supply of which is subject to the no-objection procedure laid down in paragraph 4.

6.   It notes with satisfaction that the Government of Iraq has assured Mr. Ahtisaari's mission that it would accept a system of monitoring of imports and their utilization. The Secretary-General is requested, in consultation with the Government of Iraq and the ICRC, to arrange for such a system of on the spot monitoring to proceed in conjunction with the despatch of United Nations personnel to Iraq to supervise the effective utilization, for the benefit of the civilian population in all areas, of all imports to be established under the responsibility of the United Nations.

2 - 2

0276

외 무 부

종 별 :

번 호 : UNW-0688   일 시 : 91 0325 2030

수 신 : 장 관(국연,중동일,법규,기정,해기)

발 신 : 주 유엔대사

제 목 : 걸프사태(안보리)

연: UNW-0667

1. 연호 3.22. 안보리 재재위원회의 대 이락 금수일부 완화 결정과 관련 원종찬참 사관이 동위원회 의장국인 오지리 대표부(G.JANDL서기관)로 부터 입수한 참고사항은 아래와같음.

가. 3.22 제재 완화 조치는 식품류(FOODSTUFFS) 에 대해서는 형식적인 반입 봉보만으로 충분하므로 실질적인 금수해제를 의미함.(의약품은 처음부터 제재대상에서제외), 연호 민수용의 인도적품목의 경우 절차상 이의 불제기(NO-OBJECTION)를 요건으로 하고있어 일정한 경우 불허 결정을 유보하고 있으나, 동절차의 취지는 반입을용이하게하려는데 있음.

나. 90.8월 대 이락 제제 결정이후 제재위원회가 접수한 반입신청 또는 봉보 현황은 다음과같음.

1)반입신청:식품류 9개국(예멘, 터키 인도 이란벨지움 독일 리비아 요르단 그리스), 전부허가

2)반입봉보 :의약품 (오지리 일본 독일 덴마크 모리타니아 리비아 인도등), 제재대상이 아니므로 제재위원회의 참고를 위한 봉보

다. 금 3.25. 현재 안보리 의장(P. HOHENFELLNER) 은 인도적 목적을 위한 상기 제 재조치 완화 결정과관련 후속 및 추가조치 문제를 이사국들과 개별 협의중임.

이사국들중 쿠바, 예멘은 인도적 품목에 관한 금수 전면해제 및인도적 원조공여에 관한 결의안 제출 가능성을 시사하고 있음. (UNW-0491 첨부 3참조)

2. 한편 현재 안보리 상임 이사국들간에 정식 휴전결의 문안 교섭이 계속 진행중인 것으로알려짐.

3. 금 3.25. 배포된 표제 관련 주요 안보리 문서는다음과 같음.

국기국   중아국   국기국   안기부   공보처

PAGE 1   91.03.26   11:23 CT

외신 1과 통제관

0277

가. 이란 대사의 사무총장앞 3.23.자 서한(S/22379):이락에 대한 내정간섭 부인,이락의 잔혹행위비난

나. 이락대사의 사무총장앞 3.24.자 서한(S/22380):미국의 이락군용기 격추 및 미군용기의 이락영공 비행비난.끝

(대사 노창희-국장)

PAGE 2

0278

외 무 부

종 별 :

번 호 : UNW-0694   일 시 : 91 0326 1830

수 신 : 장 관(국연,중동일,기정)

발 신 : 주 유엔 대사

제 목 : 걸프사태(경제제재 조치)

연: UNW-0632

안보리 결의 661호 (경제제재조치) 이행에 따른 자국의 특별한 경제문제와 관련 연호 개도국 및 동구권 21개국은 안보리 의장앞으로 3.22.자 공동각서 (S/22382)를 제출한바, 동각서내용을 별첨송부함.

첨부:상기 각서: UNW(F)-132

끝

(대사 노창희-국장)

국기국   1차보   중아국   정문국   안기부

PAGE 1   91.03.27   10:47 WG
                                 외신 1과 롱제관

0279

UNW-6694   UNW(斤)-132   10326 (handwritten)   S/22382
철부   (국연·중동일·기저)   English
                                                           Page 3

<u>Annex</u>

MEMORANDUM

1.   By resolution 669 (1990), the Security Council entrusted its Committee
established by resolution 661 (1990) with the task of examining requests for
assistance under the provisions of Article 50 of the Charter of the United
Nations. It was the first time that a large number of States addressed the
Security Council on the basis of this Article.

2.   All the 21 States addressing the Security Council under Article 50 of the
Charter emphasized their full adherence to the relevant Security Council
resolutions relating to the Gulf crisis and their solidarity with the international
community. They expressed their firm determination to continue to comply fully
with the provisions of resolution 661 (1990), in spite of the grave economic,
financial and commercial losses incurred as a result of implementation of
sanctions, which are estimated at more than $US 30 billion.

3.   The Security Council Committee considered the cases referred to it and by the
recommendations adopted, launched individual appeals to all States and specialized
agencies of the United Nations and international financial institutions to provide
urgent assistance to the affected States in order to mitigate the adverse economic
and social problems confronted by them.

4.   The problems affecting these countries persist, and in certain respects have
been aggravated, while the appeals launched pursuant to the recommendations of the
Security Council Committee and addressed to all concerned by the Secretary-General,
have not evoked responses commensurate with the urgent needs of the affected
countries.

5.   Assistance to the affected countries in accordance with Article 50 of the
Charter would reaffirm international solidarity and unity.

6.   The 21 States launch a collective appeal, particularly to all donor States, to
respond urgently and effectively in providing assistance to the affected countries
by allocating additional financial resources both through bilateral channels and by
supporting the actions of the competent organs and specialized agencies of the
United Nations system.

7.   The 21 States most seriously affected believe that it is essential that all
Member States, as well as the United Nations, the specialized agencies and other
international organizations of the United Nations system, take all appropriate
action to cooperate with them in the fields of trade, employment, economic
assistance and other areas, in order to alleviate the difficult economic problems
facing them.

8.   The affected countries believe that, given the magnitude of the difficulties
they face, the Security Council should give renewed attention to these problems
with a view to finding quick and effective solutions.

-----

1 -1

0280

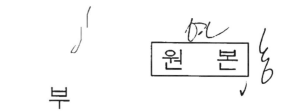

외 무 부

종 별 :

번 호 : UNW-0715 일 시 : 91 0327 2030

수 신 : 장 관(국연,중동일,기정,해기)

발 신 : 주 유엔 대사

제 목 : 걸프사태(안보리)

연: UNW-697

1. 금 3.27 오후 현재 상임이사국들간 연호 휴전결의문안 교섭이 계속되고 있는바, 소련측이 약간의 문안수정을 제기하고 있는 것으로 알려짐.

2. 상기와같이 공식적인 상임이사국 합의문안이 나오지 않는 상태이나, 연호 교섭문안과 관련 비상임이사국 (비동맹국가)들이 동 문안중 국경보장, 경제제재 (특히, 인도적 품목에 대한 허가제), 이락 군사력제한 정도 문제에 대해 상당히 유보적인 반응을 보이고 있는 것으로 알려짐.

3. 한편, M.AHTISAARI 조사단은 금주중 쿠웨이트 조사임무를 마칠 예정이며, A.FARAH 조사단도 다음주 귀환할 것으로 보임.

4. 표제관련 금 3.27 배포된 주요 안보리문서는 다음과 같음.

가. 사무총장의 안보리 의장앞 3.26자 서한 (S/22387): 쿠웨이트 재산반환 관련 업무담당관 지정 (R.FORAN 사무차장보)

나. 쿠웨이트 대사의 사무총장앞 3.26자 서한 (S/22389): 팔레스타인계 주민 탄압사실 부인

다. 이란대사의 사무총장앞 3.26자 서한 (S/22401): 이락에 대한 간섭사실 부인, 이락측의 이란-이락간 휴전협정 위반사례 제기

첨부: 상기 휴전결의(안)관련 3.27자 NYT 지사설. 끝

(대사 노창희-국장)

국기국   1차보   중아국   정문국   안기부   공보처

PAGE 1

The U.N. Squeezes Iraq

The United Nations seems about to crown military success in the Persian Gulf with hard but equitable peace terms. The conditions for a cease-fire set forth in a draft resolution before the Security Council are remarkable in both their sweep and precision. For Iraq, the price for cessation of hostilities is willingness to destroy terror weapons, pay a portion of its oil revenues into a U.N.-administered reparations fund and recognize the inviolability of Kuwait's frontiers.

The council's five permanent members — the United States, the Soviet Union, Britain, France and China — are close to final agreement on this landmark resolution. That would clear the way for likely approval by the council as a whole, meaning that Iraq will actually be held accountable for its high crimes against the family of nations.

The cease-fire terms would put U.N. observers in a demilitarized zone between Iraq and Kuwait, so that U.S. forces could withdraw to the safer confines of Kuwait and out of a crossfire in Iraq.

If Saddam Hussein rejects U.N. terms, the state of war will continue; so will the presence of foreign forces on Iraqi soil. Punitive economic sanctions would also remain in place, with an exception allowed for "materials and supplies for essential civilian needs." These levers provide real pressure against a tyrannical regime fighting for its life against Kurdish and Shiite insurgents.

Yet if Saddam Hussein accepts the harsh terms, he will be ending a war in which Iraq gained

nothing with a peace in which Iraq's military power has been radically reduced, a dire outcome for which he would be personally accountable to the Iraqi people. It is a fittingly bitter dilemma, and his only real choice may be compliance.

The U.N.'s draft terms are deservedly punitive and preventive in calling for the destruction and removal of chemical and biological weapons, plus all ballistic delivery systems — i.e. Scuds. This would be subject to on-site scrutiny by a special commission. Iraq would also be required to renounce nuclear weapons and place all its weapons-grade nuclear material under international custody for removal.

As compensation to victims of Iraqi aggression, a percentage of Iraq's petroleum revenues would be allotted to a special international fund to meet claims for injuries to people and property, including damage to the environment. The principle is surely just, though it may be some time before a devastated Iraq can make a substantial contribution. Every bit as just is insistence that Baghdad once and for all recognize, as it did in 1963, the sovereign frontiers of Kuwait.

From every vantage, these seem the outlines for a safe and reasonable settlement that is consistent with U.N. resolutions and responsive to security fears of Iraq's neighbors. And by their rigor and breadth, these are terms calculated to discourage other regional bullies with covetous designs on vulnerable smaller states.

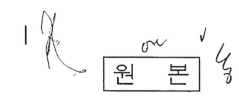

외 무 부

종 별 :

번 호 : UNW-0697　　　　　　　　　　일 시 : 91 0326 1930

수 신 : 장 관(국연,중동일,기정,해기)

발 신 : 주 유엔 대사

제 목 : 걸프사태(안보리)

1.미,영등 관련국 대표부 및 당지언론보도에 의하면, 안보리 상임이사국들간의 정식휴전 결의문안 협의가 막바지에 이른것으로 보이는바 (빠르면 3.27 문안 타결가능성) , 이락의 군사력제한 및 63년 이락-쿠웨이트간 국경합의 보장문제가 주요쟁점이 되어온 것으로 알려짐. 3.26오후현재 상기 상임이사국 (PERM-5) 간 교섭문안은 당관에서 입수한 별첨초안을 참조바람. (동 문안에 대해 미,영,불은 일단이의 없다고하며, 소련은 본부훈령 대기중, 중국은 입장유보 중인것으로 알려짐.)

2.인도적 원조수요 파악을 위한 유엔조사단 (단장:M.AHTISAARI 사무차장)은 이락방문 (3.10-17)에 이어 현재 쿠웨이트에서 조사활동중인바, 금주중 임무를 마칠수 있을 것으로 알려짐.

3.금 3.26 배포된 표제관련 주요 안보리문서는 다음과같음.

가.3.21.자 이락대사의 안보리 의장앞 서한 (S/22370): 이락 혁명위 쿠웨이트 병합 무효조치관련 관보게재(3.18) 통보

나.3.21.자 이락대사의 안보리 의장앞 서한 (S/22375): 쿠웨이트 금괴, 지폐, 주화반환예정 (10억불 이상 상당)

다.3.22자 쿠웨이트 대사의 안보리 의장앞 서한 (S/22395): 이락측의 안보리결의 686 호 이행상의문제점 (쿠웨이트 억류자송환, 쿠웨이트병합무효화, 재산반환, 배상책임)

라.3.25.자 이락대사의 사무총장앞 서한 (S/22384):미군용기의 이락상공 비행비난.

첨부:상기 교섭문안: UNW(F)-133

끝

(대사 노창희-국장)

국기국　　1차보　　　중아국　　정문국　　안기부　　공보처
　　　　　2차보

=UNW-0697
첨부
15:10, March 26, 1991

U/NW(F)-133   10326   1930
(국연. 중동의. 기정. 해기)
                                    총 20 매

DRAFT ELEMENTS OF THE NEXT RESOLUTION
ON GULF SECURITY

The Security Council,

A. Recalling its resolutions 660 (1990), 661 (1990), 662 (1990), 664 (1990), 665 (1990), 666 (1990), 667 (1990), 669 (1990), 670 (1990), 674 (1990), 677 (1990), 678 (1990) and 686 (1991),

B. Welcoming the restoration to Kuwait of its sovereignty, independence, and territorial integrity and the return of its legitimate government,

C. Affirming the commitment of all Member States to the sovereignty, territorial integrity and political independence of Kuwait and Iraq, and noting the intention expressed by the member states cooperating with Kuwait under paragraph 2 of resolution 678 (1990) to bring their military presence in Iraq to an end as soon as possible consistent with paragraph 8 of

20-1

0284

- 2 -

resolution 686 (1991),

D. <u>Reaffirming</u> the need to be assured of Iraq's peaceful intentions in light of its unlawful invasion and occupation of Kuwait,

E. <u>Taking note</u> of the letter sent by the Foreign Minister of Iraq on 27 February 1991 (S/22275) and those sent pursuant to resolution 686 (1991) (S/22276, S/22273, S/22330, S/22321, S/22320), in particular the letter dated .... concerning Iraq's fulfillment of the requirements in resolution 686 (1991),

F. <u>Noting</u> that Iraq and Kuwait, as independent sovereign states, signed at Baghdad on 4 October 1963 "Agreed Minutes Regarding the Restoration of Friendly Relations, Recognition and Related Matters," thereby recognizing formally the boundary between Iraq and Kuwait and the allocation of islands, which were registered with the United Nations in accordance with Article 102 of the Charter and in which Iraq recognized the independence and complete sovereignty of the State of Kuwait within its borders as specified and accepted in the letter of the Prime Minister of Iraq dated 21 July 1932, and as accepted by the Ruler of Kuwait in his letter dated 10 August 1932,

G. <u>Conscious</u> of the need for demarcation of the said boundary,

20-2   0285

- 3 -

H. Conscious also of the statements by Iraq threatening to use
weapons in violation of its obligations under the Geneva
Protocol for the Prohibition of the Use in War of Asphyxiating,
Poisonous or Other Gases, and of Bacterioligical Methods of
Warfare, signed at Geneva on 17 June 1925, and of its prior use
of chemical weapons and affirming that grave consequences would
follow any further use by Iraq of such weapons,

I. Recalling that Iraq has subscribed to the Declaration
adopted by all States participating in the Conference of States
Party to the 1925 Geneva Protocol and Other International
States, held at Paris January 7-11, 1989, establishing the
objective of universal elimination of chemical and biological
weapons,

J. Recalling further that Iraq has signed the Convention on
the Prohibition of the Development, Production and Stockpiling
of Bacteriological (Biological) and Toxin weapons and on Their
Destruction, of 10 April 1972,

K. Noting the importance of Iraq ratifying this convention,

L. Noting moreover the importance of all states adhering to
this convention and encouraging its forthcoming Review

2o-3   0286

- 4 -

Conference to reinforce the authority, efficiency and universal scope of the convention;

M. Stressing the importance of urgent progress being made by the Conference on Disarmament in completing work on a Convention on the Universal Prohibition of Chemical Weapons and of universal adherence thereto,

N. Aware of the use by Iraq of ballistic missiles in unprovoked attacks,

O. Concerned that Iraq has attempted to acquire materials for a nuclear weapons program contrary to its obligations under the Treaty on the Non-Proliferation of Nuclear Weapons of 1 July 1968,

P. Recalling also the objective of the establishment of a nuclear weapons free zone in the region of the Middle East,

Q. Conscious of the threat which weapons of mass destruction pose to peace and security in the area and of the need to work towards the establishment in the Middle East of a zone free of such weapons, including through a dialogue among the states of the region,

26-4   0287

- 5 -

R. <u>Conscious also</u> of the objective of achieving balanced and
comprehensive control of armaments in the region,

S. <u>Noting</u> that resolution 686 (1991) marked the lifting of the
measures imposed by resolution 661 (1990) in so far as they
applied to Kuwait,

T. <u>Noting</u> that despite the progress being made in fulfilling
the obligations of resolution 686 (1990), many Kuwaiti and
third country nationals are still not accounted for and
property remains unreturned,

U. <u>Recalling</u> the International Convention against the Taking
of Hostages, opened for signature at New York on December 18,
1979, which categorizes all acts of taking hostages as
manifestations of international terrorism,

V. <u>Deploring</u> threats made by Iraq during the recent conflict
to make use of terrorism against targets outside Iraq and the
taking of hostages by Iraq,

W. <u>Taking note</u> of the Report of the Secretary-General
of 20 March 1991, and conscious of the desirability of meeting
humanitarian needs in Kuwait and Iraq in the immediate
post-crisis environment,

20-5   0288

- 6 -

X. Bearing in mind its responsibility to restore international
peace and security in the area as set out in resolution 678
(1990) and therefore conscious of the need to take the
following measures,

Y. Acting under Chapter VII of the Charter,

1. Affirms all thirteen resolutions noted above, except as
expressly changed below to achieve the goals of this
resolution, including a formal cease-fire;

A

2. Demands that Iraq and Kuwait respect the inviolability of
the international boundary and the allocation of islands set
out in the "Agreed Minutes Between the State of Kuwait and the
Republic of Iraq Regarding the Restoration of Friendly
Relations and Related Matters," signed at Baghdad on 4 October
1963;

3. Calls on the Secretary-General to make arrangements with
Iraq and Kuwait to demarcate the boundary between Iraq and
Kuwait, drawing on appropriate material including the map
contained in Security Council document S/...... and to report

2 0 - 6

0289

- 7 -

back to the Security Council within one month;

4. Decides to guarantee the inviolability of the above
mentioned international boundary and allocation of islands
taking as appropriate all necessary measures to that end in
accordance with the Charter;

B

5. Requests the Secretary General, after consulting with Iraq
and Kuwait, to submit within three days to the Security Council
for its approval a plan for the immediate deployment of a
United Nations observer unit to monitor the Khor Abdullah and a
demilitarized zone extending 10 kilometers into Iraq and 5
kilometers into Kuwait from the boundary referred to in the
"Agreed Minutes Between the State of Kuwait and the Republic of
Iraq Regarding the Restoration of Friendly Relations,
Recognition and Related Matters" of October 4, 1963; to deter
violations of the boundary through its presence in and
surveillance of the demilitarized zone; to observe any hostile
or potentially hostile action mounted from the territory of one
state to the other; and for the Secretary-General to report
regularly to the Council on the operations of the unit, and
immediately if there are serious violations of the zone or
potential threats to peace;

2-0-7

0290

- 8 -

6. <u>Notes</u> that the deployment of the United Nations observer unit as soon as possible will establish the conditions for the forces of the member states cooperating with Kuwait in accordance with resolution 678 (1990) to bring their military presence in Iraq to an end consistent with resolution 686 (1991);

<u>C</u>

7. <u>Requires</u> that Iraq unconditionally accept the destruction, removal, or rendering harmless, under international supervision, of:

    (a) all chemical and biological weapons and all stocks of agents;

    (b) all ballistic missile systems;

and all subsystems and components and all research, development, support and manufacturing facilities related to the above,

8. <u>Decides</u>, for the implementation of paragraph 7 above, the following:

20-A   0291

- 9 -

a) Iraq shall submit to the Secretary General, within
fifteen days of the adoption of this resolution, a
declaration of the locations, amounts and types of all
items specified in paragraph 7 and agree to urgent, on-site
inspection as specified below;

b) the Secretary-General, in consultation with the
appropriate Governments and, where appropriate, with the
Director General of the World Health Organization (WHO),
within 45 days of the passage of this resolution, shall
develop, and submit to the Council for approval, a plan
calling for the completion of the following acts within 45
days of such approval:

(i) the forming of a Special Commission, which
shall carry out immediate on-site inspection of
Iraq's biological, chemical and ballistic missile
capabilities, based on Iraq's declarations and
the designation of any additional locations by
the Special Commission itself;

(ii) the destruction by Iraq, under supervision
of the Special Commission, of all its ballistic
missile systems, including their subsystems,

2 0 - 9   0292

- 10 -

components and launchers, and yielding possession
to the Special Commission for destruction,
removal or rendering harmless of all other items
notified under paragraph 8 (a) above, or
otherwise required by the Special Commission;

9. Requires that Iraq unconditionally undertake not to use,
develop, construct or acquire any of the items specified in
paragraph 7 above and requests the Secretary General, in
consultation with the Special Commission, to develop a plan for
the future on-going monitoring and verification of Iraq's
compliance with this paragraph, to be submitted to the Council
for approval within 120 days of the passage of this resolution;

10. Requires that Iraq unconditionally agree not to acquire or
develop nuclear weapons or nuclear weapons-usable material or
any subsystems or components or any research, development,
support or manufacturing facilities related to the above; to
submit to the Secretary-General and the Director General of the
International Atomic Energy Agency (IAEA) within 15 days of the
adoption of this resolution a declaration of the locations,
amounts, and types of all items specified above; to place all
of its nuclear weapons-usable materials under the exclusive
control, for custody and removal, of the IAEA, with the
assistance and cooperation of the Special Commission as

20-10   0293

- 11 -

provided for in the plan of the Secretary-General discussed in
paragraph 8 above; to accept, in accordance with the
arrangements provided for in paragraph 11 below, the
destruction, removal, or rendering harmless of all items
specified above; and to accept the plan discussed in paragraph
11 below for the future ongoing monitoring and verifications of
its compliance with these undertakings;

11. Requests the Director General of the International Atomic
Energy Agency (IAEA), with the assistance and cooperation of
the Special Commission, as provided for in the plan of the
Secretary-General in paragraph 8 above, to carry out immediate
on-site inspection of Iraq's nuclear capabilities based on
Iraq's declarations and the designation of any additional
locations by the Special Commission; to develop a plan for
submission to the Security Council within 45 days calling for
the destruction, removal, or rendering harmless of all items
listed in paragraph 10 above; to carry out the plan within 45
days following approval by the Security Council; and to develop
a plan for the future ongoing monitoring and verification of
Iraq's compliance with paragraph 10 above, including an
inventory of all nuclear material in Iraq subject to the
Agency's verification and special inspections to confirm that
IAEA safeguards cover all relevant nuclear activities in Iraq,
to be submitted to the Council for approval within 120 days of

0294

2-0-11

- 12 -

the passage of this resolution;

12. <u>Invites</u> Iraq to reaffirm unconditionally its obligations under the Treaty on the Non-Proliferation of Nuclear Weapons, of 1 July 1968 and the Geneva Protocol for the Prohibition of the Use in War of Asphyxiating, Poisonous or Other Gases, and of Bacteriological Methods of Warfare, signed at Geneva on 17 June 1925 and to ratify the Convention on the Prohibition of the Development, Production, and Stockpiling of Bacteriological (Biological) and Toxin Weapons and on Their Destruction, of 10 April 1972, and notes that the actions to be taken by Iraq in paragraphs 7, 8, 9, 10, and 12 of this resolution represent steps toward the goal of establishing in the Middle East a zone free from weapons of mass destruction and ballistic missile systems and the objective of a global ban on chemical weapons;

<u>D</u>

13. <u>Requests</u> the Secretary General to report to the Security Council on the steps taken to facilitate the return of all Kuwaiti property seized by Iraq, including a list of any property which Kuwait claims has not been returned or which has not been returned intact;

<u>E</u>

20-12   0295

- 13 -

14. Reaffirms that Iraq, without prejudice to the debts and
obligations of Iraq arising prior to August 2, 1990, which will
be addressed through the usual mechanisms, is liable under
international law for any direct loss, damage, including
environmental damage and the depletion of natural resources, or
injury to foreign governments, nationals and corporations, as a
result of Iraq's unlawful invasion and occupation of Kuwait;

15. Decides that the Iraqi statements made since August 2,
1990, concerning its foreign debt are null and void;

16. Decides to create a Fund to pay compensation for claims
that fall within paragraph 14 above and to establish a
Commission that will administer the fund;

17. Directs the Secretary-General to develop and present to
the Council for decision, no later than 30 days following the
adoption of this resolution, recommendations for the Fund to
meet the requirement for the payment of claims established in
accordance with paragraph 16 above and for a program to
implement the decisions in paragraphs 14-16 above, including:
administration of the Fund; mechanisms for determining the
appropriate level of Iraq's contribution to the Fund based on a
percentage of the value of the exports of petroleum and

26-13   0296

- 14 -

petroleum products from Iraq not to exceed a figure to be
suggested to the Council by the Secretary-General, taking into
account the requirements of the people of Iraq and in
particular humanitarian needs, Iraq's payment capacity as
assessed in conjunction with the international financial
institutions taking into consideration external debt service,
and the needs of the Iraqi economy; arrangements for ensuring
that payments are made to the Fund; the process by which funds
will be allocated and claims paid; appropriate procedures for
evaluating losses, listing claims and verifying their validity
and resolving disputed claims in respect of Iraq's liability as
specified in paragraph 14 above; and the composition of the
Commission designated above;

F

18. Decides, effective immediately, that the prohibitions
against the sale or supply to Iraq of commodities or products,
and prohibitions against financial transactions related
thereto, contained in resolution 661 (1990) shall not apply to
foodstuffs notified to the Committee established in resolution
661 (1990) and, with the approval of that Committee, under
simplified and accelerated procedures, materials and supplies
for essential civilian needs as identified in the report of the
Secretary-General dated March 20, 1991 (S/22366), and in any

20-14   0297

- 15 -

further findings of humanitarian need by the Committee;

19. Decides that the Council shall review the provisions of
paragraph 18 above every sixty days in light of the policies
and practices of the Government of Iraq, including the
implementation of all relevant resolutions of the Security
Council, for the purpose of determining whether to modify
further or lift the prohibitions referred to therein;

20. Decides that upon the approval by the Security Council of
the program called for in paragraph 17 above and of the
completion by Iraq of all actions contemplated in paragraphs 7,
8, 9, 10, and 12 above, the prohibitions against the import of
commodities and products originating in Iraq and the
prohibitions against financial transactions related thereto
contained in resolution 661 (1990) shall have no further force
or effect;

21. Decides that, pending action by the Security Council under
paragraph 20 above, the Committee established under Resolution
661 shall be empowered to approve, when required to assure
adequate financial resources on the part of Iraq to carry out
the activities under paragraph 18 above, exceptions to the
prohibition against the import of commodities and products
originating in Iraq;

20-15

0298

- 16 -

22. <u>Decides</u> that, in accordance with resolution 661 (1990) and
subsequent related resolutions and until a further decision is
taken by the Council, all States shall continue to prevent the
sale or supply, or promotion or facilitation of such sale or
supply, to Iraq by their nationals, or from their territories
or using their flag vessels or aircraft, of:

  a) arms and related materiel of all types, specifically
  including the sale or transfer through other means of all
  forms of conventional military equipment, including for
  paramilitary forces, and spare parts and components and
  their means of production, for such equipment;

  b) items specified and defined in paragraph 7 and
  paragraph 10 above not otherwise covered above;

  c) technology under licensing or other transfer
  arrangements used in the production, utilization or
  stockpiling of items specified in subparagraphs a) and b)
  above;

  d) personnel or materials for training or technical
  support services relating to the design, development,
  manufacture, use, maintenance or support of items specified

2 0—16

0299

- 17 -

in subparagraphs a) and b) above;

23. Calls upon all States and international organizations to act strictly in accordance with paragraph 22, notwithstanding the existence of any contracts, agreements, licenses, or any other arrangements;

24. Calls upon all States to maintain such national controls and procedures and to take such other actions consistent with the guidelines to be established under paragraph 25 below as may be necessary to ensure compliance with the terms of paragraph 22 above, and calls upon international organizations to take all appropriate steps to assist in ensuring such full compliance;

25. Requests the Secretary General, in consultation with appropriate Governments, to develop, for approval of the Council, within 60 days, guidelines to facilitate full international implementation of paragraphs 22~24 above, and to make them available to all States and to establish a procedure for up-dating these guidelines periodically;

26 Agrees to review its decisions in paragraphs 20~23 above,

20-17

0300

- 18 -

except for the items specified and defined in paragraphs 7 and
10 above, on a regular basis and in any case 120 days following
passage of this resolution, taking into account Iraq's
compliance with this resolution and general progress towards
the control of armaments in the region;

27. Decides that all States, including Iraq, shall take the
necessary measures to ensure that no claim shall lie at the
instance of the Government of Iraq, or of any person or body in
Iraq, or of any person claiming through or for the benefit of
any such person or body, in connection with any contract or
other transaction where its performance was affected by reason
of the measures taken by the Security Council in Resolution 661
(1990) and related resolutions;

G

28. Decides that, in furtherance of its commitment to
facilitate the repatriation of all Kuwaiti and third country
nationals, Iraq shall cooperate with the International
Committee of the Red Cross, providing lists of such persons,
facilitating the access of the International Committee of the
Red Cross to all such persons wherever located or detained and
facilitating the search by the International Committee of the
Red Cross for those Kuwaiti and Third Country nationals still

20-18

0301

- 19 -

unaccounted for;

29. Invites the International Committee of the Red Cross to
keep the Secretary General apprised as appropriate of all
activities undertaken in connection with facilitating the
repatriation or return of all Kuwaiti and Third Country
nationals or their remains present in Iraq on or after August
2, 1990;

H

30. Requires Iraq to inform the Council that it will not
commit or support any act of international terrorism or allow
any organization directed toward commission of such acts to
operate within its territory and to condemn unequivocally and
renounce all acts, methods, and practices of terrorism;

I

31. Declares that, upon official notification by Iraq to the
Secretary-General and to the Security Council of its acceptance
of the provisions above, a formal ceasefire is effective
between Iraq and Kuwait and the member states cooperating with
Kuwait in accordance with resolution 678 (1990);

20-19

0302

- 20 -

32. <u>Decides</u> to remain seized of the matter and to take such
further steps as may be required for the implementation of this
resolution and to secure peace and security in the area.

10/439

0303

外務部 걸프戰 事後 對策班

題 目 : 유엔 平和維持軍派遣 움직임

91. 3. 28.
中 東 1 課

1. 유엔 平和維持軍 派遣 要請

   o 덴마크 政府는 유엔으로부터 유엔 平和維持軍의 걸프地域 派遣 要請을
     받고 이에 응하기로 하였으며 于先 1次로 13名을 派遣한후 追後 약100명을
     追加로 派遣할 豫定에 있다고 KUND ENGAARD 國防長官이 2.26 發表한바
     있음.

   o 또한 덴마크 言論은 덴마크, 스웨덴, 노르웨이, 필란드 北歐 4個國은
     240여명의 유엔 平和維持軍의 共同派遣을 準備中이라고 報道한바도 있음.

2. 北歐 4個國 立場 (現地公館 調査報告)

   가. 덴마크

      덴마크는 유엔의 要請에 따라 何時라도 平和維持軍을 派遣할 수 있도록
      준비해 놓고 있으며 最終的인 派遣與否, 時期 및 方法等은 유엔에서 平和
      維持軍 派遣에 관한 具體的인 決定에 따를 것임.

   나. 핀랜드

      핀랜드 政府는 유엔등으로 부터 要請이 있을시 平和維持軍을 걸프地域에
      派遣할 用意가 있음을 밝힘.

      그러나 現在까지 平和維持軍 派遣을 要請받은바 없으므로 自國으로서는
      平和維持軍 派遣 與否를 決定하지 않았음.

   다. 노르웨이

      유엔의 要請이 있으면 北歐諸國과 協調하여 유엔監視團 및 平和維持軍을
      걸프地域에 派遣한다는 것이 基本 方針임.

   라. 스웨덴

      스웨덴 政府는 유엔으로부터 要請받을 경우, 單獨이든 北歐 4個國 共同이든
      유엔 平和維持軍을 걸프地域에 派遣할 豫定

앙고재	91년 3월 동과	담 당	과 장	심의관	국 장	차관보	차 관	장 관
					전결			

0304

3. 유엔 監視團 및 平和維持軍 派遣與否

　　가. 유엔 監視團

　　　　休戰이 公式的으로 成立되는 경우, 休戰 遵守與否를 MONITOR 하기위해

　　　　維持되며 武裝하지 않은 將校級 構成한 小規模 水準

　　　　유엔측 構想은 各國 10명정도를 要請할 豫定

　　　　- 無關 또는 이란, 이라크 休戰監視團으로 이미 現地에 派遣되어 있는

　　　　　1-2명 追加 可能性

　　　　- 노르웨이 11명, 덴마크 13명 可能視

　　나. 平和維持軍

　　　　유엔 平和維持軍 交戰 當事國인 쿠웨이트, 이라크, 사우디등 當事國의

　　　　要請과 유엔의 決議가 우선되어야 하나 아직 未決定 狀態

4. 觀察 및 評價

　　o 北歐 4個國은 유엔으로 부터 유엔 監視團 또는 平和維持軍의 걸프地域

　　　派遣 要請이 있을시 派遣 준비중에 있음.

　　o 그러나 유엔 安保理가 休戰 決議案을 아직 採擇하지 않은 狀態이기 때문에

　　　同 決議案 採擇時까지는 待機狀態인 것으로 보임.

　　o 유엔 安保理 5個 常任理事國들은 걸프 休戰 決議案에 大體的으로 合意

　　　到達한 狀態인바, 조만간 同 休戰 決議案이 採擇될 경우, 유엔은 유엔

　　　監視團(UN Observer Unit)을 걸프地域에 派遣 多國籍軍을 유엔 監視團으로

　　　代替할 것으로 보며 北歐 4個國이 積極 參與할 것으로 보임.

주 국 련 대 표 부

주국련 20313- 200   1991. 3. 28.

수신 장관

참조 국제기구조약국장, 중동아프리카국장

제목 걸프사태 (안보리)

표제사태 관련 안보리 문서를 별첨과 같이 송부합니다.

첨 부 : 상기문서. 끝.

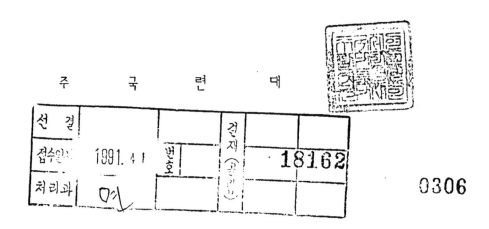

0306

UNITED NATIONS

 Security Council

S

Distr.
GENERAL

S/22362
20 March 1991

ORIGINAL: ENGLISH

LETTER DATED 18 MARCH 1991 FROM THE PERMANENT REPRESENTATIVE OF
THE ISLAMIC REPUBLIC OF IRAN TO THE UNITED NATIONS ADDRESSED TO
THE SECRETARY-GENERAL

I have the honour to enclose herewith a copy of the note verbale dated
12 November 1991, file No. 90-51/5901L, from the Interests Section of the Islamic
Republic of Iran at Washington addressed to the Embassy of the People's Democratic
Republic of Algeria concerning violations of principles of international law by the
United States Naval Forces stationed in the Persian Gulf and the Sea of Oman.

It would be highly appreciated if this letter and its annex were circulated as
a document of the Security Council.

(_Signed_) Kamal KHARRAZI
Ambassador
Permanent Representative

91-08907 2214h (E)   /...

0307

<u>Annex</u>

<u>Note verbale dated 21 November 1990 from the Interests Section
of the Islamic Republic of Iran at Washington addressed to the
Embassy of Algeria at Washington</u>

The Interests Section of the Islamic Republic of Iran at Washington presents its compliments to the Embassy of the Democratic and Popular Republic of Algeria and has the honour to quote the attached message in two copies, the original text and an unofficial translation, received from the Ministry of Foreign Affairs of the Islamic Republic of Iran. It is respectfully requested that the original text of the messages be transmitted to the United States Department of State and our office be informed of their response.

0307-1

/...

Enclosure

According to information received from officials of the Government of the
Islamic Republic of Iran, United States warships positioned in the Sea of Oman and
the Persian Gulf have created a nuisance for Iranian sea patrolling aircraft and
American aircraft have intercepted routine sea patrolling missions of Iranian
aircraft on the following dates and locations.

A. Warnings by United States warships

1.   On 11 August 1990, at 0927 hours, a United States warship warned the pilot of
     an Iranian sea patrolling aircraft, whose position was N2517 and E5732, not to
     get closer to the warship.

2.   On 11 August 1990, at 0940 hours, a United States warship warned the pilot of
     an Iranian sea patrolling aircraft, whose position was N2457 and E5825, not to
     get closer to the warship.

3.   On 12 August 1990, at 1348 hours, three United States warships at the position
     of N2545 and E5642 warned the pilot of an Iranian sea patrolling aircraft,
     whose position was N2614 and E5650, not to get closer to the warships.

4.   On 12 August 1990, at 1435 hours, three United States warships at the position
     of N2405 and E5747 warned the pilot of an Iranian sea patrolling aircraft,
     whose position was N2431 and E5747, not to get closer to the warships.

5.   On 13 August 1990, at 0910 hours, six United States warships at the position
     of N2448 and E5755 warned the pilot of an Iranian sea patrolling aircraft,
     whose position was N2653 and E5723, not to get closer to the warships.

6.   On 17 August 1990, at 0947 hours, six United States warships at the position
     of N2444 and E5826 warned the pilot of an Iranian sea patrolling aircraft,
     whose position was N2506 and E5804, not to get closer to the warships.

7.   On 18 August 1990, at 0958 hours, a United States warship at the position of
     N2555 and E5825 warned the pilot of an Iranian sea patrolling aircraft, whose
     position was N2455 and E5730, not to get closer to the warship and to change
     its course.

8.   On 20 August 1990, at 0942 hours, a United States warship at the position of
     N2410 and E5824 warned the pilot of an Iranian sea patrolling aircraft, whose
     position was N2445 and E5750, not to get closer to the warship.

B. Interceptions by United States aircraft

1.   On 8 August 1990, at 1000 hours, two United States aircraft (an F-14 and an
     F-18) intercepted an Iranian sea patrolling aircraft, whose position was N2403
     and E5917, for a period of 40 minutes.

0307-2   /...

2.   On 13 August 1990, at 0950 hours, a United States P3F aircraft intercepted an Iranian sea patrolling aircraft, whose position was N2354 and E5913, for a period of five minutes.

3.   On 22 August 1990, at 0955 hours, two United States F-14 aircraft intercepted an Iranian sea patrolling aircraft, whose position was N2552 and E5640, for a period of 10 minutes.

     The Government of the Islamic Republic of Iran protests such illegal actions by the United States Government and demands an explanation of these unlawful interventions.

0308

Security Council

Distr.
GENERAL

S/22366
20 March 1991

ORIGINAL: ENGLISH

LETTER DATED 20 MARCH 1991 FROM THE SECRETARY-GENERAL ADDRESSED TO THE PRESIDENT OF THE SECURITY COUNCIL

Further to my decision to dispatch a mission in order to assess the humanitarian needs arising in Iraq and in Kuwait in the immediate post-crisis environment, I have the honour to inform you that the mission, led by Under-Secretary-General Martti Ahtisaari and comprising representatives of appropriate United Nations agencies and programmes, visited Iraq in the period from 10 to 17 March 1991.

In the light of the wish of the members of the Security Council to be kept informed of the progress of the mission (S/22322), I have the honour to transmit herewith, for their consideration, the report prepared by Mr. Ahtisaari concerning his visit to Iraq.

The Mission will commence its visit to Kuwait on 22 March 1991. I shall of course convey to you as soon as possible the report on that visit.

(Signed) Javier PEREZ de CUELLAR

Annex

<u>Report to the Secretary-General on humanitarian needs in Kuwait
and Iraq in the immediate post-crisis environment by a mission
to the area led by Mr. Martti Ahtisaari, Under-Secretary-General
for Administration and Management, dated 20 March 1991</u>

CONTENTS

0310

/...

INTRODUCTION

1.   You asked me to travel, as a matter of urgency, to Kuwait and Iraq to assess humanitarian needs there in the immediate post-crisis environment, and to bring with me a team comprising representatives of the appropriate United Nations agencies and programmes. Your decision was announced in a press statement of 1 March 1991.

2.   On 3 March 1991, the President of the Security Council made a statement on behalf of the Council, in which it welcomed your announcement and invited you to keep it informed in the shortest possible time of the progress of this mission, in respect of which it pledged to take immediate action (S/22322).

3.   In the days immediately preceding my departure, I consulted with all concerned parties, and met on 4 and 5 March 1991 with the Permanent Representative of Iraq to the United Nations, H.E. Dr. Abdul Amir A. Al-Anbari, and with the Chargé d'affaires of Kuwait to the United Nations, Ambassador Mohammad Saad Al-Sallal. Each pledged the full cooperation of his Government but mentioned logistical difficulties and communication problems with his capital. In my meeting with the representative of Kuwait I expressed a preference to travel there first. He, however, responded that his Government anticipated receiving a mission led by Mr. Abdulrahim Farah to assess losses and damages during the Iraqi occupation of Kuwait. His authorities preferred to receive that mission first. Thus, he believed that it would be more practical for my mission to travel first to Iraq before proceeding to Kuwait. He appreciated my desire to go first to his country and hoped that the mission could be received there in the near future.

4.   I departed from New York on 7 March. The mission assembled at Geneva the following day. It comprised representatives not only of the Secretariat, but also of the United Nations Children's Fund (UNICEF), the United Nations Development Programme (UNDP), the Office of the United Nations Disaster Relief Coordinator (UNDRO), the Office of the United Nations High Commissioner for Refugees (UNHCR), the Food and Agriculture Organization of the United Nations (FAO) and the World Health Organization (WHO). On my way to the Middle East, I consulted at Geneva with Mr. Claudio Caratsch, Vice-President of the International Committee of the Red Cross (ICRC). The mission travelled to Amman on 9 March and arrived at Baghdad on 10 March. At Amman, I was received by His Highness Crown Prince Hassan and by His Excellency Mr. Taher Al-Masri, Foreign Minister of Jordan. The mission remained in Iraq until 17 March. On that date I travelled to Bahrain while awaiting the outcome of consultations in New York and your further instructions. In Bahrain I met with the Foreign Minister, His Excellency Sheikh Mohamed bin Mubarak Al Khalifa. On 19 March you instructed me to return to New York. Leaving the remainder of the mission in Bahrain whilst awaiting the decision of the Kuwaiti Government, I departed that day and arrived in New York on 20 March. The Kuwaiti authorities have now informed you that the mission is expected to depart Bahrain for Kuwait on or about 22 March.

0311   /...

I. MODUS OPERANDI IN IRAQ

5.   The mission began its work immediately upon arrival at Baghdad on 10 March, first linking up with local UNDP and UNICEF representatives and, later that day, meeting with His Excellency Mr. Mohamed Sa'eed Al-Sahaf, Minister of State for Foreign Affairs, and senior officials of the relevant government departments and of local authorities. Joint working groups were established with the various United Nations specialist members of the mission. These held their first meetings that same evening to establish work programmes. Field work was undertaken from 11 to 16 March at various locations in and around Baghdad. A longer field trip was made by a group from the mission, led by myself, to Mosul, 400 kilometres north-west of Baghdad, and I myself also inspected numerous locations in Greater Baghdad. I and members of the mission held meetings with representatives of foreign diplomatic missions at Baghdad and with senior representatives of ICRC. Members of the mission also met with representatives of several non-governmental organizations (NGOs) who had made their way to Iraq to see the situation for themselves. I held final meetings in respect of the specialist teams' work with the Foreign Minister, His Excellency Mr. Tariq Aziz, and with the Minister of State and the participating senior officials, on the evening of 16 March.

6.   The Iraqi authorities were fully cooperative in regard to the activities of the five specialist working groups. These dealt with: food and agriculture; water, sanitation and health; transportation and communications; energy; and refugees and other vulnerable groups. Members were able to inspect all locations and facilities that they had requested to see in the Baghdad area and in several other governorates, and could also engage in independent field research in wholesale and retail markets and undertake household surveys. However, the Government was unable to accede to my request that we visit Souera, Moussayeb, Basrah, Nasiriyah and Kirkuk. In respect of some, the problems were said to be logistical; in regard to others, concern for security was conveyed. I expressed regret at our inability to cover the whole country, because it was important that the United Nations should be able to assess the humanitarian needs of the entire population of Iraq in all regions. The authorities also expressed their regret on this subject, and we agreed that locally based United Nations staff would travel to these areas as soon as conditions permitted. It has, however, been possible to infer from information available from various other sources that needs are unlikely to vary greatly from what we ourselves observed, but it is reported that conditions may be substantially worse in certain locations.

II. SUMMARY OF FINDINGS AND RECOMMENDATIONS IN REGARD TO IRAQ

7.   A summary of the mission's findings and conclusions is set out below. It is based upon a number of internal working papers, technical annexes, visits to sites and oral reports by mission specialists.

0312

/...

A. General remarks

8.   I and the members of my mission were fully conversant with media reports regarding the situation in Iraq and, of course, with the recent WHO/UNICEF report on water, sanitary and health conditions in the Greater Baghdad area. It should, however, be said at once that nothing that we had seen or read had quite prepared us for the particular form of devastation which has now befallen the country. The recent conflict has wrought near-apocalyptic results upon the economic infrastructure of what had been, until January 1991, a rather highly urbanized and mechanized society. Now, most means of modern life support have been destroyed or rendered tenuous. Iraq has, for some time to come, been relegated to a pre-industrial age, but with all the disabilities of post-industrial dependency on an intensive use of energy and technology.

9.   My mandate was limited to assessing the need for urgent humanitarian assistance. It did not extend to the huge task of assessing the requirements for reconstructing Iraq's destroyed infrastructure, much less, to developmental matters. Accordingly, my report to you, in its several technical sections, seeks with as much exactitude as possible to convey the extent of needs in the primary areas of humanitarian concern: for safe water and sanitation, basic health and medical support; for food; for shelter; and for the logistical means to make such support actually available. Underlying each analysis is the inexorable reality that, as a result of war, virtually all previously viable sources of fuel and power (apart from a limited number of mobile generators) and modern means of communication are now, essentially, defunct. The far-reaching implications of this energy and communications' vacuum as regards urgent humanitarian support are of crucial significance for the nature and effectiveness of the international response.

10.   These conditions, together with recent civil unrest in some parts of the country, mean that the authorities are as yet scarcely able even to measure the dimensions of the calamity, much less respond to its consequences, because they cannot obtain full and accurate data. Additionally, there is much less than the minimum fuel required to provide the energy needed for movement or transportation, irrigation or generators for power to pump water and sewage. For instance, emergency medical supplies can be moved to health centres only with extreme difficulty and, usually, major delay. Information regarding local needs is slow and sparse. Most employees are simply unable to come to work. Both the authorities and the trade unions estimate that approximately 90 per cent of industrial workers have been reduced to inactivity and will be deprived of income as of the end of March. Government departments have at present only marginal attendance. Prior to recent events, Iraq was importing about 70 per cent of its food needs. Now, owing to the fuel shortage, the inability to import and the virtual breakdown of the distribution system, the flow of food through the private sector has been reduced to a trickle, with costs accelerating upwards. Many food prices are already beyond the purchasing reach of most Iraqi families. Agricultural production is highly mechanized, and much land depends on pumped-water irrigation. Should the main harvest in June 1991 be seriously affected by a lack of energy to drive machines and pump water, then an already grave situation will be further aggravated. As shown below, prospects for the 1992 harvest could, for combined reasons, be in at least as much jeopardy. Having regard to the nature of

/...

0313

Iraq's society and economy, the energy vacuum is an omnipresent obstacle to the success of even a short-term, massive effort to maintain life-sustaining conditions in each area of humanitarian need.

B. Food and agriculture

11. Mission members held working sessions with counterparts from the relevant ministries, visited social centres where various vulnerable groups are cared for, agricultural production areas, a seed production centre, a veterinary health centre and a dairy production unit. The mission noted that Iraq has been heavily dependent on food imports which have amounted to at least 70 per cent of consumption needs. Seed was also imported. Sanctions decided upon by the Security Council had already adversely affected the country's ability to feed its people. New measures relating to rationing and enhanced production were introduced in September 1990. These were, however, in turn, negatively affected by the hostilities which impacted upon most areas of agricultural production and distribution.

12. Food is currently made available to the population both through government allocation and rations, and through the market. The Ministry of Trade's monthly allocation to the population of staple food items fell from 343,000 tons in September 1990 to 182,000 tons, when rationing was introduced, and was further reduced to 135,000 tons in January 1991 (39 per cent of the pre-sanctions level). While the mission was unable to gauge the precise quantities still held in government warehouses, all evidence indicates that flour is now at a critically low level, and that supplies of sugar, rice, tea, vegetable oil, powdered milk and pulses are currently at critically low levels or have been exhausted. Distribution of powdered milk, for instance, is now reserved exclusively for sick children on medical prescription.

13. Livestock farming has been seriously affected by sanctions because many feed products were imported. The sole laboratory producing veterinary vaccines was destroyed during the conflict, as inspected by the mission. The authorities are no longer able to support livestock farmers in the combat of disease, as all stocks of vaccine were stated to have been destroyed in the same sequence of bombardments on this centre, which was an FAO regional project.

14. The country has had a particular dependence upon foreign vegetable seeds, and the mission was able to inspect destroyed seed warehouses. The relevant agricultural authorities informed the mission that all stocks of potatoes and vegetable seeds had been exhausted. Next season's planting will be jeopardized if seeds are not provided before October 1991.

15. This year's grain harvest in June is seriously compromised for a number of reasons, including failure of irrigation/drainage (no power for pumps, lack of spare parts); lack of pesticides and fertilizers (previously imported); and lack of fuel and spare parts for the highly-mechanized and fuel-dependent harvesting machines. Should this harvest fail, or be far below average, as is very likely barring a rapid change in the situation, widespread starvation conditions become a real possibility.

0314   /...

16. The official programme for the support of socially dependent groups of the population (the elderly, disabled, mothers and children, hospital patients, orphans, refugees, etc.) is affected by the overall grave deficiencies in the food situation.

17. The mission had the opportunity to conduct independent research relating to household costs and living standards in Baghdad. Such standards have declined rapidly in the last months, while food and fuel prices have climbed dramatically. Price increases in the August to January period reflected shortages of supply, but since January there has been a further acceleration of price increases reflecting both supply shortages and the breakdown of the transport system. Interviews with private wholesale food distributors revealed that their stocks are near depletion and they no longer have an organized private transport capacity, owing to fuel shortages. The government-initiated rationing system was designed to provide families with a fraction of their basic necessities at prices comparable to those prevailing before August. The system allows families either 5 kilograms per person, per month, of flour or 3 loaves of baked bread; 10 kilograms per family, per month, of liquid cooking gas; 1 bar of soap per person, per month, etc. However, independent surveys conducted by the mission in several diverse areas of Baghdad showed that many families cannot draw their full rations, since the distribution centres are often depleted and they have great difficulty in travelling to other centres. The quality of food distributed has itself deteriorated to the point of causing health problems. Most families also reported that they could not meet their needs through the private markets. Despite official price controls, the independent market surveys conducted by the mission showed hyperinflation since August. The price of most basic necessities has increased by 1,000 per cent or more. For example, flour is now 5-6 dinars per kilogram (and seemingly still rising); rice has risen to 6 dinars per kilogram; sugar to 5 dinars per kilogram; lentils to 4 dinars per kilogram; and whole milk to 10 dinars. In contrast to this hyperinflation, many incomes have collapsed. Many employees cannot draw salaries, the banking system has in large measure closed down and withdrawals are limited to 100 dinars per month. The minimum monthly wage was 54 dinars and the average monthly salary of a civil servant was 70 dinars. In short, most families lack access to adequate rations or the purchasing power to meet normal minimal standards.

18. The mission recommends that, in these circumstances of present severe hardship and in view of the bleak prognosis, sanctions in respect of food supplies should be immediately removed, as should those relating to the import of agricultural equipment and supplies. The urgent supply of basic commodities to safeguard vulnerable groups is strongly recommended, and the provision of major quantities of the following staples for the general population: milk, wheat flour, rice, sugar, vegetable oil and tea. These are required to meet minimum general requirements until the next harvest. Safeguarding the harvest means the urgent importation of fertilizers, pesticides, spare parts, veterinary drugs, agricultural machinery and equipment, etc. The mission was able to quantify many of these needs. The disappearance of vegetables from the country's markets also appears likely by the summer, and seed importation is crucial.

19. The mission observes that, without a restoration of energy supplies to the agricultural production and distribution sectors, implementation of many of the above recommendations would be to little effect. Drastic international measures across the whole agricultural spectrum are most urgent.

C. Water, sanitation and health

20. As regards water, prior to the crisis Baghdad received about 450 litres per person supplied by seven treatment stations purifying water from the Tigris river. The rest of the country had about 200-250 litres per person per day, purified and supplied by 238 central water-treatment stations and 1,134 smaller water projects. All stations operated on electric power; about 75 per cent had standby diesel-powered generators. Sewage was treated to an acceptable standard before being returned to the rivers.

21. With the destruction of power plants, oil refineries, main oil storage facilities and water-related chemical plants, all electrically operated installations have ceased to function. Diesel-operated generators were reduced to operating on a limited basis, their functioning affected by lack of fuel, lack of maintenance, lack of spare parts and non-attendance of workers. The supply of water in Baghdad dropped to less than 10 litres per day but has now recovered to approximately 30-40 litres in about 70 per cent of the area (less than 10 per cent of the overall previous use). Standby generating capacity is out of order in several pumping stations and cessation of supplies will therefore ensue if current machinery goes out of order for any reason (spare parts are not available owing to sanctions). As regards the quality of water in Baghdad, untreated sewage has now to be dumped directly into the river - which is the source of the water supply - and all drinking-water plants there and throughout the rest of the country are using river water with high sewage contamination. Recently, the water authority has begun to be able to improve the quality of drinking water by adding more of the remaining stock of alum and chlorine after assurances from UNICEF and ICRC that emergency aid would be provided. Chemical tests are now being conducted at the stations but no bacteriological testing and control is possible because of the lack of electricity necessary for the functioning of laboratories, the shortage of necessary chemicals and reagents and the lack of fuel for the collection of samples. No chlorine tests are being conducted because of the lack of fuel for sampling. While the water authority has warned that water must be boiled, there is little fuel to do this, and what exists is diminishing. Cool winter conditions have prevailed until recently.

22. Only limited information is available to authorities regarding the situation in the remainder of the country because all modern communications systems have been destroyed and information is now transmitted and received (in this sector as in all others) by person-to-person contact. In those areas where there are no generators, or generators have broken down, or the fuel supply is exhausted, the population draws its water directly from polluted rivers and trenches. This is widely apparent in rural areas, where women and children can be seen washing and filling water receptacles. The quantity and quality of water produced by treatment centres is very variable and in many locations there are no chemicals available for

0316   /...

purification. No quality control - chlorine testing, chemical testing or bacteriological testing - is being conducted.

23. The mission identified the various problems mentioned above: heavy sewage-pollution of water intakes; absence or acute shortage of water-treatment chemicals, especially aluminium sulphate (alum) and chlorine; lack of power to operate equipment; lack or shortage of diesel to run generators; inability to repair generators because of lack of spare parts; in some instances a total absence of generators; the destruction of some stations; absence of water-testing; lack of a health surveillance system in respect of communicable, and, especially, water-borne diseases. A further major problem, now imminent, is the climate. Iraq has long and extremely hot summers, the temperature often reaching 50 degrees Celsius. This has two main implications: (a) the quantity of water must be increased, and a minimum target of 50 litres per person per day has to be attained (this entails a gross output of 65 litres per person at the source); and (b) the heat will accelerate the incubation of bacteria, and thus the health risks ascribable to the water quality (already at an unacceptable level) will be further exacerbated - especially viewed in the overall sanitary circumstances which have already led to a fourfold increase in diarrhoeal disease incidence among children under five years of age, and the impact of this on their precarious nutritional status.

24. As regards sanitation, the two main concerns relate to garbage disposal and sewage treatment. In both cases, rapidly rising temperatures will soon accentuate an existing crisis. Heaps of garbage are spread in the urban areas and collection is poor to non-existent. The work of collection vehicles is hampered by lack of fuel, lack of maintenance and spare parts and lack of labour, because workers are unable to come to work. Incinerators are in general not working, for these same reasons, and for lack of electric power. Insecticides, much needed as the weather becomes more torrid, are virtually out of stock because of sanctions and a lack of chemical supplies. As previously stated, Iraqi rivers are heavily polluted by raw sewage, and water levels are unusually low. All sewage treatment and pumping plants have been brought to a virtual standstill by the lack of power supply and the lack of spare parts. Pools of sewage lie in the streets and villages. Health hazards will build in the weeks to come.

25. As regards health conditions, the mission reviewed the situation since the special joint WHO-UNICEF mission in February 1991. It found that the recommendations made in that report (S/22328), subsequently approved by the Security Council Committee established by resolution 661 (1990) concerning the situation between Iraq and Kuwait, were well-founded. The mission also identified any further immediate health problems that needed to be addressed over the next three to six months. It also identified constraints that hamper the implementation of the already-agreed recommendations of the joint mission. It found that health conditions in Baghdad and throughout the country remain precarious. A major factor is the water and sanitation situation described above. Additionally, the total lack of telephone communication and drastically reduced transport capability pose other problems to the health system since basic information on communicable diseases cannot be collected and disseminated, and essential drugs, vaccines and medical supplies cannot be distributed efficiently to the country. Mission health

/...

0317

experts therefore focused especially on control and prevention of communicable diseases; water quality control; and logistics support for an effective distribution system from Baghdad to outlying regions of vaccines, drugs and medical supplies, as well as infant formula.

26. There is an urgent need to establish a national surveillance and reporting capacity for communicable diseases. This would require the establishment of sentinel sites that can test for the major communicable diseases, as well as the capacity to collate and analyse resulting data on a national scale in a timely manner. Communications, functional laboratories, including necessary chemicals and reagents, and transport and power resources are essential to provide for this emergency humanitarian need. The question of water quality control has already been described. The fourfold increase in incidence of diarrhoeal diseases amongst young children reported by the WHO/UNICEF mission has been reconfirmed by findings recently obtained in 11 sentinel sites in Baghdad. The water and sanitation situation contributes to this problem which must be expected to increase as the summer approaches. The mission concluded that a catastrophe could be faced at any time if conditions do not change. It assessed the detailed requirements for water quality control. As for logistics, this sector is at present especially affected by the same problems that exist in the rest of society.

27. The mission's recommendations regarding water, sanitation and health, on an urgent humanitarian basis, are as follows:

(a) For water, needs have to be calculated in such a way as to permit a minimum quantity of safe water through the hot season from April to September. Assistance, similar to that approved earlier, should be provided to cities outside Baghdad, including the necessary quantities of fuel for generators and transport; lubricants for engines; aluminium sulphate; chlorine; generators for water stations; skid-mounted river water treatment units; chemical dosing pumps; gas chlorinators; pump sets; spare parts; collars for water pipes; and reagents for chemical tests;

(b) For sanitation needs, these include: fuel and spare parts for garbage collection trucks, as well as insecticides; fuel and spare parts for the sewage disposal system (all of which is mechanical and imported); and hoses for drawing water with tanker-trucks;

(c) As regards medical needs, the mission concluded that a number of items were essential to deal with urgent humanitarian needs and established requirements. They include the provision of essential drugs and vaccines, as approved earlier, on a more extended scale, chemicals and reagents, generators, battery-operated incubators, means of alternative communication, requirements for the reinstitution of the cold chain for vaccines, and some vehicles;

(d) Without fuel, power and communications, the needed measures indicated above could, however, prove more or less ineffectual. Estimates of related fuel requirements have been made by the mission.

0318   /...

D. Refugees and other vulnerable groups

28. Conditions described above affect the whole population of Iraq and, most especially, low-income groups. The mission paid particular attention to the plight of especially vulnerable groups, whether Iraqi or non-Iraqi. Thus, it found that care for orphans, the elderly and the handicapped had been in many instances disrupted, with residents of institutions having had to be moved and regrouped at various locations. It recommends the urgent implementation of a humanitarian programme aimed at enabling some 25 orphanages and 71 other social welfare centres to resume their normal activities and at providing their beneficiaries with essential relief supplies, and specifies essential inputs for this purpose.

29. As regards the displaced and the homeless, the authorities themselves have not yet been able fully to assess the impact of the recent hostilities. They have, however, calculated that approximately 9,000 homes were destroyed or damaged beyond repair during the hostilities, of which 2,500 were in Baghdad and 1,900 were in Basrah. This has created a new homeless potential total of 72,000 persons. Official help is now hampered by the conditions described throughout this report and, especially, a virtual halt in the production of local building materials and the impossibility to import. The input of essential materials should be permitted.

30. The mission was unable, in the time available and having regard to the incomplete data in the hands of the authorities, to ascertain the number of foreign workers of Arab and other nationalities still resident in Iraq. It has been estimated that approximately 750,000 were still present in January 1991. It can at this stage be no more than a matter of surmise whether a number of those remaining may be in need of support to return to their countries of origin.

31. Some 64,000 Iranian nationals, protected under either the Fourth Geneva Convention relative to the Protection of Civilian Persons in Time of War of 14 August 1949, or the 1951 Convention relating to the Status of Refugees, had previously resided in three camps in Iraq. There has been substantial dislocation of some of these persons. Others have indicated their desire for repatriation. Limited relief assistance is urgently needed for some of those who have been obliged to leave one of the camps. Additionally, some 80,000 Palestinians are resident in Iraq, including a group of 35,000 considered as refugees benefiting from the protection of the Iraqi Government. It has been reported that several hundred Palestinians have recently come to Baghdad from Kuwait and are now in need of emergency assistance. Certain measures have been developed to provide urgent assistance to those most in need.

E. Logistics: transportation, communications and energy

32. The mission examined transportation, communications and energy facilities, as it increasingly emerged that adequate logistics and energy would be essential to support and make effective emergency humanitarian assistance.

33. As regards transportation, the fact that the country has been on a war footing almost continuously since 1980 has undermined its capacity. At present, Iraq's

0319   /...

sole available surface transport link with the outside world is via Amman to Aqaba. (It has been reported that a bridge has recently been destroyed on the Iskenderun/Mersin road to Iraq from Turkey; and the ports of Basrah and Umm Qasr are currently out of use; nor has there for some years been any direct cargo traffic to Iraq via the Syrian Arab Republic.) Internal transportation by road is now severely affected by a lack of spare parts and tyres and, above all, by a lack of fuel. Some internal railway capability still exists on the Baghdad-Mosul line. The mission was informed that a total of 83 road bridges had been destroyed and a number were inspected.

34. As regards communications, the mission was informed that all internal and external telephone systems had been destroyed, with the exception of a limited local exchange in one town. It had the opportunity to inspect a number of war-damaged or destroyed facilities and experienced for itself the situation in the Greater Baghdad and other urban areas. Communication in Iraq is now on a person-to-person basis, as mail services have also disintegrated.

35. The role of energy in Iraq is especially important because of the level of its urbanization (approximately 72 per cent of the population lives in towns), its industrialization, and its prolonged, very hot, summers. Pre-war energy consumption consisted of oil and refined products (85 per cent), electricity (14.8 per cent) and other sources (0.2 per cent). About 30 per cent of electric power generation was hydro-power. Bombardment has paralysed oil and electricity sectors almost entirely. Power output and refineries' production is negligible and will not be resumed until the first repair phase is complete. The limited and sporadic power supply in some residential areas and for health facilities is provided by mobile generators. There have, officially, been virtually no sales of gasoline to private users since February. The mission was told that the only petrol, oil and lubricants (POL) products now available are heating oil (rationed to 60 litres per month, per family) and liquefied petroleum gas (LPG), which is rationed to one cylinder per month, per family. The authorities stated that stocks of these two products are close to exhaustion and that their distribution is expected to cease within the next 2-4 weeks. While work is under way to clear sites and assess damages, lack of communications and transport is retarding this activity. Initial inspections are said to show that necessary repairs to begin power generation and oil refining at minimal levels may take anywhere from 4 to 13 months. Minimal survival level to undertake humanitarian activities would require approximately 25 per cent of pre-war civilian domestic fuel consumption. Its absence, given the proximate onset of hot weather conditions, may have calamitous consequences for food, water supply and for sanitation; and therefore for health conditions. It seems inescapable that these fuel imports must take place urgently, and units and spare parts will also be required to enable Iraq to meet its own humanitarian needs as soon as possible. Under optimal circumstances it would be difficult or impossible for such needs to be provided from other sources given all the circumstances of that country's economy and social conditions, and bearing also in mind the limited bulk transportation possibilities that are likely to exist for the foreseeable future.

36. During my final meetings in Baghdad on 16 March I made reference to the need to be able to assess the effective utilization of all inputs that might in future

0320   /...

be established under the responsibility of the United Nations. The Government assured the mission that it would accept a system of monitoring of imports and their utilization.

F. Observations

37. The account given above describes as accurately as the mission has been able, using all sources, including much independent observation, to ascertain the situation, which, within the time available and the travel limitations referred to earlier, was perceived to exist in regard to urgent humanitarian needs in Iraq during the week of 10-17 March. I, together with all my colleagues, am convinced that there needs to be a major mobilization and movement of resources to deal with aspects of this deep crisis in the fields of agriculture and food, water, sanitation and health. Yet the situation raises, in acute form, other questions. For it will be difficult, if not impossible, to remedy these immediate humanitarian needs without dealing with the underlying need for energy, on an equally urgent basis. The need for energy means, initially, emergency oil imports and the rapid patching up of a limited refining and electricity production capacity, with essential supplies from other countries. Otherwise, food that is imported cannot be preserved and distributed; water cannot be purified; sewage cannot be pumped away and cleansed; crops cannot be irrigated; medicaments cannot be conveyed where they are required; needs cannot even be effectively assessed. It is unmistakable that the Iraqi people may soon face a further imminent catastrophe, which could include epidemic and famine, if massive life-supporting needs are not rapidly met. The long summer, with its often 45 or even 50 degree temperatures (113-122 degrees Fahrenheit), is only weeks away. Time is short.

0321

UNITED
NATIONS

S

Security Council

Distr.
GENERAL

S/22367
20 March 1991

ORIGINAL: ENGLISH

LETTER DATED 20 MARCH 1991 FROM THE PERMANENT REPRESENTATIVE OF
KUWAIT TO THE UNITED NATIONS ADDRESSED TO THE SECRETARY-GENERAL

I should like to refer to the letter dated 19 March 1991 from the President of the Security Council addressed to Your Excellency concerning the modalities for the return of property from Iraq to Kuwait, which shall be arranged through your Office (S/22361).

To facilitate accounting for the Kuwaiti property seized by Iraq, lists from the different government agencies will be forwarded to you promptly. To this end, I should like to enclose the preliminary list forwarded to the President of the Security Council on 14 March 1991. That list comprises the assessment of the following government agencies: Libraries, Kuwait Central Bank, Kuwait Airways Corporation, and Ministry of Justice and Legal Affairs. Additional information from the above agencies is due shortly.

I should appreciate it if you would arrange for this letter to be circulated as a document of the Security Council.

(Signed) Mohammad A. ABULHASAN
Ambassador
Permanent Representative

91-08994 2236e (E)

/...

0322

<u>Annex</u>

A. <u>Central Bank of Kuwait</u>

1. Over 1,269,232.168 ounces of gold

2. Gold and silver coins

B. <u>Kuwait Airways Corporation</u>

<u>Registration number</u>	<u>Type of aircraft</u>
1. 9K - AIB	Boeing 767-200 ER
2. 9K - AIC	Boeing 767-200 ER
3. 9K - AHA	Airbus A310-200
4. 9K - AHB	Airbus A310-200
5. 9K - AHC	Airbus A310-300
6. 9K - AHD	Airbus A310-200
7. 9K - AHE	Airbus A310-200
8. 9K - AHF	Airbus A300-200
9. 9K - AHG	Airbus A300-200
10. 9K - AHI	Airbus A300-200
11. 9K - AGA	HS 125
12. 9K - AGB	HS 125
13. 9K - AEG	Gulf Stream GIII
14. 9K - AEH	Gulf Stream GIII
15. 9K - AFA	Boeing B727-200

C. <u>Libraries</u>

1. Institute for Arabic Manuscripts

2. Educational Library for Arab Gulf States

0323 /...

3.   Libraries of Kuwait University

4.   Library and archives of the <u>Magazine of Gulf and Arabian Peninsula Studies</u>

5.   School libraries

6.   Public libraries

7.   Library and manuscripts of the Arab Heritage Department - National
     Council for Culture, Arts and Literature

8.   Library of the Arab Planning Institute

D.   <u>Ministry of Justice and Legal Affairs</u>

1.   All documents relating to real estate ownership

2.   All duplicates and reproductions of documents, including those recorded
     on microfilms

3.   All originals and registries of general and exclusive powers of attorney

4.   All documents pertaining to the original contracts founding corporations
     of all types

5.   All documents related to judicial courts, offices of public prosecution
     and the Information Centre of the Ministry of Justice

6.   All documents related to the Public Authority of Minors' Affairs,
     including all the records

7.   All files of civil, commercial and penal lawsuits and all their documents

8.   All files of the Directorate of Experts

0324

UNITED NATIONS

Security Council

S

Distr.
GENERAL

S/22371
21 March 1991
ENGLISH
ORIGINAL: ARABIC

IDENTICAL LETTERS DATED 20 MARCH 1991 FROM THE PERMANENT
REPRESENTATIVE OF IRAQ TO THE UNITED NATIONS ADDRESSED
RESPECTIVELY TO THE SECRETARY-GENERAL AND THE PRESIDENT
OF THE SECURITY COUNCIL

On instructions from my Government, I have the honour to transmit herewith a
letter dated 20 March 1991 from Mr. Tariq Aziz, Deputy Prime Minister and Minister
for Foreign Affairs of the Republic of Iraq, concerning the infiltration of large
numbers of armed groups into Iraq from a neighbouring State and their engagement in
acts of widespread subversion, murder, destruction, arson and pillage in a number
of Iraqi governorates.

We should be grateful if you would have this letter and its annex circulated
as a document of the Security Council.

(Signed) Dr. Abdul Amir AL-ANBARI
Ambassador
Permanent Representative

Annex

<u>Letter dated 20 March 1991 from the Deputy Prime Minister
and Minister for Foreign Affairs of Iraq addressed to the
President of the Security Council</u>

I have the honour to draw your attention and the attention of the members of the international community to the fact that, immediately after the announcement of the cessation of military operations by the armed forces of the United States and its allies, large numbers of armed and organized groups infiltrated into the country from a neighbouring State, as already indicated in the address by the President of the Republic of 16 March 1991. These groups engaged in widespread acts of subversion, murder, destruction, arson and pillage in the governorates of Basra, Meisan, Dhi Qar, Qadisiya, Karbala, Najaf, Muthanna and Babil and the same thing happened a few days later in the governorates of Sulaimaniya, Irbil and Dohuk.

It is noteworthy that the neighbouring State from the territory of which these groups came has not concealed its sympathy, as expressed in statements by its officials, with the acts committed by these groups. These armed groups have engaged in widespread sabotage operations, including the destruction and pillage of hospitals, universities, schools, court-houses, food warehouses, official government offices, public utilities such as electricity and water supply and fire-fighting facilities and other public service institutions, as well as the large-scale destruction and pillage of houses, commercial establishments, vehicles and other private property.

The losses suffered by State institutions and citizens as a result of these deliberate criminal acts are estimated at very large amounts. Moreover, these criminal acts have created an extremely serious situation from the standpoint of the living conditions, health and welfare of several million Iraqi citizens who have already suffered greatly from the damage caused by the military operations, as indicated in the letter which I sent to you on 3 March 1991.

The purpose of this letter is to give you a general idea of the nature of the losses suffered by Iraq as a result of these deliberate acts of sabotage. We will subsequently be providing you with detailed information concerning these losses.

Accept, Sir, the assurances of our highest consideration.

(<u>Signed</u>) Tariq AZIZ
Deputy Prime Minister and
Minister for Foreign Affairs of
the Republic of Iraq

0326

Security Council

Distr.
GENERAL

S/22379
23 March 1991

ORIGINAL: ENGLISH

LETTER DATED 22 MARCH 1991 FROM THE PERMANENT REPRESENTATIVE
OF THE ISLAMIC REPUBLIC OF IRAN TO THE UNITED NATIONS
ADDRESSED TO THE SECRETARY-GENERAL

Upon instructions from my Government, and with reference to public statements made by a number of Iraqi officials and insinuations made in the letters addressed to Your Excellency from the Foreign Minister and Permanent Representative of Iraq, contained in Security Council documents S/22371 and S/22364 respectively, I have the honour to bring the following to your attention.

The Islamic Republic of Iran pursued vigorously an active policy of neutrality in the tragic conflict in the Persian Gulf, while taking every possible measure in order to bring the bloodshed and destruction of Iraq and the region to a speedy end and mitigate the suffering of the innocent people of Iraq. In this context, in addition to its intense diplomatic efforts, my Government, in coordination with the Security Council Sanctions Committee, has dispatched several shipments of humanitarian assistance including medicine and foodstuff to Iraq.

The Government of the Islamic Republic of Iran, in response to allegations of dubious character, has declared at the highest level that, in line with its Constitution, it does not seek to interfere in the internal affairs of Iraq, and has categorically rejected all such irresponsible allegations. Furthermore, in accordance with the same principles governing its foreign policy and consistent with the very strong and clear position it adopted against bombardment of civilian areas in Iraq by allied forces, the Islamic Republic of Iran cannot remain but alarmed at numerous reports of horrifying attacks by government forces against innocent civilians as well as reported desecration of holy shrines and prominent religious personalities. Such concerns are shared by Muslims all over the world, and by the international community in general.

I will be grateful if this letter were circulated as a document of the Security Council.

(Signed) Kamal KHARRAZI
Ambassador ·
Permanent Representative

91-09371 2391b (E)

0327

**UNITED
NATIONS**

Security Council

S

Distr.
GENERAL

S/22380
24 March 1991
ENGLISH
ORIGINAL: ARABIC

LETTER DATED 23 MARCH 1991 FROM THE PERMANENT REPRESENTATIVE OF
IRAQ TO THE UNITED NATIONS ADDRESSED TO THE SECRETARY-GENERAL

On instructions from my Government and further to the letter which I addressed
to you on 20 March 1991 concerning the continuing overflight of Iraqi territory by
United States military aircraft, I have the honour to inform you that to date
81 formations have flown a total of 171 sorties. The operations have been
concentrated in the areas of southern Baghdad, Al-Qadisiyah, eastern Baghdad,
Al-Habbaniyah, Al-Ramadi, Tikrit, Kut, Karbala, Khanaqin and Al-Najaf. The
formations flew at an altitude of between 3,000 and 7,500 metres at a speed of
720 kilometres per hour. In addition, United States military aircraft shot down
two PC-9 aircraft in northern Iraq.

I should be grateful if you would arrange for this letter to be circulated as
a document of the Security Council.

(Signed)   Abdul Amir AL-ANBARI
Ambassador
Permanent Representative

91-09404 2244e (E)

0328

UNITED NATIONS

Security Council

S

Distr.
GENERAL

S/22384
25 March 1991
ENGLISH
ORIGINAL: ARABIC

**LETTER DATED 25 MARCH 1991 FROM THE PERMANENT REPRESENTATIVE OF
IRAQ TO THE UNITED NATIONS ADDRESSED TO THE SECRETARY-GENERAL**

On instructions from my Government, and further to my letter dated
24 March 1991 concerning ongoing violations of Iraqi airspace by aircraft belonging
to the United States Air Force, I have the honour to inform you that, up to
24 March 1991, this United States air activity has amounted to 134 sorties by 62
formations. These overflights, at altitudes ranging from 7 to 8 km and at a speed
of 750 kph, have focused on the city of Baghdad, Kut, Rutbah and Rozazah.

I should be grateful if you would have this letter circulated as a document of
the Security Council.

(Signed) Dr. Abdul Amir AL-ANBARI
Ambassador
Permanent Representative

91-09519 2330j (E)

0329

**UNITED
NATIONS**

Security Council

Distr.
GENERAL

S/22385
25 March 1991

ORIGINAL: ENGLISH

S

LETTER DATED 22 MARCH 1991 FROM THE SECRETARY-GENERAL ADDRESSED
TO THE PRESIDENT OF THE SECURITY COUNCIL

I have the honour to refer to my statement yesterday in informal consultations
of the Security Council in which I announced my decision to appoint a successor to
Ambassador Gunnar Jarring as Special Representative to the Middle East.
Ambassador Jarring announced his retirement from this position in a letter
addressed to me on 11 January 1991.

I should like to confirm my decision, effective today, to appoint
Ambassador Edouard Brunner of Switzerland as Special Representative to the Middle
East in accordance with paragraph 3 of Security Council resolution 242 of
22 November 1967.

(Signed) Javier PEREZ de CUELLAR

91-09525 2223f (E)

0330

UNITED
NATIONS

General Assembly   Security Council

Distr.
GENERAL

A/45/986
S/22389
26 March 1991
ENGLISH
ORIGINAL: ARABIC

GENERAL ASSEMBLY
Forty-fifth session
Agenda items 23 and 153
QUESTION OF PALESTINE
IRAQI AGGRESSION AND THE CONTINUED
  OCCUPATION OF KUWAIT IN FLAGRANT
  VIOLATION OF THE CHARTER OF THE
  UNITED NATIONS

SECURITY COUNCIL
Forty-sixth year

<u>Letter dated 26 March 1991 from the Permanent Representative of
Kuwait to the United Nations addressed to the Secretary-General</u>

On instructions from my Government, I wish to inform you as follows:

In recent months, and even after the liberation of Kuwait, some irresponsible
parties have been seeking to sow discord by reiterating biased statements directed
against the State, the Government and the people of Kuwait, which suffered greatly
as a result of a tyrannical occupation to which Kuwaitis and other residents,
entire residential districts and their population, as well as the land, the air and
the sea, fell victim. On the eve of the liberation of Kuwait, these parties began
to warn of a "massacre" and lamented in advance the fate of certain groups, while
remaining silent concerning the emigration of about 100,000 Palestinians, the
confiscation of their property and even the death of some of them during the
tyrannical Iraqi occupation of Kuwait. We observe leaders seeking to spread
sedition instead of extending a helping hand; at the present time, they are
treating Kuwait and its population in a malevolent and hostile manner, instead of a
spirit of friendship and brotherhood. They are spreading rumours concerning the
treatment of non-Kuwaiti residents who, in actual fact, feel an intense desire to
see the re-establishment of peace and security for all Kuwaiti and non-Kuwaiti
residents.

Since the recovery of its authority over its national territory, the
Government of Kuwait has been diligently endeavouring to restore security and
stability and protect its nationals and other residents in accordance with the law
and in a manner consistent with international conventions. While exercising its

91-09696 2211g (E)

/...

0331

powers in regard to the process of repopulation, as well as reconstruction, the Government has affirmed that every member of society is legally responsible for his actions and that no violations will be permitted against nationals or other residents. In confirmation of this policy, the Government invited the International Committee of the Red Cross to visit any detainees in Kuwait, to interview them in private and to submit reports to the authorities for the investigation of any violations of their rights. Furthermore, the Government appointed a representative of the Ministry of Justice at each detention centre to monitor and investigate any allegation concerning violation of the rights of nationals or other residents of any nationality.

While lamenting its martyrs and attempting to extinguish the flames which the aggressor and its allies kindled in the land and in the hearts of our people, Kuwait calls upon all persons to extinguish the flames of sedition which are being fanned by biased parties and to help it to normalize the situation in the true interests not only of Kuwait but of the world as a whole.

I should be grateful if you would kindly have this letter circulated as a document of the General Assembly, under items 23 and 153, and of the Security Council.

(Signed) Mohammad A. ABULHASAN
Permanent Representative

0332

UNITED NATIONS

Security Council

S

Distr.
GENERAL

S/22394
22 March 1991

ORIGINAL: ENGLISH

LETTER DATED 21 MARCH 1991 FROM THE PERMANENT REPRESENTATIVE OF
KUWAIT TO THE UNITED NATIONS ADDRESSED TO THE PRESIDENT OF THE
SECURITY COUNCIL

Further to my letter of 14 March 1991, I should like to forward the assessment by the Ministry of Information of Kuwaiti property seized or damaged by Iraq.

I should appreciate it if you would arrange for this letter to be circulated as a document of the Security Council.

(Signed) Mohammad A. ABULHASAN
Ambassador
Permanent Representative

91-09246 2209g (E)

/...

Annex I

Ministry of Information

[Original: Arabic]

1. Stored materials

    Radio spare parts
    Television spare parts
    Paper and envelopes
    Supplies and stationery
    Printed materials
    Accessories and furniture

2. Office furniture, typewriters, copying machines, etc.

3. Cars, trucks and lifts

4. Printing presses of the old and new Government printing offices

5. Stolen television and radio programmes (it must be mentioned that this figure is the total spent for the production of programmes over the past 10 years; also, it should be noted that it is difficult to estimate the value of some documentary programmes and films)

6. Loss of revenue from the sale of periodicals such as the magazine Al-Arabi, revenue from television advertising and the revenue of the Government printing office

7. Value of the buildings of the Ministry of Information which are unfit for use, including the buildings of the Kuwait Museum, the Planetarium and the three theatres

8. Losses due to the destruction of the television transmitting stations at al-Mitla', Rawdhatain and Failaka, the studios and their contents and the cinema building and all its equipment

9. Radio transmitting stations at Maqwa', Kabd and Juyun, together with the related studios and their contents

10. Spare parts for the engineering services

    Note: These estimates do not include the costs stemming from the losses sustained by the National Museum and the Islamic Museum, which housed cultural treasures that cannot be valued in material terms. A full study is being conducted at present for the purpose of establishing estimates of these possessions, which we shall furnish to you upon its completion.

0334

/...

Annex II

Ministry of Information

Furniture, typewriters and copying machines stolen

Furniture

    Leaders' offices
    Civil servants' offices
    Copying machines
    Typewriters
    Television sets
    Videos
    Word-processing equipment
    Rugs and carpets

/...

0335

Annex III

Ministry of Information

List of equipment of transmitting stations and studios of the Ministry of Information

I. Radio

1. Kabd short-wave transmitting station

The Iraqi authorities dismantled and plundered the four new transmitters which were in this station, each having a capacity of 500 kilowatts. They also destroyed the station buildings housing all the other transmitters, of which there were seven: six had a capacity of 500 kilowatts, while the seventh had a capacity of 250 kilowatts. In addition, the antenna grids were destroyed. Consequently, the losses at this station are estimated as follows:

-   500-kilowatt transmitters and related equipment

-   250-kilowatt transmitters and related equipment

-   Antenna grid

-   Buildings required for housing the said equipment and transmitters, with all their appurtenances

2. Kabd medium-wave transmitting station

The transmitter buildings and the buildings of the power generating station at this station were destroyed, along with the power supply rooms of the (a) and (b) antennas. The replacement cost of this station is as follows:

-   750-kilowatt transmitters and related equipment

-   1.5-megawatt generator

-   Refrigerator and fire-fighting equipment and other installations

-   Transmitter and generator buildings

3. Maqwa' transmitting station

The new units in this station and the new antennas were dismantled and stolen, as well as the power supply rooms and other equipment in this station; also, the building constructed to house this equipment was destroyed.

In addition, the old building at this station, housing its power supply equipment, was destroyed.

0336

/...

4. Radio broadcasting studios, including transmitting, recording, editing and music studios, the music room, main control, electronic maintenance, outside broadcast, the ministry telephone exchange, reception and frequency monitoring: the equipment located in these places were dismantled and stolen.

II. Television

Transmitting

1. Al-Mitla' transmitting station

This station was destroyed in its entirety, along with the old station adjacent to it which serves as a stand-by.

2. Failaka transmitting station

The old and new buildings of this station were destroyed, and the new equipment in the old buildings was stolen. In addition, the main transmitting tower suffered damage to cables ... in four places. The cost of the buildings and equipment and of the repair of the damage to the transmitting tower amounts to:

Studios

The various equipment was stolen from all the television and cinema studios.

1. Production studios

(80 m, 500 m, 800 m) 4 x 1.5

2. News broadcasting studios

(No. 1, No. 2 and News)

3. Editing centre

4. Telecine and video recording

5. Main control and teletext

6. Outside broadcast, including seven vehicles equipped for broadcasting: 7 x 1.5 million

7. Engineering communications

8. Cinema (all the laboratories and equipment in the cinema building)

9. Portable cameras

0337

/...

Annex IV

Ministry of Information

List of radio broadcasting studios

Location	Description	Number	Estimated cost	Total
Broadcasting studio	Sound recorders - Mixer Microphones - Additional auxiliary equipment	12		
Production studio	Recorders - Mixer - Microphones Echo chambers - Additional auxiliary equipment	4		
Drama studio	Recorders - Mixer - Microphones Echo and special effects equipment - Additional equipment	2		
Music studio	24-channel recorders and ordinary recorders 24-channel mixer - Echo chambers Noise-reduction equipment Other auxiliary eqiupment	2		
Music room	Recorders and mixer - Sound equipment - Dubbing equipment Lighting equipment - Chairs and additional auxiliary equipment	1		
Main control	Special radios - Cassette recordings - Miscellaneous auxiliary equipment			
Electronic maintenance	Special testing equipment Miscellaneous equipment and appliances for testing broadcasting equipment and measuring equipment for audio processing - Optic fibre testing equipment			
Outside broadcast	Portable recorders and portable mixer - Amplifiers - Portable special-effects equipment Miscellaneous additional equipment 4 vehicles fully equipped for radio broadcasting			

0338

/...

Location	Description	Number	Estimated cost	Total
Ministry telephone exchange	Telephones - Computer equipment Special testing equipment			
Receiving and frequency equipment				

0339   /...

Annex V

Ministry of Information

2 complete television cameras
4 VHS video cassette recorders
2 Betamax video cassette recorders
2 Umatik recorders
13 1-inch video recorders
2 visual-effects devices
1 sound-effects device
1 machine control device
3 sound recorders
4 speakers
2 electronic printing machines
1 electronic graphics plotter
2 microphones

Subtitle section

8 dubbing devices
6 monochrome monitors
6 VHS video cassette recorders
4 colour monitors
2 colour television sets

0340

/...

Annex VI

Ministry of Information

Thefts from the cinema building

1. Filmline negative film developer
2. Three Filmline positive film developers
3. Colour corrector
4. Two 16-mm film printers
5. One 35-mm film printer
6. Special-effects device
7. Six Prévosts
8. Two Shelburger mixers
9. Four 35-mm projectors
10. Three 16-mm projectors
11. Ten 35-mm and 16-mm sound playback machines
12. Four 35-mm and 16-mm sound recording and re-recording machines
13. One 16-mm optical sound transmitter
14. One 35-mm optical sound transmitter

0341

/...

Annex VII

Ministry of Information

Note: Equipment that may be recovered, subject to inspection and verification of its serviceability and of the fact that no parts are missing, if in the same sound condition as before it was stolen. This equipment includes the following:

1.   Radio

Broadcasting studios

48 studio sound recorders
12 studio sound mixers
48 studio microphones
48 ancillary items

Production studios

16 studio sound recorders
4 studio sound mixers
16 studio microphones
4 ancillary items

Drama studios

8 studio sound recorders
2 sound mixers
8 microphones
2 echo chambers
2 ancillary and effects devices

Music studio

2 24-channel recorders
8 regular studio recorders
2 24-channel sound mixers
2 echo chambers
2 other ancillary devices

Music room

4 music-room sound recorders
1 music-room sound mixer
4 dubbing systems
Complete lighting system
Full audio system
450 luxury chairs

0342

/...

Outside broadcasting

4 vehicles fully equipped for remote broadcasting

2. Television

Production studios

15 cameras complete with accessories
4 image mixers
3 effects devices
8 video recording devices
350 spotlights
20 sound mixers
5 lighting control panels
1 electronic dubbing device
38 colour monitors
38 microphones complete with accessories
5 colour television sets
Complete audio system

Broadcasting studios

9 cameras complete with accessories
3 image mixers
12 colour monitors
36 monochrome monitors
19 microphones
3 dubbing devices
2 slide projectors
1 computerized slide projector
1 graphics device
3 special-effects devices
12 sound recorders
6 audio turntables
2 image-enhancement devices
2 electronic printing machines
Complete audio system
120 spotlights

Engineering liaison section

30 microwave devices
50 walkie-talkies
1 mobile tower vehicle
4 microwave vehicles
6 videotape recorders
2 computers
10 inspection and metering devices
15 monitors
10 sound recorders

0343

/...

Video recording and telecine section

39 video recording devices
2 16/35-mm telecine devices

Main control and teletext

2 image system converters
2 SECAM-to-PAL converters
2 PAL-to-SECAM converters
1 colour control device
2 complete teletext devices
8 colour television sets

Outside broadcasting

8 vehicles fully equipped for remote television broadcasting (including one whose contents were stolen and which was set on fire)

Portable cameras

30 complete portable cameras
15 complete portable recorders (video recorders)
4 large, fixed video recorders
30 complete lighting units
3 image mixers
18 sound mixers
85 microphones

Montage centre

3 image mixers
4 sound mixers
14 colour monitors
1 monochrome monitor

Lighting

300 spotlights in the production studios, together with control panel
120 spotlights in the broadcasting studios, together with control panel
270 spotlights kept in the lighting stores
3,150 light bulbs kept in the lighting stores
4 lighting control panels kept in the lighting stores
2 lighting vehicles containing:
  45 spotlights
   2 lighting control panels
  28 light stands

About 50 spotlights in the broadcasting room, together with control panel

0344   /...

Cutting section

4 colour monitors
4 monochrome monitors
3 sets of earphones
6 speakers
8 colour televisions
8 VHS video cassette recorders
4 Betamax video cassette recorders
2 Umatik video cassette recorders
2 2-inch video recorders
1 slow-speed video recorder
6 microphones with stands

UNITED NATIONS

Security Council

S

Distr.
GENERAL

S/22401
26 March 1991

ORIGINAL: ENGLISH

LETTER DATED 26 MARCH 1991 FROM THE PERMANENT REPRESENTATIVE OF
THE ISLAMIC REPUBLIC OF IRAN TO THE UNITED NATIONS ADDRESSED TO
THE SECRETARY-GENERAL

Upon instructions from my Government, and with reference to the letter of the Permanent Representative of Iraq contained in Security Council document S/22397, I have the honour to bring the following to your attention.

The Islamic Republic of Iran categorically rejects the baseless, irresponsible and potentially dangerous allegations contained in the above-mentioned letter. Iran fully observes the terms of cease-fire and has closely monitored the developments in border region in view of the special circumstances inside Iraq and possible abuse of the situation by suspicious elements. I should point out, however, that since the outbreak of recent hostilities between Iraq and the allied forces, there have been frequent instances of technical and in cases serious Iraqi violations of the terms of cease-fire between Iran and Iraq. My Government will, in due course and in line with its past practice, provide the details of these violations which include infiltrations into Iranian territory, violations of airspace and territorial waters of the Islamic Republic of Iran and firing of artillery across the border into Iranian territory.

As I clearly stated in my letter of 22 March 1991 (S/22379), the Islamic Republic of Iran, which pursued a policy of neutrality in the course of the recent war, does not interfere in the internal affairs of Iraq and has rejected the allegations advanced in order to distract international attention from the internal difficulties faced by the Iraqi authorities as well as reports of horrifying measures adopted by Iraqi armed forces against Iraqi civilians.

It will be highly appreciated if this letter were circulated as a document of the Security Council.

(Signed) Kamal KHARRAZI
Ambassador
Permanent Representative

91-09690 2840a (E)

0346

UNITED NATIONS

A S

General Assembly   Security Council

Distr.
GENERAL

A/46/122
S/22403
27 March 1991

ORIGINAL: ENGLISH

GENERAL ASSEMBLY
Forty-sixth session
Item 72 of the preliminary list*
UNITED NATIONS RELIEF AND WORKS
  AGENCY FOR PALESTINE REFUGEES
  IN THE NEAR EAST

SECURITY COUNCIL
Forty-sixth year

<u>Letter dated 26 March 1991 from the Permanent Representative of
Japan to the United Nations addressed to the Secretary-General</u>

I have the honour to transmit herewith the text of the decision made on
26 March 1991 by the Government of Japan to make a donation to the Gulf
crisis-related emergency food distribution programme of the United Nations Relief
and Works Agency for Palestine Refugees in the Near East (see annex).

I should be grateful if you would arrange to have the text of the present
letter and its annex circulated as an official document of the General Assembly,
under item 72 of the preliminary list, and of the Security Council.

(<u>Signed</u>) Yoshio HATANO
Ambassador Extraordinary
and Plenipotentiary
Permanent Representative of
Japan to the United Nations

---

*   A/46/50.

91-09776   2212g (E)

/...

0347

ANNEX

Donation of the Government of Japan to the Gulf crisis-related
emergency food distribution programme of the United Nations
Relief and Works Agency for Palestine Refugees in the Near East

1. The Government of Japan, in response to a request from the United Nations
Relief and Works Agency for Palestine Refugees in the Near East (UNRWA), decided on
Tuesday, 26 March 1991, to make a contribution of 1.37 billion yen (approximately
$US 10 million) from its reserve fund in support of the efforts of UNRWA on behalf
of Palestinians living in the West Bank and the Gaza Strip.

2. The Palestinians in the West Bank and the Gaza Strip are facing deteriorating
economic conditions and food shortages because of the cessation of income remitted
by migratory workers in the Gulf region, the decrease in economic assistance from
nations in the Gulf region, and the curfew imposed by the Israeli authorities in
the occupied territories as a result of the Gulf crisis. UNRWA established an
emergency food distribution programme for 295,000 households (about 1.7 million
people) in the West Bank and the Gaza Strip for the three-month period that began
in mid-January this year in order to address the problem of malnutrition among the
Palestinian people, and it has sent requests to various countries in the world for
donations towards the sum of about $US 33 million needed to implement the said
programme. On 7 March, a letter from the Acting Commissioner-General of UNRWA was
dispatched to the Japanese Government requesting a contribution to the programme.

3. In response, the Government of Japan, in a humanitarian effort to help
eliminate the problem of malnutrition among the Palestinians caused by the Gulf
crisis, has decided to extend this emergency aid. The Japanese donation is the
largest donation from a single country and is second only to that of the European
Community.

0348

UNITED
NATIONS

Security Council

Distr.
GENERAL

S/22406
27 March 1991

ORIGINAL: ENGLISH

LETTER DATED 26 MARCH 1991 FROM THE PERMANENT REPRESENTATIVE
OF KUWAIT TO THE UNITED NATIONS ADDRESSED TO THE PRESIDENT
OF THE SECURITY COUNCIL

I have the honour to enclose herewith a statement made by
H.E. Dr. Badr Jassem Al-Yaqoub, Minister of Information and Minister of State for
National Assembly Affairs, on behalf of the Government of Kuwait.

I should appreciate it if you would arrange for this letter to be circulated
as an official document of the Security Council.

(Signed) Mohammad A. ABULHASAN
Ambassador
Permanent Representative

91-09860 2845a (E)   /...

0349

Annex

[Original: Arabic]

Statement made by Dr. Badr Jassem Al-Yaqoub, Kuwaiti Minister
of Information and Minister of State for National Assembly
Affairs, on 26 March 1991

Dr. Badr Jassem Al-Yaqoub, the Kuwaiti Minister of Information and Minister of State for National Assembly Affairs, has made the following statement concerning the rumours that are circulating in some political and media circles to the effect that Kuwait is mistreating its Palestinian brothers residing in Kuwait:

"1. These strategems, lies and allegations which are being circulated to the detriment of Kuwait under the present circumstances are merely a continuation of the hostile policy that has been pursued by well-known parties since the beginning of the criminal Iraqi invasion of Kuwait's territory. We are fully confident that world public opinion will not be deceived by these strategems, that it will realize their underlying aims and objectives and that it will be able to separate the wheat from the chaff.

2. Kuwait has always diligently endeavoured to apply the law fully to all Kuwaiti and non-Kuwaiti residents alike, without discrimination among them on grounds of race, origin or affiliation. Anyone who infringes or violates the sacrosanct provisions of the law is subject to its penalties in keeping with the principle of the rule of law and public order in the State, as is the practice throughout the world.

3. If certain acts have been committed against Kuwaiti or other residents in the circumstances that Kuwait has been experiencing, these matters will be referred to the judicial authorities for judgement in accordance with the law and Kuwait's consistent practice.

Kuwait wishes to assure world public opinion, at all levels from leaders to Governments, peoples and organizations, that it will maintain its tradition as a land of security, justice and peace and that, even under the present circumstances that it is experiencing in the aftermath of the criminal aggression against its territory, Kuwait is perfectly willing to receive all petitions and claims concerning any allegedly unlawful practices against residents of Kuwait, so that appropriate measures can be taken in this regard in accordance with the provisions of the law. Kuwait also affirms its full willingness to receive representatives of international humanitarian bodies and organizations in order to examine this question."

0350

UNITED NATIONS

S

Security Council

Distr.
GENERAL

S/22407
27 March 1991
ENGLISH
ORIGINAL: ARABIC

LETTER DATED 27 MARCH 1991 FROM THE PERMANENT REPRESENTATIVE OF
IRAQ TO THE UNITED NATIONS ADDRESSED TO THE SECRETARY-GENERAL

On instructions from my Government, and further to my letter dated
25 March 1991 concerning ongoing violations of Iraqi airspace by aircraft belonging
to the United States Air Force, I have the honour to inform you that these United
States air operations on 25 and 26 March 1991 took the following form:

I.   On 25 March 1991

1.   The United States air operations amounted to 138 sorties flown by 65
formations.

2.   The aircraft flew at altitudes of 2-9 km and at a speed of 800 kph.

3.   The aircraft types were identified as F.14s and F.15s.

4.   The enemy aircraft focused on the areas of southern Baghdad, northern Baghdad
and the city of Baghdad.

5.   The objective of the enemy aircraft was to engage in surveillance and
provocation, since they flew over the city of Baghdad several times.

II.   On 26 March 1991

1.   The United States air operations amounted to 126 sorties flown by 63
formations.

2.   The aircraft flew at altitudes of 2-8 km and at a speed of 800 kph.

3.   The aircraft types were identified as F.14s and F.15s.

4.   The enemy aircraft focused on the city of Baghdad, southern Baghdad, northern
Baghdad and the western region.

91-09866   2213g (E)

/...

0351

5.   The objective of the enemy aircraft was to engage in surveillance and provocation, since they flew over the city of Baghdad several times.

I should be grateful if you would kindly have this letter circulated as a document of the Security Council.

Accept, Sir, etc.

(Signed) Abdul Amir AL-ANBARI
Ambassador
Permanent Representative

0352

United Nations

Press Release

Department of Public Information • News Coverage Service • New York

DEV/1864
22 March 1991

UNDP APPROVES $4 MILLION GULF CRISIS PROGRAMME

NEW YORK, 21 March (UNDP) -- The United Nations Development Programme (UNDP) yesterday approved a Special Programme of up to $4 million to help identify and meet the urgent relief, rehabilitation and development needs of the countries affected by the Gulf crisis.

The Programme will respond to five major areas of need, identified in consultation with the affected countries, UNDP field offices, United Nations agencies and others: immediate humanitarian needs, primarily emergency relief in Kuwait and Iraq; immediate and medium-term human needs, especially the socio-economic reintegration of returnees; rehabilitation of institutions and infrastructure, particularly in Kuwait and Iraq; economic management, where necessary, to rechart socio-economic strategies; and environmental recovery.

Initial funds have already been allocated under the Special Programme to meet emergency relief needs in Iraq and Kuwait, including medicine, water and sanitation. Funds have also been earmarked in response to requests from both Jordan and the Philippines for assistance, in cooperation with the United Nations specialized agencies, to reintegrate returnee families. Special attention will be paid to the situation of women-headed households and other vulnerable groups. The UNDP is also responding to requests from Bahrain and Qatar for assistance to address the environmental consequences of the war, especially the oil spill in the Gulf.

For other affected countries in the Middle East, Asia, Africa and Eastern and Central Europe, Programme funds will be used to assist Governments to assess the impact of the Gulf crisis and to launch plans of action in critical areas, drawing on the expertise of the United Nations system.

UNDP Resident Representatives -- who also serve as Resident Coordinators for the United Nations system -- will play central roles in working with the Governments of affected countries to mobilize the resources of the United Nations development system and to coordinate assistance.

"The main challenge", said UNDP Administrator, William H. Draper III, "is to link the issues of peace, security and development in the post-war period, and, by so doing, heal the wounds of war".

(more)

2385P

0353

Press Release DEV/1864
22 March 1991

To meet this challenge, "we must respond with the moral and material support commensurate with the scale of the need", said Mohamed A. Nour, UNDP Assistant Administrator and Director, Regional Bureau for Arab States and Europe. Mr. Nour chairs the Gulf Task Force established by the Administrator in February to respond to development needs in the post-war period. The first report of the Gulf Task Force was presented to the February session of UNDP's Governing Council.

* *** *

0354

2385P

United Nations

Press Release

Department of Public Information • News Coverage Service • New York

FAO/3508
27 March 1991

FAO ANNOUNCES EMERGENCY FOOD AID FOR VULNERABLE GROUPS IN IRAQ; FOOD SUPPLY SITUATION DETERIORATES IN COUNTRY

ROME, 26 March (FAO) -- Vulnerable groups in Iraq whose numbers have risen by 50 per cent because of the war will be provided emergency food aid worth over $17 million, the Food and Agriculture Organization (FAO) announced today.

"The food situation in Iraq is increasingly becoming so desperate that people are turning to cereals normally used for animal feed", FAO Director-General Edouard Saouma said in a statement. "Worst affected are the vulnerable groups whose survival now critically depends on large-scale emergency food aid."

Referring to a recent on-the-spot assessment of crop prospects, he said that although a large area had been planted, the outlook for grain harvest was poor. "The agricultural sector has been seriously disrupted by the war, as well as by shortage of inputs and farm labour", he added.

Mr. Saouma, on recommendation of World Food Programme (WFP) Executive Director James Ingram, approved an emergency food aid allocation totalling $17,126,097.

A shipment of 29,400 tons of cereals, 1,470 tons of vegetable oil, 1,000 tons of canned fish or meat, 56 tons of cheese, 1,800 tons of pulses, 340 tons of enriched dried skimmed milk and 1,100 tons of sugar will be supplied from WFP resources to a total of 735,000 war-affected vulnerable persons, including orphans, mothers, the elderly and the disabled.

According to FAO, local food production in Iraq represents only about 25 to 30 per cent of consumption requirements. Stocks of basic foods are reportedly being depleted, while cereals normally used for animal feed are now being also used for human feeding. Milk powder is now exclusively distributed to sick children on medical prescription. On the open market, prices are reportedly extremely high with wheat flour 40 times more expensive than rationed wheat flour.

(more)

0355

2440P

For information media—not an official record

Apart from the vulnerable groups, others are also suffering from shortages, especially those who cannot afford to pay open market prices, and are restricted to subsist on the constantly decreasing rationing system. It is estimated that those dependent on the rationing system would need some 365,000 tons of basic food commodities until the next harvest in June, according to FAO.

* *** *

0356

외 무 부

종 별 :

번 호 : UNW-0733   일 시 : 91 0329 0200

수 신 : 장 관(국연,중동일,기정)

발 신 : 주 유엔 대사

제 목 : 안보리

연: UNW-0701

안보리는 금 3.28 오후 비공식 협의를 갖고 M.AHTISAARI 조사단의 쿠웨이트 방문 결과 및 사이프러스 문제를 검토한바, 동 주요 결과를 아래보고함.

1. A. AHTISAARI 조사단 쿠웨이트 방문: 별첨보고서를 접수하였으나, 실질토의는 없었음.

2. 사이프러스 문제: 연호 사무총장 보고와 관련 의장성명 발표문에 합의한바, 동 성명문 내용은 추보위계임.

첨부:상기 보고서: UNW(F)-140

끝

(대사 노창희-국장)

국기국	1차보	중아국	정문국	안기부	이주국	장관	차관	청와대	1차보, 2차보

UNW(府)-140   10329 0200
(국연. 중동일. 기정)   총16매

UNW-0733 의
첨부물

Report to the Secretary-General on humanitarian needs in Kuwait
in the immediate post-crisis environment by a mission to the
area led by Mr. Martti Ahtisaari, Under-Secretary-General for
Administration and Management, dated 28 March 1991

CONTENTS

16-1

0358

- 2 -

INTRODUCTION

1.   You asked me to travel, as a matter of urgency, to Kuwait and Iraq to assess humanitarian needs there in the immediate post-crisis environment, and to bring with me a team comprising representatives of the appropriate United Nations agencies and programmes. Your decision was announced in a press statement of 1 March 1991.

2.   On 3 March 1991, the President of the Security Council made a statement on behalf of the Council, in which it welcomed your announcement and invited you to keep it informed in the shortest possible time of the progress of this mission, in respect of which it pledged to take immediate action (S/22322).

3.   I submitted a report to you on the first part of my mission, that relating to Iraq, on 20 March 1991 and, in a letter of that date, you transmitted it to the President of the Security Council (S/22366). As noted in your letter, the Mission was to commence its visit to Kuwait on 22 March 1991, and you stated that you would convey the report on that visit as soon as possible.

4.   After consultations at headquarters, I myself departed for the mission area on 23 March, arriving in Kuwait on 25 March. I was received there by the Minister of Planning of the Kuwaiti Government, Mr. Suleiman Abdul-Razaq Al-Mutawa, and by members of the mission, who had remained in Bahrain after my departure for headquarters on 19 March and had preceded me to Kuwait on 23 March.

5.   In Kuwait, the Mission comprised representatives of the Secretariat, UNDP, UNDRO, UNHCR, WFP and FAO. It received substantial assistance from Mr. Abdulrahim Abby Farah and members of his mission who were at the time in Kuwait looking into the subject of damages undergone by Kuwait during events subsequent to 2 August 1990 and, in particular, from the technical knowledge and experience of members of Mr. Farah's mission from UNEP. It was also materially assisted by representatives of UNICEF's office in the Arab Gulf States, and by a WHO mission which was also in the country at that time. The mission completed its work in Kuwait on 27 March and departed on that date. I returned to New York today, 28 March 1991.

16-2

0359

- 3 -

I. MODUS OPERANDI IN KUWAIT

6.   In close consultation with myself, members of the mission who had remained in Bahrain while I was undertaking consultations in New York began their work immediately upon arrival in Kuwait on 23 March 1991. Teams began to meet with Kuwaiti officials in the fields of food, agriculture, water, sanitation, health, transportation, communications, energy and environmental matters, and to visit various sites and locations throughout Kuwait. Upon my arrival on 25 March 1991 I was briefed by senior members of the mission and immediately met for a working session with Mr. Suleiman Abdul-Razaq Al-Mutawa, Minister of Planning in the Government of Kuwait. With him, I was then briefed at Camp Freedom by Brigadier-General Mooney, U.S. Army, and members of the Kuwaiti Joint Task Force. I met that evening with Mr. Sheikh Nasser As-Sabah, Minister of State in the Kuwaiti Foreign Ministry, and other Ministers. On 26 March I was received by His Highness, Sheikh Saad Al-Abdullah As-Salim As-Sabah, Crown Prince and Prime Minister of Kuwait. I also met with Mr. Abdul-Wahab Al-Fozan, Minister of Health, and with representatives of the diplomatic community. I toured the city of Kuwait and, by helicopter, many parts of the country, and saw conditions there. Members of the mission accompanied me on these visits and inspections, and continued and completed their technical work in the country. With the excellent cooperation of Mr. Farah and his team I and my mission had access to relevant aspects of its technical findings, upon which certain parts of this report also draw. I was briefed by Dr. Daniel Tarantola, of a WHO mission that had been invited to the country by the Government of Kuwait in regard to their assessment of health conditions and needs.

7.   The Kuwaiti authorities afforded the mission their fullest cooperation.

II. SUMMARY OF FINDINGS AND RECOMMENDATIONS IN REGARD TO KUWAIT

8.   A summary of the mission's findings and conclusions is set out below. It is based upon a number of internal working papers, technical annexes, visits to sites, and oral reports

16-3

0360

- 4 -

by members of the mission and by other United Nations' specialists present at the time in Kuwait.

A. General remarks

9.   Kuwait is scarred by the ravages of illegal occupation and, subsidiarily, of war. At least two-thirds of the population present on 2 August 1990 are now scattered throughout the world. Those who remained have fresh memory of a brutal occupation and the sacking and pillaging of their homes, their resources and their environment. Many vividly recount inhuman or degrading treatment undergone by themselves or family members. I and my mission saw for ourselves prolific evidence of arson, looting, malicious destruction of homes, businesses, markets, museums, libraries, and all that a nation cherishes. Kuwait's coast is disfigured by broken buildings and rolls of barbed wire; its beaches made lethal by hundreds of thousands of mines. Above it hangs a thick cloud of oily dark smoke that, on some days, brings a chilly twilight at noon, as well as still-uncharted perils to health. No one knows exactly how many of its oil-wells are on fire: - but at least half, perhaps six to seven hundred, belching flames and smoke. From the air, the horizon sometimes comprises only black clouds and pillars of fire, torched in a final deliberate onslaught by retreating troops. The environmental havoc still cannot be authoritatively assessed. But its consequences are already felt by neighbouring countries, and may affect yet others still more distant. Rivers, ponds and even lakes of spilling oil lie on the sand and edge towards the wadis, the roads and the sea. Power stations, oil refineries, communications' facilities, water-desalination plants have been destroyed by war or vandalised so that they are irreparable. Harbours are blocked, ships sunk, cranes toppled. Life-preserving medical equipment - even ambulances - have been removed; mainframe computers have been ripped out of Government offices and carried off.

10.   This scene of devastation - some being calculated, much wanton - was, I learned, even worse four weeks ago, when Kuwaitis began to return to their liberated country. For much has already been done, as the following paragraphs will show, to put Kuwait back on the road to reconstruction. Food supplies are being brought in and distributed, though both officials and observers say that such distribution has at times been somewhat uneven. Some water and power have been restored. Petrol is being made available, free of charge, even for

16-4

0361

- 5 -

private vehicles. Telephone communications have been partly re-established, and
international traffic will soon follow. Assessment of damages to homes, businesses and
economic facilities and resources is under way, and much contracting for reconstruction has
already been completed. Means of internal and external transportation are starting to
function, in a limited fashion, even though there may still be limited air- and seaport
capability, and many vehicles were stolen or destroyed. Teams of specialists are beginning to
assess and remedy the oilfield disasters. A Kuwaiti Government is in place (at this time, on
a caretaker basis) and, despite vast logistical and all other species of practical problems, is
drawing up plans for reconstruction. It is working closely with a Joint Kuwaiti Task Force,
comprising elements of the armed forces allied with Kuwait in the recent conflict, that was
established in December 1990 to plan for the time when liberation should have taken place.
The allied element of the Joint Task Force comprises civil affairs elements of the US,
British, French, Canadian and Saudi Arabian armed forces, with medical, communications,
police, transportation, intelligence, aviation, finance, engineering and sanitation specialists
and teams from those Governments. At a briefing on 25 March 1991 General Mooney of
the U.S. Army and some of his senior staff described the work of the Joint Task Force in
regard to water, food and medical supplies, sanitation, power, telecommunications and
transportation, as well as in regard to damage assessment and surveys during the period from
December 1990 to date. He said that contracts worth more than US$550 million had already
been signed for work in these various areas. The Joint Task Force said that they believed
that the country had now largely overcome the emergency phase and that they anticipated
that power and communications would be effectively restored by mid-April in Kuwait City,
and that most services would be functioning throughout the country in between three and six
months. The oil industry would take longest to restore. The Minister of Planning called the
burning of the oil-wells "the crime of all centuries", because of its multifarious negative
consequences - health, environmental, economic - short- and long-term, for Kuwait and other
countries as well. General Mooney said that the amount of unexploded mines and other
ordnance was colossal. There was, he added, a good military programme for clearance, but
said that he had never seen so much of this hazard before. Many members of the mission
saw unexploded weaponry during their work in Kuwait. The Task Force said that clearance
of the quantities left behind exceeded the capabilities of the allied forces.

11.   Kuwaiti Government ministers told me that they were taking the opportunity to
review questions of population composition and the future of the work-force. Prior to 2

16-5

0362

- 6 -

August 1990 the population was about 2.3 million, of whom about 700 thousand were
Kuwaiti nationals (about 30%). Most of the population had left the country during the
period of occupation and conflict. At the time of my mission to Kuwait, estimates of the
remaining population varied between 600 and 700 thousand, of whom perhaps one-third
were Kuwaitis. The authorities have recommended that their exiled countrymen not return
to Kuwait for three months to allow for essential services to be rehabilitated, and spoke of
the possibility that the future permanent population should be limited, with others being in
the country on a more or less short-term basis. They planned that return from exile should
keep pace with the gradual resumption of economic activity, the re-establishment of basic
social amenities and reduction of environmental health hazards. While the mission was in
Kuwait this policy had not yet been finalised.

12.   As during the previous mission to Iraq, we focussed our initial attention upon the
basic areas of humanitarian concern: - the need for shelter, food supplies, clean water,
sanitation and adequate health support, as well as on the logistical capability to make these
effective for the people as a whole. Particular local conditions may create additional
hazards. The account which follows regarding the situation in these various areas of basic
concern is affected in one form or another by the general factors which I have sketched
above. Kuwait, with the assistance of the Governments cooperating with it in the Joint Task
Force, is steadily assessing its needs and seeking to overcome them within the parameters
which it is establishing. My recommendations are formulated in the spirit of cooperation
with which my mission was received and welcomed, and in the context of the assistance of
which the international community is, I believe, capable.

B. Food and Agriculture

13.   Prior to August 1990, Kuwait imported approximately 95% of its food needs, with
local agriculture and fisheries playing only a minor role in the national economy (0.7% of
GDP in 1989). The country had established a six months' strategic food reserve which was
substantially looted during the occupation. Despite this, a sufficient quantity remained to
sustain the population until liberation.

16-6

0363

- 7 -

14.   Emergency food plans for the next three months are hypothesised upon a population of 800,000. The country is organised into forty consumer cooperatives, each having a food distribution centre. The state-run Kuwait Supply Company has, since liberation, imported large amounts of food. These staples are distributed directly to the cooperatives and then made available, free of charge, to their members. Apart from this, items such as meat, fruits, vegetables and eggs are sold at subsidised prices, and in some instances made available free of charge, to cooperative members. Private retail facilities are now also beginning to open. Some shortages, apparently due to delivery delays, have been noted in respect of baby products and, on the whole, only logistical and administration bottlenecks at frontiers have hampered the general reinstitution of supplies.

15.   However, the overall situation has not as yet permitted the re-instatement of the domestic agricultural and fisheries industries whose expansion had been encouraged in recent years. The spread of oil across the land towards the sea, and the heavily mined coastal areas, have bleak implications for the future of this sector.

16.   The mission concluded that the Kuwaiti Government has already established an effective food system aimed at ensuring proper standards of nourishment and preventing suffering amongst the whole population of Kuwait, although it heard a number of complaints that there had been discrimination against certain groups, especially in the days immediately following liberation. It does not appear that any further external food aid is required by Kuwait.

C. Water, Sanitation and Health

17.   Kuwait's water supply depends largely on desalination and partly on artesian reservoirs. Moderate damage was done to the infrastructure by events subsequent to 2 August 1990, and the mission saw one desalination plant which appeared to have been wrecked by the departing forces and was said to be irreparable. Water has, however, been available in limited quantities and areas since liberation. The Joint Task Force informed the mission that it had distributed 11.75 million litres since that time in bulk or bottles. As power was restored, supplies were slowly returning to normal and reaching more

16-7

0364

- 8 -

neighbourhoods. The authorities believed that the situation would return to normal in a matter of weeks. It remains necessary, however, to monitor the quality of water being supplied, having regard to all the circumstances including the various current environmental problems.

18.   As regards sanitation, the country's three major plants suffered no structural damage and only superficial repairs are required. The Joint Task Force estimated that it would be fully operational, having been thoroughly tested, by the end of March. A contract for the collection of garbage has been concluded and this is being undertaken.

19.   Prior to 2 August 1990 the standard of health care in Kuwait was one of the highest in the world. The national health services had gradually expanded their scope by creating diagnostic and treatment facilities for non-communicable diseases which required a constantly increasing level of technical sophistication and amount of resources. This was reflected by the number and quality of health facilities, the efficiency of the emergency care services and the creation of centres specialising in a wide range of advanced medical techniques. Six regional and 9 specialised hospitals, 72 health centres and several medico-social institutions in the country were providing medical care and rehabilitation services to the entire population, free of charge. Over 3,200 doctors and 9,900 nurses - the great majority being foreign - were providing such services, with a ratio to the population of around 2.3 million which compared favourably with most countries in the world. Many of the medical technicians whose skilled work helped to make this advanced system work were also from overseas.

20.   The immediate consequence of the invasion was the departure from Kuwait of a very large number of medical personnel. The situation is now critical as regards, especially, nursing and technical staff, and the mission was told that the authorities were seeking to recruit several hundred nurses from abroad. The environment is also medically challenging, having especial regard to pollution and widely-prevalent explosives. Many hospitals, specialist clinics and health centres are either closed down or are operating at reduced capacity. There was little structural damage to the health facilities, which were also used by the occupying forces, but advanced equipment was removed and some destruction was carried out by departing troops. Despite these major difficulties, existing medical, surgical

16-8

0365

- 9 -

and dental facilities are able to deal with the most urgent needs of a population which is temporarily reduced in size.

21.   A WHO team, together with the Ministry of Public Health, has developed a plan of action for an emergency response period covering the next three months. During this time the situation would be re-assessed and further plans formulated. The plan deals with reconstruction of the health care infrastructure (both human and material); the development of surveillance centres during a critical period for the appearance of health hazards; environmental health systems; disease prevention and control, particular vigilance being required during the current period; the establishment of a post war programme to deal with post-war trauma of various kinds; and the provision of essential drugs. As to this last, while large quantities have been received from various sources, some are at or beyond expiration date, thus requiring careful inventory and verification of shipments. Other short-term needs include the resumption of diagnostic facilities and a blood bank; meeting the high demand from the population for health information and education; the restoration of emergency medical are including intensive care units; and the reinstatement of managerial, coordinating and technical skills to rehabilitate and reconstruct the health infrastructure. In this regard, the secondment of staff on a multilateral or bilateral basis to the Ministry of Public Health, and the creation of coordinating committees, are urgently required.

22.   A UNICEF mission arrived in Kuwait on 1 March to provide emergency relief assistance to children. The outcome of its work was a decision to mount an airlift of urgently needed vaccines and cold chain equipment, and the fielding of a team to assist the Government of Kuwait in dealing with the psychological trauma effects of war on children. Members of the UNICEF team briefed me and the members of my mission on 25 March 1991.

D. Environmental Questions

23.   Kuwait has between 1200 and 1400 oil wells (estimates vary). According to local sources, between 500 and 800 were premeditatedly set on fire in the last days of February by the retreating forces. They pour huge clouds of dark oily smoke into the skies, and their flames can be seen for many miles. Damaged wells are also pouring crude oil onto the

16-9

0366

- 10 -

desert and rivers or lakes of oil are moving forward towards roads, towns and the sea. Several, which have gone out, have had to be set on fire again in order to reduce the flow of oil onto the land. The smoke from the fires forms a dense cloud ceiling at various heights up to about 12,000 feet. Depending upon weather conditions, the smoke is visible in a number of other Persian Gulf littoral States, and I am informed that its impact could spread beyond the Gulf area. The authorities have sought international help in bringing the situation under control and a number of firms, representing 80% or more of the world's present oil-well firefighting capacity, are at present in Kuwait. Work has begun on dealing with the fires, and new equipment is in some instances being built for this purpose. It is, however, made more difficult by land mines and unexploded ordnance in the surrounding areas. No authoritative estimate can as yet be given of the time that will be needed to restore the situation. It is possible that some wells could self-extinguish as water begins to be drawn into them from surrounding strata. It is estimated that about 4 - 6 million barrels of oil are burning each day.

24.   Environmental protection agencies of the allied governments have inspected the situation but there is as yet no certainty regarding the hazards to the atmosphere, to the adjacent territories, or to health. The presence of smoke clouds has appeared to lower temperatures locally. They move according to climatic conditions, especially the wind, and have been reported from several other Gulf States. Depending upon atmospheric conditions, environmentalists believe that these clouds could spread further afield.

25.   While the mission was unable to make or find any scientific assessment of the impact on health of these emissions, local anecdotal evidence relates to skin, eye and lung ailments, and the situation is being actively studied. It seems clear that monitoring, on a regional basis, is urgently required of the environmental, including health, aspects of the oil-well fires, and that a national infrastructure should be created in Kuwait to assess and communicate related data.

26.   Urgent steps are being taken in Kuwait to prevent unignited oil from reaching the sea, thereby creating a further potential marine disaster.

27.   As regards mines and other unexploded ordnance, the situation is extremely grave. A number of deaths and injuries have already been reported both among private persons and

16-10

0367

- 11 -

among military engineers seeking to neutralise mines. Some maps showing the location of minefields have been handed over to the Kuwaiti authorities. However, both urban and outlying areas are reported to have a plethora of live bombs, rockets, grenades and other unexploded devices. The authorities also stated that explosive booby-traps had been scattered. As regards mines, many thousands have been laid on and around beaches, along the border between Kuwait and Saudi Arabia, and in other areas. It appears that they are of a non-ferrous composition, thus being especially difficult to locate using orthodox mine-detecting equipment. They are, moreover, reported to be at least semi-buoyant. If this be so, the future location of at least some may be anticipated to depend upon tides and currents, and to present a threat to the coasts of other Gulf States. My mission was told that engineering detachments of the allied Governments were currently engaged in dealing with the threat from mines and other unexploded ordnance, and members indeed saw military personnel remove some from the area of mission headquarters. However, the onerous task was stated to be too great for the combined resources of the allied Governments, and other engineering concerns were being contacted.

28.   I believe that the threat to the civilian population of Kuwait (and possibly of other nearby States), as well as to livestock, requires urgent coordinated action in support of the endeavours of the Government, which is clearly deeply concerned over the situation. Already, a public education programme has been instituted to warn of the dangers, and many areas, including the intensively mined region on the Saudi Arabian border, may need permanent fencing with crossing points. It may also be necessary to develop medical resources for those unfortunate occasions when prevention has failed. This could include the creation of specialist units to deal with injuries, and an immediate rescue operation capability.

29.   I believe that the ordnance problem is of such gravity that every possible assistance, both through the United Nations and on a bilateral basis, should be extended to assist the Kuwaiti authorities with this programme on an emergency basis. Without it, an acute danger could remain for years to come. In my opinion, this may be one of the most urgent humanitarian needs, as summer begins and the population, adults and children, begins to return to their country from exile.

16 - 11

0368

- 12 -

E. Refugees and other Vulnerable Groups

30.   The mission was informed that the Government is in the process of formulating a
policy with regard to its manpower requirements with a view to reducing Kuwait's overall
dependence on foreign labour. Such review of policies and practices had not been completed
at the time of the mission's departure. Depending on its outcome, a revision might affect
some categories of workers, and, perhaps, some national groups, who might either wish to be
re-admitted, or whose residence could be discontinued as a result of loss of employment.

31.   During a meeting with His Highness the Crown Prince and Prime Minister Sheikh
Saad Al-Abdullah As-Salim As-Sabah on 26 March 1991 I alluded to reports emanating from
Kuwait, especially in the days immediately following liberation, containing allegations
affecting non-Kuwaitis including Palestinians. The Joint Task Force had also mentioned
these matters in the briefing given to me, and representatives of the authorities had
emphasised steps being taken to ensure non-discriminatory treatment for the whole
population. These included strengthening the police presence, and deploying officials of the
Ministry of Justice to each police station. His Highness assured me that many fabrications
had been circulated on this subject and said that he was himself meeting that evening with a
large Palestinian delegation to hear their concerns and provide every possible reassurance.
In a statement issued shortly before my departure, the Minister of Information and Minister
of State for Kuwaiti National Council Affairs, Dr. Badr Jassem Ya'Coub, emphasised that
Kuwait would apply its laws equally and without discrimination on grounds of race, origin or
descent. The rule of law would be upheld, and whoever infringed it would be punished in
accordance with its provisions. The statement concluded that "Even in the current
circumstances which it is experiencing as a result of the evil aggression against its territory,
Kuwait is fully prepared to receive all requests and claims regarding any practice believed to
be illegal to which residents in Kuwait may have been subjected, in order that the
appropriate measures regarding such practices may be taken in accordance with the precepts
of the law. Kuwait also reaffirms that it is fully prepared to receive representatives from
competent international bodies and organizations in order to examine this matter".

32.   The mission looked into reports of numbers of displaced persons at the Kuwait-Iraq
border, and held discussions with the Kuwait authorities, with representatives of the

16-12

0369

- 13 -

International Committee of the Red Cross, the Kuwaiti Red Crescent, the International Organisation for Migration, and with the Civil Administration of the U.S. Army concerning these persons, and others without documentation. It visited a temporary camp at Abdili in northern Kuwait and the border post of Safwan.

33.   The Abdili camp accommodated approximately 1,000 persons at the time of the visit, some in tents provided through the Kuwaiti Red Crescent and some in makeshift shelters. Food and medical assistance is also provided by the Kuwaiti Red Crescent. The camp population was composed of some 450 Egyptian nationals who were in the process of being registered for repatriation, 50 persons of various other nationalities and up to 500 Iraqis who arrived prior to a decision by the Kuwaiti authorities to admit only third country nationals at the border check point. Several thousand Iraqis are also reported displaced to the Iraqi border town of Safwan, fleeing areas of civil unrest in major cities of southern Iraq, in search of security and shelter. Most of them are accommodated in vacated premises within the city and benefit from food and medical assistance dispensed by military forces. A temporary tented camp located on the outskirts of Safwan, had already received 200 newcomers only 24 hours after it had been established. This may be indicative of a reported sizeable movement of displaced persons towards the southern tip of Iraq. The mission was also informed of the presence on Kuwaiti territory and at the border with Iraq of several thousand undocumented persons, known as "Bedoons", who had previously been working in Kuwait and would now wish to regain either Kuwaiti citizenship or residence.

34.   In the circumstances described above, and having regard to the type of humanitarian problem observed developing at the border, the mission believes that urgent action may be required including consideration by the High Commissioner for Refugees of the establishment of an office in Kuwait. In this connection, the mission is also mindful of a possible need for rapid repatriation, assistance or protection, and of the status of the Iraqi territory adjacent to Kuwait in relation to the Geneva Conventions. It would also be desirable, in my opinion, for UNHCR to initiate consultations, along with the International Committee of the Red Cross and the International Organisation for Migration, with the Kuwaiti authorities and, as appropriate, the civil administration of the occupying forces, in order to define the most appropriate assistance or protection measures for all categories of person who may be in need.

16-13

0370

- 14 -

F. Logistics: transportation, communications and energy

35.   According to surveys undertaken by the U.S. Army's Corps of Engineers, Kuwait's roads underwent moderate damage during the events from August 1990 to February 1991 with bomb craters, surface damage by tracked vehicles, and damage to three bridges. As regards Kuwait International Airport, runways and taxiways are only slightly damaged, if at all. However, the landing system, terminals and the other buildings have undergone serious damage and the control tower has been destroyed. Kuwait's two commercial ports of Shuwaikh and Shuaiba are currently being assessed. There are sunken ships and mines, and dock facilities have been seriously affected. The mission was informed that repairs to these various facilities were anticipated to be complete before the end of 1991 at a total cost of around US$13 million. All the work is expected to be covered by bilateral agreements between Kuwait and the United States, and by commercial sub-contracting.

36.   The Kuwaiti vehicle fleet suffered major losses during the period. It is estimated that there were around 800 thousand motor vehicles in the country in 1990, of which about 85% were private cars. Approximately two-thirds of this asset was reported stolen, looted or vandalised. The loss of public and private vehicles is very apparent. For instance, all Kuwait City's fire-engines and the Government's stock of ambulances were removed from the country. The mission was also informed that the authorities are organising large-scale procurement of replacement vehicles.

37.   As regards communications, major damage was caused by war, vandalism and looting to most forms of telecommunications. The Joint Task Force's surveys showed that about one third of the facilities were moderately to severely damaged. Contracts for repair and replacement have already been signed to a total value of US$23.7 million with leading international private companies. As of 15 March, 57% of the capacity of the telecommunication facilities had been restored. There is now also a limited international service with the possibility for the whole population of free calling, within certain criteria.

38.   Prior to August 1990, Kuwaiti oil production was at the rate of approximately 2 million barrels per day. Currently, at least half its oilwells are on fire; many others are severely damaged. It is estimated that between 4 and 6 million barrels per day are currently

16-14

0371

- 15 -

being lost and there was, at the time of the mission's presence in the country, no production of crude oil or refined products. However, certain reserves are in storage and are being replenished by imports. Repairs to certain facilities are under way and, it is anticipated, production may be resumed by the end of April to a sufficient degree to sustain adequate supplies of electricity and other services to the population. The timing of a return to previous levels of production is problematical.

39.   Electrical supplies have already been restored to most of Kuwait. Its previous power system was regarded as one of the most advanced in the world, with a highly-developed grid system. All four of its power stations were damaged during the events. Repairs are under way, as well as to more than 40 substations which incurred varying degrees of damage.

40.   My mission has concluded that, despite severe damage done to the nation's transportation, communications' and energy resource-base, the process of repair and replacement has already proceeded to such a degree that they are fully capable of providing adequate support for humanitarian needs.

G. Observations

41.   There can be no doubt that a deliberate attempt was made to extinguish Kuwait, its national identity, the pride of its people in their history and achievements. The manner of destruction, with its coordinated vandalism and massive looting, leaves an indelible image. It was a privilege for me and the members of my team to witness the rebirth of a nation, however painful the circumstances. Already, with the cooperation of its friends and allies, the country has made remarkable progress in dealing with immediate humanitarian needs. It is now moving swiftly towards meeting the major tasks of reconstruction. Therefore, little in the way of traditional humanitarian aid is immediately required of the international community at large. Certain vital assistance, as described above, is, however, urgently necessary so that the suffering of the population of Kuwait is not further prolonged, and so that it and its neighbours can again live in good health and peace.

16 - 15

0372

- 16 -

42.   Finally, I should like to place on record my appreciation to the executive heads of UNDP, UNICEF, UNHCR, UNDRO, UNEP, WFP, FAO and WHO for the cooperation which permitted a mission of so wide a range of specialisations and experience to work with me in Iraq and Kuwait. I believe it most important that the United Nations family of organisations establish ever-closer coordination, and matters of emergency humanitarian assistance provide an excellent area in which this can be further developed. I was especially fortunate in the members assigned to this mission. Their objectivity, expertise and professionalism, often under trying circumstances, and the excellent spirit of cooperation, reminded me once again of the great reservoir of experience and dedication available to the United Nations.

16-16

0373

외 무 부

종 별 :

번 호 : UNW-0734

일 시 : 91 0329 0200

수 신 : 장 관(국연,중동일,기정,해기)

발 신 : 주유엔대사

제 목 : 걸프사태(안보리)

연: WUN-0715

1. 금 3.28 오후 현재 상임이사국들간 연호휴전결의 문안교섭이 거의 합의
단계에이른것으로 알려진바, 남은 쟁점은 별첨문안 본문8항 B) 미사일
조항(일정사정거리이하의 미사일일부 허용여부 문제)인 것으로 알려짐.

2. 안보리는 상기 결의안 문제관련 4.1.(월)비공식 협의예정임.

첨부:상기 휴전결의 교섭문안: UNW(F)-141

끝

(대사 노창희-국장)

국기국	장관	차관	1차보	2차보	미주국	중아국	정와대	안기부
공보처								

PAGE 1

91.03.29 16:33

외신 1과 통제관

0374

UNW(府)-141   0329 0200
(국연·중동일·기정·해기)

총21매
UNW-0734 의
첨부욱

11:45, March 28, 1991

DRAFT ELEMENTS OF THE NEXT RESOLUTION
ON GULF SECURITY

The Security Council,

A. Recalling its resolutions 660 (1990), 661 (1990), 662
(1990), 664 (1990), 665 (1990), 666 (1990), 667 (1990), 669
(1990), 670 (1990), 674 (1990), 677 (1990), 678 (1990) and 686
(1991),

B. Welcoming the restoration to Kuwait of its sovereignty,
independence, and territorial integrity and the return of its
legitimate government,

C. Affirming the commitment of all Member States to the
sovereignty, territorial integrity and political independence
of Kuwait and Iraq, and noting the intention expressed by the
member states cooperating with Kuwait under paragraph 2 of
resolution 678 (1990) to bring their military presence in Iraq
to an end as soon as possible consistent with paragraph 8 of

21-1

0375

MAR 29 '91 01:45 KOREAN MISSION

P.2

- 2 -

resolution 686 (1991),

D. Reaffirming the need to be assured of Iraq's peaceful
intentions in light of its unlawful invasion and occupation of
Kuwait,

E. Taking note of the letter sent by the Foreign Minister of
Iraq on 27 February 1991 (S/22275) and those sent pursuant to
resolution 686 (1991) (S/22273, S/22276, S/22320, S/22321,
S/22330), in particular the letter dated .... concerning
Iraq's fulfillment of the requirements in resolution 686 (1991),

F. Noting that Iraq and Kuwait, as independent sovereign
states, signed at Baghdad on 4 October 1963 "Agreed Minutes
Regarding the Restoration of Friendly Relations, Recognition
and Related Matters," thereby recognizing formally the boundary
between Iraq and Kuwait and the allocation of islands, which
were registered with the United Nations in accordance with
Article 102 of the Charter and in which Iraq recognized the
independence and complete sovereignty of the State of Kuwait
within its borders as specified and accepted in the letter of
the Prime Minister of Iraq dated 21 July 1932, and as accepted
by the Ruler of Kuwait in his letter dated 10 August 1932,

G. Conscious of the need for demarcation of the said boundary,

21-2

0376

- 3 -

H. <u>Conscious also</u> of the statements by Iraq threatening to use
weapons in violation of its obligations under the Geneva
Protocol for the Prohibition of the Use in War of Asphyxiating,
Poisonous or Other Gases, and of Bacteriological Methods of
Warfare, signed at Geneva on 17 June 1925, and of its prior use
of chemical weapons and affirming that grave consequences would
follow any further use by Iraq of such weapons,

I. <u>Recalling</u> that Iraq has subscribed to the Declaration
adopted by all States participating in the Conference of States
Party to the 1925 Geneva Protocol and Other International
States, held at Paris January 7-11, 1989, establishing the
objective of universal elimination of chemical and biological
weapons,

J. <u>Recalling further</u> that Iraq has signed the Convention on
the Prohibition of the Development, Production and Stockpiling
of Bacteriological (Biological) and Toxin weapons and on Their
Destruction, of 10 April 1972,

K. <u>Noting</u> the importance of Iraq ratifying this convention,

L. <u>Noting</u> moreover the importance of all states adhering to
this convention and encouraging its forthcoming Review

21-3

0377

- 4 -

Conference to reinforce the authority, efficiency and universal
scope of the convention,

M. Stressing the importance of (urgent progress being made) by
the Conference on Disarmament (in completing work) on a
Convention on the Universal Prohibition of Chemical Weapons and
of universal adherence thereto,

N. Aware of the use by Iraq of ballistic missiles in
unprovoked attacks,

O. Concerned (by the reports in the hands of Member States) that
Iraq has attempted to acquire materials for a nuclear weapons
program contrary to its obligations under the Treaty on the
Non-Proliferation of Nuclear Weapons of 1 July 1968,

P. Recalling also the objective of the establishment of a
nuclear weapons free zone in the region of the Middle East,

Q. Conscious of the threat which all (of the above noted)
weapons of mass destruction pose to peace and security in the
area and of the need to work towards the establishment in the
Middle East of a zone free of such weapons,

R. Conscious also of the objective of achieving balanced and

21-4

0378

- 5 -

comprehensive control of armaments in the region,

S. Conscious further of the importance of achieving the
objectives noted above using all available means, including a
dialogue among the states of the region,

T. Noting that resolution 686 (1991) marked the lifting of the
measures imposed by resolution 661 (1990) in so far as they
applied to Kuwait,

U. Noting that despite the progress being made in fulfilling
the obligations of resolution 686 (1990), many Kuwaiti and
third country nationals are still not accounted for and
property remains unreturned,

V. Recalling the International Convention against the Taking
of Hostages, opened for signature at New York on December 18,
1979, which categorizes all acts of taking hostages as
manifestations of international terrorism,

W. Deploring threats made by Iraq during the recent conflict
to make use of terrorism against targets outside Iraq and the
taking of hostages by Iraq,

X. Taking note of the Report of the Secretary-General   21.-5

0379

- 6 -

of 20 March 1991, and conscious of the desirability of meeting
humanitarian needs in Kuwait and Iraq in the immediate
post-crisis environment,

Y. _Bearing_ in mind its objective of restoring international
peace and security in the area as set out in recent Council
resolutions,

Z. _Conscious of_ the need to take the following measures acting
under Chapter VII of the Charter,

1. _Affirms_ all thirteen resolutions noted above, except as
expressly changed below to achieve the goals of this
resolution, including a formal cease-fire;

A

2. _Demands_ that Iraq and Kuwait respect the inviolability of
the international boundary and the allocation of islands set
out in the "Agreed Minutes Between the State of Kuwait and the
Republic of Iraq Regarding the Restoration of Friendly
Relations and Related Matters," signed at Baghdad on 4 October
1963;

3. _Calls on_ the Secretary-General to lend his assistance to

21-6

0380

- 7 -

make arrangements with Iraq and Kuwait to demarcate the
boundary between Iraq and Kuwait, drawing on appropriate
material including the map contained in Security Council
document S/...... and to report back to the Security Council
within one month;

4. **Decides** to guarantee the inviolability of the above
(allocation of, island)
mentioned international boundary and to take as appropriate all
necessary measures to that end in accordance with the Charter;

B

5. **Requests** the Secretary General, after consulting with Iraq
and Kuwait, to submit within three days to the Security Council
for its approval a plan for the immediate deployment of a
United Nations observer unit to monitor the Khor Abdullah and a
demilitarized zone extending 10 kilometers into Iraq and 5
kilometers into Kuwait from the boundary referred to in the
"Agreed Minutes Between the State of Kuwait and the Republic of
Iraq Regarding the Restoration of Friendly Relations,
Recognition and Related Matters" of October 4, 1963; to deter
violations of the boundary through its presence in and
surveillance of the demilitarized zone; to observe any hostile
or potentially hostile action mounted from the territory of one
state to the other; and for the Secretary-General to report

21-7

0381

- 8 -

regularly to the Council on the operations of the unit, and
immediately if there are serious violations of the zone or
potential threats to peace;

6. Notes that the deployment of the United Nations observer
unit as soon as possible will establish the conditions for the
forces of the member states cooperating with Kuwait in
accordance with resolution 678 (1990) to bring their military
presence in Iraq to an end consistent with resolution 686
(1991);

C

7. Invites Iraq to reaffirm unconditionally its obligations
under the Geneva Protocol for the Prohibition of the Use in War
of Asphyxiating, Poisonous or Other Gases, and of
Bacteriological Methods of Warfare, signed at Geneva on 17 June
1925, and to ratify the Convention on the Prohibition of the
Development, Production, and Stockpiling of Bacteriological
(Biological) and Toxin Weapons and on Their Destruction, of 10
April 1972;

(Requires)

8. Decides that Iraq shall unconditionally accept the
destruction, removal, or rendering harmless, under
international supervision, of:

𝒹1-β

0382

- 9 -

(a) all chemical and biological weapons and all stocks of
agents;

(b) all .... missile systems capable of delivering
weapons of mass destruction;

(all ballistic missile system)

and all subsystems and components and all research,
development, support and manufacturing facilities related to
the above,

9. Decides, for the implementation of paragraph 8 above, the
following:

a) Iraq shall submit to the Secretary General, within
fifteen days of the adoption of this resolution, a
declaration of the locations, amounts and types of all
items specified in paragraph 8 and agree to urgent, on-site
inspection as specified below;

b) the Secretary-General, in consultation with the
appropriate Governments and, where appropriate, with the
Director General of the World Health Organization (WHO),
within 45 days of the passage of this resolution, shall
develop, and submit to the Council for approval, a plan

21-9

0383

- 10 -

calling for the completion of the following acts within 45
days of such approval:

(i) the forming of a Special Commission, which
shall carry out immediate on-site inspection of
Iraq's biological, chemical and missile *(ballistic)*
capabilities, based on Iraq's declarations and
the designation of any additional locations by
the Special Commission itself;

(ii) the destruction by Iraq, under supervision
of the Special Commission, of all its missile *(ballistic)*
(System) capabilities, including their subsystems,
components and launchers, and yielding possession
to the Special Commission for destruction,
removal or rendering harmless, taking into
account the requirements of public safety, of all
other items notified under paragraph 9 (a) above,
or otherwise required by the Special Commission;

(iii) the provision by the Special Commission of
the assistance and cooperation to the Director
General of the International Atomic Energy Agency
(IAEA) required in paragraphs 12 and 13 below;

21 — 10

0384

- 11 -

(Requires)

10. <u>Decides</u> that Iraq |shall| unconditionally undertake not to use, develop, construct or acquire any of the items specified in paragraph 8 above and requests the·Secretary General, in consultation with the Special Commission, to develop a plan for the future on-going monitoring and verification of Iraq's compliance with this paragraph, to be submitted to the Council for approval within 120 days of the passage of this resolution;

11. <u>Invites</u> Iraq to reaffirm unconditionally its obligations under the Treaty on the Non-Proliferation of Nuclear Weapons, of 1 July 1968;

(Requires)

12. <u>Decides</u> that Iraq |shall| unconditionally agree not to acquire or develop nuclear weapons or nuclear weapons-usable material or any subsystems or components or any research, development, support or manufacturing facilities related to the above; to submit to the Secretary-General and the Director General of the International Atomic Energy Agency (IAEA) within 15 days of the adoption of this resolution a declaration of the locations, amounts, and types of all items specified above; to place all of its nuclear weapons-usable materials under the exclusive control, for custody and removal, of the IAEA, with the assistance and cooperation of the Special Commission as provided for in the plan of the Secretary-General discussed in paragraph 9(b) above; to accept, in accordance with the

0385

- 12 -

arrangements provided for in paragraph 13 below, (urgent on-site
inspection and) the destruction, removal, or rendering harmless
(as appropriate) of all items specified above; and to accept the
plan discussed in paragraph 13 below for the future ongoing
monitoring and verification of its compliance with these
undertakings;

13.   Requests the Director General of the International Atomic
Energy Agency (IAEA) (through the Secretary-General,) with the
assistance and cooperation of the Special Commission as
provided for in the plan of the Secretary-General in paragraph
9(b) above, to carry out immediate on-site inspection of Iraq's
nuclear capabilities based on Iraq's declarations and the
designation of any additional locations by the Special
Commission; to develop a plan for submission to the Security
Council within 45 days calling for the destruction, removal, or
rendering harmless as appropriate of all items listed in
paragraph 12 above; to carry out the plan within 45 days
following approval by the Security Council; and to develop a
plan, taking into account the rights and obligations of Iraq
under the Treaty on the Non-Proliferation of Nuclear Weapons,
of 1 July 1968, for the future ongoing monitoring and
verification of Iraq's compliance with paragraph 12 above,
including an inventory of all nuclear material in Iraq subject
to the Agency's verification and special inspections to confirm
that IAEA safeguards cover all relevant nuclear activities in

0386

- 13 -

Iraq, to be submitted to the Council for approval within 120 days of the passage of this resolution;

14. Takes note that the actions to be taken by Iraq in paragraphs 8, 9, 10, 11, 12 and 13 of this resolution represent steps toward the goal of establishing in the Middle East a zone free from weapons of mass destruction and all missiles for their delivery and the objective of a global ban on chemical weapons;

D

15. Requests the Secretary General to report to the Security Council on the steps taken to facilitate the return of all Kuwaiti property seized by Iraq, including a list of any property which Kuwait claims has not been returned or which has not been returned intact;

E

16. Reaffirms that Iraq, without prejudice to the debts and obligations of Iraq arising prior to August 2, 1990, which will be addressed through the normal mechanisms, is liable under international law for any direct loss, damage, including environmental damage and the depletion of natural resources, or

21-13

0387

- 14 -

injury to foreign governments, nationals and corporations, as a
result of Iraq's unlawful invasion and occupation of Kuwait;

17. Decides that the Iraqi statements made since August 2,
1990, concerning its foreign debt are null and void;

18. Decides to create a Fund to pay compensation for claims
that fall within paragraph 16 above and to establish a
Commission that will administer the fund;

19. Directs the Secretary-General to develop and present to
the Council for decision, no later than 30 days following the
adoption of this resolution, recommendations for the Fund to
meet the requirement for the payment of claims established in
accordance with paragraph 18 above and for a program to
implement the decisions in paragraphs 16, 17, and 18 above,
including: administration of the Fund; mechanisms for
determining the appropriate level of Iraq's contribution to the
Fund based on a percentage of the value of the exports of
petroleum and petroleum products from Iraq not to exceed a
figure to be suggested to the Council by the Secretary-General,
taking into account the requirements of the people of Iraq and
in particular humanitarian needs, Iraq's payment capacity as
assessed in conjunction with the international financial
institutions taking into consideration external debt service,

21—14

0388

- 15 -

and the needs of the Iraqi economy; arrangements for ensuring
that payments are made to the Fund; the process by which funds
will be allocated and claims paid; appropriate procedures for
evaluating losses, listing claims and verifying their validity
and resolving disputed claims in respect of Iraq's liability as
specified in paragraph 16 above; and the composition of the
Commission designated above;

P

20. Decides, effective immediately, that the prohibitions
against the sale or supply to Iraq of commodities or products,
and prohibitions against financial transactions related
thereto, contained in resolution 661 (1990) shall not apply to
foodstuffs notified to the Committee established in resolution
661 (1990) and, with the approval of that Committee, under
simplified and accelerated procedures, materials and supplies
for essential civilian needs as identified in the report of the
Secretary-General dated March 20, 1991 (S/22366), and in any
further findings of humanitarian need by the Committee;

21. Decides that the Council shall review the provisions of
paragraph 20 above every sixty days in light of the policies
and practices of the Government of Iraq, including the
implementation of all relevant resolutions of the Security

21-15

0389

- 16 -

Council, for the purpose of determining whether to modify
further or lift the prohibitions referred to therein;

22. Decides that upon the approval by the Council of the
program called for in paragraph 19 above and of the completion
by Iraq of all actions contemplated in paragraphs 8, 9, 10, 11,
12, and 13 above, the prohibitions against the import of
commodities and products originating in Iraq and the
prohibitions against financial transactions related thereto
contained in resolution 661 (1990) shall have no further force
or effect;

23. Decides that, pending action by the Council under
paragraph 22 above, the Committee established under Resolution
661 shall be empowered to approve, when required to assure
adequate financial resources on the part of Iraq to carry out
the activities under paragraph 20 above, exceptions to the
prohibition against the import of commodities and products
originating in Iraq;

24. Decides that, in accordance with resolution 661 (1990) and
subsequent related resolutions and until a further decision is
taken by the Council, all States shall continue to prevent the
sale or supply, or promotion or facilitation of such sale or
supply, to Iraq by their nationals, or from their territories

21-16

0390

- 17 -

or using their flag vessels or aircraft, of:

    a) arms and related materiel of all types, specifically
including the sale or transfer through other means of all
forms of conventional military equipment, including for
paramilitary forces, and spare parts and components and
their means of production, for such equipment;

    b) items specified and defined in paragraph 8 and
paragraph 12 above not otherwise covered above;

    c) technology under licensing or other transfer
arrangements used in the production, utilization or
stockpiling of items specified in subparagraphs a) and b)
above;

    d) personnel or materials for training or technical
support services relating to the design, development,
manufacture, use, maintenance or support of items specified
in subparagraphs a) and b) above;

25. <u>Calls upon</u> all States and international organizations to
act strictly in accordance with paragraph 24 above,
notwithstanding the existence of any contracts, agreements,
licenses, or any other arrangements;

21-17

0391

- 18 -

26. Requests the Secretary General, in consultation with
appropriate Governments, to develop within 60 days, for
approval of the Council, guidelines to facilitate full
international implementation of paragraphs 24 and 25 above and
paragraph 27 below, and to make them available to all States
and to establish a procedure for up-dating these guidelines
periodically;

27. Calls upon all States to maintain such national controls
and procedures and to take such other actions consistent with
the guidelines to be established by the Security Council under
paragraph 26 above as may be necessary to ensure compliance
with the terms of paragraph 24 above, and calls upon
international organizations to take all appropriate steps to
assist in ensuring such full compliance;

28. Agrees to review its decisions in paragraphs 22, 23, 24,
and 25 above, except for the items specified and defined in
paragraphs 8 and 12 above, on a regular basis and in any case
120 days following passage of this resolution, taking into
account Iraq's compliance with this resolution and general
progress towards the control of armaments in the region;

29. Decides that all States, including Iraq, shall take the

21-18

0392

- 19 -

necessary measures to ensure that no claim shall lie at the
instance of the Government of Iraq, or of any person or body in
Iraq, or of any person claiming through or for the benefit of
any such person or body, in connection with any contract or
other transaction where its performance was affected by reason
of the measures taken by the Security Council in Resolution 661
(1990) and related resolutions;

<u>G</u>

30. <u>Decides</u> that, in furtherance of its commitment to
facilitate the repatriation of all Kuwaiti and third country
nationals, Iraq\shall/cooperate with the International
Committee of the Red Cross, providing lists of such persons,
facilitating the access of the International Committee of the
Red Cross to all such persons wherever located or detained and
facilitating the search by the International Committee of the
Red Cross for those Kuwaiti and Third Country nationals still
unaccounted for;

31. <u>Invites</u> the International Committee of the Red Cross to
keep the Secretary General apprised as appropriate of all
activities undertaken in connection with facilitating the
repatriation or return of all Kuwaiti and Third Country
nationals or their remains present in Iraq on or after August

21-19

0393

- 20 -

2, 1990;

H

32. Requires Iraq to inform the Council that it will not commit or support any act of international terrorism or allow any organization directed toward commission of such acts to operate within its territory and to condemn unequivocally and renounce all acts, methods, and practices of terrorism;

I

33. Declares that, upon official notification by Iraq to the Secretary-General and to the Security Council of its acceptance of the provisions above, a formal cease-fire is effective between Iraq and Kuwait and the member states cooperating with Kuwait in accordance with resolution 678 (1990);

34. Decides to remain seized of the matter and to take such further steps as may be required for the implementation of this resolution and to secure peace and security in the area.

10/439

21-20

0394

28 March 1991

Note by the President

Following consultations of the Council, the President of the
Security Council issued the following statement on behalf of the
members of the Council on 28 March 1991:

The members of the Council have considered the
Secretary-General's report on his mission of good offices in
Cyprus. They are unanimous in expressing their full support of his
current efforts.

The members of the Council agree with the Secretary-General's
assessment of the current situation, including the main issues that
remain to be clarified before an outline can be completed, and
encourage him to continue his efforts along the lines he has
proposed, by making suggestions to facilitate the discussions.

The members of the Council reaffirm Security Council resolution
649 (1990) and the mandate for the Secretary-General's mission of
good offices as set out in resolution 367 (1975); and recall that
that resolution 649 (1990) reaffirmed in particular Security Council
resolution 367 (1975) as well as the Council's support for the 1977
and 1979 high-level agreements between the leaders of the two
communities. This should continue to serve as the basis for the
Secretary-General's effort to arrive at an agreed outline.

The members of the Council urge all concerned to act in a
manner consistent with resolution 649 (1990), to cooperate fully
with the Secretary-General and to continue the discussions that have
taken place over the past few months in order to resolve without
delay the outstanding issues.

The members of the Council welcome the Secretary-General's
intention to submit a further report by early July 1991 on his
effort to arrive at an agreed outline of an overall settlement. The
members of the Council will decide, in the light of the situation at
that time, on any further measures for proceeding that may be
necessary.

21-21

0395

외 무 부

종 별 :

번 호 : UNW-0734   일 시 : 91 0329 0200

수 신 : 장 관(국연,중동일,기정,해기)

발 신 : 주유엔대사

제 목 : 걸프사태(안보리)

연: WUN-0715

1. 금 3.28 오후 현재 상임이사국들간 연호휴전결의 문안교섭이 거의 합의 단계에이른것으로 알려진바, 남은 쟁점은 별첨문안 본문8항 B) 미사일 조항(일정사정거리이하의 미사일일부 허용여부 문제)인 것으로 알려짐.

2. 안보리는 상기 결의안 문제관련 4.1.(월)비공식 협의예정임.

첨부:상기 휴전결의 교섭문안: UNW(F)-141

끝

(대사 노창희-국장)

국기국 공보처	장관	차관	1차보	2차보	미주국	중아국	정와대	안기부

PAGE 1   91.03.29   16:33

외신 1과 통제관

0396

UNW(有)-141   10329 0200
(국연·중동일. 기정. 해기)

총21매
#UNW-0734의
첨부물

11:45, March 28, 1991

DRAFT ELEMENTS OF THE NEXT RESOLUTION
ON GULF SECURITY

The Security Council,

A. Recalling its resolutions 660 (1990), 661 (1990), 662
(1990), 664 (1990), 665 (1990), 666 (1990), 667 (1990), 669
(1990), 670 (1990), 674 (1990), 677 (1990), 678 (1990) and 686
(1991),

B. Welcoming the restoration to Kuwait of its sovereignty,
independence, and territorial integrity and the return of its
legitimate government,

C. Affirming the commitment of all Member States to the
sovereignty, territorial integrity and political independence
of Kuwait and Iraq, and noting the intention expressed by the
member states cooperating with Kuwait under paragraph 2 of
resolution 678 (1990) to bring their military presence in Iraq
to an end as soon as possible consistent with paragraph 8 of

21—1

0397

- 2 -

resolution 686 (1991),

D. Reaffirming the need to be assured of Iraq's peaceful
intentions in light of its unlawful invasion and occupation of
Kuwait,

E. Taking note of the letter sent by the Foreign Minister of
Iraq on 27 February 1991 (S/22275) and those sent pursuant to
resolution 686 (1991) (S/22273, S/22276, S/22320, S/22321,
S/22330), in particular the letter dated .... concerning
Iraq's fulfillment of the requirements in resolution 686 (1991),

F. Noting that Iraq and Kuwait, as independent sovereign
states, signed at Baghdad on 4 October 1963 'Agreed Minutes
Regarding the Restoration of Friendly Relations, Recognition
and Related Matters,' thereby recognizing formally the boundary
between Iraq and Kuwait and the allocation of islands, which
were registered with the United Nations in accordance with
Article 102 of the Charter and in which Iraq recognized the
independence and complete sovereignty of the State of Kuwait
within its borders as specified and accepted in the letter of
the Prime Minister of Iraq dated 21 July 1932, and as accepted
by the Ruler of Kuwait in his letter dated 10 August 1932,

G. Conscious of the need for demarcation of the said boundary,

21-2

0398

- 3 -

H. Conscious also of the statements by Iraq threatening to use
weapons in violation of its obligations under the Geneva
Protocol for the Prohibition of the Use in War of Asphyxiating,
Poisonous or Other Gases, and of Bacteriological Methods of
Warfare, signed at Geneva on 17 June 1925, and of its prior use
of chemical weapons and affirming that grave consequences would
follow any further use by Iraq of such weapons,

I. Recalling that Iraq has subscribed to the Declaration
adopted by all States participating in the Conference of States
Party to the 1925 Geneva Protocol and Other International
States, held at Paris January 7-11, 1989, establishing the
objective of universal elimination of chemical and biological
weapons,

J. Recalling further that Iraq has signed the Convention on
the Prohibition of the Development, Production and Stockpiling
of Bacteriological (Biological) and Toxin weapons and on Their
Destruction, of 10 April 1972,

K. Noting the importance of Iraq ratifying this convention,

L. Noting moreover the importance of all states adhering to
this convention and encouraging its forthcoming Review

21-3

0399

- 4 -

Conference to reinforce the authority, efficiency and universal
scope of the convention,

M. Stressing the importance of urgent progress being made by
the Conference on Disarmament in completing work on a
Convention on the Universal Prohibition of Chemical Weapons and
of universal adherence thereto,

N. Aware of the use by Iraq of ballistic missiles in
unprovoked attacks,

O. Concerned by the reports in the hands of Member States that
Iraq has attempted to acquire materials for a nuclear weapons
program contrary to its obligations under the Treaty on the
Non-Proliferation of Nuclear Weapons of 1 July 1968,

P. Recalling also the objective of the establishment of a
nuclear weapons free zone in the region of the Middle East,

Q. Conscious of the threat which all of the above noted
weapons of mass destruction pose to peace and security in the
area and of the need to work towards the establishment in the
Middle East of a zone free of such weapons,

R. Conscious also of the objective of achieving balanced and

21-4

0400

- 5 -

comprehensive control of armaments in the region,

S. Conscious further of the importance of achieving the
objectives noted above using all available means, including a
dialogue among the states of the region,

T. Noting that resolution 686 (1991) marked the lifting of the
measures imposed by resolution 661 (1990) in so far as they
applied to Kuwait,

U. Noting that despite the progress being made in fulfilling
the obligations of resolution 686 (1990), many Kuwaiti and
third country nationals are still not accounted for and
property remains unreturned,

V. Recalling the International Convention against the Taking
of Hostages, opened for signature at New York on December 18,
1979, which categorizes all acts of taking hostages as
manifestations of international terrorism,

W. Deploring threats made by Iraq during the recent conflict
to make use of terrorism against targets outside Iraq and the
taking of hostages by Iraq,

X. Taking note of the Report of the Secretary-General 2/ -5

0401

- 6 -

of 20 March 1991, and conscious of the desirability of meeting
humanitarian needs in Kuwait and Iraq in the immediate
post-crisis environment,

Y. Bearing in mind its objective of restoring international
peace and security in the area as set out in recent Council
resolutions,

Z. Conscious of the need to take the following measures acting
under Chapter VII of the Charter,

1. Affirms all thirteen resolutions noted above, except as
expressly changed below to achieve the goals of this
resolution, including a formal cease-fire;

A

2. Demands that Iraq and Kuwait respect the inviolability of
the international boundary and the allocation of islands set
out in the "Agreed Minutes Between the State of Kuwait and the
Republic of Iraq Regarding the Restoration of Friendly
Relations and Related Matters," signed at Baghdad on 4 October
1963;

3. Calls on the Secretary-General to lend his assistance to

21-6

0402

- 7 -

make arrangements with Iraq and Kuwait to demarcate the
boundary between Iraq and Kuwait, drawing on appropriate
material including the map contained in Security Council
document S/...... and to report back to the Security Council
within one month;

4. **Decides** to guarantee the inviolability of the above
mentioned international boundary and to take as appropriate all
necessary measures to that end in accordance with the Charter;

B

5. **Requests** the Secretary General, after consulting with Iraq
and Kuwait, to submit within three days to the Security Council
for its approval a plan for the immediate deployment of a
United Nations observer unit to monitor the Khor Abdullah and a
demilitarized zone extending 10 kilometers into Iraq and 5
kilometers into Kuwait from the boundary referred to in the
"Agreed Minutes Between the State of Kuwait and the Republic of
Iraq Regarding the Restoration of Friendly Relations,
Recognition and Related Matters" of October 4, 1963; to deter
violations of the boundary through its presence in and
surveillance of the demilitarized zone; to observe any hostile
or potentially hostile action mounted from the territory of one
state to the other; and for the Secretary-General to report

21-7

0403

- 8 -

regularly to the Council on the operations of the unit, and immediately if there are serious violations of the zone or potential threats to peace;

6. Notes that the deployment of the United Nations observer unit as soon as possible will establish the conditions for the forces of the member states cooperating with Kuwait in accordance with resolution 678 (1990) to bring their military presence in Iraq to an end consistent with resolution 686 (1991);

C

7. Invites Iraq to reaffirm unconditionally its obligations under the Geneva Protocol for the Prohibition of the Use in War of Asphyxiating, Poisonous or Other Gases, and of Bacteriological Methods of Warfare, signed at Geneva on 17 June 1925, and to ratify the Convention on the Prohibition of the Development, Production, and Stockpiling of Bacteriological (Biological) and Toxin Weapons and on Their Destruction, of 10 April 1972;

8. Decides that Iraq shall unconditionally accept the destruction, removal, or rendering harmless, under international supervision, of:

0404

- 9 -

(a) all chemical and biological weapons and all stocks of agents;

(b) all .... missile systems capable of delivering weapons of mass destruction;

and all subsystems and components and all research, development, support and manufacturing facilities related to the above,

9. Decides, for the implementation of paragraph 8 above, the following:

a) Iraq shall submit to the Secretary General, within fifteen days of the adoption of this resolution, a declaration of the locations, amounts and types of all items specified in paragraph 8 and agree to urgent, on-site inspection as specified below;

b) the Secretary-General, in consultation with the appropriate Governments and, where appropriate, with the Director General of the World Health Organization (WHO), within 45 days of the passage of this resolution, shall develop, and submit to the Council for approval, a plan

21-9

0405

- 10 -

calling for the completion of the following acts within 45
days of such approval:

(i) the forming of a Special Commission, which
shall carry out immediate on-site inspection of
Iraq's biological, chemical and missile
capabilities, based on Iraq's declarations and
the designation of any additional locations by
the Special Commission itself;

(ii) the destruction by Iraq, under supervision
of the Special Commission, of all its missile
capabilities, including their subsystems,
components and launchers, and yielding possession
to the Special Commission for destruction,
removal or rendering harmless, taking into
account the requirements of public safety, of all
other items notified under paragraph 9 (a) above,
or otherwise required by the Special Commission;

(iii) the provision by the Special Commission of
the assistance and cooperation to the Director
General of the International Atomic Energy Agency
(IAEA) required in paragraphs 12 and 13 below;

21-10

0406

- 11 -

10. <u>Decides</u> that Iraq shall unconditionally undertake not to use, develop, construct or acquire any of the items specified in paragraph 8 above and requests the Secretary General, in consultation with the Special Commission, to develop a plan for the future on-going monitoring and verification of Iraq's compliance with this paragraph, to be submitted to the Council for approval within 120 days of the passage of this resolution;

11. <u>Invites</u> Iraq to reaffirm unconditionally its obligations under the Treaty on the Non-Proliferation of Nuclear Weapons, of 1 July 1968;

12. <u>Decides</u> that Iraq shall unconditionally agree not to acquire or develop nuclear weapons or nuclear weapons-usable material or any subsystems or components or any research, development, support or manufacturing facilities related to the above; to submit to the Secretary-General and the Director General of the International Atomic Energy Agency (IAEA) within 15 days of the adoption of this resolution a declaration of the locations, amounts, and types of all items specified above; to place all of its nuclear weapons-usable materials under the exclusive control, for custody and removal, of the IAEA, with the assistance and cooperation of the Special Commission as provided for in the plan of the Secretary-General discussed in paragraph 9(b) above; to accept, in accordance with the 21-11

0407

- 12 -

arrangements provided for in paragraph 13 below, urgent on-site
inspection and the destruction, removal, or rendering harmless
as appropriate of all items specified above; and to accept the
plan discussed in paragraph 13 below for the future ongoing
monitoring and verification of its compliance with these
undertakings;

13. Requests the Director General of the International Atomic
Energy Agency (IAEA) through the Secretary-General, with the
assistance and cooperation of the Special Commission as
provided for in the plan of the Secretary-General in paragraph
9(b) above, to carry out immediate on-site inspection of Iraq's
nuclear capabilities based on Iraq's declarations and the
designation of any additional locations by the Special
Commission; to develop a plan for submission to the Security
Council within 45 days calling for the destruction, removal, or
rendering harmless as appropriate of all items listed in
paragraph 12 above; to carry out the plan within 45 days
following approval by the Security Council; and to develop a
plan, taking into account the rights and obligations of Iraq
under the Treaty on the Non-Proliferation of Nuclear Weapons,
of 1 July 1968, for the future ongoing monitoring and
verification of Iraq's compliance with paragraph 12 above,
including an inventory of all nuclear material in Iraq subject
to the Agency's verification and special inspections to confirm
that IAEA safeguards cover all relevant nuclear activities in

21-12

0408

- 13 -

Iraq, to be submitted to the Council for approval within 120 days of the passage of this resolution;

14. <u>Takes note</u> that the actions to be taken by Iraq in paragraphs 8, 9, 10, 11, 12 and 13 of this resolution represent steps toward the goal of establishing in the Middle East a zone free from weapons of mass destruction and all missiles for their delivery and the objective of a global ban on chemical weapons;

<u>D</u>

15. <u>Requests</u> the Secretary General to report to the Security Council on the steps taken to facilitate the return of all Kuwaiti property seized by Iraq, including a list of any property which Kuwait claims has not been returned or which has not been returned intact;

<u>E</u>

16. <u>Reaffirms</u> that Iraq, without prejudice to the debts and obligations of Iraq arising prior to August 2, 1990, which will be addressed through the normal mechanisms, is liable under international law for any direct loss, damage, including environmental damage and the depletion of natural resources, or

21-13

0409

- 14 -

injury to foreign governments, nationals and corporations, as a
result of Iraq's unlawful invasion and occupation of Kuwait;

17. Decides that the Iraqi statements made since August 2,
1990, concerning its foreign debt are null and void;

18. Decides to create a Fund to pay compensation for claims
that fall within paragraph 16 above and to establish a
Commission that will administer the fund;

19. Directs the Secretary-General to develop and present to
the Council for decision, no later than 30 days following the
adoption of this resolution, recommendations for the Fund to
meet the requirement for the payment of claims established in
accordance with paragraph 18 above and for a program to
implement the decisions in paragraphs 16, 17, and 18 above,
including: administration of the Fund; mechanisms for
determining the appropriate level of Iraq's contribution to the
Fund based on a percentage of the value of the exports of
petroleum and petroleum products from Iraq not to exceed a
figure to be suggested to the Council by the Secretary-General,
taking into account the requirements of the people of Iraq and
in particular humanitarian needs, Iraq's payment capacity as
assessed in conjunction with the international financial
institutions taking into consideration external debt service,

21-14

0410

- 15 -

and the needs of the Iraqi economy; arrangements for ensuring
that payments are made to the Fund; the process by which funds
will be allocated and claims paid; appropriate procedures for
evaluating losses, listing claims and verifying their validity
and resolving disputed claims in respect of Iraq's liability as
specified in paragraph 16 above; and the composition of the
Commission designated above;

                              F

20. **Decides**, effective immediately, that the prohibitions
against the sale or supply to Iraq of commodities or products,
and prohibitions against financial transactions related
thereto, contained in resolution 661 (1990) shall not apply to
foodstuffs notified to the Committee established in resolution
661 (1990) and, with the approval of that Committee, under
simplified and accelerated procedures, materials and supplies
for essential civilian needs as identified in the report of the
Secretary-General dated March 20, 1991 (S/22366), and in any
further findings of humanitarian need by the Committee;

21. **Decides** that the Council shall review the provisions of
paragraph 20 above every sixty days in light of the policies
and practices of the Government of Iraq, including the
implementation of all relevant resolutions of the Security

                                        21-15

- 16 -

Council, for the purpose of determining whether to modify
further or lift the prohibitions referred to therein;

22. Decides that upon the approval by the Council of the
program called for in paragraph 19 above and of the completion
by Iraq of all actions contemplated in paragraphs 8, 9, 10, 11,
12, and 13 above, the prohibitions against the import of
commodities and products originating in Iraq and the
prohibitions against financial transactions related thereto
contained in resolution 661 (1990) shall have no further force
or effect;

23. Decides that, pending action by the Council under
paragraph 22 above, the Committee established under Resolution
661 shall be empowered to approve, when required to assure
adequate financial resources on the part of Iraq to carry out
the activities under paragraph 20 above, exceptions to the
prohibition against the import of commodities and products
originating in Iraq;

24. Decides that, in accordance with resolution 661 (1990) and
subsequent related resolutions and until a further decision is
taken by the Council, all States shall continue to prevent the
sale or supply, or promotion or facilitation of such sale or
supply, to Iraq by their nationals, or from their territories

21-16

0412

- 17 -

or using their flag vessels or aircraft, of:

a) arms and related materiel of all types, specifically
including the sale or transfer through other means of all
forms of conventional military equipment, including for
paramilitary forces, and spare parts and components and
their means of production, for such equipment;

b) items specified and defined in paragraph 8 and
paragraph 12 above not otherwise covered above;

c) technology under licensing or other transfer
arrangements used in the production, utilization or
stockpiling of items specified in subparagraphs a) and b)
above;

d) personnel or materials for training or technical
support services relating to the design, development,
manufacture, use, maintenance or support of items specified
in subparagraphs a) and b) above;

25. ·Calls upon all States and international organizations to
act strictly in accordance with paragraph 24 above,
notwithstanding the existence of any contracts, agreements,
licenses, or any other arrangements;   21-17

0413

- 18 -

26. Requests the Secretary General, in consultation with
appropriate Governments, to develop within 60 days, for
approval of the Council, guidelines to facilitate full
international implementation of paragraphs 24 and 25 above and
paragraph 27 below, and to make them available to all States
and to establish a procedure for up-dating these guidelines
periodically;

27. Calls upon all States to maintain such national controls
and procedures and to take such other actions consistent with
the guidelines to be established by the Security Council under
paragraph 26 above as may be necessary to ensure compliance
with the terms of paragraph 24 above, and calls upon
international organizations to take all appropriate steps to
assist in ensuring such full compliance;

28. Agrees to review its decisions in paragraphs 22, 23, 24,
and 25 above, except for the items specified and defined in
paragraphs 8 and 12 above, on a regular basis and in any case
120 days following passage of this resolution, taking into
account Iraq's compliance with this resolution and general
progress towards the control of armaments in the region;

29. Decides that all States, including Iraq, shall take the

21-18

0414

- 19 -

necessary measures to ensure that no claim shall lie at the
instance of the Government of Iraq, or of any person or body in
Iraq, or of any person claiming through or for the benefit of
any such person or body, in connection with any contract or
other transaction where its performance was affected by reason
of the measures taken by the Security Council in Resolution 661
(1990) and related resolutions;

G

30. Decides that, in furtherance of its commitment to
facilitate the repatriation of all Kuwaiti and third country
nationals, Iraq shall cooperate with the International
Committee of the Red Cross, providing lists of such persons,
facilitating the access of the International Committee of the
Red Cross to all such persons wherever located or detained and
facilitating the search by the International Committee of the
Red Cross for those Kuwaiti and Third Country nationals still
unaccounted for;

31. Invites the International Committee of the Red Cross to
keep the Secretary General apprised as appropriate of all
activities undertaken in connection with facilitating the
repatriation or return of all Kuwaiti and Third Country
nationals or their remains present in Iraq on or after August

21-19

0415

- 20 -

2, 1990;

H

32. Requires Iraq to inform the Council that it will not commit or support any act of international terrorism or allow any organization directed toward commission of such acts to operate within its territory and to condemn unequivocally and renounce all acts, methods, and practices of terrorism;

I

33. Declares that, upon official notification by Iraq to the Secretary-General and to the Security Council of its acceptance of the provisions above, a formal cease-fire is effective between Iraq and Kuwait and the member states cooperating with Kuwait in accordance with resolution 678 (1990);

34. Decides to remain seized of the matter and to take such further steps as may be required for the implementation of this resolution and to secure peace and security in the area.

10/439

21-20

0416

28 March 1991

Note by the President

Following consultations of the Council, the President of the
Security Council issued the following statement on behalf of the
members of the Council on 28 March 1991:

The members of the Council have considered the
Secretary-General's report on his mission of good offices in
Cyprus. They are unanimous in expressing their full support of his
current efforts.

The members of the Council agree with the Secretary-General's
assessment of the current situation, including the main issues that
remain to be clarified before an outline can be completed, and
encourage him to continue his efforts along the lines he has
proposed, by making suggestions to facilitate the discussions.

The members of the Council reaffirm Security Council resolution
649 (1990) and the mandate for the Secretary-General's mission of
good offices as set out in resolution 367 (1975); and recall that
that resolution 649 (1990) reaffirmed in particular Security Council
resolution 367 (1975) as well as the Council's support for the 1977
and 1979 high-level agreements between the leaders of the two
communities. This should continue to serve as the basis for the
Secretary-General's effort to arrive at an agreed outline.

The members of the Council urge all concerned to act in a
manner consistent with resolution 649 (1990), to cooperate fully
with the Secretary-General and to continue the discussions that have
taken place over the past few months in order to resolve without
delay the outstanding issues.

The members of the Council welcome the Secretary-General's
intention to submit a further report by early July 1991 on his
effort to arrive at an agreed outline of an overall settlement. The
members of the Council will decide, in the light of the situation at
that time, on any further measures for proceeding that may be
necessary.

2/-2/

0417

	정 리 보 존 문 서 목 록					
기록물종류	일반공문서철	등록번호	2017060007	등록일자		2017-06-05
분류번호	731.33	국가코드	XF	보존기간		30년
명 칭	걸프사태 관련 유엔안전보장이사회 동향, 1990-91. 전5권					
생 산 과	국제연합과/중동1과	생산년도	1990~1991	담당그룹		
권 차 명	V.5 1991.4월					
내용목차	* 1991.4.3 미국측 휴전 결의안 채택 (안보리 결의 687호) 4.5 이라크의 자국민 유혈 진압 규탄 (프랑스 제출) 결의안 4.6 이라크, 안보리 휴전 결의(안보리 결의 687호) 수락 4.12 휴전 결의 발효 확인 회신 이라크 전달					

0001

외 무 부

종 별 :

번 호 : UNW-0754   일 시 : 91 0401 1930

수 신 : 장 관(국연,중동일,기정)

발 신 : 주 유엔 대사

제 목 : 걸프사태(안보리)

연: UNW-0734

1. 금 4.1.오후 현재 연호 교섭문안 본문 8항 B)미사일 조항과 관련, 상임이사국들간 협의가 계속 진행중이며, 사정거리 150 KM 이하 미사일은 허용하는 방향으로 논의되고있는 것으로 알려짐.

2. 안보리 이사국중 비동맹 7개국 (간사:자이르) 은 상기 교섭문안에 대한 일부수정안을 실무급수준에서 준비중인 것으로 알려지고있음.동비동맹 내부 검토를 위해 인도, 쿠바가 각각제시한 내용은 당관에서 입수한 별첨자료 참조바람

3. 안보리는 4.1.18:00 상기 휴전결의안 문제 토의를 위해 비공식협의를 개최하였으나 실질토의는 없었으며 4.2. 비공식협의 속개예정임.

4. 한편 영국측은 쿠웨이트-이락국경문제 관련 별첨 3.28자 사무총장앞 서한을 안보리문서로 배포하였음.

첨부:1.인도수정안내용

2.쿠바수정안내용

3.영국측안보리문서: UNW(F)-145

끝

(대사 노창희-국장)

국기국   1차보   중아국   정문국   안기부

PAGE 1   91.04.02   10:22 WG

외신 1과 통제관

0002

인도수정안 UNW(유)-145 104의 1930

(국연·동봉인·기재) 충11매

Amendments proposed on "Draft Elements of the

"11.45, March 28, 1991".

PREAMBULAR PARAS

C - Delete in the end "consistent with

paragraph 8 of resolution 686(1991)".

H - Delete in the end "and affirming that

grave consequences would follow any

further use by Iraq of such weapons".

L, M & P, Q, R, S - Delete.

X - After "Taking note" insert "with grave

concern",

- Substitute "desirability of meeting

humanitarian needs in Kuwait and Iraq

in the immediate post-crisis environment"

by "urgent need to meet humanitarian

needs in Iraq and Kuwait".

OPERATIVE PARAS

1 - Substitute the text "expressly changed

below ... a formal cease-fire" by

"specified below".

2 - After "signed" insert "by them in the

exercise of their sovereignty"

- Add in the end "and registered with the

United Nations as published in U.N.

document------"

3 - Substitute by a new text to read,

11-1

0003

2

"<u>Calls</u> on Iraq and Kuwait, with the
assistance of the Secretary General, to
proceed immediately to demarcate the
boundary between them, drawing on
appropriate material, including the map
contained in Security Council document
S/_____; and requests the Secretary
General to extend all assistance as
appropriate for this purpose and report
on the progress to it within one month".

4 - Delete.

5 - Substitute in the first line "after
consulting" by "in consultation".

6 - Substitute by a new text to read, "<u>Decides</u>
that with the deployment of the UN observer
unit, the members States cooperating with
Kuwait in accordance with resolution
678(1990) will bring their military
presence in Iraq to an end".

14- Delete

17- Substitute "the Iraqi statements made
since August 2, 1990, concerning" by "all
Iraqi statements repudiating".

  - Add in the end "and demands that Iraq
scrupulously adhere to all its obligations
concerning servicing and repayment of its
foreign debt".

19- After "needs of the Iraqi economy" insert

7/ - 2

0004

3

"for reconstruction and development".

20- Substitute "notified to the Committee established in resolution 661 (1990) and, with the approval of that Committee, under simplified and accelerated procedures", by "and".

21- Delete.

22- Substitute by a new text to read, "<u>Decides</u> that upon the acceptance by Iraq of this resolution, all prohibitions against Iraq in terms of resolution 661(1990), save as provided in paragraph 24 herein, shall have no further force or effect".

23- Delete

28- Delete in the end "and general progress towards the control of armaments in the region".

30- Substitute "cooperate with" by "extend all necessary cooperation to".

11-3   0005

쿠바수정안

<u>DRAFT AMENDMENTS TO THE DRAFT ELEMENTS OF THE NEXT RESOLUTION ON GULF SECURITY
AS PRESENTED TO THE NON-ALIGNED CAUCUS BY THE DELEGATIONS OF THE UNITED
STATES, THE UNITED KINGDOM AND THE SOVIET UNION ON 28 MARCH 1991.</u>

<u>PREAMBLE:</u>

<u>Paragraph D:</u> Replace by the following: "<u>Reaffirming</u> the need to adopt all
necessary measures to guarantee peace and security to all States in the Middle
East, and the Gulf in particular, through the peaceful solution of outstanding
conflicts and hotbeds of tension in the Region,".

<u>Paragraph G:</u> Replace by the following: "<u>Conscious</u> of the need for Iraq and
Kuwait to undertake the necessary negotiations, in conformity with resolution
660 (1990) of the Security Council for the solution of all outstanding
problems between them, including the boundary between both countries on the
basis of the agreements they have previously reached on the said issue,".

<u>Paragraph H:</u> Replace by the following: "<u>Affirming</u> the need for all countries
to fulfill their obligations under the Geneva Protocol for the Prohibition of
the Use in War of Asphyxiating, Poisonous and Other Gases, and of
Bacteriological Methods of Warfare, signed at Geneva on 17 June 1925, and
<u>concerned</u> by the worldwide existence of enormous arsenals and stockpiles
of the above mentioned weapons,".

<u>Paragraph I:</u> Replace by the following: "<u>Reaffirming</u> the commitment of all
States participating in the Conference of States Party to the 1925 Geneva
Protocol and Other International States, held at Paris on January 7 to 11,
1989, with the objective of universal elimination of chemical and biological
weapons,".

<u>Paragraph J:</u> Replace by the following: "<u>Reaffirming further</u> the obligations
of all States that have signed the Convention on the Prohibition of the
Development, Production and Stockpiling of Bacteriological (Biological) and
Toxin Weapons and on Their Destruction, of 10 April 1972,".

11-4   0006

2.

Paragraph K: Replace by the following: "Fully conscious of the importance for the preservation of international peace and security in general, and in the region in particular, for all States, including Iraq and other countries in the Middle East, to sign and ratify all the previously mentioned International Instruments and to fully comply by their provisions,".

Paragraph L: Replace by the following: "Encouraging the reinforcement of the authority, efficiency and universal scope of the Convention on the Prohibition of the Development, Production and Stockpiling of Bacteriological (Biological) and Toxin Weapons and on their Destruction, of 10 April 1972, through its forthcoming Review Conference,".

Paragraph Q: At the end of the paragraph, after the comma, add the following: "as a step towards the objective of the international community of achieving general and complete disarmament and, in particular, its priority of achieving nuclear disarmament and the destruction of all weapons of mass destruction,".

Paragraph R: At the end of the paragraph, after the comma, add the following: "as a contribution to the aim of significantly reducing military arsenals and the production of weapons worldwide, and to devoting resources towards productive efforts, in particular the development of developing countries,".

Paragraph S: 1.- Second line, between the words "all available" and "means", add the word "peaceful".

2.- Second line, replace the words "including a" by "for fostering a".

3.- At the end of the paragraph, after the comma, add the following: "with the aim of achieving Agreements that would ensure a comprehensive, just and lasting peace in the area,".

Paragraph W: First line, replace the word "Deploring" by the following: "Reaffirming its abhorrence of all acts of terrorism, of all origins, and its rejection of all such acts, including...".

11-5

0007

3.

OPERATIVE SECTION:

<u>Paragraph 1</u>: Replace lines 2 and 3 by the following: "already fulfilled in accordance with the provisions thereof, or overtaken by events;".

<u>Between paragraphs 1 and 2</u>: Insert a new paragraph with the following text: "<u>Declares</u> that upon adoption of the present resolution, a formal cease-fire is effective between Iraq and Kuwait and the member States cooperating with Kuwait in accordance with resolution 678 (1990);".

<u>Paragraph 2</u>: 1.- Line 1, replace the words "respect the inviolability of" by the following: "undertake negotiations regarding...".

2.- At the end of the paragraph, replace the semicolon by the following: "and in the meantime <u>decides</u> to consider the boundary existing on August 1, 1990, as a provisional boundary exclusively for the provisions of the present resolution that might so require;".

<u>Paragraph 3</u>: 1.- Page 7, line 1, replace the words "make arrangements with Iraq and Kuwait to demarcate" by the following: "Iraq and Kuwait in the negotiations they will undertake with the purpose of demarcating...".

2.- Page 7, line 5, between the words "Security Council" and "within one month", add the words "on the results of his assistance to Iraq and Kuwait and on any other issue regarding the demarcation of boundaries between both countries that he considers should be brought before the Council,".

<u>Paragraph 4</u>: Lines 1 and 2, replace the words "above mentioned international boundary" by the following: "of the international boundary freely determined in negotiations between both countries".

11-6

0008

4.

Paragraph 5: line 6, replace the words "from the boundary referred to in the" by the following: "from the provisional boundary as specified in paragraph 2 above, pending the conclusion of negotiations regarding the...".

Paragraph 6: At the end of the paragraph, replace the semicolon by a comma, and add the following: "as soon as the United Nations observer unit is fully deployed and operational".

Paragraph 7: 1.- Line 1, between the words "_Invites_" and "Iraq", insert the following: "all countries including". Accordingly, replace the word "its" in the first line by "their".

                2.- Line 5, between the words "1925, and" and "to ratify the Convention", insert the following "_urges_ all countries to sign, and when appropriate, including Iraq, to ratify...".

Paragraph 8: Line 1, between the words "_Decides_" and "that Iraq shall", insert the following: "as a first step towards the full elimination of weapons of mass destruction and weapon systems incompatible with the aim of achieving a comprehensive, just and lasting peace in the Middle East,".

Paragraph 11: Replace by the following: "_Invites_ all States having signed and ratified the Treaty on the Non-Proliferation of Nuclear Weapons, of 1 July 1968, to reaffirm their obligations under that Treaty, and States that have not signed nor ratified it, to abide by its provisions;".

Paragraph 12: Between the word "that Iraq" and "shall unconditionally", insert the following: "as a first step towards achieving the goal of having a region totally free from nuclear weapons and other weapons of mass destruction,".

11-7

0009

5.

Paragraph 14: Replace by the following: "Requests the Secretary General to immediately undertake consultations with the countries in the region, countries with a presence in the region and all other interested countries, including the Permanent Members of the Security Council for the convening, not later that 120 days after the adoption of this resolution, of an International Conference with the goal of establishing in the Middle East a zone free from nuclear weapons and other weapons of mass destruction and all missiles for their delivery;".

Paragraph 16: Page 14, line 1, between the words "nationals and corporations" and "as a result", insert the following: "in Kuwait,".

Paragraph 20: Replace by the following: "Decides, effective immediately, that resolutions 661 (1990) and 670 (1990) of the Security Council be considered null and void owing to the non existence at present of conditions that prompted their approval and, that, thus, all prohibitions contained in the said resolutions are no longer in effect;".

Paragraphs 21, 22 and 23: Should be deleted.

Paragraph 24: Lines 1 and 2, delete the comma after the words "Decides that" and delete the following phrase: "in accordance with resolution 661 (1990) and subsequent related resolutions and...".

Paragraph 28: 1.- Delete the numbers "22, 23".
         2.- Line 5, delete the following phrase: "Iraq's compliance with this resolution and".

0010

6.

Paragraph 32: Replace by the following: "Requires all States, including Iraq, to reaffirm their commitment not to commit or support any act of international terrorism by their official agencies or allow any organization directed towards commission of such acts to operate within their territory and to condemn unequivocally and renounce all acts, methods and practices of terrorism;".

Paragraph 33: Should be deleted.

* * * * *

11-9   0011

**UNITED
NATIONS**

S

Security Council

Distr.
GENERAL

S/22412
28 March 1991

ORIGINAL: ENGLISH

LETTER DATED 28 MARCH 1991 FROM THE PERMANENT REPRESENTATIVE OF
THE UNITED KINGDOM OF GREAT BRITAIN AND NORTHERN IRELAND TO THE
UNITED NATIONS ADDRESSED TO THE SECRETARY-GENERAL

I am sending you with this letter a set of 10 sheets in the K7611 Series of topographic maps of Kuwait* produced, on a scale of 1:50,000, by the United Kingdom Director General of Military Survey. The numbers of the sheets are:

```
5348 -   I Edition 2 .
5348 - III      "    3
5349 -  II      "    3
5449 -   I      "    3
5449 - III      "    1
5449 -  IV      "    3
5449 -   I      "    2
5549 -  IV      "    2
5649 -   I      "    4
5649 -  IV      "    3
```

The maps have been produced on the basis of the letter of the Prime Minister of Iraq of 21 July 1932 and the letter of the Ruler of Kuwait of 10 August 1932.

As you know those letters do not offer a precise description of the boundary on the ground. You will also notice that the maps carry the standard Director General of Military Survey note as follows:

"Maps produced under the direction of the Director General of Military Survey are not to be taken as necessarily representing the view of the UK Government on boundaries or political status."

Nevertheless, I hope they will be of use in connection with any demarcation of the Kuwait-Iraq boundary.

---

*   The maps may be consulted in Room S-3200A, extension 3-5048.

91-10029 2335j (E)   /...

11-16   0012

S/22412
English
Page 2

    I should be grateful if you would arrange for this letter to be circulated as a document of the Security Council.

                      (Signed) D. H. A. HANNAY

-----

11 - 11

0013

외 무 부

종 별 :

번 호 : UNW-0756

일 시 : 91 0401 2000

수 신 : 장 관(국연,중동일,기정)

발 신 : 주 유엔 대사

제 목 : 걸프사태(경제제재조치)

지난 3.22. 인도적 품목에대한 안보리제재 위원회의 대이락 금수 완화조치 관련 비정부간 기구 (NGO) 들의 대이락 인도적원조공여시 절차문제 (NGO 본부 소재국책임)에 관한 3.26동 제재위원회 결정내용을 별첨송부함.

첨부:상기 제재위원회 결정: UNW(F)-147

끝

(대사 노창희-국장) G

국기국   1차보   중아국   정문국   청와대   안기부

91.04.02   10:24
외신 1과 통제관

0014

**UNITED
NATIONS**

Security Council

**Distr.
GENERAL**

**S/22419
28 March 1991**

ORIGINAL: ENGLISH

NOTE BY THE SECRETARY-GENERAL

At the request of the Chairman of the Security Council Committee established by resolution 661 (1990) concerning the situation between Iraq and Kuwait, I have the honour to bring to the attention of all States the attached decision of the Committee with regard to the procedure to be followed by non-governmental organizations wishing to provide humanitarian assistance to the civilian population of Iraq.

91-10071 2402b (E)

/...

외 무 부

종   별 :

번   호 : UNW-0762   일   시 : 91 0402 1830

수   신 : 장 관(국연,중동일,기정)

발   신 : 주 유엔 대사

제   목 : 걸프사태(안보리)

연: UNW-0734,0754

1. 금 4.2. 미국은 그간의 상임이사국 (PERM-5)들간 협의결과를 기초로 휴전결의 초안을 안보리문서 (S/22430) 로 배포한바, 동 미측제출초안은 연호 교섭문안을 다음과 같이 일부 보완내지 수정한것임.

가.보완

1)미사일 조항(본문 8항 B)

사정거리 150 KM 이하 탄도미사일 허용

2)국경조항(본문 3항)

참고 기준자료의 하나로 연호 영국 안보리문서 (S/22412: 관련지도)명시

나.자구수정

1)전문: M,N,Q,X

2) 본문:2, 3, 5, 8, 9, 10, 17, 22, 30 항

2.미대표부 F.URBANCIC 담당관에 의하면, 상기 미측안의 공동제안국들이 곧 나올것이라고함.한편 동 담당관은 인도측이 지난주말 상임이사국 교섭문안에 수정의견을 제시해온바, 미측은 동의견을 상기안에 일부 반영하였다함. (전문 X, 본문 2,17, 30 항)

3.안보리는 금 4.2.12:00 경 휴전결의안 문제토의를 위해 비공식협의를 개최하였으나, 연호비동맹 이사국 7개국 (CAUCUS) 간 내부협의가 진행중인 관계로 동일 오후 비공식협의를 다시갖기로하고 일단 오전 협의를 마쳤음.

4.동 오전협의시 불란서는 이락 내전과 관련된 최근의 사태발전 (유혈진압격화) 문제를 제기한바, 이사국들의 특기할 반응은 없었던것으로 알려짐.동 문제에 관해서는 의장이 이사국들과 개별협의를 가질예정이라고함. (가능한 조치로서는 상기

국기국   1차보   중아국   정문국   청와대   안기부

휴전결의안에 반영하는 방법, 별개 결의안 추진 , 또는 의장성명 채택방안이 있으나 앞의 두가지 가능성은 크지 않은것으로 알려짐)

5.한편 상기 이락 내전사태와 관련, 4.2.유엔사무총장은 대변인을 통해 특히 난민증가에 우려를 표명하고, 자제및 평화적 해결을 강조하였음.

6.금 4.2. 이락은 미측의 자국 영공침범 (S/22422), 유적지 훼손가능성 (S/22423) 에 관한 안보리문서를 배포하였음.한편 이락측의 이란-이락 휴전협정 위반 사례를 비난하는 이란문서(S/22426) 도 배포되었음.

첨부:1.휴전결의안 미측초안

2.이락내전사태 관련사무총장 성명내용: UNW(F)-148

끝

(대사 노창희-국장)

UNW(F)-148   10402 1A70
(국연. 중동일. 기정)

**UNITED
NATIONS**

총9대   **S**

Security Council

PROVISIONAL

S/22430
1 April 1991

ORIGINAL: ENGLISH

<u>United States of America: draft resolution</u>

<u>The Security Council</u>,

A.   <u>Recalling</u> its resolutions 660 (1990), 661 (1990), 662 (1990), 664 (1990), 665 (1990), 666 (1990), 667 (1990), 669 (1990), 670 (1990), 674 (1990), 677 (1990), 678 (1990) and 686 (1991),

B.   <u>Welcoming</u> the restoration to Kuwait of its sovereignty, independence, and territorial integrity and the return of its legitimate government,

C.   <u>Affirming</u> the commitment of all Member States to the sovereignty, territorial integrity and political independence of Kuwait and Iraq, and noting the intention expressed by the Member States cooperating with Kuwait under paragraph 2 of resolution 678 (1990) to bring their military presence in Iraq to an end as soon as possible consistent with paragraph 8 of resolution 686 (1991),

D.   <u>Reaffirming</u> the need to be assured of Iraq's peaceful intentions in light of its unlawful invasion and occupation of Kuwait,

E.   <u>Taking note</u> of the letter sent by the Foreign Minister of Iraq on 27 February 1991 (S/22275) and those sent pursuant to resolution 686 (1991) (S/22273, S/22276, S/22320, S/22321, S/22330), in particular the letter dated ... concerning Iraq's fulfilment of the requirements in resolution 686 (1991),

F.   <u>Noting</u> that Iraq and Kuwait, as independent sovereign States, signed at Baqhdad on 4 October 1963 "Agreed Minutes Regarding the Restoration of Friendly Relations, Recognition and Related Matters", thereby recognizing formally the boundary between Iraq and Kuwait and the allocation of islands, which were registered with the United Nations in accordance with Article 102 of the Charter and in which Iraq recognized the independence and complete sovereignty of the State of Kuwait within its borders as specified and accepted in the letter of the Prime Minister of Iraq dated 21 July 1932, and as accepted by the Ruler of Kuwait in his letter dated 10 August 1932,

G.   <u>Conscious</u> of the need for demarcation of the said boundary,

91 10310   32782 (E)   /...

UNW-0762 의
  천부물   7 -1   0018

S/22430
English
Page 2

H.   Conscious also of the statements by Iraq threatening to use weapons in
violation of its obligations under the Geneva Protocol for the Prohibition of the
Use in War of Asphyxiating, Poisonous or Other Gases, and of Bacteriological
Methods of Warfare, signed at Geneva on 17 June 1925, and of its prior use of
chemical weapons and affirming that grave consequences would follow any further use
by Iraq of such weapons,

I.   Recalling that Iraq has subscribed to the Declaration adopted by all States
participating in the Conference of States Parties to the 1925 Geneva Protocol and
Other Interested States, held at Paris from 7 to 11 January 1989, establishing the
objective of universal elimination of chemical and biological weapons,

J.   Recalling further that Iraq has signed the Convention on the Prohibition of
the Development, Production and Stockpiling of Bacteriological (Biological) and
Toxin Weapons and on Their Destruction, of 10 April 1972,

K.   Noting the importance of Iraq ratifying this Convention,

L.   Noting moreover the importance of all States adhering to this Convention and
encouraging its forthcoming Review Conference to reinforce the authority,
efficiency and universal scope of the convention,

M.   Stressing the importance of an early conclusion by the Conference on
Disarmament of its work on a Convention on the Universal Prohibition of Chemical
Weapons and of universal adherence thereto,

N.   Aware of the use by Iraq of ballistic missiles in unprovoked attacks and
therefore of the need to take specific measures in regard to such missiles located
in Iraq,

O.   Concerned by the reports in the hands of Member States that Iraq has attempted
to acquire materials for a nuclear-weapons programme contrary to its obligations
under the Treaty on the Non-Proliferation of Nuclear Weapons of 1 July 1968,

P.   Recalling the objective of the establishment of a nuclear-weapons-free zone in
the region of the Middle East,

Q.   Conscious of the threat which all weapons of mass destruction pose to peace
and security in the area and of the need to work towards the establishment in the
Middle East of a zone free of such weapons,

R.   Conscious also of the objective of achieving balanced and comprehensive
control of armaments in the region,

S.   Conscious further of the importance of achieving the objectives noted above
using all available means, including a dialogue among the States of the region,

T.   Noting that resolution 686 (1991) marked the lifting of the measures imposed
by resolution 661 (1990) in so far as they applied to Kuwait,

/...

9 - 2

0019

U. Noting that despite the progress being made in fulfilling the obligations of resolution 686 (1991), many Kuwaiti and third country nationals are still not accounted for and property remains unreturned,

V. Recalling the International Convention against the Taking of Hostages, opened for signature at New York on 18 December 1979, which categorizes all acts of taking hostages as manifestations of international terrorism,

W. Deploring threats made by Iraq during the recent conflict to make use of terrorism against targets outside Iraq and the taking of hostages by Iraq,

X. Taking note with grave concern of the reports of the Secretary-General of 20 March 1991 (S/22366) and 28 March 1991 (S/22409), and conscious of the necessity to meet urgently the humanitarian needs in Kuwait and Iraq in the immediate post-crisis environment,

Y. Bearing in mind its objective of restoring international peace and security in the area as set out in recent Council resolutions,

Z. Conscious of the need to take the following measures acting under Chapter VII of the Charter,

1. Affirms all thirteen resolutions noted above, except as expressly changed below to achieve the goals of this resolution, including a formal cease-fire;

A

2. Demands that Iraq and Kuwait respect the inviolability of the international boundary and the allocation of islands set out in the "Agreed Minutes Between the State of Kuwait and the Republic of Iraq Regarding the Restoration of Friendly Relations, Recognition and Related Matters", signed by them in the exercise of their sovereignty at Baghdad on 4 October 1963 and registered with the United Nations and published by the United Nations in document 7063, United Nations Treaty Series, 1964;

3. Calls on the Secretary-General to lend his assistance to make arrangements with Iraq and Kuwait to demarcate the boundary between Iraq and Kuwait, drawing on appropriate material including the map transmitted by Security Council document S/22412 and to report back to the Security Council within one month;

4. Decides to guarantee the inviolability of the above-mentioned international boundary and to take as appropriate all necessary measures to that end in accordance with the Charter;

B

5. Requests the Secretary-General, after consulting with Iraq and Kuwait, to submit within three days to the Security Council for its approval a plan for the immediate deployment of a United Nations observer unit to monitor the Khor Abdullah

/...

9 - 3

0020

S/22430
English
Page 4

and a demilitarized zone, which is hereby established, extending 10 kilometres into Iraq and 5 kilometres into Kuwait from the boundary referred to in the "Agreed Minutes Between the State of Kuwait and the Republic of Iraq Regarding the Restoration of Friendly Relations, Recognition and Related Matters" of 4 October 1963; to deter violations of the boundary through its presence in and surveillance of the demilitarized zone; to observe any hostile or potentially hostile action mounted from the territory of one State to the other; and for the Secretary-General to report regularly to the Council on the operations of the unit, and immediately if there are serious violations of the zone or potential threats to peace;

6.   Notes that the deployment of the United Nations observer unit as soon as possible will establish the conditions for the forces of the Member States cooperating with Kuwait in accordance with resolution 678 (1990) to bring their military presence in Iraq to an end consistent with resolution 686 (1991)

and to ratify the Convention on the Prohibition of the Development, Production and Stockpiling of Bacteriological (Biological) and Toxin Weapons and on Their Destruction, of 10 April 1972;

8.   Decides that Iraq shall unconditionally accept the destruction, removal, or rendering harmless, under international supervision, of:

(a)   all chemical and biological weapons and all stocks of agents and all related subsystems and components and all research, development, support and manufacturing facilities;

(b)   all ballistic missiles with a range greater than 150 kilometres and related major parts, and repair and production facilities;

9.   Decides, for the implementation of paragraph 8 above, the following:

(a)   Iraq shall submit to the Secretary-General, within fifteen days of the adoption of this resolution, a declaration of the locations, amounts and types of all items specified in paragraph 8 and agree to urgent, on-site inspection as specified below;

and, where appropriate, with the Director-General of the World Health Organization (WHO), within 45 days of the passage of this resolution, shall develop, and submit to the Council for approval, a plan calling for the completion of the following acts within 45 days of such approval.

(i)   the forming of a Special Commission, which shall carry out immediate on-site inspection of Iraq's biological, chemical and missile

/...

9 — 4

0021

capabilities, based on Iraq's declarations and the designation of any
additional locations by the Special Commission itself;

(ii)   the yielding by Iraq of possession to the Special Commission for
destruction, removal or rendering harmless, taking into account the
requirements of public safety, of all items specified under
paragraph 8 (a) above including items at the additional locations
designated by the Special Commission under paragraph 9 (b) (i) above and
the destruction by Iraq, under supervision of the Special Commission, of
all its missile capabilities including launchers as specified under
paragraph 8 (b) above;

(iii) the provision by the Special Commission of the assistance and cooperation
to the Director-General of the International Atomic Energy Agency (IAEA)
required in paragraphs 12 and 13 below;

10.   Decides that Iraq shall unconditionally undertake not to use, develop,
construct or acquire any of the items specified in paragraphs 8 and 9 above and
requests the Secretary-General, in consultation with the Special Commission, to
develop a plan for the future ongoing monitoring and verification of Iraq's
compliance with this paragraph, to be submitted to the Council for approval within
120 days of the passage of this resolution;

11.   Invites Iraq to reaffirm unconditionally its obligations under the Treaty
on the Non-Proliferation of Nuclear Weapons, of 1 July 1968;

12.   Decides that Iraq shall unconditionally agree not to acquire or develop
nuclear weapons or nuclear-weapons-usable material or any subsystems or components
or any research, development, support or manufacturing facilities related to the
above; to submit to the Secretary-General and the Director-General of the
International Atomic Energy Agency (IAEA) within 15 days of the adoption of this
resolution a declaration of the locations, amounts, and types of all items
specified above; to place all of its nuclear-weapons-usable materials under the
exclusive control, for custody and removal, of the IAEA, with the assistance and
cooperation of the Special Commission as provided for in the plan of the
Secretary-General discussed in paragraph 9 (b) above; to accept, in accordance with
the arrangements provided for in paragraph 13 below, urgent on-site inspection and
the destruction, removal, or rendering harmless as appropriate of all items
specified above; and to accept the plan discussed in paragraph 13 below for the
future ongoing monitoring and verification of its compliance with these
undertakings;

13.   Requests the Director-General of the International Atomic Energy Agency
(IAEA) through the Secretary-General, with the assistance and cooperation of the
Special Commission as provided for in the plan of the Secretary-General in
paragraph 9 (b) above, to carry out immediate on-site inspection of Iraq's nuclear
capabilities based on Iraq's declarations and the designation of any additional
locations by the Special Commission; to develop a plan for submission to the
Security Council within 45 days calling for the destruction, removal, or rendering
harmless as appropriate of all items listed in paragraph 12 above; to carry out the

/...

9 - 5.   0022

S/22430
English
Page 6

plan within 45 days following approval by the Security Council; and to develop a
plan, taking into account the rights and obligations of Iraq under the Treaty on
the Non-Proliferation of Nuclear Weapons, of 1 July 1968, for the future ongoing
monitoring and verification of Iraq's compliance with paragraph 12 above, including
an inventory of all nuclear material in Iraq subject to the Agency's verification
and special inspections to confirm that IAEA safeguards cover all relevant nuclear
activities in Iraq, to be submitted to the Council for approval within 120 days of
the passage of this resolution;

14. Takes note that the actions to be taken by Iraq in paragraphs 8, 9, 10,
11, 12 and 13 of this resolution represent steps towards the goal of establishing
in the Middle East a zone free from weapons of mass destruction and all missiles
for their delivery and the objective of a global ban on chemical weapons;

D

15. Requests the Secretary-General to report to the Security Council on the
steps taken to facilitate the return of all Kuwaiti property seized by Iraq,
including a list of any property which Kuwait claims has not been returned or which
has not been returned intact;

E

16. Reaffirms that Iraq, without prejudice to the debts and obligations of
Iraq arising prior to 2 August 1990, which will be addressed through the normal
mechanisms, is liable under international law for any direct loss, damage,
including environmental damage and the depletion of natural resources, or injury to
foreign Governments, nationals and corporations, as a result of Iraq's unlawful
invasion and occupation of Kuwait;

17. Decides that all Iraqi statements made since 2 August 1990, repudiating
its foreign debt are null and void, and demands that Iraq scrupulously adhere to
all of its obligations concerning servicing and repayment of its foreign debt;

18. Decides to create a Fund to pay compensation for claims that fall within
paragraph 16 above and to establish a Commission that will administer the Fund;

19. Directs the Secretary-General to develop and present to the Council for
decision, no later than 30 days following the adoption of this resolution,
recommendations for the Fund to meet the requirement for the payment of claims
established in accordance with paragraph 18 above and for a programme to implement
the decisions in paragraphs 16, 17, and 18 above, including: administration of the
Fund; mechanisms for determining the appropriate level of Iraq's contribution to
the Fund based on a percentage of the value of the exports of petroleum and
petroleum products from Iraq not to exceed a figure to be suggested to the Council
by the Secretary-General, taking into account the requirements of the people of
Iraq and in particular humanitarian needs, Iraq's payment capacity as assessed in
conjunction with the international financial institutions taking into consideration
external debt service, and the needs of the Iraqi economy; arrangements for
ensuring that payments are made to the Fund; the process by which funds will be

/...

9－6

0023

allocated and claims paid; appropriate procedures for evaluating losses, listing claims and verifying their validity and resolving disputed claims in respect of Iraq's liability as specified in paragraph 16 above; and the composition of the Commission designated above;

E

20. Decides, effective immediately, that the prohibitions against the sale or supply to Iraq of commodities or products, and prohibitions against financial transactions related thereto, contained in resolution 661 (1990) shall not apply to foodstuffs notified to the Committee established under resolution 661 (1990) or, with the approval of that Committee, under simplified and accelerated procedures, to materials and supplies for essential civilian needs as identified in the report of the Secretary-General dated 20 March 1991 (S/22366), and in any further findings of humanitarian need by the Committee;

21. Decides that the Council shall review the provisions of paragraph 20 above every sixty days in light of the policies and practices of the Government of Iraq, including the implementation of all relevant resolutions of the Security Council, for the purpose of determining whether to modify further or lift the prohibitions referred to therein;

22. Decides that upon the approval by the Council of the programme called for in paragraph 19 above and upon Council agreement that Iraq has completed all actions contemplated in paragraphs 8, 9, 10, 11, 12, and 13 above, the prohibitions against the import of commodities and products originating in Iraq and the prohibitions against financial transactions related thereto contained in resolution 661 (1990) shall have no further force or effect;

23. Decides that, pending action by the Council under paragraph 22 above, the Committee established under resolution 661 (1990) shall be empowered to approve, when required to assure adequate financial resources on the part of Iraq to carry out the activities under paragraph 20 above, exceptions to the prohibition against the import of commodities and products originating in Iraq;

24. Decides that, in accordance with resolution 661 (1990) and subsequent related resolutions and until a further decision is taken by the Council, all States shall continue to prevent the sale or supply, or promotion or facilitation of such sale or supply, to Iraq by their nationals, or from their territories or using their flag vessels or aircraft, of:

(a) arms and related matériel of all types, specifically including the sale or transfer through other means of all forms of conventional military equipment, inlcuding for paramilitary forces, and spare parts and components and their means of production, for such equipment;

(b) items specified and defined in paragraph 8 and paragraph 12 above not otherwise covered above;

/...

9 - 7

0024

(c) technology under licensing or other transfer arrangements used in the production, utilization or stockpiling of items specified in subparagraphs (a) and (b) above;

(d) personnel or materials for training or technical support services relating to the design, development, manufacture, use, maintenance or support of items specified in subparagraphs (a) and (b) above;

25. Calls upon all States and international organizations to act strictly in accordance with paragraph 24 above, notwithstanding the existence of any contracts, agreements, licences, or any other arrangements;

26. Requests the Secretary-General, in consultation with appropriate Governments, to develop within 60 days, for approval of the Council, guidelines to facilitate full international implementation of paragraphs 24 and 25 above and paragraph 27 below, and to make them available to all States and to establish a procedure for updating these guidelines periodically;

27. Calls upon all States to maintain such national controls and procedures and to take such other actions consistent with the guidelines to be established by the Security Council under paragraph 26 above as may be necessary to ensure compliance with the terms of paragraph 24 above, and calls upon international organizations to take all appropriate steps to assist in ensuring such full compliance;

28. Agrees to review its decisions in paragraphs 22, 23, 24, and 25 above, except for the items specified and defined in paragraphs 8 and 12 above, on a regular basis and in any case 120 days following passage of this resolution, taking into account Iraq's compliance with this resolution and general progress towards the control of armaments in the region;

29. Decides that all States, including Iraq, shall take the necessary measures to ensure that no claim shall lie at the instance of the Government of Iraq, or of any person or body in Iraq, or of any person claiming through or for the benefit of any such person or body, in connection with any contract or other transaction where its performance was affected by reason of the measures taken by the Security Council in resolution 661 (1990) and related resolutions;

G

30. Decides that, in furtherance of its commitment to facilitate the repatriation of all Kuwaiti and third country nationals, Iraq shall extend all necessary cooperation to the International Committee of the Red Cross, providing lists of such persons, facilitating the access of the International Committee of the Red Cross to all such persons wherever located or detained and facilitating the search by the International Committee of the Red Cross for those Kuwaiti and third country nationals still unaccounted for;

31. Invites the International Committee of the Red Cross to keep the Secretary-General apprised as appropriate of all activities undertaken in

/...

9 - 8

0025

S/22430
English
Page 9

connection with facilitating the repatriation or return of all Kuwaiti and third country nationals or their remains present in Iraq on or after 2 August 1990;

H

    32. Requires Iraq to inform the Council that it will not commit or support any act of international terrorism or allow any organization directed towards commission of such acts to operate within its territory and to condemn unequivocally and renounce all acts, methods, and practices of terrorism;

I

    33. Declares that, upon official notification by Iraq to the Secretary-General and to the Security Council of its acceptance of the provisions above, a formal cease-fire is effective between Iraq and Kuwait and the Member States cooperating with Kuwait in accordance with resolution 678 (1990);

    34. Decides to remain seized of the matter and to take such further steps as may be required for the implementation of this resolution and to secure peace and security in the area.

-----

9 - 9   0026

외 무 부

종 별 :

번 호 : UNW-0774

일 시 : 91 0403 0030

수 신 : 장 관(국연,중동일,기정)

발 신 : 주 유엔 대사

제 목 : 걸프사태(안보리)

연: UNW-0762

1. 안보리는 금 4.2.오후 휴전결의안 관련 상임이사국 (PERM-5),
비동맹이사국(CAUCUS 7개국)간 교섭을 진행한바, 결국 합의에 이르지 못하고 23:00경
4.3.오전 공식 회의를 개최키로하고 금일협의를 종료하였음.

2.상기 교섭과정에서 비동맹이사국들은 별첨 수정내용을 제시한 것으로
알려졌으며, 미측은 일부 내용에 대해서만 수용용의를 표명하였다고함.

3.연호 미측안 (S/22430) 에 대해, 영.소련이 공동제안국에 참여 의사를 밝혔으며,
동 공동제안국은 추가될 전망임.

4.한편 연호 이락사태와 관련 불란서는 별도의 결의안을 추진중인 것으로
알려졌으며, 터키가 동 사태 토의를 위한 안보리 회의소집을 요청하여왔다고함.

첨부:1.비동맹이사국 수정제시내용

2.불란서결의안초안: UNW(F)-149

끝

(대사 노창희-국장)

국기국   1차보   중아국   정문국   청와대   안기부   장관 차관

PAGE 1

91.04.03   14:47 WG

외신 1과 통제관

0027

첨부1. 비동맹이사국 수정제시내용   UNW(厈)-149 10403 003~
(국련.중동일.기知)
총3매

Amendments generally accepted by members of the Non-Aligned Caucus to the draft elements of the next resolution on the Gulf

Para.2   replaced by the following:

No   "Demands that Iraq and Kuwait undertake immediate negotiations, on the basis of para.3 of resolution 660 (1990), regarding the international boundary and the allocation of islands, taking into account of pertinent documents, specially the agreed minutes between the state of Kuwait and the representative of Iraq regarding the restoration of friendly relations and related matters "signed by them at Baghdad on 4 October 1963, in exercise of their sovereignty and as registered in the United Nations (Treaty Series ......).

Paras.3   Replaced by:

1/0   "Calls on Iraq and Kuwait, utilizing the good offices of the Secretary-General to conclude their negotiations expeditiously and thereafter to undertake immediately the demarkation of the boundary between them, and requests the Secretary-General to extend all appropriate assistance to them and to report periodically on the progress to the Council.

Para.4   Deleted:

Para.5   1) Line 1 - replace the words "after consulting with" by the phrase "with the prior consent of.   NO

2) Lines 6 to 9 - replace the phrase starting with the words "referred to" until "of 4 October 1963" by the following: "existing on August 1, 1990 pending the conclusion of the negotiations referred to in Para.2 above".

Para.6   Replaced by the following:

"Decides that as soon as the Secretary-General notifies the Council on the completion of the deployment of the UN Observer Unit and its operation the member States cooperating with Kuwait in accordance with resolution 678 (1990) will bring their military presence in Iraq to an end".

Para.14   Replaced by the following:

"Encourages the countries of the region to undertake all necessary negotiations geared at facilitating the total elimination of nuclear and all other weapons of mass destruction and all missiles for their delivery from the region.

Para.16   On page 14, Line 1, insert the words "in Kuwait" after the word "corporations".

N-0774 의
수록   3-1   0028

-2-

Para.17   1)   Replace the word "the" by "all".   *Bone*

         2)   Delete the words "made since 2 August 1990".   *OK*

Para.19   Lines 12 to 13 - delete the words "and in particular, *NO* humanitarian needs".

Para.20   Lines 5, 6 and 7 - replace the phrase from "foodstuffs" to "procedures" with the following - "medicine, health supplies, *NO* foodstuffs and".

Para.21   To be deleted. *?*

Para.22   replaced by the following:
"Decides that upon the formal ceasefire becoming effective and the deployment of the United Nations Observer Unit, or the *N/O* other prohibitions contained in resolution 661 (1990) shall have no further force or effect, excepting those included in para.24 below".

/Para.23   Deleted. *N/O*

Para.28   Replaced by the following:
"Agrees to review its decisions contained in this resolution *NO* on a regular basis and in any case 120 days following passage of this resolution".

Para 32   Lines 2, 3 and 4 - delete the phrase from "or allow" to "its *N/O* territory".

Para.33   Replaced by the following:
"Declares that upon adoption of the present resolution, a formal cessation of hostilities is effective between Iraq and Kuwait, and the member States cooperating with Kuwait in accordance with resolution 678 (1990)".

Insert the following Para. between Paras. 33 and 34 "affirms that the unique circumstances concerning the situation between Iraq and Kuwait on account of the blatant violation of the UN Charter and norms of *OK* international relations have required unprecedented actions by the international community which do not set undue precedents". *?*

3 — 2   0029

첨부 2.
불란서 결의안 초안

The Security council

    <u>Gravely</u> concerned by the exactions committed against Iraqi civilians, in particular in areas of kurdish populations...

    <u>Condemns</u> all forms of repression in Iraq, demands that the iraqi authorities put an end to it without delay and that they engage in a dialogue without exclusion for the respect of the rights and the realization of the legitimate aspirations of the Iraqi people in all its components.

    <u>Requests</u> the Secretary general to pursue its humanitarian mission in Iraq and to report in particular on the situation of the kurdish population.

    <u>Demands</u> that the iraqi authorities cooperate with the Secretary general to this end.

3-3

0030

외 무 부

종 별 : 지 급

번 호 : UNW-0787   일 시 : 91 0403 2000

수 신 : 장 관(국연,중동일,기정)

발 신 : 주 유엔 대사

제 목 : 걸프사태(안보리)

  연: UNW-0762,0774

  1. 안보리는 금 4.3.(수) 12:00-16:30 공식회의를 개최하여 연호 미측 휴전결의안 (S/22430)을 표결한바, 찬 12 (중국포함), 반 1 (쿠바), 기권2 (예멘,에쿠아돌)로 채택되었음. (안보리 687 호결의)

  2.상기 회의 주요경과는 다음과같음.

  가.의제채택(S/AGENDA/2981)

  나.쿠웨이트, 이락 토의참가 요청처리: 안보리의사규칙 37조에 의거 양국 토의참가허용

  다.미측안 공동제안국 추가:원제안국인 미, 영, 불, 루마니아에 벨지움, 자이르추가(총 6개국)

  라.쿠웨이트, 이락 발언

  1)쿠웨이트:휴전결의안 의의 강조, 이락책임, 쿠웨이트 재건노력 언급

  2)이락:다국적군의 월권, 이락국민 피해, 휴전결의안상의 문제점 (국경문제 강제, 배상부담, 이락의 배상청구권, 이락 군사력의 일방적 제한, 경제제재 존속), 대미비난.

  마.표결전 발언

  1)예멘:이락국민 피해, 휴전결의안문제점 (국경문제는 당사국간 합의 및 ICJ 를 통한 해결이 합당, 지역 군사력 균형파괴 우려, 경제제재 해제지연, 다국적군의 철수장 기화우려), 아랍제국간 유대회복

  2)자이르: 휴전결의안 지지

  3)짐바베: 지역전반의 군비제한 필요, 경제제재완화 (인도적 목적), 휴전결의안본문 32항 (테러리즘)해석유보 (민족해방 운동에 불영향)

국기국   1차보   중아국   정문국   청와대   안기부

PAGE 1   91.04.04   10:59 WG

외신 1과 통제관

0031

4)쿠바:휴전결의안 문제점 (안보리의 국경문제개입은 유엔헌장 위반이며 660호결의의 양국간협의 원칙에도 상치, 일방적 군사력제한부당, 이락이 쿠웨이트 철수한 이상 경제조치 존속 근거없음. 배상문제는 ICJ 를 통해처리), 안보리관련 결의안 이행에따른 21개국의 경제난 문제언급, 본건 결의안 반대

5)인도:경제제재조치 완화 (인도적목적), 국경조항은 쿠웨이트-이락간 기존합의 (62년)에 근거한 것으로 이해 (당사국간 합의원칙 확인)

6)코트디브와르:휴전결의안 지지

바.표결후 발언

1)미국: 휴전결의안 취지 및 특징설명, 아랍.이스라엘 문제해결 노력

2)프랑스:이락내전 관련 유혈진압 문제제기 (특히, 쿠드족 탄압)

3)중국: 경제제재 조기해제, 외군철수추진, 지역국가간 해결노력

4)쏘련: 그간 확전방지를 위한 자국노력, 국경문제에 관한 당사국간 합의원칙 확인, 아랍-이스라엘 문제 해결 기여 용의

5)에쿠아돌: 휴전결의안중 국경조항 유보 (당사국간합의원칙)

6)영국: 이락의 군사비과다 (개발 재원으로전용가능), 내란유혈진압 규탄

7)오스트리아: 내란 유혈진압과 관련한 불.터어키의 안보리조치 요청지지, 이락에 대한 유엔평화유지군참여 용의, 아랍-이스라엘 및 팔레스타인 문제해결 노력

8)루마니아: 이락의 본건 결의안 조속 수락촉구, 안보리관련 결의안 이행에 따른 21개국 경제난문제언급, 이락의 외채상환 의무

9)벨지움: 이락 내전관련 소수민족 탄압문제제기, 경제제재 완화(인도적 목적)

아.쿠웨이트 및 이락발언

1)쿠웨이트: 이락발언중 이락의 피해, 이락의 청구권, 국경문제 언급 반박

2)이락: 이락의 소수민족 융화노력 언급, 인접국의개입비난, 난민귀환 문제협조용의

3.금일 채택된 상기 휴전결의안은 연호 기존 미측안을 비동맹이사국들의 의견을 일부 반영하여 약간의 수정을가한것임.(수정조항:전문: E,X, 본문:6,19,20,21항)

4.연호 이락내전 유혈진압 사태와관련한 불,터어키의 안보리 조치요청 문제에 대해서는 현재 이사국들간 개별협의가 진행중인 것으로 알려짐.

5.금일 표결에서 에쿠아돌이 기권한것과 관련, 동국 대표부 관계관에게 그 경위를 문의한바, 동관계관은 국경문제는 당사자간에 타결되어야한다는 원칙을 지지하며

PAGE 2

0032

동국으로서는 페루와의 국경문제에 미칠수있는 영향을 고려해야할 입장에 있다고말함.

　　첨부:상기 휴전결의: UNW(F)-150

　　끝

　(대사 노창희-국장)

PAGE 3

0033

UNITED NATIONS

UNW(F)-150   10403   2000   총 9 메
(국연 즉도원. 기점)

Security Council

Distr.
GENERAL

S/22430
2 April 1991

ORIGINAL: ENGLISH

<u>France, Romania, United Kingdom of Great Britain and Northern
Ireland and United States of America: draft resolution</u>

<u>The Security Council</u>,

<u>Recalling</u> its resolutions 660 (1990), 661 (1990), 662 (1990), 664 (1990),
665 (1990), 666 (1990), 667 (1990), 669 (1990), 670 (1990), 674 (1990), 677 (1990),
678 (1990) and 686 (1991),

<u>Welcoming</u> the restoration to Kuwait of its sovereignty, independence, and
territorial integrity and the return of its legitimate government,

<u>Affirming</u> the commitment of all Member States to the sovereignty, territorial
integrity and political independence of Kuwait and Iraq, and noting the intention
expressed by the Member States cooperating with Kuwait under paragraph 2 of
resolution 678 (1990) to bring their military presence in Iraq to an end as soon as
possible consistent with paragraph 8 of resolution 686 (1991),

<u>Reaffirming</u> the need to be assured of Iraq's peaceful intentions in light of
its unlawful invasion and occupation of Kuwait,

<u>Taking note</u> of the letter sent by the Foreign Minister of Iraq on
27 February 1991 (S/22275) and those sent pursuant to resolution 686 (1991)
(S/22273, S/22276, S/22320, S/22321 and S/22330),

<u>Noting</u> that Iraq and Kuwait, as independent sovereign States, signed at
Baghdad on 4 October 1963 "Agreed Minutes Regarding the Restoration of Friendly
Relations, Recognition and Related Matters", thereby recognizing formally the
boundary between Iraq and Kuwait and the allocation of islands, which were
registered with the United Nations in accordance with Article 102 of the Charter
and in which Iraq recognized the independence and complete sovereignty of the State
of Kuwait within its borders as specified and accepted in the letter of the Prime
Minister of Iraq dated 21 July 1932, and as accepted by the Ruler of Kuwait in his
letter dated 10 August 1932,

<u>Conscious</u> of the need for demarcation of the said boundary,

91-10541 3290Z (E)   /...

INW-0787 의
첨부물   9-1

0034

Conscious also of the statements by Iraq threatening to use weapons in violation of its obligations under the Geneva Protocol for the Prohibition of the Use in War of Asphyxiating, Poisonous or Other Gases, and of Bacteriological Methods of Warfare, signed at Geneva on 17 June 1925, and of its prior use of chemical weapons and affirming that grave consequences would follow any further use by Iraq of such weapons,

Recalling that Iraq has subscribed to the Declaration adopted by all States participating in the Conference of States Parties to the 1925 Geneva Protocol and Other Interested States, held at Paris from 7 to 11 January 1989, establishing the objective of universal elimination of chemical and biological weapons,

Recalling further that Iraq has signed the Convention on the Prohibition of the Development, Production and Stockpiling of Bacteriological (Biological) and Toxin Weapons and on Their Destruction, of 10 April 1972,

Noting the importance of Iraq ratifying this Convention,

Noting moreover the importance of all States adhering to this Convention and encouraging its forthcoming Review Conference to reinforce the authority, efficiency and universal scope of the convention,

Stressing the importance of an early conclusion by the Conference on Disarmament of its work on a Convention on the Universal Prohibition of Chemical Weapons and of universal adherence thereto,

Aware of the use by Iraq of ballistic missiles in unprovoked attacks and therefore of the need to take specific measures in regard to such missiles located in Iraq,

Concerned by the reports in the hands of Member States that Iraq has attempted to acquire materials for a nuclear-weapons programme contrary to its obligations under the Treaty on the Non-Proliferation of Nuclear Weapons of 1 July 1968,

Recalling the objective of the establishment of a nuclear-weapons-free zone in the region of the Middle East,

Conscious of the threat which all weapons of mass destruction pose to peace and security in the area and of the need to work towards the establishment in the Middle East of a zone free of such weapons,

Conscious also of the objective of achieving balanced and comprehensive control of armaments in the region,

Conscious further of the importance of achieving the objectives noted above using all available means, including a dialogue among the States of the region,

Noting that resolution 686 (1991) marked the lifting of the measures imposed by resolution 661 (1990) in so far as they applied to Kuwait,

/...

9-2

Noting that despite the progress being made in fulfilling the obligations of resolution 686 (1991), many Kuwaiti and third country nationals are still not accounted for and property remains unreturned,

Recalling the International Convention against the Taking of Hostages, opened for signature at New York on 18 December 1979, which categorizes all acts of taking hostages as manifestations of international terrorism,

Deploring threats made by Iraq during the recent conflict to make use of terrorism against targets outside Iraq and the taking of hostages by Iraq,

Taking note with grave concern of the reports of the Secretary-General of 20 March 1991 (S/22366) and 28 March 1991 (S/22409), and conscious of the necessity to meet urgently the humanitarian needs in Kuwait and Iraq,

Bearing in mind its objective of restoring international peace and security in the area as set out in recent Council resolutions,

Conscious of the need to take the following measures acting under Chapter VII of the Charter,

1.   Affirms all thirteen resolutions noted above, except as expressly changed below to achieve the goals of this resolution, including a formal cease-fire;

A

2.   Demands that Iraq and Kuwait respect the inviolability of the international boundary and the allocation of islands set out in the "Agreed Minutes between the State of Kuwait and the Republic of Iraq Regarding the Restoration of Friendly Relations, Recognition and Related Matters", signed by them in the exercise of their sovereignty at Baghdad on 4 October 1963 and registered with the United Nations and published by the United Nations in document 7063, United Nations Treaty Series, 1964;

3.   Calls on the Secretary-General to lend his assistance to make arrangements with Iraq and Kuwait to demarcate the boundary between Iraq and Kuwait, drawing on appropriate material including the map transmitted by Security Council document S/22412 and to report back to the Security Council within one month;

4.   Decides to guarantee the inviolability of the above-mentioned international boundary and to take as appropriate all necessary measures to that end in accordance with the Charter;

B

5.   Requests the Secretary-General, after consulting with Iraq and Kuwait, to submit within three days to the Security Council for its approval a plan for the immediate deployment of a United Nations observer unit to monitor the Khor Abdullah

/...

9-3

0036

S/22430
English
Page 4

and a demilitarized zone, which is hereby established, extending 10 kilometres into
Iraq and 5 kilometres into Kuwait from the boundary referred to in the "Agreed
Minutes Between the State of Kuwait and the Republic of Iraq Regarding the
Restoration of Friendly Relations, Recognition and Related Matters" of
4 October 1963; to deter violations of the boundary through its presence in and
surveillance of the demilitarized zone; to observe any hostile or potentially
hostile action mounted from the territory of one State to the other; and for the
Secretary-General to report regularly to the Council on the operations of the unit,
and immediately if there are serious violations of the zone or potential threats to
peace;

6.   Notes that as soon as the Secretary-General notifies the Council of the
completion of the deployment of the United Nations observer unit, the conditions
will be established for the Member States cooperating with Kuwait in accordance
with resolution 678 (1990) to bring their military presence in Iraq to an end
consistent with resolution 686 (1991);

C

7.   Invites Iraq to reaffirm unconditionally its obligations under the Geneva
Protocol for the Prohibition of the Use in War of Asphyxiating, Poisonous or Other
Gases, and of Bacteriological Methods of Warfare, signed at Geneva on 17 June 1925,
and to ratify the Convention on the Prohibition of the Development, Production and
Stockpiling of Bacteriological (Biological) and Toxin Weapons and on Their
Destruction, of 10 April 1972;

8.   Decides that Iraq shall unconditionally accept the destruction, removal,
or rendering harmless, under international supervision, of:

(a)   all chemical and biological weapons and all stocks of agents and all
related subsystems and components and all research, development, support and
manufacturing facilities;

(b)   all ballistic missiles with a range greater than 150 kilometres and
related major parts, and repair and production facilities;

9.   Decides, for the implementation of paragraph 8 above, the following:

(a)   Iraq shall submit to the Secretary-General, within fifteen days of the
adoption of this resolution, a declaration of the locations, amounts and types of
all items specified in paragraph 8 and agree to urgent, on-site inspection as
specified below;

(b)   the Secretary-General, in consultation with the appropriate Governments
and, where appropriate, with the Director-General of the World Health Organization
(WHO), within 45 days of the passage of this resolution, shall develop, and submit
to the Council for approval, a plan calling for the completion of the following
acts within 45 days of such approval:

(i)   the forming of a Special Commission, which shall carry out immediate
on-site inspection of Iraq's biological, chemical and missile

/...

9-4

0037

capabilities, based on Iraq's declarations and the designation of any
additional locations by the Special Commission itself;

(ii)   the yielding by Iraq of possession to the Special Commission for
       destruction, removal or rendering harmless, taking into account the
       requirements of public safety, of all items specified under
       paragraph 8 (a) above including items at the additional locations
       designated by the Special Commission under paragraph 9 (b) (i) above and
       the destruction by Iraq, under supervision of the Special Commission, of
       all its missile capabilities including launchers as specified under
       paragraph 8 (b) above;

(iii) the provision by the Special Commission of the assistance and cooperation
       to the Director-General of the International Atomic Energy Agency (IAEA)
       required in paragraphs 12 and 13 below;

10.   Decides that Iraq shall unconditionally undertake not to use, develop,
construct or acquire any of the items specified in paragraphs 8 and 9 above and
requests the Secretary-General, in consultation with the Special Commission, to
develop a plan for the future ongoing monitoring and verification of Iraq's
compliance with this paragraph, to be submitted to the Council for approval within
120 days of the passage of this resolution;

11.   Invites Iraq to reaffirm unconditionally its obligations under the Treaty
on the Non-Proliferation of Nuclear Weapons, of 1 July 1968;

12.   Decides that Iraq shall unconditionally agree not to acquire or develop
nuclear weapons or nuclear-weapons-usable material or any subsystems or components
or any research, development, support or manufacturing facilities related to the
above; to submit to the Secretary-General and the Director-General of the
International Atomic Energy Agency (IAEA) within 15 days of the adoption of this
resolution a declaration of the locations, amounts, and types of all items
specified above; to place all of its nuclear-weapons-usable materials under the
exclusive control, for custody and removal, of the IAEA, with the assistance and
cooperation of the Special Commission as provided for in the plan of the
Secretary-General discussed in paragraph 9 (b) above; to accept, in accordance with
the arrangements provided for in paragraph 13 below, urgent on-site inspection and
the destruction, removal, or rendering harmless as appropriate of all items
specified above; and to accept the plan discussed in paragraph 13 below for the
future ongoing monitoring and verification of its compliance with these
undertakings;

13.   Requests the Director-General of the International Atomic Energy Agency
(IAEA) through the Secretary-General, with the assistance and cooperation of the
Special Commission as provided for in the plan of the Secretary-General in
paragraph 9 (b) above, to carry out immediate on-site inspection of Iraq's nuclear
capabilities based on Iraq's declarations and the designation of any additional
locations by the Special Commission; to develop a plan for submission to the
Security Council within 45 days calling for the destruction, removal, or rendering
harmless as appropriate of all items listed in paragraph 12 above; to carry out the

/...

9-5

0038

S/22430
English
Page 6

plan within 45 days following approval by the Security Council; and to develop a
plan, taking into account the rights and obligations of Iraq under the Treaty on
the Non-Proliferation of Nuclear Weapons, of 1 July 1968, for the future ongoing
monitoring and verification of Iraq's compliance with paragraph 12 above, including
an inventory of all nuclear material in Iraq subject to the Agency's verification
and inspections to confirm that IAEA safeguards cover all relevant nuclear
activities in Iraq, to be submitted to the Council for approval within 120 days of
the passage of this resolution;

14. Takes note that the actions to be taken by Iraq in paragraphs 8, 9, 10,
11, 12 and 13 of this resolution represent steps towards the goal of establishing
in the Middle East a zone free from weapons of mass destruction and all missiles
for their delivery and the objective of a global ban on chemical weapons;

D

15. Requests the Secretary-General to report to the Security Council on the
steps taken to facilitate the return of all Kuwaiti property seized by Iraq,
including a list of any property which Kuwait claims has not been returned or which
has not been returned intact;

E

16. Reaffirms that Iraq, without prejudice to the debts and obligations of
Iraq arising prior to 2 August 1990, which will be addressed through the normal
mechanisms, is liable under international law for any direct loss, damage,
including environmental damage and the depletion of natural resources, or injury to
foreign Governments, nationals and corporations, as a result of Iraq's unlawful
invasion and occupation of Kuwait;

17. Decides that all Iraqi statements made since 2 August 1990, repudiating
its foreign debt are null and void, and demands that Iraq scrupulously adhere to
all of its obligations concerning servicing and repayment of its foreign debt;

18. Decides to create a Fund to pay compensation for claims that fall within
paragraph 16 above and to establish a Commission that will administer the Fund;

19. Directs the Secretary-General to develop and present to the Council for
decision, no later than 30 days following the adoption of this resolution,
recommendations for the Fund to meet the requirement for the payment of claims
established in accordance with paragraph 18 above and for a programme to implement
the decisions in paragraphs 16, 17, and 18 above, including: administration of the
Fund; mechanisms for determining the appropriate level of Iraq's contribution to
the Fund based on a percentage of the value of the exports of petroleum and
petroleum products from Iraq not to exceed a figure to be suggested to the Council
by the Secretary-General, taking into account the requirements of the people of
Iraq and in particular humanitarian needs, Iraq's payment capacity as assessed in
conjunction with the international financial institutions taking into consideration
external debt service, and the needs of the Iraqi economy; arrangements for
ensuring that payments are made to the Fund; the process by which funds will be

/...

9-6

allocated and claims paid; appropriate procedures for evaluating losses, listing claims and verifying their validity and resolving disputed claims in respect of Iraq's liability as specified in paragraph 16 above; and the composition of the Commission designated above;

F

20. <u>Decides</u>, effective immediately, that the prohibitions against the sale or supply to Iraq of commodities or products other than medicine and health supplies, and prohibitions against financial transactions related thereto, contained in resolution 661 (1990) shall not apply to foodstuffs notified to the Committee established by resolution 661 (1990) or, with the approval of that Committee, under the simplified and accelerated "no-objection" procedure, to materials and supplies for essential civilian needs as identified in the report of the Secretary-General dated 20 March 1991 (S/22366), and in any further findings of humanitarian need by the Committee;

21. <u>Decides</u> that the Council shall review the provisions of paragraph 20 above every sixty days in light of the policies and practices of the Government of Iraq, including the implementation of all relevant resolutions of the Security Council, for the purpose of determining whether to reduce or lift the prohibitions referred to therein;

22. <u>Decides</u> that upon the approval by the Council of the programme called for in paragraph 19 above and upon Council agreement that Iraq has completed all actions contemplated in paragraphs 8, 9, 10, 11, 12, and 13 above, the prohibitions against the import of commodities and products originating in Iraq and the prohibitions against financial transactions related thereto contained in resolution 661 (1990) shall have no further force or effect;

23. <u>Decides</u> that, pending action by the Council under paragraph 22 above, the Committee established under resolution 661 (1990) shall be empowered to approve, when required to assure adequate financial resources on the part of Iraq to carry out the activities under paragraph 20 above, exceptions to the prohibition against the import of commodities and products originating in Iraq;

24. <u>Decides</u> that, in accordance with resolution 661 (1990) and subsequent related resolutions and until a further decision is taken by the Council, all States shall continue to prevent the sale or supply, or promotion or facilitation of such sale or supply, to Iraq by their nationals, or from their territories or using their flag vessels or aircraft, of:

(a) arms and related <u>matériel</u> of all types, specifically including the sale or transfer through other means of all forms of conventional military equipment, including for paramilitary forces, and spare parts and components and their means of production, for such equipment;

(b) items specified and defined in paragraph 8 and paragraph 12 above not otherwise covered above;

/...

9-7

0040

(c) technology under licensing or other transfer arrangements used in the production, utilization or stockpiling of items specified in subparagraphs (a) and (b) above;

(d) personnel or materials for training or technical support services relating to the design, development, manufacture, use, maintenance or support of items specified in subparagraphs (a) and (b) above;

25. Calls upon all States and international organizations to act strictly in accordance with paragraph 24 above, notwithstanding the existence of any contracts, agreements, licences, or any other arrangements;

26. Requests the Secretary-General, in consultation with appropriate Governments, to develop within 60 days, for approval of the Council, guidelines to facilitate full international implementation of paragraphs 24 and 25 above and paragraph 27 below, and to make them available to all States and to establish a procedure for updating these guidelines periodically;

27. Calls upon all States to maintain such national controls and procedures and to take such other actions consistent with the guidelines to be established by the Security Council under paragraph 26 above as may be necessary to ensure compliance with the terms of paragraph 24 above, and calls upon international organizations to take all appropriate steps to assist in ensuring such full compliance;

28. Agrees to review its decisions in paragraphs 22, 23, 24, and 25 above, except for the items specified and defined in paragraphs 8 and 12 above, on a regular basis and in any case 120 days following passage of this resolution, taking into account Iraq's compliance with this resolution and general progress towards the control of armaments in the region;

29. Decides that all States, including Iraq, shall take the necessary measures to ensure that no claim shall lie at the instance of the Government of Iraq, or of any person or body in Iraq, or of any person claiming through or for the benefit of any such person or body, in connection with any contract or other transaction where its performance was affected by reason of the measures taken by the Security Council in resolution 661 (1990) and related resolutions;

G

30. Decides that, in furtherance of its commitment to facilitate the repatriation of all Kuwaiti and third country nationals, Iraq shall extend all necessary cooperation to the International Committee of the Red Cross, providing lists of such persons, facilitating the access of the International Committee of the Red Cross to all such persons wherever located or detained and facilitating the search by the International Committee of the Red Cross for those Kuwaiti and third country nationals still unaccounted for;

31. Invites the International Committee of the Red Cross to keep the Secretary-General apprised as appropriate of all activities undertaken in

/...

9-8

connection with facilitating the repatriation or return of all Kuwaiti and third
country nationals or their remains present in Iraq on or after 2 August 1990;

H

32. _Requires_ Iraq to inform the Council that it will not commit or support
any act of international terrorism or allow any organization directed towards
commission of such acts to operate within its territory and to condemn
unequivocally and renounce all acts, methods, and practices of terrorism;

I

33. _Declares_ that, upon official notification by Iraq to the
Secretary-General and to the Security Council of its acceptance of the provisions
above, a formal cease-fire is effective between Iraq and Kuwait and the Member
States cooperating with Kuwait in accordance with resolution 678 (1990);

34. _Decides_ to remain seized of the matter and to take such further steps as
may be required for the implementation of this resolution and to secure peace and
security in the area.

9-9

0042

↓ GE02 9447783A001 (1301/   )

FROM: A1UNITNB

.

15248-04 -- PART I OF PART IV --
     I HAVE THE HONOUR TO TRANSMIT HEREWITH THE TEXT OF
RESOLUTION 687 (1991) ADOPTED BY THE SECURITY COUNCIL AT
ITS 2981ST MEETING ON 3 APRIL 1991.
QUOTE

                    RESOLUTION 687 (1991)
     ADOPTED BY THE SECURITY COUNCIL AT ITS 2981ST MEETING ON
                       3 APRIL 1991

THE SECURITY COUNCIL
     RECALLING ITS RESOLUTIONS 660 (1990) OF 2 AUGUST 1990; 661
(1990) OF 6 AUGUST 1990; 662 (1990) OF 9 AUGUST 1990; 664 (1990) OF
18 AUGUST 1990; 665 (1990) OF 25 AUGUST 1990; 666 (1990) OF 13
SEPTEMBER 1990; 667 (1990) OF 16 SEPTEMBER 1990; 669 (1990) OF 24
SEPTEMBER 1990; 670 (1990) OF 25 SEPTEMBER 1990; 674 (1990) OF 29
OCTOBER 1990; 677 (1990) OF 28 NOVEMBER 1990; 678 (1990) OF 29
NOVEMBER 1990 AND 686 (1991) OF 2 MARCH 1991;
     WELCOMING THE RESTORATION TO KUWAIT OF ITS SOVEREIGNTY,
INDEPENDENCE, AND TERRITORIAL INTEGRITY AND THE RETURN OF ITS
LEGITIMATE GOVERNMENT,
     AFFIRMING THE COMMITMENT OF ALL MEMBER STATES TO THE
SOVEREIGNTY, TERRITORIAL INTEGRITY AND POLITICAL INDEPENDENCE
OF KUWAIT AND IRAQ, AND NOTING THE INTENTION EXPRESSED BY THE
MEMBER STATES COOPERATING WITH KUWAIT UNDER PARAGRAPH 2 OF
RESOLUTION 678 (1990) TO BRING THEIR MILITARY PRESENCE IN IRAQ
TO AN END AS SOON AS POSSIBLE CONSISTENT WITH PARAGRAPH 8 OF
RESOLUTION 686 (1991),

0043

INTENTIONS IN LIGHT OF ITS UNLAWFUL INVASION AND OCCUPATION
OF KUWAIT,

TAKING NOTE OF THE LETTER SENT BY THE FOREIGN MINISTER OF
IRAQ ON 27 FEBRUARY 1991 (S/22275) AND THOSE SENT PURSUANT TO
RESOLUTION 686 (1991) (S/22273, S/22276, S/22320, S/22321 AND
S/22330),

NOTING THAT IRAQ AND KUWAIT, AS INDEPENDENT SOVEREIGN STATES
SIGNED AT BAGHDAD ON 4 OCTOBER 1963 QUOTE AGREED MINUTES REGARDING
THE RESTORATION OF FRIENDLY RELATIONS, RECOGNITION AND RELATED
MATTERS UNQUOTE, THEREBY RECOGNIZING FORMALLY THE BOUNDARY
BETWEEN IRAQ AND KUWAIT AND THE ALLOCATION OF ISLANDS, WHICH WERE
REGISTERED WITH THE UNITED NATIONS IN ACCORDANCE WITH ARTICLE
102 OF THE CHARTER AND IN WHICH IRAQ RECOGNIZED THE INDEPENDENCE
AND COMPLETE SOVEREIGNTY OF THE STATE OF KUWAIT WITHIN ITS BORDERS
AS SPECIFIED AND ACCEPTED IN THE LETTER OF THE PRIME MINISTER OF
IRAQ DATED 21 JULY 1932, AND AS ACCEPTED BY THE RULER OF KUWAIT
IN HIS LETTER DATED 10 AUGUST 1932,

CONSCIOUS OF THE NEED FOR DEMARCATION OF THE SAID BOUNDARY,

CONSCIOUS ALSO OF THE STATEMENTS BY IRAQ THREATENING TO USE
WEAPONS IN VIOLATION OF ITS OBLIGATIONS UNDER THE GENEVA
PROTOCOL FOR THE PROHIBITION OF THE USE IN WAR OF ASPHYXIATING,
POISONOUS OR OTHER GASES; AND OF BACTERIOLOGICAL METHODS OF
WARFARE, SIGNED AT GENEVA ON 17 JUNE 1925, AND OF ITS PRIOR USE
OF CHEMICAL WEAPONS AND AFFIRMING THAT GRAVE CONSEQUENCES WOULD
FOLLOW ANY FURTHER USE BY IRAQ OF SUCH WEAPONS,

RECALLING THAT IRAQ HAS SUBSCRIBED TO THE DECLARATION ADOPTED
BY ALL STATES PARTICIPATING IN THE CONFERENCE OF STATES PARTIES
TO THE 1925 GENEVA PROTOCOL AND OTHER INTERESTED STATES, HELD AT
PARIS FROM 7 TO 11 JANUARY 1989, ESTABLISHING THE OBJECTIVE OF
UNIVERSAL ELIMINATION OF CHEMICAL AND BIOLOGICAL WEAPONS,

RECALLING FURTHER THAT IRAQ HAS SIGNED THE CONVENTION ON THE
PROHIBITION OF THE DEVELOPMENT, AND PRODUCTION AND STOCKPILING OF
BACTERIOLOGICAL (BIOLOGICAL) AND TOXIN WEAPONN AND ON THEIR
DESTRUCTION, OF 10 APRIL 1972,

NOTING THE IMPORTANCE OF IRAQ RATIFYING THIS CONVENTION,

NOTING MOREOVER THE IMPORTANCE OF ALL STATES ADHERING TO THIS
CONVENTION AND ENCOURAGING ITS FORTHCOMING REVIEW CONFERENCE TO
REINFORCE THE AUTHORITY, EFFICIENCY AND UNIVERSAL SCOPE OF THE
CONVENTION,

STRESSING THE IMPORTANCE OF AN EARLY CONCLUSION BY THE
CONFERENCE ON DISAR═ ENT OF ITS WORK ON CONVEN═ N ON THE
UNIVERSAL PROHIBITION OF CHEMICAL WEAPONS AND OF UNIVERSAL
ADHERENCE THERETO,

AWARE OF THE USE BY IRAQ OF BALLISTIC MISSILES IN UNPROVOKED
ATTACKS AND THEREFORE OF THE NEED TO TAKE SPECIFIC MEASURES IN
REGARD TO SUCH MISSILES LOCATED IN IRAQ,

CONCERNED BY THE REPORTS IN THE HANDS OF MEMBER STATES THAT
IRAQ HAS ATTEMPTED TO ACQUIRE MATERIALS FOR A NUCLEAR-WEAPONS
PROGRAMME CONTRARY TO ITS OBLIGATIONS UNDER THE TREATY ON THE
NON-PROLIFERATION OF NUCLEAR WEAPONS OF 1 JULY 1968,

RECALLING THE OBJECTIVE OF THE ESTABLISHMENT OF A
NUCLEAR-WEAPONS-FREE ZONE IN THE REGION OF THE MIDDLE EAST,

CONSCIOUS OF THE THREAT WHICH ALL WEAPONS OF MASS DESTRUCTION
POSE TO PEACE AND SECURITY IN THE AREA AND OF THE NEED TO WORK
TOWARDS THE ESTABLISHMENT IN THE MIDDLE EAST OF A ZONE FREE
OF SUCH WEAPONS,

CONSCIOUS ALSO OF THE OBJECTIVE OF ACHIEVING BALANCED AND
COMPREHENSIVE CONTROL OF ARMAMENTS IN THE REGION,

CONSCIOUS FURTHER OF THE IMPORTANCE OF ACHIEVING THE
OBJECTIVES NOTED ABOVE USING ALL AVAILABLE MEANS, INCLUDING
A DIALOGUE AMONG THE STATES OF THE REGION,

NOTING THAT RESOLUTION 686 (1991) MARKED THE LIFTING
OF THE MEASURES IMPOSED BY RESOLUTION 661 (1990) IN SO FAR AS
THEY APPLIED TO KUWAIT,

NOTING THAT DESPITE THE PROGRESS BEING MADE IN FULFILLING THE
OBLICATION OF RESOLUTION 686 (1991), MANY KUWAITI AND THIRD COUNTRY
NATIONALS ARE STILL NOT ACCOUNTED FOR AND PROPERTY REMAINS
UNRETURNED,

RECALLING THE INTERNATIONAL CONVENTION AGAINST THE TAKING OF
HOSTAGES, OPENED FOR SIGNATURE AT NEW YORK ON 18 DECEMBER 1979,
WHICH CATEGORIZES ALL ACTS OF TAKING HOSTAGES AS MANIFESTATIONS
OF INTERNATIONAL TERRORISM,

DEPLORING THREATS MADE BY IRAQ DURING THE RECENT CONFLICT
TO MAKE USE OF TERRORISM AGAINST TARGETS OUTSIDE IRAQ AND THE
TAKING OF HOSTAGES BY IRAQ,

3

0045

TAKING NOTE WITH GRAVE CONCERN OF THE REPORTS OF THE
SECRETARY-GENERAL OF 20 MARCH 1991 (S/22366) AND 28 MARCH 1991
(S/22409), AND CONSCIOUS OF THE NECESSITY TO MEET URGENTLY THE
HUMANITARIAN NEEDS IN KUWAIT AND IRAQ,
    BEARING IN MIND ITS OBJECTIVE OF RESTORING INTERNATIONAL
PEACE AND SECURITY IN THE AREA AS SET OUT IN RECENT COUNCIL
RESOLUTIONS,
    CONSCIOUS OF THE NEED TO TAKE THE FOLLOWING MEASURES ACTING
UNDER CHAPTER VII OF THE CHARTER,

END OF PART I OF PART IV, OTHER PARTS FOLLOW
COL CKD
GBS AME M4007

=0405910630GMT

NN NN

00
↑ WOIMUBU K24651

4

0046

↓ IIX2504701-2866(UNNY:WUCA2866)
  TXT466 78724651
   WUCA2866 NYKU963 UNNY:WUCA2866
  TLXCAB
  78724651 24651//78724652 24652

   WUCA2866 MFX0598
   GS CABKS
  .NEWYORK (UNNY) 0626 GMT 04/05/91
  ETATPRIORITE
   HIS EXCELLENCY
   THE MINISTER FOR FOREIGN AFFAIRS
   OF THE REPUBLIC OF KOREA
   MINISTRY OF FOREIGN AFFAIRS
   SEOUL (REPUBLIC OF KOREA)
  BT
  15248-04 -- PART II OF PART IV --
  (CONT'D) CHAPTER VII OF THE CHARTER, ETC ETC

       1. AFFIRMS ALL THIRTEEN RESOLUTIONS NOTED ABOVE, EXCEPT AS
  EXPRESSLY CHANGED BELOW TO ACHIEVE THE GOALS OF THIS RESOLUTION,
  INCLUDING A FORMAL CEASE-FIRE SEMICOLON
       2. DEMANDS THAT IRAQ AND KUWAIT RESPECT THE INVIOLABILITY OF
  THE INTERNATIONAL BOUNDARY AND THE ALLOCATION OF ISLANDS SET OUT IN
  THE ''AGREED MINUTES BETWEEN THE STATE OF KUWAIT AND THE REPUBLIC
  OF IRAQ REGARDING THE RESTORATION OF FRIENDLY RELATIONS, RECOGNITION
  AND RELATED MATTERS'', SIGNED BY THEM IN THE EXERCISE OF THEIR
  SOVEREIGNTY AT BAGHDAD ON 4 OCTOBER 1963 AND REGISTERED WITH THE
  UNITED NATIONS AND PUBLISHED BY THE UNITED NATIONS IN DOCUMENT
  7063, UNITED ANTIONS TREATY SERIES, 1964 SEMICOLON
       3. CALLS ON THE SECRETARY-GENERAL TO LEND HIS ASSISTANCE TO
  MAKE ARRANGEMENTS WITH IRAQ AND KUWAIT TO DEMARCATE THE BOUNDARY
  BETWEEN IRAQ AND KUWAIT, DRAWING ON APPROPRIATE MATERIAL INCLUDING
  THE MAP TRANSMITTED BY SECURITY COUNCIL DOCUMENT S/22412 AND TO
  REPORT BACK TO THE SECURITY COUNCIL WITHIN ONE MONTH SEMICOLON

5

ABOVE-MENTIONED INTERNATIONAL BOUNDARY AND TO TAKE AS APPROPRIATE
ALL NECESSARY MEASU ▇ TO THAT END IN ACCORDAN▭ ITH THE
CHARTER SEMICOLON

5. REQUESTS THE SECRETARY-GENERAL, AFTER CONSLUTING WITH IRAQ
AND KUWAIT, TO SUBMIT WITHIN THREE DAYS TO THE SECURITY COUNCIL
FOR ITS APPROVAL A PLAN FOR THE IMMEDIATE DEPLOYMENT OF A UNITED
NATIONS OBSERVER UNIT TO MONITOR THE KHOR ABDULLAH AND A
DEMILITARIZED ZONE, WHICH IS HEREBY ESTABLISHED, EXTENDING 10
KILOMETRES INTO IRAQ AND 5 KILOMETRES INTO KUWAIT FROM THE
BOUNDARY REFERRED TO IN THE ''AGREED MINUTES BETWEEN THE STATE
OF KUWAIT AND THE REPUBLIC OF IRAQ REGARDING THE RESTORATION
OF FRIENDLY RELATIONS, RECOGNITION AND RELATED MATTERS '' OF
4 OCTOBER 1963 SEMICOLON TO DETER VIOLATIONS OF THE BOUNDARY
THROUGH ITS PRESENCE IN AND SURVEILLANCE OF THE DEMILITARIZED
ZONE SEMICOLON TO OBSERVE ANY HOSTILE OR POTENTIALLY HOSTILE
ACTION MOUNTED FROM THE TERRITORY OF ONE STATE TO THE OTHER
SEMICOLON AND FOR THE SECRETARY-GENERAL TO REPORT REGULARLY TO
THE COUNCIL ON THE OPERATIONS OF THE UNIT, AND IMMEDIATELY IF
THERE ARE SERIOUS VIOLATIONS OF THE ZONE OR POTENTIAL THREATS
TO PEACE SEMICOLON

6. NOTES THAT AS SOON AS THE SECRETARY-GENERAL NOTIFIES THE
COUNCIL OF THE COMPLETION OF THE DEPLOYMENT OF THE UNITED NATIONS
OBSERVER UNIT, THE CONDITIONS WILL BE ESTABLISHED FOR THE MEMBER
STATES COOPERATING WITH KUWAIT IN ACCORDANCE WITH RESOLUTION 678
(1990) TO BRING THEIR MILITARY PRESENCE IN IRAQ TO AN END
CONSISTENT WITH RESOLUTION 686 (1991) SEMICOLON

7. INVITES IRAQ TO REAFFIRM UNCONDITIONALLY ITS OBLIGATIONS
UNDER THE GENEVA PROTOCOL FOR THE PROHIBITION OF THE USE IN WAR OF
ASPHYXIATING, POISONOUS OR OTHER GASES, AND OF BACTERIOLOGICAL
METHODS OF WARFARE, SIGNED AT GENEVA ON 17 JUNE 1925, AND TT
RATIFY THE CONVENTION ON THE PROHIBITION OF THE DEVELOPMENT,
PRODUCTION AND STOCKPILING OF BACTERIOLOGICAL (BIOLOGICAL) AND
TOXIN WEAPONS AND ON THEIR DESTRUCTION, OF 10 APRIL 1972 SEMICOLON

8. DECIDES THAT IRAQ SHALL UNCONDITIONALLY ACCEPT THE
DESTRUCTION, REMOVAL, OR RENDERING HARMLESS, UNDER INTERNATIONAL
SUPERVISION, OF :

6

(A) ALL CHEMICAL AND BIOLOGICAL WEAPONS AND ALL STOCKS OF AGENTS AND ALL RELATED SUBSYSTEMS AND COMPONENTS AND ALL RESEARCH, DEVELOPMENT, SUPPORT AND MANUFACTURING FACILITIES SEMICOLON

(B) ALL BALLISTIC MISSILES WITH A RANGE GREATER THAN 150 KILOMETRES AND RELATED MAJOR PARTS, AND REPAIR AND PRODUCTION FACILITIES SEMICOLON

9. DECIDES FOR THE IMPLEMENTATION OF PARAGRAPH 8 ABOVE, THE FOLLOWING :

(A) IRAQ SHALL SUBMIT TO THE SECRETARY-GENERAL, WITHIN FIFTEEN DAYS OF THE ADOPTION OF THIS RESOLUTION, A DECLARATION OF THE LOCATIONS, AMOUNTS AND TYPES OF ALL ITEMS SPECIFIED IN PARAGRAPH 8 AND AGREE TO URGENT, ON-SITE INSPECTION AS SPECIFIED BELOW SEMICOLON

(B) THE SECRETARY-GENERAL, IN CONSULTATION WITH THE APPROPRIATE GOVERNMENTS AND, WHERE APPROPRIATE, WITH THE DIRECTOR-GENERAL OF THE WORLD HEALTH ORGANIZATION (WHO), WITHIN 45 DAYS OF THE PASSAGE OF THIS RESOLUTION, SHALL DEVELOP, AND SUBMIT TO THE COUNCIL FOR APPROVAL, A PLAN CALLING FOR THE COMPLETION OF THE FOLLOWING ACTS WITHIN 45 DAYS OF SUCH APPROVAL:

(I) THE FORMING OF A SPECIAL COMMISSION, WHICH SHALL CARRY OUT IMMEDIATE ON-SITE INSPECTION OF IRAQ'S BILOGICAL, CHEMICAL AND MISSILE CAPABILITIES, BASED ON IRAQ'S DECLARATIONS AND THE DESIGNATION OF ANY ADDITIONAL LOCATIONS BY THE SPECIAL COMMISSION ITSELF SEMICOLON

(II) THE YIELDING BY IRAQ OF POSSESSION TO THE SPECIAL COMMISSION FOR DESTRUCTION, REMOVAL OR RENDERING HARMLESS, TAKING INTO ACCOUNT THE REQUIREMENTS OF PUBLIC SAFETY, OF ALL ITEMS SPECIFIED UNDER PARAGRAPH 8 (A) ABOVE INCLUDING ITEMS AT THE ADDITIONAL LOCATIONS DESIGNATED BY THE SPECIAL COMMISSION UNDER PARAGRAPH 9 (B) (I) ABOVE AND THE DESTRUCTION BY IRAQ, UNDER SUPERVISION OF THE SPECIAL COMMISSION, OF ALL ITS MISSILE CAPABILITIES INCLUDING LAUNCHERS AS SPECIFIED UNDER PARAGRAPH 8 (B) ABOVE SEMICOLON

(III) THE PROVISION BY THE SPECIAL COMMISSION OF THE ASSISTANCE AND COOPERATION TO THE DIRECTOR-GENERAL OF THE INTERNATIONAL ATOMIC ENERGY AGENCY (IAEA) REQUIRED IN PARAGRAPHS 12 AND 13 BELOW SEMICOLON

END OF PART II OF PART IV, PART III AND IV FOLLOWS
COL CKD
GBS AME M4008

7

↓ IIX2504701-2976(UNNY:WUCA2976)

TXO794 78724651

WUCA2976 NYKU098 UNNY:WUCA2976

TLXCAB

78724651 24651

WUCA2976 MCX6575

SS CABKS

.NEWYORK (UNNY) 1956 GMT 04/05/91

ETATPRIORITE

HIS EXCELLENCY

THE MINISTER FOR FOREIGN AFFAIRS

OF THE REPUBLIC OF KOREA

MINISTRY OF FOREIGN AFFAIRS

SEOUL (REPUBLIC OF KOREA)

BT

15248-04 (PART THREE OF FOUR)

10. DECIDES THAT IRAQ SHALL UNCONDITIONALLY UNDERTAKE NOT TO USE,
DEVELOP, CONSTRUCT OR ACQUIRE ANY OF THE ITEMS SPECIFIED INPARAGRAPHS
8 AND 9 ABOVE AND REQUESTS THE SECRETARY-GENERAL, IN CONSULTATION
WITH THE SPECIAL COMMISION, TO DEVELOP A PLAN FOR THE FUTURE ONGOING
MONITORING AND VERIFICATION OF IRAQ'S COMPLIANCE WITH THIS PARAGRAPH,
TO BE SUBMITTED TO THE COUNCIL FOR APPROVAL WITHIN 120 DAYS OF THE
PASSAGE OF THIS RESOLUTION=

11. INVITES IRAQ TO REAFFIRM UNCONDITIONALLY ITS OBLIGATIONS UNDER
THE TREATY ON THE NON-PROLIFERATION OF NUCLEAR WEAPONS, OF 1 JULY
1968=

12. DECIDES THAT IRAQ SHALL UNCONDITIONALLY AGREE NOT TO ACQUIRE
OR DEVELOP NUCLEAR WEAPONS OR NUCLEAR-WEAPONS-USABLE MATERIAL OR ANY
SUBSYSTEMS OR COMPONENTS OR ANY RESEARCH, DEVELOPMENT, SUPPORT OR
MANUFACTURING FACILITIES RELATED TO THE ABOVE= TO SUBMIT TO THE
SECRETARY-GENERAL AND THE DIRECTOR-GENERAL OF THE INTERNATIONAL
ATOMIC ENERGY AGENCY (IAEA) WITHIN 15 DAYS OF THE ADOPTION OF THIS
RESOLUTION A DECLARATION OF THE LOCATIONS, AMOUNTS, AND TYPES OF ALL

0050

MATERIALS UNDER THE EXCLUSIVE CONTROL, FOR CUSTODY ND REMOVAL, OF THE
IAEA, WITH THE SSISTANCE AND COOPERATION OF THE SPECIAL COMMISSION AS
PROVIDED FOR IN THE PLAN OF THE SECRETARY-GENERAL DISCUSSED IN
PARAGRAPH 9 (B) ABOVE= TO ACCEPT, IN ACCORDANCE WITH THE ARRANGEMENTS
PROVIDED FOR IN PARAGRAPH 13 BELOW, URGENT ON-SITE INSPECTION AND THE
DESTRUCTION, REMOVAL, OR RENDERING HARMLESS AS APPROPRIATE OF ALL
ITEMS SPECIFIED ABOVE= AND TO ACCEPT THE PLAN DISCUSSED IN PARAGRAPH
13 BELOW FOR THE FUTURE ONGOING MONITORING AND VERIFICATION OF ITS
COMPLIANCE WITH THESE UNDERTAKINGS=

13. REQUESTS THE DIRECTOR-GENERAL OF THE INTERNATIONAL ATOMIC
ENERGY AGENCY (IAEA) THROUGH THE SECRETARY-GENERAL, WITH THE
ASSISTANCE AND COOPERATION OF THE SPECIAL COMMISSION AS PROVIDED FOR
IN THE PLAN OF THE SECRETRY-GENERAL IN PARAGRAPH 9 (B) ABOVE, TO
CARRY OUT IMMEDIATE ON-SITE INSPECTION OF IRAQ'S NUCLEAR CAPABILITIES
BASED ON IRAQ'S DECLARATIONS AND THE DESIGNATION OF ANY ADDITIONAL
LOCATIONS BY THE SPECIAL COMMISSION= TO DEVELOP A PLAN FOR SUBMISSION
TO THE SECURITY COUNCIL WITHIN 45 DAYS CALLING FOR THE DESTRUCTION,
REMOVAL, OR RENDERING HARMLESS AS APPROPRIATE OF ALL ITEMS LISTED IN
PARAGRAPH 12 ABOVE= TO CARRY OUT THE PLAN WITHIN 45 DAYS FOLLOWING
APPROVAL BY THE SECURITY COUNCIL= AND TO DEVELOP A PLAN, TAKING INTO
ACCOUNT THE RIGHTS AND OBLIGATIONS OF IRAQ UNDER THE TREATY ON
THE NON-PROLIFERATION OF NUCLEAR WEAPONS, OF 1 JULY 1968, FOR THE
FUTURE ONGOING MONITORING AND VERIFICATION OF IRAQ'S COMPLIANCE WITH
PARAGRAPH 12 ABOVE, INCLUDING AN INVENTORY OF ALL NUCLEAR MATERIAL IN
IRAQ SUBJECT TO THE AGENCY'S VERIFICATION AND INSPECTIONS TO CONFIRM
THAT IAEA SAFEGUARDS COVER ALL RELEVANT NUCLEAR ACTIVITIES IN IRAQ,
TO BE SUBMITTED TO THE COUNCIL FOR APPROVAL WITHIN 120 DAYS OF THE
PASSAGE OF THIS RESOLUTION=

14. TAKES NOTE THAT THE ACTIONS TO BE TAKEN BY IRAQ IN PARAGRAPHS
8, 9, 10, 11, 12 AND 13 OF THIS RESOLUTION REPRESENT STEPS TOWARDS
THE GOAL OF ESTABLISHING IN THE MIDDLE EAST A ZONE FREE FROM WEAPONS
OF MASS DESTRUCTION AND ALL MISSILES FOR THEIR DELIVERY AND THE
OBJECTIVE OF A GLOBAL BAN ON CHEMICAL WEAPONS=

D

15. REQUESTS THE SECRETARY-GENERAL TO REPORT TO THE SECURITY
SOUNCIL ON THE STEPS TAKEN TO FACILITATE THE RETURN OF ALL KUWAITI
PROPERTY SEIZED BY IRAQ, INCLUDING A LIST OF ANY PROPERTY WHICH
KUWAIT CLAIMS HAS NOT BEEN RETURNED OR WHICH HAS NOT BEEN RETURNED
INTACT=

9

F

16. REAFFIRMS THAT IRAQ, WITHOUT PREJUDICE TO THE DEBTS AND
OBLIGATIONS OF IRAQ ISING PRIOR TO 2 AUGUST 1990, WHICH WILL BE
ADDRESSED THROUGH THE NORMAL MECHANISMS, IS LIABLE UNDER
INTERNATIONAL LAW FOR ANY DIRECT LOSS, DAMAGE, INCLUDING
ENVIRONMENTAL DAMAGE AND THE DEPLETION OF NATURAL RESOURCES, OR
INJURY TO FOREIGN GOVERNMENTS, NATIONALS AND CORPORATIONS, AS A
RESULT OF IRAQ'S UNLAWFUL INVASION AND OCCUPATION OF KUWAIT=

17. DECIDES THAT ALL IRAQI STATEMENTS MADE SINCE 2 AUGUST 1990,
REPUDIATING ITS FOREIGN DEBT ARE NULL AND VOID, AND DEMANDS THAT IRAQ
SCRUPULOUSLY ADHERE TO ALL OF ITS OBLIGATIONS CONCERNING SERVICING
AND REPAYMENT OF ITS FOREIGN DEBT=

18. DECIDES TO CREATE A FUND TO PAY COMPENSATION FOR CLAIMS THAT
FALL WITHIN PARAGRAPH 16 ABOVE AND TO ESTABLISH A COMMISSION THAT
WILL ADMINISTER THE FUND=

19. DIRECTS THE SECRETARY-GENERAL TO DEVELOP AND PRESENT TO THE
COUNCIL FOR DECISION, NO LATER THAN 30 DAYS FOLLOWING THE ADOPTION OF
THIS RESOLUTION, RECOMMENDATIONS FOR THE FUND TO MEET THE REQUIREMENT
FOR THE PAYMENT OF CLAIMS ESTABLISHED IN ACCORDNCE WITH PARAGRAPH 18
ABOVE AND FOR A PROGRAMME TO IMPLEMENT THE DECISIONS IN PARAGRAPHS
16, 17, AND 18 ABOVE, INCLUDING: ADMINISTRATION OF THE FUND=
MECHANISMS FOR DETERMINING THE APPROPRIATE LEVEL OF IRAQ'S
CONTRIBUTION TO THE FUND BASED ON A PERCENTAGE OF THE VALUE OF THE
EXPORTS OF PETROLEUM AND PETROLEUM PRODUCTS FROM IRAQ NOT TO EXCEED A
FIGURE TO BE SUGGESTED TO THE COUNCIL BY THE SECRETARY-GENERAL,
TAKING INTO ACCOUNT THE REQUIREMENTS OF THE PEOPLE OF IRAQ,
IRAQ'S PAYMENT CAPACITY AS ASSESSED IN CONJUNCTION WITH THE
INTERNATIONAL FINANCIAL INSTITUTIONS TAKING INTO CONSIDERATION
EXTERNAL DEBT SERVICE, AND THE NEEDS OF THE IRAQI ECONOMY=
ARRANGEMENTS FOR ENSURING THAT PAYMENTS ARE MADE TO THE FUND= THE
PROCESS BY WHICH FUNDS WILL BE ALLOCATED AND CLAIMS PAID= APPROPRIATE
PROCEDURES FOR EVALUATING LOSSES, LISTING CLAIMS AND VERIFYING THEIR
VALIDITY AND RESOLVING DISPUTED CLAIMS IN RESPECT OF IRAQ'S LIABILITY
AS SPECIFIED IN PARAGRAPH 16 ABOVE= AND THE COMPOSITION OF THE
COMMISSION DESIGNATED ABOVE=

F

10

0052

THE SALE OR SUPPLY TO IRAQ OF COMMODITIES OR PRODUCTS, OTHER THAN
MEDICINE AND HEALTH SUPPLIES, AND PROHIBITIONS AGAINST FINANCIAL
TRANSACTIONS RELATED THERETO, CONTAINED IN RESOLUTION 661 (1990)
SHALL NOT APPLY TO FOODSTUFFS NOTIFIED TO THE COMMITTEE ESTABLISHED
BY RESOLUTION 661 (1990) OR, WITH THE APPROVAL OF THAT COMMITTEE,
UNDER THE SIMPLIFIED AND ACCELERATED ''NO-OBJECTION'' PROCEDURE, TO
MATERIALS AND SUPPLIES FOR ESSENTIAL CIVILIAN NEEDS AS IDENTIFIED IN
THE REPORT OF THE SECRETARY-GENERAL DATED 20 MARCH 1991 (S/22366),
AND IN ANY FURTHER FINDINGS OF HUMANITARIAN NEED BY THE COMMITTEE=

21. DECIDES THAT THE COUNCIL SHALL REVIEW THE PROVISIONS OF
PARAGRAPH 20 ABOVE EVERY SIXTY DAYS IN LIGHT OF THE POLICIES AND
PRACTICES OF THE GOVERNMENT OF IRAQ, INCLUDING THE IMPLEMENTATION OF
ALL RELEVANT RESOLUTIONS OF THE SECURITY COUNCIL, FOR THE PURPOSE OF
DETERMINING WHETHER TO REDUCE OR LIFT THE PROHIBITIONS REFERRED TO
THEREIN=

22. DECIDES THAT UPON THE APPROVAL BY THE COUNCIL OF THE PROGRAMME
CALLED FOR IN PARAGRAPH 19 ABOVE AND UPON COUNCIL AGREEMENT THAT IRAQ
HAS COMPLETED ALL ACTIONS CONTEMPLATED IN PARAGRAPHS 8, 9, 10, 11,
12, AND 13 ABOVE, THE PROHIBITIONS AGAINST THE IMPORT OR COMMODITIES
AND PRODUCTS ORIGINATING IN IRAQ AND THE PROHIBITIONS AGAINST
FINANCIAL TRANSACTIONS RELATED THERETO CONTAINED IN RESOLUTION 661
(1990) SHALL HAVE NO FURTHER FORCE OR EFFECT=

23. DECIDES THAT, PENDING ACTION BY THE COUNCIL UNDER PARAGRAPH 22
ABOVE, THE COMMITTEE ESTABLISHED BY RESOLUTION 661 (1990) SHALL BE
EMPOWERED TO APPROVE, WHEN REQUIRED TO ASSURE ADEQUATE FINANCIAL
RESOURCES ON THE PART OF IRAQ TO CARRY OUT THE ACTIVITIES UNDER
PARAGRAPH 20 ABOVE, EXCEPTIONS TO THE PROHIBITION AGAINST THE IMPORT
OF COMMODITIES AND PRODUCTS ORIGINATING IN IRAQ=

24. DECIDES THAT, IN ACCORDANCE WITH RESOLUTION 661 (1990) AND
SUBSEQUENT RELATED RESOLUTIONS AND UNTIL A FURTHER DECISION IS TAKEN
BY THE COUNCIL, ALL STATES SHALL CONTINUE TO PREVENT THE SALE OR
SUPPLY, OR PROMOTION OR FACILITATION OF SUCH SALE OR SUPPPLY, TO IRAQ
BY THEIR NATIONALS, OR FROM THEIR TERRITORIES OR USING THEIR FLAG
VESSELS OR AIRCRAFT, OF:

(END OF PART THREE OF FOUR - PART FOUR TO FOLLOW)
COL CKD
GBS AME M4009

0053

SE02 9447809A001 (1379/   )

FROM: AIUNITNA

15248-04 (PART FOUR OF FOUR)

(A) ARMS AND RELATED MATERIEL OF ALL TYPES, SPECIFICALLY INCLUDING
THE SALE OR TRANSFER THROUGH OTHER MEANS OF ALL FORMS OF CONVENTIONAL
MILITARY EQUIPMENT, INCLUDING FOR PARAMILITARY FORCES, AND SPARE
PARTS ND COMPONENTS AND THEIR MEANS OF PRODUCTION, FOR SUCH
EQUIPMENT=

(B) ITEMS SPECIFIED AND DEFINED IN PARAGRAPH 8 AND PARAGRAPH 12
ABOVE NOT OTHERWISE COVERED ABOVE=

(C) TECHNOLOGY UNDER LICENSING OR OTHER TRANSFER ARRANGEMENTS USED
IN THE PRODUCTION, UTILIZATION OR STOCKPILING OF ITEMS SPECIFIED IN
SUBPARAGRAPHS (A) AND (B) ABOVE=

(D) PERSONNEL OR MATERIALS FOR TRAINING OR TECHNICAL SUPPORT
SERVICES RELATING TO THE DESIGN, DEVELOPMENT, MANUFACTURE, USE,
MAINTENANCE OR SUPPORT OF ITEMS SPECIFIED IN SUBPARAGRAPHS (A) AND
(B) ABOVE=

25. CALLS UPON ALL STATES AND INTERNATIONAL ORGANIZATIONS TO ACT
STRICTLY IN ACCORDANCE WITH PARAGRAPH 24 ABOVE, NOTWITHSTANDING THE
EXISTENCE OF ANY CONTRACTS, AGREEMENTS, LICENCES, OR ANY OTHER
ARRANGEMENTS=

26. REQUESTS THE SECRETARY-GENERAL, IN CONSULTATION WITH
APPROPRIATE GOVERNMENTS, TO DEVELOP WITHIN 60 DAYS, FOR APPROVAL OF
THE COUNCIL, GUIDELINES TO FACILITATE FULL INTERNATIONAL
IMPLEMENTATION OF PARAGRAPHS 24 AND 25 ABOVE AND PARAGRAPH 27 BELOW,
AND TO MAKE THEM AVAILABLE TO ALL STATES AND TO ESTABLISH A PROCEDURE
FOR UPDATING THESE GUIDELINES PERIODICALLY=

0054

27. CALLS UPON ALL STATES TO MAINTAIN SUCH NATIONAL CONTROLS AND
PROCEDURES AND TO TAKE SUCH OTHER ACTIONS CONSISTENT WITH THE
GUIDELINES TO BE ESTABLISHED BY THE SECURITY COUNCIL UNDER PARAGRAPH
26 ABOVE AND MAY BE NECESSARY TO ENSURE COMPLIANCE WITH THE TERMS OF
PARAGRAPH 24 ABOVE, AND CALLS UPON INTERNATIONAL ORGANIZATIONS TO
TAKE ALL APPROPRIATE STEPS TO ASSIST IN ENSURING SUCH FULL
COMPLIANCE=

28. AGREES TO REVIEW ITS DECISIONS IN PARAGRAPHS 22, 23, 24, AND
25 ABOVE, EXCEPT FOR THE ITEMS SPECIFIED AND DEFINED IN PARAGRAPHS 8
AND 12 ABOVE, ON A REGULAR BASIS AND IN ANY CASE 120 DAYS FOLLOWING
PASSAGE OF THIS RESOLUTION, TAKING INTO ACCOUNT IRAQ'S COMPLIANCE
WITH THIS RESOLUTION AND GENERAL PROGRESS TOWARDS THE CONTROL OF
ARMAMENTS IN THE REGION=

29. DECIDES THAT ALL STATES, INCLUDING IRAQ, SHALL TAKE THE
NECESSARY MEASURES TO ENSURE THAT NO CLAIM SHALL LIE AT THE INSTANCE
OF THE GOVERNMENT OF IRAQ, OR OF ANY PERSON OR BODY IN IRAQ, OR OF
ANY PERSON CLAIMING THROUGH OR FOR THE BENEFIT OF ANY SUCH PERSON OR
BODY, IN CONNECTION WITH ANY CONTRACT OR OTHER TRANSACTION WHERE ITS
PERFORMANCE WAS AFFECTED BY REASON OF THE MEASURES TAKEN BY THE
SECURITY COUNCIL IN RESOLUTION 661 (1990) AND RELATED RESOLUTIONS=

G

30. DECIDES THAT, IN FURTHERANCE OF ITS COMMITMENT TO FACILITATE
THE REPATRIATION OF ALL KUWAITI AND THIRD COUNTRY NATIONALS, IRAQ
SHALL EXTEND ALL NECESSARY COOPERATION TO THE INTERNATIONAL COMMITTEE
OF THE RED CROSS, PROVIDING LISTS OF SUCH PERSONS, FACILITATING THE
ACCESS OF THE INTERNATIONAL COMMITTEE OF THE RED CROSS TO ALL SUCH
PERSONS WHEREVER LOCATED OR DETAINED AND FACILITATING THE SEARCH BY
THE INTERNATIONAL COMMITTEE OF THE RED CROSS FOR THOSE KUWAITI AND
THIRD COUNTRY NATIONALS STILL UNACCOUNTED FOR=

31. INVITES THE INTERNATIONAL COMMITTEE OF THE RED CROSS TO KEEP
THE SECRETARY-GENERAL APPRISED AS APPROPRIATE OF ALL ACTIVITIES
UNDERTAKEN IN CONNECTION WITH FACILITATING THE REPATRIATION OR RETURN
OF ALL KUWAITI AND THIRD COUNTRY NATIONALS OR THEIR REMAINS PRESENT
IN IRAQ ON OR AFTER 2 AUGUST 1990=

H

32. REQUIRES IRAQ TO INFORM THE COUNCIL THAT IT WILL NOT COMMIT OR
SUPPORT ANY ACT OF INTERNATIONAL TERRORISM OR ALLOW ANY ORGANIZATION
DIRECTED TOWARDS COMMISSION OF SUCH ACTS TO OPERATE WITHIN ITS
TERRITORY AND TO CONDEMN UNEQUIVOCALLY AND RENOUNCE ALL ACTS,
METHODS, AND PRACTICES OF TERRORISM=

13

0055

33. DECLARES THAT, UPON OFFICIAL NOTIFICATION BY IRAQ TO THE
SECRETARY-GENERAL AN —O THE SECURITY COUNCIL O——TS ACCEPTANCE OF
THE PROVISIONS ABOVE, A FORMAL CEASE-FIRE IS EFFECTIVE BETWEEN IRAQ
AND KUWAIT AND THE MEMBER STATES COOPERATING WITH KUWAIT IN
ACCORDANCE WITH RESOLUTION 678 (1990)=

34. DECIDES TO REMAIN SEIZED OF THE MATTER AND TO TAKE SUCH
FURTHER STEPS AS MAY BE REQUIRED FOR THE IMPLEMENTATION OF THIS
RESOLUTION AND TO SECURE PEACE AND SECURITY IN THE AREA.+
(END OF PART FOUR OF FOUR)

UNQUOTE

HIGHEST CONSIDERATION.

JAVIER PEREZ DE CUELLAR
SECRETARY-GENERAL

COL CKO
GBS A—E Y4C1D

14
-END-

0056

<del>0055</del>

외 무 부

종 별 :

번 호 : UNW-0805   일 시 : 91 0404 2000

수 신 : 장관(국연,중동일,기정)

발 신 : 주유엔대사

제 목 : 걸프사태(유엔 쿠웨이트 피해조사단)

　　1. 지난 3주간 쿠웨이트 현지에서 이락점령기간중 쿠웨이트의 인명, 재산피해 상황을 조사해온 유엔대표단 (단장: A. FARAH 전 사무차장)은 4.4.일단 철수하기로 하였으며, 동 조사내용중 인권관련 부분 보완을 위해 2-3 개월후 유엔인권센타와 협조하여 쿠웨이트를 재방문 계획인것으로 알려졌음.

　　2. 동 대표단은 당지 귀임후 사무총장에게 금번 쿠웨이트 방문 조사결과를 보고예정이라고함. 끝

　　(대사 노창희-국장)

국기국			1차보	2차보	중아국	정문국	안기부

PAGE 1   91.04.05   12:04 CG

외신 1과 통제관

0057

외 무 부

종 별 :

번 호 : UNW-0806

일 시 : 91 0404 2000

수 신 : 장관(국연,중동일,기정)

발 신 : 주유엔대사

제 목 : 걸프사태(안보리 휴전결의 후속조치)

　　1.유엔사무총장은 4.3. 안보리 687 호 결의채택에따라 동결의 이행 관련 업무를 총괄 할 기획단 (COORDINATING GROUP) 을 사무국내에 설치키로 한바, 동 기획단은 사무차장 7명, 차장보 2명으로 구성되며총장 부재시에는 V.DAYAL 사무차장(비서실장)이주재하게 됨.

　　2.한편, 상기 687호 결의 본문 5항 유엔옵서버단 배치문제와 관련 M .GOULDING 사무차장 (특정문제 담당)이 동 배치계획을 준비중이며, 본건계획은 4.5 또는 4.6. 안보리에 제출될 예정이라고 함. 동 유엔옵서버단은 UNIKOM (UNITED NATIONS IRAQ-KUWAIT OBSERVATION MISSION) 으로 명명될 것으로 알려짐.

　　3.표제휴전결의 개요와 후속이행 일정에 관한 금 4.4.자 NYT, WP 지 자료및 NYT관련사설을 참고로 별첨송부함.

　　첨부:상기 자료및 사설: UNW(F)-153

　　끝

　　(대사 노창희-국장)

국기국	장관	차관	1차보	2차보	중아국	안기부

PAGE 1

91.04.05　12:05 CG

외신 1과 통제관

0058

UNW(A)-153   10404 2000   총 3 대
(국연. 중동원. 기점)

THE RESOLUTION IN BRIEF
PRINCIPAL POINTS OF THE SECURITY COUNCIL RESOLUTION

■ Recognizes and guarantees the international borders stated in a 1963 treaty signed by Iraq and Kuwait.

■ Requests the secretary general to submit a plan for the immediate deployment of a U.N. observer unit to monitor the Khor Abdullah and a demilitarized zone extending 6 miles into Iraq and 3 miles into Kuwait.

■ Decides that Iraq shall "unconditionally accept the destruction, removal or rendering harmless" of all chemical and biological weapons, related components and facilities; and all ballistic missiles with a range greater than 150 kilometers, related components and facilities. This will be conducted under international supervision and guaranteed by on-site inspections. Iraq must provide U.N. inspectors with locations, numbers and types of weapons, components and facilities covered.

■ Forbids Iraq from using, developing or acquiring these weapons, and requests the secretary general to develop a plan for ongoing monitoring and verification.

■ Decides that Iraq must destroy or render harmless any nuclear weapons, and must agree unconditionally not to acquire or develop nuclear weapons or related components.

■ Requests the secretary general to report on steps taken to facilitate the return of all Kuwaiti property seized by Iraq.

■ Reaffirms that Iraq is liable under international law for losses and damage (including environmental) associated with the invasion and occupation of Kuwait.

■ Creates a fund to compensate claims, and establishes a commission to administer the fund.

■ Directs the secretary general to recommend the appropriate level of Iraq's contribution to the fund, based on a percentage of its oil exports.

■ Lifts the prohibition against the sale of foodstuffs to Iraq.

■ Directs the Security Council to review sanctions against Iraq every 60 days to determine whether they should be modified or lifted.

■ Retains sanctions against selling or supplying arms and materiel to Iraq, until further notice.

■ Decides that Iraq shall aid the International Committee of the Red Cross in its search for missing Kuwaitis and other victims of war.

■ Requires Iraq to condemn and renounce terrorism, halt support for international terrorism and forbid any organization committing terrorism from operating on Iraqi territory.

■ Declares that a cease-fire will become effective when Iraq officially notifies the secretary general and the Security Council that it accepts these terms.

THE WASHINGTON POST

의

3 — 1

0059

The U.N.'s Timetable

The schedule set forth in United Nations Security Council resolution 687 that would govern a cease-fire in the Persian Gulf war. The cease-fire would take effect when Iraq accepts the resolution.

☐ IMMEDIATELY
Sanctions on food imports are lifted and restrictions on imports of other emergency civilian goods are eased.

☐ BY FRIDAY
Secretary-General Javier Pérez de Cuéllar must submit plans for a U.N. observer force to monitor a buffer zone extending six miles into Iraq and three miles into Kuwait.

☐ BY APRIL 17
Iraq must provide lists of locations, amounts and types of its chemical and biological weapons, material that could be used in nuclear weapons, and ballistic missiles with a range greater than 90 miles.

☐ BY MAY 2
The Security Council must approve a fund to pay compensation for war damages. The fund would be fed by an unspecified percentage of Iraq's oil revenues. A commission would administer the fund, taking into account Iraq's needs and its foreign debt.

☐ BY MAY 17
The Secretary General and the International Atomic Energy Agency must submit plans to the Council for a special commission to conduct inspections of Iraq's weapons of mass destruction and, within another 45 days destroy them.

☐ MAY 17 OR LATER
The Security Council must lift its ban on Iraqi exports, including oil, if Baghdad has handed over its dangerous weapons and nuclear materials for destruction or removal and the Council has accepted the reparations payment plan.

■ BY JUNE 1
The Secretary General must submit guidelines to the Security Council for implementation of a new arms embargo against Iraq.

■ JUNE 1 AND EVERY 60 DAYS THEREAFTER
The Security Council must review restrictions on non-military goods imported to Iraq and decide whether to modify them, in light of the policies and practices.

■ BY AUGUST
The Security Council must review its ban on some conventional weapons, taking into account Iraq's compliance with this resolution and general progress toward the control of armaments in the region.

3-2

0060

The War's Not Over Yet

Saddam Hussein's war against the world won't finally end until he accepts the cease-fire terms voted yesterday by the United Nations Security Council. But those terms are so tough and comprehensive that the Iraqi dictator might well refuse, or at least stall, even as tens of thousands of refugees flee from his rule. Where would that leave the victorious Desert Storm allies, now eager to pull out of Iraq and go home?

At the least, Iraqi defiance would mean a continued embargo on its oil exports. That alone might force Iraq, broke as well as broken, to come around. But Saddam Hussein must contemplate a still more painful alternative: that the coalition forces in Iraq could at any time resume their pulverizing bombardment of his tanks and artillery.

•

Bowing to the U.N. terms would compel Iraq to scrap its chemical, biological and nuclear weapons, accept the inviolability of Kuwait's frontiers, pay a portion of its oil earnings into a reparations fund, renounce terrorism, accept restrictions on future arms purchases and destroy its ballistic missiles.

Iraq's compliance would be closely monitored, and a blue-helmeted United Nations peacekeeping force would be deployed in the region under what an awed Soviet delegate described as "the mother of all resolutions."

The impressive global support for these cease-fire terms at least tempers the bitterest frustration of the Persian Gulf war — the allies' inability to protect Kurdish and Shiite rebels from Saddam Hussein's vengeful butchery.

It is now plain that Iraq used its conscripts as fodder in the 100-hour war, and pulled back crack armored units for use against rebels. That being so, it's likely that the allies could not have saved the insurgents with anything short of full-scale, and endless, intervention.

President Bush spoke with obvious discomfort yesterday about the resulting barbaric reprisals. He joined in condemnation of Iraq's massacre of civilians and pleaded with the Iraqi Army "to take matters into its own hands" by getting rid of Saddam Hussein. At the same time, Mr. Bush said plainly that America and its partners had no wish to plunge into an Iraqi civil war — a sentiment he would have done well to express as clearly in previous speeches exhorting Iraqis to rebel against Saddam Hussein.

France is proposing a Security Council resolution that would deal separately with Iraq's internal strife and link any easing of sanctions to Baghdad's treatment of dissidents. Another way for the world to help would be to facilitate safe haven for the columns of Iraqi refugees who are now streaming into Iran, Turkey and occupied Iraqi territory. But in the longer term, the tough U.N. cease-fire terms offer the surest way of moderating the internal behavior of its rulers.

By compelling Iraq to reduce military expenditures, the Security Council peace terms will make any Baghdad regime less of a threat to its neighbors, or its own peoples. But first things first; whether because of continued economic pressure or fear of renewed military operations, Iraq must be made to accept those terms.

3-3

외 무 부

종 별 :

번 호 : UNW-0808

일 시 : 91 0404 2030

수 신 : 장 관(국연,중동일,기정)

발 신 : 주 유엔대사

제 목 : 걸프사태(안보리)

연: UNW-0787

1. 안보리는 4.3. 휴전결의(687 호) 를 채택한데 이어 금 4.4.오후 비공식협의를 개최하여 이락 내전 유혈진압사태와 관련한 연호 불.터어키의 안보리조치 요청을 검토중에 있음.

2.금일 20:00 현재 불란서의 별첨 결의안초안(이락당국의 자국민탑압규탄, 난민구호호소)을 협의하고 있는바,중.소.인도.쿠바.예멘등이 동 문안에 이의가 있는것으로 알려지고 있으며, 표결은 4.5(금) 에나 있을것으로 관측됨.

첨부:1.불란서 결의안초안,

2.터키안보리소집요청서한,

3.이락측 서한: UNW(F)-154

끝

(대사 노창희-국장)

국기국   1차보   중아국   정문국   안기부

PAGE 1

91.04.05   12:07 WH

외신 1과 통제관

UNITED
NATIONS

UNW(Fr)-154 10404 2030

ORIGINAL: FRENCH

FRANCE: DRAFT RESOLUTION

The Security Council,

Mindful of its duties and its responsibilities under the Charter of the United

Gravely concerned by the repression of the Iraqi civilian population in many parts of Iraq, including most recently in Kurdish populated areas which led to a massive flow of refugees towards and across international frontiers and to cross border incursions, which threaten international peace and security in the region,

Deeply disturbed by the magnitude of the human suffering involved,

Taking note of the letters sent by the Permanent Representatives of Turkey and Iran to the United Nations dated 2 April 1991 and 3 April 1991, respectively (documents S/22435 and S/22436),

Reaffirming the commitment of all Member States to the sovereignty, territorial integrity and political independence of Iraq and of all States in the area,

Bearing in mind the Secretary-General's report of 20 March 1991 (S/22366),

1. Condemns the repression of the Iraqi civilian population in many parts of Iraq, including most recently in Kurdish populated areas, the consequences of which threaten international peace and security in the region;

2. Demands that Iraq immediately end this repression and engage in an open dialogue to ensure that the human and political rights of all Iraqi citizens are respected;

3. Insists that Iraq allow immediate access by international humanitarian organizations to all those in need of assistance in all parts of Iraq and to make available all necessary facilities for their operations;

3056E

/...

INW-0번 of
첨부목.

5 — 1

S/22442
English
Page 2

    4.   <u>Requests</u> the Secretary-General to pursue his humanitarian efforts in Iraq and to report forthwith on the plight of the Iraqi civilian population, and in particular the Kurdish population, suffering from the repression in all its forms inflicted by the Iraqi authorities;

    5.   <u>Requests further</u> the Secretary-General to use all the resources at his disposal, including those of the relevant United Nations agencies, to address urgently the critical needs of the refugees and displaced Iraqi population;

    6.   <u>Appeals</u> to all Member States and to all humanitarian organizations to contribute to these humanitarian relief efforts;

    7.   <u>Demands</u> that Iraq cooperate with the Secretary-General to these ends;

    8.   <u>Decides</u> to remain seized of the matter.

-----

5 - 2

0064

UNITED
NATIONS

S

Security Council

Distr.
GENERAL

S/22435
3 April 1991

ORIGINAL: ENGLISH

LETTER DATED 2 APRIL 1991 FROM THE PERMANENT REPRESENTATIVE OF
TURKEY TO THE UNITED NATIONS ADDRESSED TO THE PRESIDENT OF THE
SECURITY COUNCIL

Upon instructions from my Government, I have the honour to inform you that owing to the action taken by the Iraqi army against the local population in Northern Iraq, approximately 220,000 Iraqi citizens, many of them women and children, are currently massed along the Turkish border.

It is apparent that the Iraqi Government forces are deliberately pressing these people towards the Turkish border in order to drive them out of their country. These actions violate all norms of behaviour towards civilian populations and constitute an excessive use of force and a threat to the region's peace and security. In the course of the Iraqi operations, which are being carried out with the support of helicopters and artillery, many mortar shells have actually landed on Turkish territory.

Turkey is taking appropriate action to bring urgent humanitarian assistance to the affected Iraqi civilians. It is expected that the heavy burden of caring for these victims of repression will be shared by international organizations as well as by those countries in a position to assist.

I request that a meeting of the Security Council be convened immediately to consider this alarming situation and to adopt the necessary measures to put an end to this inhuman repression being carried out on a massive scale.

(Signed) Mustafa AKŞIN
Ambassador
Permanent Representative

91-10567 2240h (E)

5-3

0065

**UNITED
NATIONS**

 Security Council

S

Distr.
GENERAL

S/22440
3 April 1991
ENGLISH
ORIGINAL: ARABIC

LETTER DATED 3 APRIL 1991 FROM THE PERMANENT REPRESENTATIVE OF
IRAQ TO THE UNITED NATIONS ADDRESSED TO THE SECRETARY-GENERAL

On instructions from my Government, I have the honour to draw attention to the actions of certain circles within the Security Council aimed at disrupting the internal security of my country, and to clarify that groups of saboteurs have taken advantage of the situation created by the military operations conducted against Iraq with the authorization of the Security Council to infiltrate, with outside support and following plans drawn up abroad, into towns in the south and the north of Iraq. These groups have committed abominable criminal acts directed against the life and security of the inhabitants, their property and their honour, and State property and officials.

Since the State is called upon to assume the obligations and responsibility incumbent on it of restoring public order throughout the country and putting an end to the sabotage and the criminal acts perpetrated against the population by armed groups, it had to take the necessary measures to restore public order in the southern and northern provinces. Now that the authority of the State and of the law has been restored in the south and the north, the security measures that had to be taken to suppress the rebellion and the sabotage operations have achieved their objective.

My country's Government reiterates that the vast majority of inhabitants of Iraq's towns and villages have not collaborated with the groups of saboteurs. Some of them may however have been victims of the campaign of terror and lies disseminated by the saboteurs or have been compelled by armed force to leave the country - as has happened on other occasions - serving as a shield for the above-mentioned groups or a means of facilitating their escape abroad.

The Iraqi Government is in a position to affirm that the inhabitants of the towns and provinces where public order has been restored have nothing to fear in terms of their personal safety, their property or their legal rights, whether or not they remained in the towns and villages in question. The authorities will bring to book and prosecute only those who have been responsible for murders, fires, rapes or theft, or have taken up arms against the State and the law.

91-10684   2264e (E)   /...

5 — 4

0066

S/22440
English
Page 2

    My country's Government invites all those of its citizens who have had to leave their homes or their places of residence to return to their town or village in Iraq in full security and full dignity. In this connection, the Iraqi authorities are prepared to cooperate with any third party.

    The Iraqi Government also appeals to the Governments of neighbouring countries to cooperate with it in restoring the situation and reinstating public order so as to avoid the relations they maintain with Iraq being affected. It also calls on the foreign circles which have discovered their humanitarian vocation to stop exploiting the sufferings of the Iraqi population for political and basely self-interested purposes.

    I should be grateful if you would have the text of this letter circulated as a document of the Security Council.

(Signed) Abdul Amir AL-ANBARI
Ambassador
Permanent Representative

-----

5 — 5

0067

외 무 부

종 별 :

번 호 : UNW-0813   일 시 : 91 0405 1630

수 신 : 장 관(국연,중동일,기정)

발 신 : 주 유엔 대사

제 목 : 걸프사태 (안보리 휴전결의 후속조치)

    연: UNW-0806

    1. 금 4.5.자 NYT 지 보도에 의하면, 안보리 휴전결의 (687호)에 의거한 유엔 옵서버단 (UNIKOM) 에 안보리 상임이사국 5개국이 모두참여할 예정이라고 함. 또한 동보도에 따르면 유엔사무총장은 A.KHAN 전난민고등 판무관에게 이락 및 쿠웨이트에 대한 인도적 원조문제를 총괄하는 임무를 맡길 계획이라고함.

    2.사무총장 대변인에 의하면 사무총장은 4.6.(토)상기 옵서버단 배치계획 관련 보고서를 안보리에 제출 예정이나 이와관련 안보리 회의가 동일 개최될지는 현재 결정되지 않았다고 함.옵서버단의 구성, 경비문제는 동 보고서에 포함되지 않으며, 추후 (6.8.경) 보완 수록될것 이라고함.

    3.한편 4.5. WP 지는 당지 외교소식봉을 인용, 이락의 상기 휴전결의 수락 전망에 관해 별첨기사를 게재한바 참고바람. 끝

    (대사 노창희-국장)

    첨부: FAX (UNW(F)-0155)

국기국   1차보   중아국   정문국   안기부

외신 1과 통제관

0068

5 April 1991

PRESS BRIEFING BY EDOUARD BRUNNER, SPECIAL REPRESENTATIVE TO MIDDLE EAST

Following his recent appointment as the Secretary-General's Special Representative to the Middle East, Ambassador Edouard Brunner of Switzerland briefed correspondents at today's noon briefing.

Mr. Brunner said he was starting his new position with a meeting with the Secretary-General this afternoon, and a round of talks with the representatives of the member States of the Security Council. He would leave tomorrow for Geneva, after which he would visit the capitals of the permanent members of the Security Council. He would not visit the Middle East until May, "most probably with the Secretary-General", he added.

Although much activity at the moment centred around events in the Gulf, he said, the Middle East was still in the minds of many people and he would try and learn more about their thoughts on how to solve the issue during talks in the next weeks.

In reply to a question, Ambassador Brunner said he was not familiar with the plan proposed by the Government of Israel for a preliminary conference between Israel and Arab representatives. However, he would discuss any thoughts on the matter with the parties involved.

Did he see it as his ultimate goal to convene a Middle East peace conference in accordance with Security Council resolutions 242 (1967) and 338 (1973)? Mr. Brunner was asked. The goal for the time being, he said, was to bring peace to the area.

When asked whether the United States was considering convening a conference chaired by the Soviet Union and the United States, not under the United Nations chapeau, to lead to bilateral contacts, he said he had not heard of this.

To a question on what he thought the main difference between his role and that of Gunnar Jarring would be, and whether he expected to play a more active role than his predecessor, Mr. Brunner said events in the region had determined the extent of Mr. Jarring's role. There was much talk now of windows of opportunity, he said, but he did not know "how wide open these windows will be". He would be active in proportion to the possibilities, he added.

He was asked what made him think he could eventually be more active than Mr. Jarring. He did not think that, he answered. He could only hope. Before giving an assessment of any possible activities, he would have to hear from the principal actors in the region on what their thoughts were.

In reply to a question, he said many people realized after the war in the Gulf that a serious effort would have to be made to bring peace to the

(more)

3114B

0069

region. How that should be done, he could not say at this moment. He added
that deadlocks had existed within the United Nations and the Security Council
on this particular problem until a few months ago, but now a different
atmosphere prevailed between the permanent members of the Council, which led
to more hope.

He was asked how he thought the Gulf war affected his mission and whether
he agreed with the general assessment that it improved the chances of peace in
the Middle East. Ambassador Brunner said that before the war, the chances
were estimated as being rather slim, and no one was very hopeful. But he had
begun to hear from many parts of the world the phrase "window of opportunity"
following the Gulf war.

Asked whether his mandate precluded talks with the Palestine Liberation
Organization (PLO), he said that was one of the questions he would discuss
with the Secretary General this afternoon.

When asked to share some of the thinking of United States Secretary of
State James A. Baker, Mr. Brunner said the American approach was a very
flexible one, generally speaking, favouring a "double-track" approach, but the
details needed to be worked on. What was important was that the United States
had shown very quickly after the war its intention to try seriously to bring
about peace in the region. He personally believed that something visible had
to happen in the next six months to show that there was progress.

A correspondent referred to the provision made for the elimination of
Iraq's weapons of mass destruction in setting up a mechanism for regional
security, and asked Mr. Brunner whether he could play a role in that wider
aim. He replied that there were, besides the question of talks between the
interested parties in the region, two other problems which dominated the
scene. Those were arms control in the region and the quality of those arms;
and, in a very wide sense, the economic approach to the whole region.

If there was a serious attempt at curbing the export of certain types of
arms, he said, that could, perhaps, bring about a meeting or conference to
look at that problem. However, such an approach would have to be a
multilateral one involving countries supplying arms as well as the countries
in the region.

Asked what the effects would be if there was no progress in the next six
months, Mr. Brunner said it would be a pity after all the efforts that would
be made, such as the "troika" of the European Community that travelled around
the region and the Italian/Spanish plan for a conference between countries in
the Mediterranean.

Would his mandate allow him to implement some of his own ideas?
Mr. Brunner was asked. He said he thought the Secretary-General would expect
him to make a contribution based on talks in the next weeks.

In reply to a question on what his title implied, he said it was a large
mandate, and much would depend on the situation, on what he was invited to do
or not to do, and on the role the partners in the region wished the United
Nations to play.

(more)

0070

A correspondent said Council resolution 242 (1967) included a formula for peace, and asked Mr. Brunner if he was committed to that formula. "What we are looking for in this region is peace", he replied, adding that there were many ways to bring about peace.

In reply to further questions, he said he had not been in touch with the PLO, and that for the time being he would not be going to Israel.

* *** *

0071

외 무 부

종 별 : 지 급

번 호 : UNW-0823　　　　　　　　　　　일 시 : 91 0405 2230

수 신 : 장 관(국연,중동일,기정)

발 신 : 주 유엔 대사

제 목 : 걸프사태(안보리)

연 : UNW-0808

1. 안보리는 금 4.5.(금) 17:20-20:20 공식회의를 개최하여 연호 이락의 자국민유혈진압을 규탄하는 불란서 제출결의안 (S/22448 : 벨지움, 영국공동제안)을 표결한바, 찬10, 반3 (쿠바, 짐바브웨, 예멘), 기권 2 (중,인도)로 채택되었음. (안보리 결의 688 호)

2. 상기회의 주요 경과는 다음과같음.

가. 의제 채택 (S/AGENDA/2982)

나. 토의참가 요청처리

의사규칙 37조에 의거 이락.터어키.이락등 16 개국참가초청

다. 터어키.파키스탄,이란,이락 발언

1) 터어키 : 이락의 유혈진압에 의한 난민 유입으로 지역의 안정위협, 국제적 공동대응 필요

2) 파키스탄 : 아프가니스탄 난민을 수용하고 있는 입장에서 특별한 관심.대화와 자제요청

3) 이란 : 난민 유입사태로 지역의 평화와 안전위협, 이락의 유혈탄압규탄, 유엔의 조치촉구

4) 이락 : 이락국민의 수난은 다국적군의 공습과 경제제재조치의 결과, 내전사태는 외부개입에 기인, 유엔헌장상의 내정불간섭 (2조7항)원용, 난민에 대한 사면조치 설명, 불란서 결의안반대, 유엔조사단 파견문제 제의, 경제제재 조치해제 요구

라. 표결전 발언

1) 루마니아 : 지역의 안전과 안정위협 지적, 불란서 결의안의 내정불간섭원칙 언급유의, 안보리의 연대행동 강조

국기국	1차보	중아국	정문국	청와대	안기부	장관실 차관실 그차보 미주국

PAGE 1　　　　　　　　　　　　　　　　　　　91.04.06　13:12 WG

외신 1과 통제관

0072

2)예멘: 내정불간섭 원칙준수긴요,특정종족 (쿠드족)을 대상, 국제평화와 안전위협을 구실로한 내정간섭 선례 우려, 안보리 기본임무에서 국내문제로 표류경계, 헌장을 무시한 정치적 목적 추구반대

3)짐바붸:내정간섭반대, 안보리의 인도적 문제취급 부적절

4)에쿠아돌: 인권보호는 보편적요구, 국제평화위협에 대한 대응필요, 이락측의 유엔조사단제의 유념

5)자이르:본건사태는 국제평화와 안전위협, 불란서 결의안 지지

6)코트디브와르:국제안전유지를 위한 예방활동강조, 내정불간섭 원칙재확인

7)쿠바: 내정불간섭 원칙강조, CIA 의 대이락활동 (NYT 지 보도) 비난, 인도적 문제는 총회에서 다루는것이 헌장에 합치 (특별총회소집가능), 안보리의 과두체제 비난

마.표결후 발언

1)불란서:결의안 취지및 특징언급, 대이락 규탄

2)중국:난민문제 우려표명, 내정불간섭 원칙강조, 인도적문제는 적절한 경로를 통해 취급필요

3)오스트리아: 국제평화와 안전유지는 안보리의무, 난민구호 기여용의, 터어키 국경 개방촉구

4)미국:난민구호기여 계획언급,이락측의 구호활동협조촉구

5)소련:결의안의 내정불간섭 원칙 확인유의

6)인도:자제촉구,이락측의 유엔조사단 제의주목,내정불간섭 원칙강조

7)영국:안보리 월권주장 반박, 사무총장의 난민구호 협력호소 (4.8)계획 지지, 영국측의 난민구호 활동 , 후세인이 집권하는한 이락의 국제사회 완전복귀 난망시

8)벨지움:대이락 규탄, 대화촉구

바.이태리, 독일, 룩셈브르크, 덴마크, 화란, 스페인, 스웨던, 애란, 폴투갈, 노르웨이, 카나다, 그리스 12개국은 이락측의 유혈탄압을 규탄하고 결의안 채택지지및 구호활동 참여의사를 표명하는 요지의 발언을 하였음.

3.금일 채택된 결의문안은 연호안에 4.4-5비공식 및 개별협의 과정에서 나타난 특히 중.쏘.인도의 내정불간섭 문제에 관한 우려를 고려, 일부 수정한 것임.

첨부:1.상기 결의안(S/22448)

2. 불란서 측안보리문서(S/224,2)

PAGE 2

0073

3. 이란측 안보리문서(S/22447):UNW(F)-156

끝

(대사 노창희-국장)

**UNITED
NATIONS**

UNW (F)-156 10405 2230 총50개
(국연. 동동얼 기정)

Security Council

장관실	차관실	一차관보실	二차관보실	기획실장	제이아주국	미주국	구주국	중아국	국제기구국	경제국	통상국	정문국	정보과	총무과	감사과	공보관	의전관	청와대	총리부	아기부	부처
/	/	/	/	/		/		/	0		/	/		/	/	/		/	/	/	

PROVISIONAL

S/22448
5 April 1991
ENGLISH
ORIGINAL: FRENCH

Belgium, France and United Kingdom of Great Britain
and Northern Ireland: draft resolution

The Security Council,

Mindful of its duties and its responsibilities under the Charter of the United Nations for the maintenance of international peace and security,

Also mindful of Article 2, paragraph 7, of the Charter of the United Nations,

Gravely concerned by the repression of the Iraqi civilian population in many parts of Iraq, including most recently in Kurdish populated areas which led to a massive flow of refugees towards and across international frontiers and to cross border incursions, which threaten international peace and security in the region,

Deeply disturbed by the magnitude of the human suffering involved,

Taking note of the letters sent by the representatives of Turkey and France to the United Nations dated 2 April 1991 and 4 April 1991, respectively (S/22435 and S/22442),

Taking note also of the letters sent by the Permanent Representative of the Islamic Republic of Iran to the United Nations dated 3 and 4 April 1991, respectively (S/22436 and S/22447),

Reaffirming the commitment of all Member States to the sovereignty, territorial integrity and political independence of Iraq and of all States in the area,

Bearing in mind the Secretary-General's report of 20 March 1991 (S/22366),

1.   Condemns the repression of the Iraqi civilian population in many parts of Iraq, including most recently in Kurdish populated areas, the consequences of which threaten international peace and security in the region;

2.   Demands that Iraq, as a contribution to remove the threat to international peace and security in the region, immediately end this repression and express the hope in the same context that an open dialogue will take place to ensure that the human and political rights of all Iraqi citizens are respected;

3070E

/...

UNW-0023 의
처방 안

5-1

S/22448
English
Page 2

3.   Insists that Iraq allow immediate access by international humanitarian organizations to all those in need of assistance in all parts of Iraq and to make available all necessary facilities for their operations;

4.   Requests the Secretary-General to pursue his humanitarian efforts in Iraq and to report forthwith, if appropriate on the basis of a further mission to the region, on the plight of the Iraqi civilian population, and in particular the Kurdish population, suffering from the repression in all its forms inflicted by the Iraqi authorities;

5.   Requests further the Secretary-General to use all the resources at his disposal, including those of the relevant United Nations agencies, to address urgently the critical needs of the refugees and displaced Iraqi population;

6.   Appeals to all Member States and to all humanitarian organizations to contribute to these humanitarian relief efforts;

7.   Demands that Iraq cooperate with the Secretary-General to these ends;

8.   Decides to remain seized of the matter.

5-2

0076

**UNITED
NATIONS**

S

Security Council

Distr.
GENERAL

S/22442
4 April 1991
ENGLISH
ORIGINAL: FRENCH

LETTER DATED 4 APRIL 1991 FROM THE CHARGE D'AFFAIRES A.I. OF THE
PERMANENT MISSION OF FRANCE TO THE UNITED NATIONS ADDRESSED
TO THE PRESIDENT OF THE SECURITY COUNCIL

On instructions from my Government, I have the honour to request you to convene an urgent meeting of the Security Council to discuss the serious situation resulting from the abuses being committed against the Iraqi population in several parts of Iraq, and more particularly in the Kurdish-inhabited areas. By virtue of its repercussions in the region, this situation constitutes a threat to international peace and security.

(Signed) Jean-Marc ROCHEREAU DE LA SABLIERE
Chargé d'affaires a.i.
Deputy Permanent Representative of France
to the United Nations

91-10903 2391d (E)

5-3

0077

**UNITED
NATIONS**

S

Security Council

Distr.
GENERAL

4 April 1991
S/22447

ORIGINAL: ENGLISH

LETTER DATED 4 APRIL 1991 FROM THE PERMANENT REPRESENTATIVE OF THE
ISLAMIC REPUBLIC OF IRAN TO THE UNITED NATIONS ADDRESSED TO THE
SECRETARY-GENERAL

Upon instructions from my Government, I have the honour to bring to your
urgent attention the desperate situation of Iraqi civilians who are crossing all
along the border into the Islamic Republic of Iran.

Events in Iraq and the method by which Iraqi military has dealt with the
uprising of Iraqi population has lead to uprooting and driving of hundreds of
thousands of them towards the neighbouring countries. It is estimated that about
500,000 Iraqi civilians will try to cross the borders into Iran within a very short
period of time of the next few days.

Up until noon today, more than 110,000 Iraqi civilians have already crossed
the border into Iran along the border including more than 45,000 in the North.
Hundreds of thousands of Iraqi people and their vehicles, forming a line of more
than 60 kilometres, are crossing into Iran at the only paved road at Haji Omran
border post. Thousands of other Iraqi people including elderly and children, many
on bare foot in mountainous areas in the north and under heart-breaking
circumstances are trying to escape the military attacks and find refuge in the
Islamic Republic of Iran. The influx of refugees is also continuing in the South,
albeit at a slower pace.

The Islamic Republic of Iran - in line with its long standing policy and in
spite of the hardships it is facing - has kept its borders open to Iraqi people
escaping repression so as to decrease the pressure upon them. The influx of
refugees in addition to its obvious economic and social problems has caused tension
and chaos at the borders of the Islamic Republic of Iran.

The prolongation of the situation, with its implications for Iraq's
neighbours, will have consequences that in fact threaten regional peace and
security. The magnitude of the suffering of Iraqi refugees, its international
character and its consequences for regional peace and security make a concerted
international reaction by the Security Council of the United Nations a political
and humanitarian imperative.

91-10921 2418b (E)   /...

5—4

0078

S/22447
English
Page 2

It will be highly appreciated if this letter were circulated as a document of
the Security Council.

(Signed) Kamal KHARRAZI
Ambassador
Permanent Representative

5-5

長官報告事項

報告畢

1991. 4. 6.

國際機構條約局
國際聯合課（17）

題目 : 걸프戰爭 休戰에 관한 安保理決議 採擇

유엔安保理는 91.4.3(水) 걸프戰爭 休戰에 관한 美側이 주도한
決議 687（1991)호를 採擇한 바, 同 內容 아래 報告합니다.

---

1. 決議案 共同提案國(6개국) : 美, 英, 佛, 루마니아, 벨지움, 자이르

2. 安保理 表決結果 : 찬성 12 : 반대 1(쿠바) : 기권 2(예멘, 에쿠아돌)

   * 中國도 贊成 表決함.

3. 表決後 主要國 發言槪要

   ○ 美 國 : 休戰 決議案 趣旨 및 特徵說明, 아랍-이스라엘 問題解決에
     努力 豫定

   ○ 中 國 : 經濟制裁 早期解除, 外軍 撤收, 地域國家間 問題解決 强調

   ○ 蘇 聯 : 걸프戰 확전 防止를 위한 自國 努力 說明, 國境問題에
     관한 當事國間 合意原則 强調

공	담 당	과 장	국 장	차 관 보	차 관	장 관
람						

0080

o 에쿠아돌 : 決議案 內容中 國境條項때문에 棄權(當事國間 合意原則 强調)

- 에쿠아돌-페루간의 國境問題에 미치는 影響이 棄權事由

※ 에쿠아돌의 기권관련, 등 배경들을 *[handwritten]*

4. 쿠웨이트 및 이락 發言 槪要

* 쿠웨이트.이락은 紛爭當事國으로서 安保理議事規則(37조)에 따라 投票權
없이 討議에만 參加

o 이   락 : 이락의 少數民族 融和努力 言及, 隣接國의 介入非難,
難民歸還 問題 協調要請

o 쿠웨이트 : 이락의 被害 및 請求權, 國境問題에 관한 이락의 言及
內容 反駁

5. 休戰決議 後續措置

가. *[handwritten: 조정 기구]* 企劃團(Coordinating Group) 設置

o 構   成 : 事務總長(주재), 事務次長 7명, 事務次長補 2명으로 構成

o 任   務 : 安保理決議 687호에 따라 事務局內에 同 決議 履行業務 總括

나. 유엔 옵서버단 配置 計劃 準備

o 名   稱 : UNIKOM (United Nations Iraq-Kuwait Observation
Mission)

o 準備現況 : M. Goulding 特別政治擔當 事務次長이 準備中
4.5-4.6.中 安保理에 計劃 提出 豫定

* 其他 參考事項

o 이락 內戰 流血鎭壓 事態와 關聯한 불란서, 터키의 安保理 措置 要請
問題에 대하여는 現在 理事國間 個別 協議 進行中

添 附 : 安保理決議 687호 主要內容.   끝.

안보리결의 687 (1991)호 주요내용

* 뉴욕시간 1991.4.3(수) 채택

o 1963.10.4. 이락.쿠웨이트간에 체결한 조약(Agreed Minutes Between the
  State of Kuwait and the Republic of Iraq Regarding the Restoration of
  Friendly Relations, Recognition and Related Matters) 상의 양국국경선
  상호 존중 및 보장

o 유엔사무총장은 동 결의채택후 3일이내 이락.쿠웨이트 국경지대에 양측간
  휴전감시를 임무로하는 유엔 감시단 파견계획 수립, 안보리에 제출

o 이락이 "생물.화학무기의 개발, 생산, 저장 금지에 관한 조약(1972.4.10)"
  비준토록 촉구

o 이락은 국제 감시하에 모든 생물, 화학무기 및 관련시설을 파괴 또는 철거
  하고 사정거리 150Km 이상의 미사일 및 관련부품, 시설물을 파괴 또는
  제기토록 결정

o 상기 사항의 실효적 이행확보를 위하여 유엔사무총장은
  - 이락의 생물.화학무기.시설감시를 임무로 하는 특별위원회의 설립등에
    관한 계획 수립

o 유엔사무총장은 향후 이락의 생물.화학무기의 사용, 생산, 획득방지를
  위하여 동 결의안 채택후 120일이내에 이락감시 방안을 작성, 안보리에 제출

o 이락은 일체의 핵무기 또는 핵무기관련 물자 또는 시설의 개발 및 획득 불가

o IAEA 사무처장은 유엔사무총장 및 특별위원회의 지원하에 이락이 현재
  보유하고 있는 핵관련 장비 및 시설의 사찰 즉시 실시, 제반 위험 방지조치
  실시

0082

o 유엔사무총장은 쿠웨이트 자산의 반환을 위하여 취해진 조치에 관하여
  안보리에 보고

o 이락이 90.8.2. 이후 외채에 관하여 발효한 모든 사항은 무효이며 외채
  상환의무 이행 요구

o 손해배상을 위한 기금과 기금운영을 위한 위원회 설치 및 본 결의채택후
  30일이내에 유엔사무총장은 손해배상 청구와 관련, 이락의 석유 수출능력
  및 경제상황등을 감안한 동 기금에의 기여비율등을 포함한 세부내용 작성,
  안보리에 보고

o 이락에 대한 식품, 의약품등 반입 허용 및 대이락 금수조치의 단계적 완화

o 대이락 무기류, 군수품 및 관련기술의 금수 지속 및 실효적 이행 확보

o 이락이 자국내 쿠웨이트 및 제3국 국민들의 귀환 및 실종자 확인을 위해
  국제적십자 위원회(ICRC)에 최대한 협조토록 결정

o 이락, 국제테러 행위 지원 불가

o 이락이 상기 제조항 수락시 종전 발효

0083

외 무 부

종 별 :

번 호 : UNW-0824   일 시 : 91 0407 0830

수 신 : 장관(국연,중동일,기정)

발 신 : 주 유엔대사

제 목 : 걸프사태(안보리)

　　1.4.6. 이락의 안보리 휴전결의(687호) 수락에 관한 금 4.7.자 NYT 기사를 별첨송부함.

　　2.관련사항 추보위계임.

　　첨부:상기 NYT 지 기사: UNW(F)-157

　　끝

　　(대사 노창희-국장)

국기국　1차보　　미주국　　중아국　　안기부　청와대　총리실
　　장관. 차관. 2차보

PAGE 1   91.04.07   23:38 FN
                                      외신 1과 통제관

                                        0084

DAY, APRIL 7, 1991 $1.75 beyond 75 miles from New York City, except on Long Island $1.50

BAGHDAD FORMALLY AGREES TO 'UNJUST' U.N. CONDITIONS FOR PERMANENT CEASE-FIRE

Punished but Hanging On

By PATRICK E. TYLER
Special to The New York Times

News Analysis

WASHINGTON, April 6 — Iraq's acceptance today of a punishing United Nations cease-fire resolution has forced Saddam Hussein to accept the full consequences of his arrogance and of the defeat that the United States and its allies imposed on him and his people in the Persian Gulf war.

But as stringent as the demands are in forcing Iraq to complete the destruction of its chemical, biological and nuclear industries and pay reparations to Kuwait, they have not produced the outcome that the Bush Administration continues to pursue publicly and privately: the removal of President Hussein from power.

While Mr. Hussein may take his personal survival as a victory, it is by no means a victory for the Iraqi people, who have had little to say about the course of his two decades of rule, especially on the crucial and catastrophic decisions to invade Iran in 1980, invade Kuwait in 1990, and go to war against the American-led coalition in 1991.

The Iraqi people have mortgaged a piece of their sovereignty to the United Nations and to the coalition, whose bureaucrats and inspectors will in coming months oversee the destruction of the country's high-technology military laboratories. In the name of enforcement, they also control Iraq's trade for the indefinite future as a means to garnish a suitable part of oil revenues to pay damages to Kuwait.

Even Iraq's ballistic missile program, which a few years ago instilled pride across the Arab world as a step toward pan-Arab satellites and space industries, will be dismantled and destroyed, stripping the country of weapons that all of its enemies from Tehran to Damascus to Tel Aviv still possess.

Mr. Hussein, who told a Soviet envoy on Oct. 30 that if his choice were to surrender in Kuwait or fight, he was inclined to fight, has long inspired official fear in Saudi Arabia that he would someday lead an assault by the so-called have-not Arab countries of Yemen and Jordan against the rich oil-producing emirates and monarchies of

Continued on Page 14, Column 5

TRUCE NOW OFFICIAL

Peacekeepers Ready — No U.S. Order Yet on Pullout of Troops

By ALAN COWELL
Special to The New York Times

AMMAN, Jordan, April 6 — Five weeks after the United States and its allies drove Saddam Hussein's army from Kuwait, Iraq today accepted United Nations terms for a formal cease-fire in the Persian Gulf war.

In accepting the conditions, the National Assembly in Baghdad, which follows Mr. Hussein's dictates, called the arrangement "unjust," but it acknowledged that Iraq had little choice if it was to avert further degradation.

The message of Iraqi acceptance was delivered in New York to the offices of the United Nations Secretary General and to the chairman of the Security Council by the Iraqi representative at the United Nations, Abdul Amir al-Anbari. He told reporters that Iraq accepted the terms "without conditions," but added that he considered the resolution "one-sided and unfair."

Cease-Fire Now Official

Under the terms of Security Council Resolution 687, adopted on Wednesday, Iraq's acceptance automatically activates a permanent cease-fire between the opponents in the gulf war. But the Pentagon did not immediately issue orders to American forces in the Persian Gulf region proclaiming a formal end to hostilities.

[In Houston, where he is spending the weekend, President Bush said the Iraqi letter appeared to be positive. But he said he did not want to go too far out front until we get the analysis." Mr. Bush took note of "some griping" in the Iraqi letter about the conditions. "That's just too bad," he said. "Saddam Hussein is in no position to barter."]

The Iraqi acceptance clears the way for a series of steps to insure the peace. Those include the establishment of a United Nations peacekeeping force, the destruction of Iraq's biological and chemical weapons and its long-range missiles, and the payment of Iraqi reparations to Kuwait for damages suffered after the invasion last Aug. 2.

Embargo's End in Sight

Iraq's move will also clear the way for the eventual end to the economic embargo against Baghdad, and it will ease the withdrawal of American troops occupying 15 percent of Iraqi territory in the south of the country.

The Iraqi acceptance is a major diplomatic milestone in the campaign begun by the United States and its allies last August to expel Iraqi forces

Continued on Page 14, Column 1

UNW(F)-157   10407   0830
(국련. 중동일. 기정)   총 3매

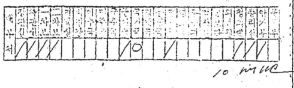

10 때
0085

3-1'

Baghdad Formally Agrees to 'Unjust' U.N. Terms

Continued From Page 1

from Kuwait and strip Mr. Hussein of the military power that made his army the most feared in the Arab world.

But the allied campaign against President Hussein has not ended the Iraqi leader's hold on power. He still appears firmly in control and his army has apparently crushed rebellions by Kurds in the north of Iraq and Shiite Muslim dissidents in the south.

Hundreds of thousands of Kurds continued to flee from the Iraqi Army today, fearing reprisals after their revolt in the north. In Baghdad, the Iraqi leader dismissed his Defense Minister and replaced him with a son-in-law, sharpening the nepotistic profile of a Government that has come to depend increasingly on clan and blood ties as the gulf crisis has unfolded.

The United States, which has declined to give the rebels direct military aid, has announced that starting on Sunday, American helicopters with Air Force cover will drop non-military supplies to Kurds stranded in northern Iraq. Other Kurdish refugees continued to enter Iran, which called again today for increased international aid.

A Rubber Stamp

The vote in the 250-seat Iraqi Parliament accepting the Security Council resolution was said by Iraqi officials to be 160 to 31, although the numbers, like the assembly itself, represent little more than window-dressing for decisions of the the Supreme Revolutionary Command Council, which met under Mr. Hussein's chairmanship last night.

"While declaring that this resolution is unjust, they have found there was no other choice than to accept it in order to defeat the American-Zionist plot," the Parliament speaker, Saadi Mehdi Saleh, said. Drawing on Koranic texts, he said, "We must sometimes, for our own good, accept that which displeases us."

The allied air war destroyed much of Iraq's roads, bridges, oil refineries, water-purification plants, electricity-generating stations, sewage plants and communications networks. To rebuild them, Iraq needs to free itself of the economic and other sanctions imposed by the United Nations after Baghdad's invasion of Kuwait.

But Resolution 687, approved by the Security Council on Wednesday and accepted by the Iraqi parliament today, makes the lifting of trade sanctions conditional on the destruction of Baghdad's chemical, biological and nuclear weapons potential under United Nations supervision.

Terms of Trade Ban

Until those capabilities are destroyed, a trade ban remains in force, and until Iraq can resume oil exports, it has no way of earning money to finance its own reconstruction. At the same time, the resolution mortgages part of

Has Iraq opened the way for its own salvation?

Iraq's oil revenues to pay reparations to Kuwait.

Baghdad's effort to quickly restore its economy may also be impeded by a separate Security Council resolution, adopted on Friday, calling on Iraq to halt its repression of the Kurds and the Shiites. Because it asserts that the international movement of Kurdish and other refugees is a threat to global security for which the Iraqi Government may be held responsible, the resolution could be used as a basis for continued sanctions against Baghdad.

While the terms of Wednesday's resolution have been widely condemned in Baghdad as an American ploy to destroy Arab military potential in the fight against Israel, the Iraqi Parliament's acceptance today seemed part of an effort by Baghdad to secure its own survival after months of crisis, war and insurrection that have brought not only destruction by allied bombing but the worst uprisings in Iraq's modern history.

Those twin civil wars have left a legacy of bitterness and fear. Iranian officials reported today, for instance, that 300,000 Iraqi Kurds had fled into Iran, braving minefields and harsh conditions to escape anticipated retribution from loyalist Iraqi units known for vengeance.

On Friday, Baghdad offered a conditional amnesty to rebellious Kurds, but Kurdish rebel officials in Damascus dismissed the offer today as what one rebel spokesman called a "sick joke."

Panoply of Revolt

Confronted by this panoply of revolt, destruction and challenge, President Hussein has rewarded family loyalty and reinforced the power of his own clansmen. Thus, Brig. Gen. Hussein Kamel, a cousin and son-in-law from the Iraqi leader's native Tikrit region, was given the Defense portfolio today, replacing a military commander, Gen. Sadeh Tuma Abbas.

General Kamel had previously been charged with building Iraq's military, now likely to be truncated all the more under the terms of the resolution.

Baker to Middle East

Special to The New York Times

HOUSTON, April 6 — Secretary of State James A. Baker 3d arrived here today to see President Bush before flying to Turkey and the Middle East.

Mr. Baker said the main purpose of his trip would be to "take advantage of the window of opportunity in the aftermath of the gulf war" to see if progress could be made on a settlement of disputes between Israelis and Arabs.

At a news conference, Mr. Bush said he did not rule out using American troops as part of a peacekeeping force in the gulf. But he said "a lot of United States troops" would not be involved, adding, "I have no intention of leaving our forces there."

3-2

Iraq Approval Starts Peace Schedule

By PAUL LEWIS
Special to The New York Times

UNITED NATIONS, April 6 — Iraq's formal acceptance of the Security Council's Persian Gulf peace offer today meets the conditions for an immediate cease-fire and clears the way for the destruction of Iraq's most dangerous weapons, the establishment of a procedure for Iraqi reparations to Kuwait and the lifting of trade sanctions against Baghdad.

The 120-day timetable for carrying out the demands was spelled out in Security Council Resolution 687, which was adopted on Wednesday. Following the schedule, Secretary General Javier Pérez de Cuéllar presented a plan today for sending a United Nations military observer force to monitor a demilitarized zone along the Iraq-Kuwait border.

As soon as the Secretary General certifies that this force has been successfully deployed, Resolution 687 provides for the allies to complete their withdrawal from the zone they occupy in southern Iraq.

United Nations officials said that they expected the Security Council to approve the proposed force on Monday or Tuesday, and that an advance party of the blue-helmeted observers should be in position within 48 hours.

The force should be fully deployed within two weeks, but officials here said the United States would probably step up the pace of the withdrawal of its forces once United Nations troops begin arriving. About 100,000 American troops are now in southern Iraq.

Relief for Refugees Promised

In his report on the proposed military observer force, the Secretary General says the 300 observers need the protection of five infantry companies against possible disorder in the area as the allies depart.

An estimated 27,000 Iraqi civilians are in the allied-occupied zone, many of them refugees from fighting between the Iraqi Army and Shiite Muslims who rose up against the Baghdad Government in the aftermath of the Gulf war.

The United Nations monitoring force has no responsibility for these refugees, and the Secretary General urged Iraq and Kuwait to send in civil police to maintain order in their respective areas of the demilitarized zone, which will extend nine miles into Iraq and three miles into Kuwait. He also promised to send urgent relief supplies to the refugees.

By April 18, or 15 full days after the adoption of Resolution 687, the peace plan requires Iraq to list the locations, amounts and types of all Iraqi chemical and biological weapons, all "nuclear weapons-usable" materials and Scud and other ballistic missiles with ranges of over 90 miles.

Reparations Plan Due in May

By May 3, the Secretary General must ask the Council to approve his plan for a special fund to regulate the flow of Iraqi reparations to Kuwait. The fund will be fed by a levy on Iraq's future oil revenues.

Next, the Secretary General must submit proposals to the Security Council by May 18, or 45 days after passage of Resolution 687, for creating a commission to develop a plan within the next 45 days for inspecting and taking possession of all Iraq's weapons of mass destruction and doing away with them.

Assets to Be Freed

In accepting Resolution 687 today, Iraq has agreed never again to try to develop chemical, biological or nuclear weapons.

After Iraq has handed over its weapons of mass destruction as well as its dangerous nuclear material and agreed to the financial compensation plans, the Security Council will lift the

Wrapping up the war starts with a 120-day U.N. countdown.

prohibition against buying Iraqi oil, allowing Baghdad to resume normal oil exports.

It will also free Iraq's frozen foreign assets, which will revert to their previous owners.

By June 2, or 60 days after approval of Resolution 687, the Secretary General must ask the Council to approve new guidelines for enforcing the continuing arms embargo against Iraq.

By the same date and every 60 days thereafter, the Security Council will review the remaining embargo against imports into Iraq of nonessential civilian goods and may modify or lift it "in the light of the policies and practices of

the Government of Iraq, including the implementation of all relevant resolutions of the Security Council."

Iraq is currently free to import food and medicine, and the Council has promised to approve all requests to buy essential civilian supplies such as spare parts for water treatment and sewage plants.

Arms Ban to Be Reviewed

The Council may also authorize it to sell enough oil to pay for these humanitarian imports.

By Aug. 1, or 120 days after passage of Resolution 687, and on a regular basis thereafter, the Security Council will review the ban on arms sales to Iraq, "taking into account Iraq's compliance with this resolution and general progress towards the control of armaments in the region."

But the ban on selling Iraq weapons of mass destruction and long-range ballistic missiles as well as the technology to develop them, will remain in effect indefinitely.

Punished but Staying

Continued From Page 1

the Arabian peninsula.

The Iraqi leader's decision to hold on to Kuwait — along with his refusal to pull out of Kuwait without a fight at the last minute, an act that would have left him still the most powerful hand in the region — may go down as one of the most colossal miscalculations in modern history.

But Mr. Hussein may well think that his mistakes, while regrettable, may be overcome. After all, he has the rebellion by Shiites in southern Iraq and by the Kurds in northern Iraq under control.

Military Stretched Thin

But the Iraqi military is stretched thin in holding onto major cities and oil-producing areas. The prospect of low-intensity guerrilla warfare that will sap the strength of the Government is a real threat to the stability Mr.

Saddam Hussein accepts the consequences.

Hussein must re-establish if he is to rebuild his country.

The humanitarian airlift that this week will send American C-130's into the mountains of northern Iraq will be dropping food, blankets and tents not only to civilian Kurdish refugees, but also to the Kurdish rebel fighters who are traveling among them. In that sense, the airlift is lending direct aid to the insurrection.

With the vote of Iraq's National Assembly today ratifying the decision to accept the cease-fire terms, Mr. Hussein has shown that he is not ready to resign and is handling decisions in the manner he has in the past. This was the same Assembly that ratified, after the fact, Mr. Hussein's decision to go into Kuwait, to release hostages taken in Kuwait and Iraq and to go to war against the coalition.

If his error in Kuwait forces Mr. Hussein to loosen the reins of control, it is unlikely that Iraqis outside the inner circle will have any role except in the civic affairs agenda: repairing electri-

eal water and sewage services, reopening schools, and providing public health services. Any attempt at debate on foreign policy in Iraq is confined to be reserved for the Revolutionary Command Council, where Mr. Hussein is likely to remain rampant.

Though a United States intelligence report two weeks ago predicted Mr. Hussein's downfall within a year, some longtime analysts inside the Government suggest that Mr. Hussein's grip on Iraq's security services, and the leadership of both the military establishment and Baath Socialist party, will protect him from any internal rivals.

These analysts and Iraqi specialists expected Mr. Hussein to accept terms he considered onerous because that was the only way to get his nation working again, by ending United Nations trade sanctions and removing the blockade on the shipment of Iraqi crude oil to world markets.

Clearing the Obstacle

Middle East specialists in the Administration and the intelligence agencies say that once the Iraqi economy is moving forward again, Mr. Hussein and his cosmetically rearranged Cabinet can be expected to try to whittle, chisel and needle their way around every obstacle that the cease-fire resolutions placed before them.

As American military forces withdraw from the region, they say, Mr. Hussein is likely to waste little time in channeling his regained oil revenues both into domestic rebuilding programs and also in repairing his military machine so he can once again put force central control throughout the country.

And politically, they say, he will seek to press United States policy in the region to use the same standard of pressure it has applied to Iraq to bring Israel into compliance with United Nations resolutions calling for the return of occupied territories.

If Mr. Hussein is able to exact any measure of revenge for the humiliation he has been made to suffer in the eyes of many in the world, it will be in the political arena. There still are millions of Palestinians, Jordanians, Yemenis and North Africans who supported him in the war and may still clamor for the same measure of justice that Washington fought for in the name of Kuwait.

외 무 부

종 별 :

번 호 : UNW-0828

수 신 : 장 관(국연,중동일,기정)

발 신 : 주 유엔 대사

제 목 : 걸프사태(안보리)

일 시 : 91 0408 1700

원 본

연: UNW-0823,0824

1. 안보리 휴전결의 (687호) 수락에 관한 이락 A.HUSSEIN 외상의 4.6.자 유엔사무총장, 안보리의장앞 서한이 금 4.8. 안보리문서로 배포된바 (S/22456) 동 상세는 별첨 참조 바람.

2.사무총장은 상기 안보리결의 본문 5항에 의거 유엔군사 옵서버단 (UNIKOM) 배치계획서를 4.5.자로 안보리에 제출한바 (S/22454), 동계획에 의하면, 초기단계에서 동 옵서버단 규모는 기간요원 (300 명) 에 지원요원 (보명,공벼,보급)을 합쳐 총1,440 이하로 하되, 동규모는 추후 조정가능하게 되어있음. 처음 6개월간 옵서버단 경비는 8,300 만불, 다음 6개월은 4,000 만불 수준으로 추정하고있음. (S/22454/ADD.1)

3. 상기 UNIKOM 배치계획관련 M.GOULDING사무차장은 4.6. 쿠웨이트, 이락측과 협의한 것으로 알려졌으며, 양국 반응은 추후 공개될 예정이라고함.본건 옵서버단 단장 (CHIEF MILITARYOBSERVER) 으로는 G.GREINDL 전 UNFICYP사령관 (오스트리아 소장)이 거론되고있음. 동옵서버단에는 안보리 상임이사국 5개국이 모두참여할 예정이며, 총 20-30 개국정도가 참여할 전망이라고함.

4.한편 사무총장은 이락 쿠르드족 난민문제와 관련 유엔조사단 파견을 검토중인 것으로 알려짐. (안보리결의 688 호참조)

5.금 4.8. 오후 안보리는 비공식협의를 갖고 상기 사무총장 UNIKOM 배치계획서를 검토할예정임.

첨부:상기 안보리문서: UNW(F)-158

끝

(대사 노창희-국장)

국기국   1차보   중아국   정문국   안기부

91.04.09   09:48 WG

외신 1과 통제관

0088

S/22456
English
Page 2

UNW(F).-158 10408 1700
(국연.중동원.기정)

총13대

Annex

Identical letters dated 6 April 1991 from the Minister for Foreign
Affairs of the Republic of Iraq addressed respectively to the
Secretary-General and the President of the Security Council

I have the honour to inform you that the Iraqi Government has taken note of
the text of Security Council resolution 687 (1991), the authors of which are the
first to recognize that it is unprecedented in the annals of the Organization, an
wishes, before stating its official position, to make a number of fundamental
comments regarding certain concepts and provisions contained therein:

I.   While in its preamble the resolution reaffirms that Iraq is an
independent sovereign State, the fact remains that a good number of its iniquitou:
provisions impair that sovereignty. In fact, the resolution constitutes an
unprecedented assault on the sovereignty, and the rights that stem therefrom,
embodied in the Charter and in international law and practice. For example, where
the question of boundaries is concerned, the Security Council has determined in
advance the boundary between Iraq and Kuwait. And yet it is well known, from the
juridical and practical standpoint, that in international relations boundary issue
must be the subject of an agreement between States, since this is the only basis
capable of guaranteeing the stability of frontiers.

Moreover, the resolution fails to take into account Iraq's view, which is wel
known to the Council, that the provisions relating to the boundary between Iraq an
Kuwait contained in the "Agreed Minutes Between the State of Kuwait and the
Republic of Iraq Regarding the Restoration of Friendly Relations, Recognition and
Related Matters" dated 4 October 1963 have not yet been subjected to the
constitutional procedures required for ratification of the Agreed Minutes by the
legislative branch and the President of Iraq, thus leaving the question of the
boundary pending and unresolved. The Council has nevertheless imposed on Iraq the
line of its boundary with Kuwait. By acting in this strange manner, the Council
itself has also violated one of the provisions of resolution 660, which served as
the basis for its subsequent resolutions. In its paragraph 3, resolution 660 calls
upon Iraq and Kuwait to resolve their differences through negotiation, and the
question of the boundary is well known to be one of the main differences. Iraq
officially informed the Council that it accepted resolution 660 and was prepared to
apply it, but the Council has gone beyond this legal position, contradicting its
previous resolution, and adopted an iniquitous resolution which imposes on Iraq, an
independent and sovereign State and a Member of the United Nations, new conditions
and a boundary line which deprive it of its right to establish its territorial
rights in accordance with the principles of international law. Thus the Council is
also depriving Iraq of its right to exercise its free choice and to affirm that it
accepts that boundary without reservation. Where the question of the boundary is
concerned, the Council resolution is an iniquitous resolution which constitutes a
dangerous precedent, a first in the annals of the international Organization and -
as some impartial members of the Council indicated in their statements when the
resolution was voted on - an assault on the sovereignty of States.

/...

-0828

13-1

0089

S/22456
English
Page 3

It is also to be noted that the United States of America, the author of the
draft resolution on which resolution 687, which imposes a solution to the
boundary-related and other differences between Iraq and Kuwait, was based, refuses
to impose any solution whatsoever on its ally, Israel, in accordance with
conventions, United Nations resolutions and international law.

Furthermore, the United States of America is preventing the Security Council
from assuming the responsibilities incumbent upon it with respect to the
Arab-Zionist conflict, the Israeli policy of annexation of the occupied Arab
territories, the establishment of settlements, the displacement of populations and
the disregard for the rights of the Palestinian people and the neighbouring Arab
countries, by vetoing any draft resolution approved by the remaining members of the
Council, for the simple reason that Israel does not want a resolution which favours
a just settlement of the conflict.

II. Iraq's position with regard to the prohibition of chemical and
bacteriological weapons is clear. It is indeed a party to the Protocol for the
Prohibition of the Use in War of Asphyxiating, Poisonous or Other Gases, and of
Bacteriological Methods of Warfare, signed at Geneva in 1925. In a statement
issued in September 1988, Iraq reiterated its attachment and adherence to the
provisions of that Protocol. It also participated in the Conference of States
Parties to the 1925 Geneva Protocol and Other Interested States, held at Paris from
7 to 11 January 1989, and signed the Declaration issued by the participating
States. On that occasion, Iraq took a position which was unanimously shared by all
the Arab countries, namely that all weapons of mass destruction, including nuclear
weapons, must be eliminated from the Middle East region.

Iraq is also a party to the Treaty on the Non-Proliferation of Nuclear
Weapons, of 1 July 1968. As the many reports of the International Atomic Energy
Agency confirm, it is applying all the provisions of the Treaty. The Security
Council resolution obliges only Iraq, and it alone, to undertake the destruction of
the non-conventional weapons left to it after the heavy destruction inflicted both
on these weapons and on the related installations by the military operations
launched against Iraq by the 30 countries of the coalition. It does not deprive
the other countries of the region, particularly Israel, of the right to possess
weapons of this type, including nuclear weapons. Moreover, the Council has ignored
its resolution 487 (1981), which calls on Israel to place all its nuclear
facilities under international safeguards, and has not sought to ensure the
implementation of that resolution in the same way as it is now seeking to impose
the position it has taken against Iraq. It is thus clear that a double standard is
being applied with respect to the elimination of weapons of mass destruction in the
region, and an attempt being made to disrupt the military balance there, and this
is, all the more apparent in that Iraq has not had recourse to weapons of this type.

The application of this provision of the resolution cannot but seriously
endanger the regional balance, as indeed was confirmed by certain impartial members
of the Security Council in their statements when the resolution was voted upon.
There can be no doubt that Israel, an expansionist aggressor country which is
occupying the territory of neighbouring countries, usurping the right of the

/...

0090

S/22456
English
Page 4

Palestinian Arab people against which it daily commits the most horrible atrocities, and refusing to comply with the resolutions of the Security Council, which it holds in contempt, as well as all the resolutions of the international Organization, will be the first to benefit from this imbalance.

Whereas the resolution emphasizes the importance of all States adhering to the Convention on the Prohibition of the Development, Production and Stockpiling of Bacteriological (Biological) and Toxin Weapons, of a Convention on the Universal Prohibition of Chemical Weapons being drafted and of universal adherence thereto, it makes no mention whatsoever of the importance of universal adherence to the convention banning nuclear weapons or of the drafting of a convention on the universal prohibition of such weapons in the region. Instead, it emphasizes the importance of instituting a dialogue among the States of the region with a view to achieving a so-called balanced and comprehensive control of armaments in the region.

Proof of the resolution's biased and iniquitous nature is afforded by the Council's use of what it terms unprovoked attacks using ballistic missiles as grounds for calling for the destruction of all ballistic missiles with a range greater than 150 kilometres and of all repair and production facilities. The term unprovoked attacks is used of attacks against Israel, a country which itself launched an unprovoked attack in 1981, destroying Iraqi nuclear installations which were used for peaceful purposes and were under international safeguards. In this connection, the Security Council considered in its resolution 487 (1981), adopted unanimously, that that attack constituted a serious threat to the entire safeguards regime of the International Atomic Energy Agency, which is the foundation of the Treaty on the Non-Proliferation of Nuclear Weapons.

It should be pointed out as well that the Council had also considered in the same resolution that Iraq was entitled to appropriate redress for the destruction it had suffered. The Council has to date taken no steps for the implementation of that resolution, whereas it imposes particularly severe and iniquitous terms and mechanisms when it comes to the redress referred to in resolution 687 (1991), without taking into account even the basic humanitarian needs of the Iraqi people.

III. Furthermore, Iraq's internal and external security has been and remains seriously threatened, in that continuing efforts are being made to interfere, by force of arms, in the country's internal affairs. Thus the measures taken by the Council against Iraq to deprive it of its lawful right to acquire weapons and military matériel for defence directly contribute to the intensification of these threats and to the destabilization of Iraq, thus endangering the country's internal and external security and hence peace, security and stability throughout the region.

IV. Whereas the Council resolution provides for mechanisms for obtaining redress from Iraq, it makes no reference to Iraq's rights to claim redress for the considerable losses it sustained and the massive destruction inflicted on civilian installations and infrastructures as a result of the abusive implementation of resolution 678 (1990), which were testified to by the delegation sent by the Secretary-General which visited Iraq recently, and have been referred to by the President of a permanent member of the Security Council (Soviet President Mikhail Gorbachev) and by all impartial observers who have seen with

/...

13-3

their own eyes the consequences of the military operations launched against Iraq.
The Council has not explained to world public opinion and the conscience of mankind
what the relationship is between its resolution 678 and the deliberate destruction
of Iraq's infrastructure - generating stations, water distribution networks,
irrigation dams, civilian bridges, telephone exchanges, factories producing
powdered milk for infants and medicines, shelters, mosques, churches, commercial
centres, residential neighbourhoods, etc. Moreover, the resolution authorizes
third parties to claim compensation from Iraq for damage that may have been caused
to them, even when such damage resulted from unfulfilment of their commitments to
Iraq immediately following the adoption of resolution 661.

Further evidence of the resolution's biased and iniquitous nature is that it
holds Iraq liable for environmental damage and the depletion of natural resources,
although this liability has not been established; on the other hand, it makes no
mention of Iraq's own right to obtain compensation for the established facts of
damage to its environment and depletion of its natural resources as a result of
more than 88,000 tons of explosives, or for the destruction of water distribution
networks, generating stations and the road network, which has spread disease and
epidemics and caused serious harm to the environment.

These provisions partake of a desire to exact vengeance and cause harm, not to
give effect to the relevant provisions of international law. The direct concrete
consequences of their implementation will affect the potential and resources of
millions of Iraqis, and deprive them of the right to live in dignity.

V. After imposing compulsory and universal sanctions against Iraq by
adopting resolution 661 (1990) in consequence, according to it, of Iraq's refusal
to comply with the provisions of resolution 660 (1990), the Council has maintained
most of them in force despite Iraq's acceptance of all the Council's resolutions
and the implementation of a good number of their provisions. The Council
resolution provides for the progressive lifting of sanctions over an unspecified
period, thus leaving broad discretionary authority to certain influential members
of the Council which have drawn up the Council's resolutions in an arbitrary manner
in order to impose them for political purposes which bear no relation to the
Charter or to international law.

In essence, this procedure means that the Council has contradicted the initial
resolution under which it imposed sanctions against Iraq, and moreover has not
taken account of the offensive launched against Iraq, whereas the interests of the
other parties have been taken into account, despite their wealth and their
considerable resources.

VI. The Council does not deal clearly and directly with the question of
withdrawal of the foreign forces occupying part of Iraqi territory, although the
resolution declares a formal cease-fire.

The very conditions invoked in support of the declaration of a formal
cease-fire also necessitate the withdrawal. The fact that the withdrawal is not
explicitly mentioned is tantamount to authorizing the occupation of Iraqi territory
for a period whose duration is at the discretion of the occupying countries, which

/...

13-4

0092

make no secret of their intention to exploit the occupation for political purposes and to make use of it as a trump card in their hand. This position on the part of the Council constitutes a flagrant violation of Iraq's sovereignty, independence and territorial integrity, and cannot be justified by any provision of resolution 678 (1990). Under this same selective, premeditated and totally unjustifiable approach, the resolution stipulates that the observer forces will be deployed in Iraq to a distance of 10 kilometres from the boundary, and only five kilometres into the territory of the other party, despite the fact that the terrain in the region is flat everywhere, with no relief features that would justify this difference of treatment.

VII. Numerous mechanisms are envisaged which will necessitate consultation in the context of the implementation of the resolution's provisions, but the resolution is not at all clear about Iraq's participation in these consultations. The fact that Iraq is concerned to the highest degree in the application of the resolution makes its effective participation in all consultations bearing on the implementation of these provisions essential. However, the Council has once again opted for an arbitrary and inequitable method.

The questions raised in the resolution and discussed in the foregoing preliminary comments constitute, in substance, an injustice, a severe assault on the Iraqi people's right to life and a flagrant denial of its inalienable rights to sovereignty and independence and its right to exercise its free choice.

In practice, the provisions of the resolution embodying the criteria of duality in international relations and the application of a double standard to questions of the same kind hold Iraq and its population hostage to the designs harboured by certain Powers to take control of their resources, set quotas for their food and clothing needs, and deprive them of their right to live in dignity in the modern society to which they aspire.

Such injustices and such assaults on the rights of a member country of the United Nations and its people cannot under any circumstances be in conformity with the purposes and objectives of the Charter. The Council had a duty to discuss the issues before it with objectivity and in accordance with the provisions of international law and the principles of justice and equity.

By adopting this unjust resolution and by this selective treatment of the Iraqi people, the Council has merely confirmed the fact that we have never ceased to emphasize, namely that the Council has become a puppet which the United States of America is manipulating in order to achieve its political designs in the region, the prime objective being to perpetuate Israel's policy of aggression and expansion, despite the empty words about peace and justice in the Middle East uttered by one or another of the Council members which voted for this resolution.

It could not be more clear to all men of honour and justice that these iniquitous and vengeful measures against Iraq are not a consequence of the events of 2 August 1990 and the subsequent period, for the essential motive underlying these measures stems from Iraq's rejection of the unjust situation imposed on the Arab nation and the countries of the region for decades, a situation which has

/..

13-5

0093

enabled Israel, a belligerent Power heavily armed with the most modern and fearsome conventional weapons and with weapons of mass destruction, including nuclear weapons, to exercise hegemony in the region. This reality confirms what Iraq had stated before the events of 2 August 1990, namely that it was the target of a plot aimed at destroying the potential it had deployed with a view to arriving at a just balance in the region which would pave the way for the institution of justice and of a lasting peace.

It is unfortunate that States whose intention was not in any way to help the United States of America and Israel attain their objectives should involuntarily have contributed to their attainment by voting for this iniquitous resolution.

As Iraq makes its preliminary comments on the juridical and legal aspects of this resolution, so as to encourage men of conscience in the countries members of the international community and world public opinion to make an effort to understand the truth as it is and the need to ensure the triumph of justice, it has no choice but to accept this resolution.

I should be grateful if you would have this letter circulated as a document of the Security Council.

(Signed) Ahmed HUSSEIN
Minister for Foreign Affairs
of Iraq

13-6

0094

UNITED
NATIONS

Security Council

Distr.
GENERAL

S/22454
5 April 1991

ORIGINAL: ENGLISH

REPORT OF THE SECRETARY-GENERAL ON THE IMPLEMENTATION OF PARAGRAPH 5 OF SECURITY COUNCIL RESOLUTION 687 (1991)

1. The present report is submitted in pursuance of Security Council resolution 687 (1991) of 3 April 1991. In paragraph 5 of that resolution, the Council established a demilitarized zone along the boundary between Iraq and Kuwait and requested the Secretary-General to submit to the Council, within three days, for approval a plan for the immediate deployment of a United Nations observer unit.

Terms of reference

2. In accordance with paragraph 5 of resolution 687 (1991), the terms of reference of the unit, which I propose should be called the "United Nations Iraq-Kuwait Observation Mission" (UNIKOM), would be:

(a) To monitor the Khor Abdullah and a demilitarized zone extending 10 kilometres into Iraq and 5 km into Kuwait from the boundary referred to in the Agreed Minutes between the State of Kuwait and the Republic of Iraq regarding the Restoration of Friendly Relations, Recognition and Related Matters of 4 October 1963; 1/

(b) To deter violations of the boundary through its presence in and surveillance of the demilitarized zone;

(c) To observe any hostile or potentially hostile action mounted from the territory of one State to the other.

General principles

3. Four essential conditions would have to be met for UNIKOM to be effective: first, it would need to have at all times the confidence and backing of the Security Council. Second, it would have to be given the necessary cooperation of the parties. Third, it would have to function as an integrated and efficient military unit. Fourth, adequate financial arrangements would have to be made to cover its costs.

91-11141 2422b (E)

/...

13-7

0095

S/22454
English
Page 2

4.   In accordance with established principles,

(a) UNIKOM would be under the command of the United Nations, vested in the
Secretary-General, under the authority of the Security Council. Command in the
field would be exercised by a Chief Military Observer appointed by the
Secretary-General with the consent of the Security Council. The Chief Military
Observer would be responsible to the Secretary-General. The Secretary-General
would report regularly to the Security Council on the operations of UNIKOM and
immediately if there were serious violations of the demilitarized zone or potential
threats to peace. All matters that might affect the nature or the continued
effective functioning of UNIKOM would be referred to the Council for its decision;

(b) UNIKOM would be composed of military contingents provided by Member
States at the request of the Secretary-General. The military contingents would be
selected in consultation with the parties and with the concurrence of the Security
Council, bearing in mind the accepted principle of equitable geographic
representation;

(c) As recommended below, the contingents would comprise armed and unarmed
military personnel. UNIKOM and its personnel would be authorized to use force only
in self-defence;

(d) UNIKOM would proceed on the assumption that the parties would take all
the necessary steps to comply with the decisions of the Security Council. It would
have to have the freedom of movement and communication and other rights and
facilities that would be necessary for the performance of its tasks. UNIKOM and
its personnel would also have to be granted all relevant privileges and immunities
provided for by the Convention on the Privileges and Immunities of the United
Nations; agreements with the host Governments concerning the status of UNIKOM would
have to be concluded without delay. The Governments of Iraq and Kuwait would be
expected to provide, free of charge, the land and premises required by UNIKOM.

Considerations relevant to the discharge of the mandate

5.   As an observation mission, UNIKOM would be required to monitor and observe and
would not be expected and, indeed, would not be authorized to take physical action
to prevent the entry of military personnel or equipment into the demilitarized
zone. Further, it is my understanding that the clause requiring UNIKOM to "observe
any hostile or potentially hostile action mounted from the territory of one State
to the other" refers to activities that can be observed in or from the Khor
Abdullah and the demilitarized zone.

6.   UNIKOM would not assume responsibilities that fall within the competence of
the host Governments and would avoid unnecessary interference in the normal
civilian life of the area. It is assumed that the Governments of Iraq and Kuwait
would each carry out all aspects of civilian administration in their respective
part of the demilitarized zone, including the maintenance of law and order. At the
same time, if UNIKOM is to be effective, it would need to have certain powers and
facilities. In this connection, the two Governments would be expected to extend to
UNIKOM full freedom of movement, on land and through the air, across the border and

/...

13-A

0096

throughout the demilitarized zone; to control movement into and out of the
demilitarized zone by requiring all traffic to be routed past United Nations
observation posts; to notify UNIKOM in advance of sea and air traffic in the
demilitarized zone and the Khor Abdullah; and to establish limitations on the right
of their citizens to bear arms in the demilitarized zone. Further details
regarding the regulation of activities in the demilitarized zone and the
Khor Abdullah would be worked out in consultation with the two Governments,
including the number and armament of police deployed in the area.

Area of operation

7. The demilitarized zone is about 200 km long, the Khor Abdullah about 40 km.
For the most part, the zone is barren and almost uninhabited, except for the
oilfields and two towns, Umm Qasr and Safwan. A small airfield is at Safwan. A
port and airfield are at Umm Qasr, which became Iraq's only outlet to the sea after
the Shatt al-Arab was blocked. A number of roads cross the demilitarized zone,
most of them in the eastern part, but the terrain makes cross-country travel easy,
and the inhabitants, particularly the bedouins, are accustomed to moving freely
throughout the area and across the border.

Concept of operation

8. In order to carry out the mandate defined by the Security Council, UNIKOM
would monitor the situation (on a continuing basis) to ensure that no military
personnel and equipment were within the demilitarized zone and that no military
fortifications and installations were maintained in it. To this end, it would:

(a) Monitor the withdrawal of any armed forces now in the zone which is to be
demilitarized;

(b) Operate observation posts on the main roads to monitor traffic into and
out of the demilitarized zone;

(c) Operate observation posts at selected locations in the demilitarized zone;

(d) Conduct patrols throughout the demilitarized zone by land and by air;

(e) Monitor the Khor Abdullah from observation posts set up on its shores and
from the air;

(f) Carry out investigations.

Requirements

9. The tasks defined above are essentially tasks for military observers.
However, in the circumstances obtaining in the UNIKOM area of operations, they
could not be carried out by military observers alone. This is for three main
reasons.

13-9

/...

0097

S/22454
English
Page 4

10.   First, the area of operations, apart from Umm Qasr and territory to the east
of it, is currently controlled by the forces of Member States cooperating with
Kuwait. As those forces bring their military presence in Iraq to an end, in
accordance with paragraph 6 of resolution 687 (1991), there is a risk that disorder
would ensue, at least for a period of time. In particular, the forces of Member
States cooperating with Kuwait are at present providing humanitarian assistance to
some tens of thousands of refugees and displaced persons, many of them in what will
become the UNIKOM area of operations. I am taking urgent steps to arrange for the
United Nations system to provide such humanitarian support as may be needed by
these people. It is also hoped that the host Governments' police forces would soon
be in a position to maintain law and order in their respective parts of the
demilitarized zone. Nevertheless, during this delicate transitional phase there
might well be a threat to the security of UNIKOM personnel, equipment and
supplies. My plan therefore includes the provision of an infantry element to
ensure UNIKOM's security at that stage.

11.   Second, I have been informed by Member States cooperating with Kuwait that
mines and unexploded ordnance are a serious hazard in the area. Considerable
effort would be required to clear areas required for UNIKOM observation posts and
other installations, to make existing roads and tracks safe for patrolling and to
establish additional tracks to enable UNIKOM to patrol the length and breadth of
the demilitarized zone. Unless satisfactory arrangements can be made to complete
this work before UNIKOM is deployed, the mission would have to include a field
engineer unit.

12.   Third, the demilitarized zone is barren and sparsely populated, the climate is
harsh and the infrastructure in the area has suffered greatly. The military
observers would therefore need a greater degree of logistic support than is the
case in areas that are more settled and have less severe climates. There would
thus be a continuing need for a logistic unit.

13.   To carry out the tasks described in paragraph 8 above, a group of 300 military
observers would be required initially, although this number would be reviewed as
the mission gained experience and refined its methods. As regards support for the
observers, my plan would be to assign temporarily to UNIKOM five infantry companies
drawn from existing peace-keeping operations in the region, with the agreement of
the troop-contributing Governments concerned. These units would provide essential
security for UNIKOM during the setting-up phase. The Chief Military Observer would
be instructed to advise me, approximately four weeks after the beginning of the
operation, whether he foresaw a continuing need for an infantry element. If he
did, I would seek the Council's authority to replace the units temporarily assigned
to UNIKOM with one or more battalions on a more permanent basis. As indicated in
paragraph 11 above, a field engineer unit would also be required if the necessary
clearance of mines and unexploded ordnance had not been completed by the time
UNIKOM was deployed. In addition, UNIKOM would have an air unit with fixed-wing
aircraft and light helicopters, a logistic unit responsible primarily for medical
care, supply and transport, and a headquarters unit. The maximum initial strength
of UNIKOM would be approximately 1,440 all ranks, of which the infantry temporarily
attached to it from already established missions would be approximately 680, and
the field engineer unit, if it is deployed, approximately 300.

/...

13-10

0098

14. UNIKOM's headquarters would need to be within the demilitarized zone, where Umm Qasr would seem to be the most suitable location. A logistic base would be established in Kuwait. The military observers and the infantry units would be deployed throughout the demilitarized zone. Liaison offices would be maintained at Baghdad and Kuwait City. At the start of the mission, liaison would also need to be maintained with the forces of the Member States cooperating with Kuwait, whose withdrawal through the demilitarized zone would need to be coordinated with UNIKOM.

15. A preliminary estimate of the cost of UNIKOM and my observations on its financing will be circulated in an addendum to the present report.

Consultations with the parties

16. As already stated, UNIKOM would be able to function effectively only with the full cooperation of the parties. In accordance with resolution 687 (1991), I have informed the Permanent Representatives of Iraq and Kuwait of the plan contained in the present report and requested their urgent confirmation that their respective Governments would cooperate with the United Nations on this basis. I will report further to the Security Council as soon as this has been received.

Notes

1/   United Nations Treaty Series, vol. 485, No. 7063.

13-11

0099

UNITED NATIONS

Security Council

Distr.
GENERAL

S/22454/Add.1
5 April 1991

ORIGINAL: ENGLISH

REPORT OF THE SECRETARY-GENERAL ON THE IMPLEMENTATION OF
PARAGRAPH 5 OF SECURITY COUNCIL RESOLUTION 687 (1991)

Addendum

Estimated cost and method of financing

1.   Should the Security Council establish the United Nations Iraq-Kuwait Observation Mission (UNIKOM) on the basis set out in the main part of the present report, it is estimated that the cost of the Mission for the first six months would be approximately $83 million. The costs of continuing UNIKOM for the following six months would be approximately $40 million. These estimates do not include additional costs that would be incurred if the infantry units temporarily assigned to UNIKOM are replaced with infantry battalions on a more permanent basis; nor do they include the costs that would be incurred if the engineer unit had to be continued beyond six months. These are preliminary estimates, which might be subject to revision as further details are clarified and/or as a result of decisions taken by the Security Council.

2.   It would be my recommendation that the costs of the Mission be considered an expense of the Organization to be borne by Member States in accordance with Article 17, paragraph 2, of the Charter. I would recommend to the General Assembly that the assessments to be levied on Member States be credited to a special account that would be established for this purpose.

3.   The capacity of the United Nations to deploy UNIKOM would depend in large measure on the availability of the financial resources necessary to meet the start-up costs of the operation. This in turn would depend not only on the appropriation of the necessary funds by the Assembly but, equally importantly, on the receipt from Member States of their assessed contributions. As is known, the payment of assessed contributions for peace-keeping operations established by the Security Council has been at rates far lower than were necessary to meet cash-flow requirements. In order to meet the start-up costs of UNIKOM, I would therefore appeal to Member States to make voluntary payments, which would be repaid as soon as sufficient assessed contributions have been received. I would also appeal to Member States to make voluntary contributions in cash and in kind for setting up and maintaining the Mission.

91-11165 2250f (E)   /...

13-12

0100

S/22454/Add.1
English
Page 2

4.   I take this opportunity to point out that the above cost estimate covers only paragraph 5 of resolution 687 (1991). The financial implications of the resolution's other provisions will become clearer after the necessary detailed examination of the manner in which these provisions may be implemented by the Secretary-General and of the various commissions to be established under the resolution. It is already apparent, however, that the aggregate financial implications of the resolution are likely to be quite substantial.

13-13

0101

외 무 부

종 별 :

번 호 : UNW-0839

일 시 : 91 0408 2300

수 신 : 장 관(국연,중동일,기정)

발 신 : 주 유엔 대사

제 목 : 걸프사태(안보리)

연: UNW-0828

안보리는 금 4.8.(월) 오후 표제사태 관련 비공식회의를 가진바, 주요결과를 아래보고함.

1. 이락의 안보리휴전결의 (687호) 수락

이락측의 수락통보 (S/22456) 에 대해 별첨 안보리 의장 회신을 4.9. 보내기로함.

2. 유엔옵서버단(UNIKOM) 배치계획

연호 사무총장 계획서를 재가하고 동 배치 계속여부 및 방식을 6개월마다 심사키로 한다는 요지의 결의안 채택문제를 명 4.9. 협의키로함.

3. 이락내 난민 보호지역 설정문제

금일 비공식 협의시 영국은 난민, 특히 쿠르드족에 대한 효과적인 구호를 위해 보호지역을 설정하는 문제를 제기한바, 미,불이 지지입장을 표명함.본건은 사무총장이 추진중인 유엔의 난민조사단 파견과도 연계, 명일 재협의가 있을예정임.

첨부:상기 안보리 의장 회신(안) 및 결의안 초안:UNW(F)-161

끝

(대사 노창희-국장)

국기국   1차보   중아국   정문국   안기부   장관실 차관실 2차보 청와대

PAGE 1

91.04.09   12:38 WG

외신 1과 통제관

0102

P.1

APR 08 '91 21:48 KOREAN MISSION

UNW(주)-161 104억 2700 총2대
(국연 중동원. 기정)

DRAFT

I have the honour to acknowledge receipt of your communication dated
6 April 1991 (document S/22456).

You thereby transmit to me the letter addressed to me by the Minister for
Foreign Affairs of Iraq, the penultimate paragraph of which contains official
notification of the acceptance by Iraq, without any specific conditions, of
resolution 687 (1991), in accordance with paragraph 33 of that resolution.

I have also taken note of the acceptance by Iraq's National Assembly, on
6 April 1991, of the aforesaid resolution.

The members of the Security Council have, lastly, asked me to note that the
conditions established in paragraph 33 of resolution 687 (1991) have now been met
and that the formal cease-fire referred to in paragraph 33 of the resolution is
therefore now effective.

3074B

#UNW-0839 의
첨부문   2-1

0103

걸프사태 관련 유엔안전보장이사회 동향, 1990-91. 전5권 (V.5 1991.4월) 529

The Security Council

Recalling its resolution 687 (1991)

1. <u>Approves</u> the report of the Secretary-General on the implementation of paragraph 5 of Security Council resolution 687 (1991) contained in document S/22454 and S/22454 add 1 of 5 April 1991;

2. <u>Notes</u> that the decision to set up the observer unit was taken in paragraph 5 of resolution 687 (1991) and can only be terminated by a decision of the Council. The Council shall therefore review the question of termination or continuation every six months;

3. <u>Decides</u> that the modalities for the initial six-month period of the United Nations Iraq-Kuwait Observation Mission shall be as set out in accordance with the above mentioned report and shall also be reviewed regularly every six months.

#1/2908

2-2

0104

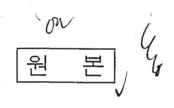

외 무 부

종 별 :

번 호 : UNW-0873   일 시 : 91 0410 2030

수 신 : 장 관(국연,중동일,기정)

발 신 : 주 유엔 대사

제 목 : 걸프사태(안보리)

　　　연: UNW-0839,0852

　　1. 지난 4.6 이락의 안보리 휴전결의 수락통보 (S/22456) 관련 금 4.10 이락측이 자국 국회의 휴전결의 수락결정 사본을 안보리 의장에게 제출해옴에 따라 동의장은 4.11 10:00 까지 이사국으로부터 이의제기가 없는경우 연호 의장명의회신 (휴전발효 확인)을 이락측에 발송예정임.

　　2. 연호 이락 난민 관련 유엔조사단은 E.SUY단장및 단원 4-5 명 (WHO, WFP, UNICEF관계자)으로 구성되며, 요르단을 경유 4.13.이락도착, 약 10일간 동국에서 조사 활동예정인 것으로 알려짐.이와관련 이락측은 유엔조사단 접수용의를 이미 표명한바 있음.

　　3.한편, 미.영의 난민 구호품 공수관련 이락은 4.7자 안보리 의장앞 A. HUSSEIN외상명의 서한에서, 이락의 당국 또는 적십자를 통하지 않는 동공수행위를 주권침해라고 비난함.(S/22459)

　　4. 연호 유엔군사 옵서버단 (UNIKOM)은 동단장이 임명되는대로 선발대가 4.12 경현지 도착예정이라고함.

　　5.다음주 사무총장 유럽방문 (ACC 정기회의참석)중 터어키 방문 가능성이 있는것으로 관측되고있음.끝

　　　(대사 노창희-국장)

국기국　　1차보　　　중아국　　　정문국　　　안기부

외 무 부

외신 1과 통제관 원 본

종 별 : 지 급

번 호 : UNW-0888   일   시 : 91 0411 2000

수 신 : 장 관(국연,중동일,기정)

발 신 : 주 유엔 대사

제 목 : 걸프사태(안보리)

연: UNW-0873

1. 휴전결의 발효를 확인하는 안보리 의장회신은 연호보고와 같이 당초 4.11 10:00 이락측에 전달 예정이었으나, 미.영국이 동 회신문안수정을 요구해 옴에 따라 안보리는 금 4.12 비공식협의 결과 별첨 회신문안에 합의한바, 동 회신은 금일 18:00안보리 의장이 이락대사에게 직접 전달하였음.

2. 상기 안보리 비공식 협의시 휴전발효 시점관련 논의가 있었는바, 미.영 등은 상기 의장회신일 (4.11) 을, 인도등은 이락의 휴전결의 (687호)수락통보일 (4.6)을 기준으로 할것을 각각주장하였음. 본건에 관해 양측간에 합의가 이루어지지 않은 결과, 상기 의장회신은 이문제에 관해 명확한 입장을 취하지 않고있음.

3. 한편 4.11 사무총장은 유엔옵서버단 단장으로 안보리 동의를 거쳐 G.GREINDL소장 (오지리)임명을 발표하였음. (S/22478,22479)

첨부:상기 안보리 의장 대이락 회신내용:UNW(F)-166

끝

(대사 노창희-국장)

국기국   1차보   중아국   정문국   청와대   안기부

PAGE 1   91.04.12   09:29 WG

외신 1과 통제관

P.4

UNW(桓)-166 10411 200
(국연.중동일 기정)   총1억

I have the honour to acknowledge receipt of your communication dated 6 April 1991 (S/22456).

You thereby transmit to me the letter addressed to me by the Minister for Foreign Affairs of Iraq, the penultimate paragraph of which contains official notification of the acceptance, irrevocable and without qualifying conditions, by Iraq of resolution 687 (1991), in accordance with paragraph 33 of that resolution.

You have subsequently confirmed to me on behalf of your Government, during our meeting on 8 April 1991, that the above-mentioned letter constitutes Iraq's irrevocable and unqualified acceptance of resolution 687 (1991) in accordance with paragraph 33 of that resolution. You have also transmitted to me the acceptance by Iraq's National Assembly on 6 April 1991 of the aforesaid resolution (S/22480), and confirmed to me, in the name of your Government, that the Revolution Command Council has used its constitutional powers to make this Decision legally binding in the Republic of Iraq.

The members of the Security Council have, accordingly, asked me to note that the conditions established in paragraph 33 of resolution 687 (1991) have been met and that the formal cease-fire referred to in paragraph 33 of that resolution is therefore effective.

The members of the Council welcome this development as a positive step towards the full implementation of resolution 687 (1991).

UNW-0888
첨부물   1-1   0107

걸프사태 관련 유엔안전보장이사회 동향, 1990-91. 전5권 (V.5 1991.4월) 533

외교문서 비밀해제: 걸프 사태 20
걸프 사태 유엔안전보장이사회 동향 3

초판인쇄 2024년 03월 15일
초판발행 2024년 03월 15일

지은이 한국학술정보(주)
펴낸이 채종준
펴낸곳 한국학술정보(주)
주 소 경기도 파주시 회동길 230(문발동)
전 화 031-908-3181(대표)
팩 스 031-908-3189
홈페이지 http://ebook.kstudy.com
E-mail 출판사업부 publish@kstudy.com
등 록 제일산-115호(2000. 6. 19)

ISBN   979-11-6983-980-8 94340
       979-11-6983-960-0 94340 (set)